LGBTQs, Media and Culture in Europe

T0298471

This collection addresses the Anglo-American bias in much LGBTQ media research and offers the reader a series of snapshots, both past and present, that detail how European LGBTQ people have used, and continue to engage with, media technologies, texts and practices. A must-read for anyone who is interested in work in this area.

—*Sharif Mowlabocus, University of Sussex*

Media matter, particularly to social minorities like lesbian, gay, bisexual, transgender and queer people. Rather than one homogenised idea of the 'global gay', what we find today is a range of historically and culturally specific expressions of gender and sexuality, which are reflected and explored across an ever increasing range of media outlets. This collection zooms in on a number of facets of this kaleidoscope, each chapter discussing the intersection of a particular European context and a particular medium with its affordances and limitations. While traditional mass media form the starting point of this book, the primary focus is on digital media such as blogs, social media and dating sites. All contributions are based on recent, original empirical research, using a plethora of qualitative methods to offer a holistic view on the ways media matter to particular LGBTQ individuals and communities. Together the chapters cover the diversity of European countries and regions, of LGBTQ communities and of the contemporary media ecology. Resisting the urge to extrapolate, they argue for specificity, contextualisation and a provincialized understanding of the connections between media, culture, gender and sexuality.

Alexander Dhoest is Associate Professor in Communication Studies at the University of Antwerp, Belgium. His research explores the significance of popular media culture in relation to social identities, focusing in particular on media and diversity.

Lukasz Szulc is a Postdoctoral Fellow of the Research Foundation Flanders at the University of Antwerp, Belgium, and Marie Curie Fellow in the Media and Communication Department at the London School of Economics and Political Science, UK.

Bart Eeckhout is Professor of English and American Literature at the University of Antwerp, Belgium. He studied at Columbia University and Ghent University and has been a visiting professor at Fordham University and New York University, USA. He is a NIAS Fellow-in-Residence for the academic year 2016–17.

Routledge Research in Cultural and Media Studies

For a full list of titles in this series, please visit www.routledge.com.

LGBTQs, Media and Culture in Europe

Edited by Alexander Dhoest,
Lukasz Szulc and Bart Eeckhout

Routledge
Taylor & Francis Group

LONDON AND NEW YORK

First published 2017
by Routledge

2 Park Square, Milton Park, Abingdon, Oxfordshire OX14 4RN
52 Vanderbilt Avenue, New York, NY 10017

Routledge is an imprint of the Taylor & Francis Group, an informa business

First issued in paperback 2019

Routledge is an imprint of the Taylor & Francis Group, an informa business

Copyright © 2017 Taylor & Francis

Library of Congress Cataloging-in-Publication Data

CIP data has been applied for.

ISBN: 978-1-138-64947-7 (hbk)
ISBN: 978-0-367-87715-6 (pbk)

Typeset in Sabon
by codeMantra

Contents

List of Figures and Tables

Figures

Tables

Foreword

Richard Dyer

Ever since there has been anything that we might recognise as LGBTQ, it has been clear that, as Alexander Dhoest, Lukasz Szulc and Bart Eeckhout put it, 'media matter for LGBTQ emancipation'.

From the mid-nineteenth century on, campaigners have referenced the signs of LGBTQ presence (in whatever was the parlance of the day), in written as well as aural-visual media. LGBTQ media presence is itself a confluence of three elements: the development of the very idea of identities (as opposed to ranks) and thus LGBTQ ones (as opposed to the universal recognition, if widespread disapproval, of same-sex and gender-diverse practices), the growth of forms of mass distribution of media products (making available to isolated LGBTQ people awareness of shared existences and desires) and the invention of photographic media (whose indexicality acts as a proof that other such people exist). Early campaigners sought equally to establish the fact and scale of our existence, now and throughout human time and space, and our worth (in establishing splendid artistic and other lineages, the 'Socrates, Sappho, Shakespeare and me' syndrome), and also to critique the way we were portrayed and the attitudes towards us in existing media. Hence the importance of banks of images and photos in early LGBTQ rights publications and treatises and the inclusion from the beginning of analysis and criticism of contemporary media productions.

The London Gay Liberation Front Manifesto of 1971 identified the media as one of the key sources of our oppression:

> The press, radio, television and advertising are used as reinforcements against us, and make possible the control of people's thoughts on an unprecedented scale. Entering everyone's home, affecting everyone's life, the media controllers, all representatives of the rich, male-controlled world, can exaggerate or suppress whatever information suits them.
>
> Under different circumstances, the media might not be the weapon of a small minority. The present controllers are therefore dedicated defenders of things as they stand. Accordingly, the images of people which they transmit in their pictures and words do not subvert, but support society's image of 'normal' man and woman. It follows that

we are characterised as scandalous, obscene perverts; as rampant, wild sex-monsters; as pathetic, doomed and compulsive degenerates; while the truth is blanketed under a conspiracy of silence.

Much of the drive for LGBTQ work on the media, from activism to analysis, is embryonic in this statement: the sense of the centrality and pervasiveness of the media, its role in the definition of sexualities, its privileging of straight ones and denigration of queer ones, the glimpse of 'different circumstances' when the media might serve our interests rather than run counter to them.

By the time of Gay and Lesbian Liberation, television was the dominant mass media form in the Western world. However, it was also one of the most highly regulated forms, partly because it was consumed in homes, by what was projected as heterosexually based nuclear families. It was cinema, the previously dominant mass media form, that loomed larger in gay liberation activism. In part as a way of competing for television audiences, cinema saw daring in matters sexual as having an edge over television; in part, the darkness of the cinema, and its separation from home, made it a haven for LGBTQ people. What would eventually become the now prolific LGBTQ film studies emerged from the regular film criticism in the early Gay and Women's Lib magazines, newspapers and flyers. Criticism of TV could only focus on absence; criticism of film could focus on what little there was, on how it could be, and gradually was, 'better'.

Film is no longer a privileged site for media analysis and struggle, although the buoyancy of LGBTQ film festivals around the world attests to a desire for occasions to come together in the same physical space to share representations and fantasies of ourselves. Nonetheless, as this collection demonstrates, it is subsequent forms, more profligate in production and outlet, that now constitute the principal sites of struggle and affirmation. Such sites, above all the internet, alter the dynamic of the dialectic of the private self and the public imaginary that is at the heart of identity formation. The internet privatises production and consumption and yet makes the global reach of connection wider than ever before; it permits both a bullying conformity of identification and a proliferation of niche recognitions; it fosters control of self-presentation and the illusion of the self as the only begetter of identity. This power play is everywhere evident in the essays in this collection.

Is there a European specificity to these developments? As Sharif Mowlabocus points out in his afterword, there is a danger in viewing European LGBTQ culture in relation to the 'Stonewall benchmark', seeing everything as a kind of catching up with the US lead in LGBTQ as with other cultural production. It would be possible to write a history indicating the importance of Europe in the development of LGBTQ identities and not least in the emergence of, at any rate, film images of emancipation: *Vingarne* (Sweden, 1916), *Anders als die Anderen* (Germany, 1919), *Mädchen in Uniform* (Germany, 1931), *In dit teken* (The Netherlands, 1949), *Olivia*

(France, 1951), *Victim* (UK, 1961) – but it would not be an uncontested history and would start to look different from 1970 onwards. European culture, including LGBTQ cultures, is produced in the context of US cultural hegemony, especially in the mass and popular media. But hegemony is by definition not irrevocably achieved dominance nor yet total saturation. The work in this collection reveals the specificity of different European media constructions and uses, the way particular cultural-historical circumstances inflect the gay liberationist agenda of coming out and visibility, the way geographically and generationally rooted situations mould and provoke different ways of handling the media.

The Gay Liberation Front Manifesto's sketch of the media could not be made today as far as (most of) Europe is concerned. In many countries, the press, radio, television and advertising are as concerned to promote (and shape and perhaps discipline) LGBTQ identities as to ignore or trample on them, and if the role of the rich and the male in media control is far from entirely dislodged, the degree of control in the hands of anyone with network access is astonishing in comparison to what was possible forty-five years ago. And, as this collection triumphantly demonstrates, not only is there no longer any craven sense of the USA as both the great mass-cultural Moloch and the gay Promised Land, there is also an awareness of the many other sources of European identities in the rest of the world and their implications for LGBTQ media and emancipation. Still, a central tenet of all the many phases of LGBTQ activism, and all its many geo-cultural specific manifestations, remains constant: 'Media matter'.

Introduction

*Alexander Dhoest, Lukasz Szulc
and Bart Eeckhout*

Although the social acceptance and legal rights of lesbian, gay, bisexual, transgender and queer people (LGBTQs) have greatly improved over the past decades, especially in the West, this is an uneven and unfinished process. The collection of case studies we present here is based on the firm belief that media matter for LGBTQ emancipation. Both traditional mass media such as film and television and, more recently, digital and social media play a significant role not only in representing LGBTQs but also in providing them with materials and spaces for the exploration and expression of identifications as well as for engaging in diverse forms of social interaction.

The Field

The key role of media for sexual and gender minorities has been acknowledged and studied in an ever-expanding literature. Richard Dyer was one of the first academics to address the topic, starting with his *Gays in Film* (1977) and continuing in later works such as *Now You See It: Studies on Lesbian and Gay Film* (1990). Whereas Dyer tended to focus on textual representations (including stereotypes) from a film studies perspective, others like Larry Gross, working in the communication studies tradition, focused more on the cultural role of television and other mass media (see e.g. *Out of the Mainstream: Sexual Minorities and the Mass Media*, 1991). In 2001, Gross published another seminal work in the field, *Up from Invisibility: Lesbians, Gay Men, and the Media in America*, in which he addressed the key importance of media in creating visibility. While acknowledging the possibility for gay and lesbian audiences to subvert and resist mainstream representations, Gross did not empirically explore these processes. This reflects a wider tendency in the field, as also noted by Fred Fejes and Kevin Petrich (1993), who discussed the representation of gays and lesbians in different media as well as their assumed – but not researched – roles in the formation of gay and lesbian identities.

From the 1990s onwards, the increased representation of gays and lesbians in mainstream media led to a growth in academic studies on the topic, which became itself rather mainstream in the 2000s (see for instance Barnhurst, 2007; Harrington, 2003). Most work continued to analyse representations, now focusing less on their negative or stereotypical nature and more on their heteronormativity (e.g. Avila-Saavedra, 2009; Battles & Hilton-Morrow, 2002; Fejes, 2000). Gradually, however, some authors started to explore how LGBTQs read and used media in the process of developing various gender and sexual identifications (e.g. Driver, 2007; Kivel & Kleiber, 2000). Moreover, the rapid extension of the internet and other digital media kick-started a whole new area of LGBTQ media research, where audiences – now defined as users – took centre stage.

From the early years of its emergence, the internet has been considered as a safe haven for sexual and gender minorities (Döring, 2009). The first ethnographic accounts portrayed the Bulletin Board System (Correll, 1995) and Internet Relay Chat (Shaw, 1997) as a virtual lesbian café or gay bar, where LGBTQs could safely explore their identities, find relevant information and enjoy the support of the community. The relative anonymity of online environments (Mehra, Merkel & Bishop, 2004; Woodland, 2000) and the authenticity of online representations of LGBTQs by LGBTQs (Gray, 2009; Gudelunas, 2012) have been recognized as key characteristics, or affordances, of such 'new' media as personal websites (Alexander, 2002) and blogs (Rak, 2005). Some scholars discuss how these affordances, particularly anonymity, enable a creative play with gender and sexual identities (McRea, 1997; Turkle, 1995). The majority, however, recognise the close intertwinement of the online and the offline (Campbell, 2004; McGlotten, 2013; Mowlabocus, 2010), and look into the role of the internet for the 'identity work' of LGBTQs (Gray, 2009), that is, the exploration, negotiation and expression of LGBTQ identities, especially before and after coming out (Szulc & Dhoest, 2013).

The internet has thus been recognised as offering LGBTQs an alternative to their long-standing invisibility and stereotyping in traditional mainstream media, a sort of 'third place', which combines 'connected sociality of public space with anonymity of the closet' (Woodland, 2000, p. 418). As supportive and empowering as this 'third place' may be, it is not free of prejudice: research indicates that issues of racism (Gosine, 2007; Lee, 2007) and sexism (Bromseth & Sundén, 2011) do not evaporate in LGBTQ communities on the internet. What is more, the fact that LGBTQs online become more visible also means they become more easily trackable, which can be used by third parties for different purposes, including commercial ones (Aslinger, 2010; Campbell, 2005) but also those related to surveillance (Phillips, 2007; Phillips & Cunningham, 2007) and censorship (Szulc, 2015). The most recent media developments have turned LGBTQ internet research towards social media (Dhoest & Szulc, 2016; Duguay, 2014; Fox & Warber, 2015) and geosocial dating sites and apps (Blackwell, Birnholtz & Abbott, 2015; Race, 2015; Roth, 2014). While the former, particularly Facebook, become less anonymous than previous online platforms and thus provoke questions about impression management and self-disclosure, the latter introduce new possibilities of overlaying physical spaces with LGBTQ-related data.

This Volume

By now, the importance of both 'old' and 'new' media for LGBTQs has been widely documented. Yet anybody who reviews the literature is able to notice its strong focus on the United States and, to a lesser degree, other Anglophone contexts. This is partly due to the fact that only English-language sources were mentioned in our survey, but it also reflects the relative dearth of English-language research on non-Anglophone contexts. Although there are some recent and important studies on the uses and roles of media for LGBTQs in other parts of the world (e.g. Berry, Martin & Yue, 2003; Görkemli, 2014; Kuntsman & Al-Qasimi, 2012; Pullen, 2012), the field strongly gravitates towards North America. Continental Europe, in particular, is conspicuously absent from the picture, notwithstanding its (at times disputably) central position in many other fields of research. As Lukasz Szulc notes in relation to LGBTQ internet studies, such quantitative dominance of US cases translates into 'the tendency of U.S. scholars writing about U.S. cases to ignore (at worst) or take for granted (at best) their research contexts' (2014, p. 2929). This tendency is obviously not unique to LGBTQ media studies but constitutes a bigger problem typical of (Western) media studies in general (Curran & Park, 2000; Goggin & McLelland, 2009; Thussu, 2009a). Responding to this problem, Daya Thussu (2009b), the editor of a volume entitled *Internationalizing Media Studies*, urges scholars to historicise media and culture, take religion seriously, break free from the hegemony of Anglo-American theorisation and go beyond a merely tokenistic engagement with non-US or non-UK contexts.

The current volume explicitly aims to contribute insights from Continental Europe to the literature on LGBTQ media representations and uses, going against the implicit universalism in this literature and adding 'provincialized' forms of knowledge (Chakrabarty, 2000) which are situated in specific cultural and historical contexts. Broadening the scope from Northern and Western Europe, which are most prominent in LGBTQ research, our collection also zooms in on countries in Eastern and Southern Europe. Alphabetically, the thirteen countries discussed are Belgium, Denmark, Germany, Ireland, Italy, Latvia, the Netherlands, Poland, Portugal, Russia, Serbia, Sweden and the United Kingdom. Each chapter reflects on the significance of cultural specifics, be it by interrogating a particular national context or comparing different national contexts, by focusing on a particular city or region or by discussing the transnational experiences of immigrants. As a whole, the volume seeks to provide a sufficiently panoramic overview of the specificity and variety of LGBTQ experiences across Europe. While media are the central object of research in all chapters, our authors take a more media-decentred approach, not analysing media in isolation but focusing on their significance for communities and users within a particular cultural context.

This volume explores an unusual variety of connections between LGBTQs and media, ranging from LGBTQs being the object of representations to their consumption and creation of media content. Each of these roles entails a form of agency and empowerment, within certain structuring limitations. These limitations are related not only to particular national and cultural contexts, with different LGBTQ rights and forms of self-organisation, but also to particular media, with their characteristic affordances. A wide range of media is discussed, starting with mass media such as television and the press, but also including music as a significant medium for LGBTQ culture. The primary focus in our case studies, however, is on digital media, in particular blogs, social media and dating sites, reflecting wider tendencies in the academic literature and indeed society today. Collectively, our contributors cover a striking diversity of possible interactions between LGBTQs and contemporary media.

While we have decided to use the acronym LGBTQ as an umbrella term to refer to sexual and gender minorities, individual chapters may use other, more particular terms, such as gay men, lesbians, LGBs, trans* people and queers. This reflects not only the range of approaches in academia today but also, importantly, the variety of subject positions taken up by sexual and gender minorities. Where possible, the authors adopt the labels preferred and used by the people they study. In this way as well, what we are able to offer is a diverse and inclusive view of the field.

Methodologically too this volume is all but uniform, as a wide range of (sometimes innovative) methods is used. The contributions aim for a deeper understanding of media in context, often by combining methods such as content analysis, discourse analysis, semiotic analysis, music analysis, image analysis, in-depth interviews, oral history interviews, surveys, netnography and participant observation. Thus, our collection offers a state-of-the-art overview of possible ways to approach the interaction between media and LGBTQs. All authors, however, prioritise a qualitative approach, which is deemed to be most suited to obtain an in-depth understanding of the meanings carried by media and their uses. And all present concrete case studies, based on empirical data favouring extensive contextualised analysis over theoretical reflection.

Diversity is at the heart of this volume, not only in pleading for the study of a broad range of people and media from different disciplinary and methodological perspectives, but also in resisting the urge to extrapolate and generalise. The chapters, as a whole, build up an argument for specificity, contextualisation and a 'provincialized' understanding of the connections between media, culture, gender and sexuality. What we have before us is a smorgasbord of historically and culturally specific expressions of gender and sexuality, which are reflected and explored across an ever increasing range of media outlets. This volume zooms in on a number of facets of this kaleidoscope, each chapter discussing the intersection of a particular European context and a particular medium with its characteristic affordances and limitations.

Structure

To guide the reader through this diverse landscape, the book is divided into five parts, each exploring a specific aspect or medium. Part I, *Histories of Representation in Mass Media and Beyond*, takes a historical approach, investigating how different media were used to represent LGBTQs, but also how LGBTQs used media to create their own cultures and communities. Páraic Kerrigan discusses the impact of Ireland's first TV broadcast of a homosexual couple in 1980, pinpointing the social relevance of mainstream representations of homosexuality, particularly in a conservative and religious country such as Ireland at the time. By portraying a gay couple in their domestic context, Kerrigan argues, this broadcast changed the heteronormative idea of domesticity. Ana Maria Brandão, Tânia Cristina Machado and Joana Afonso explore the early lesbian press in Portugal. Starting relatively late, in 1990, this press reflects transformations in Portuguese society and its emerging lesbian and gay community, including tensions between the diverging purposes of identification and political mobilisation. Extending the scope from television and magazines to music, Robbe Herreman and Alexander Dhoest complete this historical part of the volume with their analysis of a particular segment of drag culture in the Belgian city of Antwerp from the 1970s onwards. Arguing, like the preceding authors, that media played a key role in defining lesbian and gay cultures, Herreman and Dhoest analyse drag musicals as a shared form of 'gay culture' as well as of symbolic resistance to dominant structures of gender and sexuality.

Part II, *Media Consumption, Identification and Role Models*, deals with one of the key issues in LGBTQ lives, that of sexual and gender identity formation and the role contemporary media play in supporting this process. Ulrike Roth analyses how the internet facilitates the process of coming out for queer-lesbians in Germany. While acknowledging the key role played by the internet, she draws attention to its limitations and the ways in which the internet is sometimes *not* used by certain individuals in specific contexts. Marion Wasserbauer studies the importance and role of music for the creation of women's fluid non-heterosexual identities in Flanders, the northern region of Belgium. Like Roth, she points to individual differences, both in processes of identification and in the roles played by music, while also highlighting the importance of local role models. Finally, Louis Bailey, Jay McNeil and Sonja J. Ellis shift the focus to transgender people, a group which came to social, media and scholarly attention only recently. Based on the UK Trans Mental Health Study, they discuss how mainstream media representations (including television and the press) were predominantly perceived as negative and hurtful by respondents. While noting a certain amount of progress over the past years, they argue for the need to move away from cisnormative frameworks and representations.

Part III, *LGBTQs as Producers in the Digital Age: Blogging*, zooms in on online narratives about and by LGBTQs, created as alternatives to dominant discourses in the traditional media of Eastern and Southern Europe.

Evgeniya Boklage draws on the concepts of public sphere and counterpublics to assess the potential and limitations of the Russian LGBT blogging community *AntiDogma* to form a safe, open and inclusive space for discussing LGBT-relevant topics. Giulia Evolvi also employs the notion of the counterpublic with reference to blog discussions about homosexuality. By analysing both atheist and Catholic discourses, she is able to show that the internet helps to challenge the invisibility of LGBTQs in Italian mainstream media not only in favour of but also against LGBTQ rights. Finally, Joana Chojnicka offers a detailed semiotic analysis of Latvian and Polish LGBTQ and feminist blogs. In particular, she points to the importance of layout and images, and their relations with texts and denotative/connotative meanings, in articulating a variety of dissident positions online.

Part IV, *Discourses on and by LGBTQs on Social Media*, addresses the central role played by social media such as Facebook in the contemporary media landscape, also among LGBTQs. While they are generally perceived as liberating, social media also constitute a normative environment. Thus Tim Savenije demonstrates how homosexuality is often normatively referenced in Facebook comments on news stories, based on his qualitative content analysis of Dutch and Belgian news fanpages. He notes that the attitudes towards homosexuality expressed in these comments are often introduced in discussions of other topics and are strongly inspired by the immediate context of these news stories. Jakob Svensson studies a more local social medium, the Swedish gay community and dating site Qruiser, where homosexuality is equally brought up in other – in this case political – discussions. As part of the verbal 'cockfighting' taking place, 'correct' ways of being gay are used to justify political positions. Finally, Daniel Cardoso discusses how Portuguese youngsters resort to new media to find information about sexuality and gender, to engage in civic participation, but also to use pornography and sexting, as part of their identity-building relationships with new media. According to Cardoso, through their practices and discourses youngsters co-produce and shape themselves as sexual(ised) subjects, governing and disciplining their behaviours and those of others.

In Part V, *Self-Presentation and Intimacy on Online Dating Sites*, the authors take a close look at the uses of popular dating sites and apps by gay men. Lorenza Parisi and Francesca Comunello discuss the role of the geosocial app Grindr for gay men based in the urban contexts of Milan and Rome. They analyse self-disclosure practices, patterns of interactions and users' reflections on their adoption of the app, and conclude that Grindr helps gay men to update their 'queer cartographies', providing them with gay-relevant information about the physical spaces they navigate. Andrew DJ Shield too examines geosocial media, particularly Grindr and PlanetRomeo, but focuses on their role for newcomers and immigrants in the greater Copenhagen area. Comparing the uses of those 'new' media to the uses of 1970s ads in gay magazines, he points out that, 'As in the 1970s, today's online dating platforms connect potential and recent immigrants to locals, and enable cross-cultural social networks that can assist newcomers with friendship and logistical support'. Zoran Milosavljevic, in turn, investigates the strategies of disclosing or non-disclosing one's HIV status on gay dating sites in Serbia. Drawing on his interviews with users of Grindr, PlanetRomeo and Gay-Serbia.com, he shows how online strategies of (in)visibility and internet bareback subcultures may increase the risk of HIV transmission.

Last but not least, Sharif Mowlabocus offers his reflections on this book project and provides some directions for future research in LGBTQ media studies. First, he advocates intergenerational studies and projects, which would help us understand and revive the kind of intergenerational dialogue between LGBTQ people that was characteristic of the vivid pre-internet bar cultures in the West. Second, he asks for more intersectional research, which would pay close attention to diverse dimensions of LGBTQ lives, including race, ethnicity, class, age, disability and geographical location. Third, he proposes deeper engagement with issues of physical space in LGBTQ media studies, taking into account where LGBTQs use media but also how media, especially geosocial apps, can render LGBTQs visible to the extent that they become more vulnerable. Finally, Mowlabocus reminds us of the need for more non-Anglo-American studies in LGBTQ media research. Not only should such studies discuss appropriations and assimilations of globally circulating texts and media, he argues, but they should also drop the aura of exceptionality and influence thinking beyond the local. As editors of this book, we hope that the collection of chapters presented here will make a useful and thrilling contribution in this direction.

References

Alexander, J. (2002). Homo-Pages and Queer Sites: Studying the Construction and Representation of Queer Identities on the World Wide Web. *International Journal of Sexuality and Gender Studies*, 7(2/3), 85–106.

Aslinger, B. (2010). PlanetOut and the Dichotomies of Queer Media Conglomeration. In C. Pullen & M. Cooper (Eds.), *LGBT Identity and Online Mew Media* (pp. 113–124). New York: Routledge.

Avila-Saavedra, G. (2009). Nothing Queer about Queer Television: Televised Construction of Gay Masculinities. *Media, Culture & Society*, 31(1), 5–21.

Barnhurst, K. G. (Ed.) (2007). *Media Queered: Visibility and Its Discontents*. New York: Peter Lang.

Battles, K. & Hilton-Morrow, W. (2002). Gay Characters in Conventional Spaces: *Will and Grace* and the Situation Comedy Genre. *Critical Studies in Media Communication*, 19(1), 87–105.

Berry, C., Martin, F. & Yue, A. (Eds.) (2003). *Mobile Cultures: New Media in Queer Asia*. Durham, NC: Duke University Press.

Blackwell, C., Birnholtz, J. & Abbott, C. (2015). Seeing and Being Seen: Co-Situation and Impression Formation Using Grindr, a Location-Aware Gay Dating App. *New Media & Society*, 17(7), 1117–1136.

Bromseth, J. & Sundén, J. (2011). Queering Internet Studies: Intersections of Gender and Sexuality. In M. Consalvo & C. Ess (Eds.), *The Handbook of Internet Studies* (pp. 270–299). Chichester: Wiley-Blackwell.

Campbell, J. E. (2004). *Getting It On Online: Cyberspace, Gay Male Sexuality and Embodied Identity*. London: Harrington Park.

Campbell, J. E. (2005). Outing PlanetOut: Surveillance, Gay Marketing and Internet Affinity Portals. *New Media & Society, 7*(5), 663–683.

Chakrabarty, D. (2000). *Provincializing Europe: Postcolonial Thought and Historical Difference*. Princeton: Princeton University Press.

Correll, S. (1995). The Ethnography of an Electronic Bar: The Lesbian Cafe. *Journal of Contemporary Ethnography, 24*(3), 270–298.

Curran, J. & Park, M.-K. (Eds.) (2000). *De-Westernizing Media Studies*. London: Routledge.

Dhoest, A. & Szulc, L. (2016, forthcoming). Navigating Online Selves: Social, Cultural and Material Contexts of Social Media Use by Diasporic Gay Men. *Social Media & Society*.

Döring, N. M. (2009). The Internet's Impact on Sexuality: A Critical Review of 15 Years of Research. *Computers in Human Behavior, 25*, 1089–1101.

Driver, S. (2007). *Queer Girls and Popular Culture: Reading, Resisting, and Creating Media*. New York: Peter Lang.

Duguay, S. (2014). 'He Has a Way Gayer Facebook Than I Do': Investigating Sexual Identity Disclosure and Context Collapse on a Social Networking Site. *New Media & Society*. DOI: 10.1177/1461444814549930.

Dyer, R. (1977). *Gays in Film*. London: BFI.

Dyer, R. (1990). *Now You See It: Studies on Lesbian and Gay Film*. London: Routledge.

Fejes, F. (2000). Making a Gay Masculinity. *Critical Studies in Mass Communication, 17*(1), 113–116.

Fejes, F. & Petrich, K. (1993). Invisibility, Homophobia and Heterosexism: Lesbians, Gays and the Media. *Critical Studies in Mass Communication, 10*(4), 396–422.

Fox, J. & Warber, K. M. (2015). Queer Identity Management and Political Self-Expression on Social Networking Sites: A Co-Cultural Approach to the Spiral of Silence. *Journal of Communication, 65*(1), 79–100.

Goggin, G. & McLelland, M. (Eds.) (2009). *Internationalizing Internet Studies: Beyond Anglophone Paradigms*. New York: Routledge.

Görkemli, S. (2014). *Grassroots Literacies: Lesbian and Gay Activism and the Internet in Turkey*. New York: SUNY Press.

Gosine, A. (2007). Brown to Blonde at Gay.com: Passing White in Queer Cyberspace. In K. O'Riordan & D. J. Phillips (Eds.), *Queer Online: Media Technology & Sexuality* (pp. 139–153). New York: Peter Lang.

Gray, M. (2009). *Out in the Country: Youth, Media, and Queer Visibility in Rural America*. New York: NYU Press.

Gross, L. (1991). Out of the Mainstream: Sexual Minorities and the Mass Media. In M. A. Wolf & A. P. Kielwasser (Eds.), *Gay People, Sex and the Media* (pp. 19–46). New York: The Haworth Press.

Gross, L. (2001). *Up from Invisibility: Lesbians, Gay Men, and the Media in America*. New York: Columbia University Press.

Gudelunas, D. (2012). Generational Differences among Gay Men and Lesbians: Social and Media Change. Paper presented at the International Communication Association conference, Phoenix, 24–28 May.

Harrington, C. L. (2003). Homosexuality on *All My Children*: Transforming the Daytime Landscape. *Journal of Broadcasting and Electronic Media, 47*(2): 216–235.

Kivel, B. & Kleiber, D. (2000). Leisure in the Identity Formation of Lesbian/Gay Youth: Personal, but Not Social. *Leisure Sciences*, 22(4), 215–232.

Kuntsman, A. & Al-Qasimi, N. (Eds.) (2012). *Queering Middle Eastern Cyberscapes*. Special issue of the *Journal of Middle East Women's Studies*, 8(3), 1–157.

Lee, H. N. (2007). Queering Race in Cyberspace. In K. G. Barnhurst (Ed.), *Media/Queered: Visibility and Its Discontents* (pp. 243–260). New York: Peter Lang.

McGlotten, S. (2013). *Virtual Intimacies: Media, Affect, and Queer Sociality*. Albany: SUNY Press.

McRea, S. (1997). Flash Made Word: Sex, Text, and the Virtual Body. In D. Porter (Ed.), *Internet Culture* (pp. 73–86). New York: Routledge.

Mehra, B., Merkel, C. & Bishop, A. P. (2004). The Internet for Empowerment of Minority and Marginalized Users. *New Media & Society*, 6(6), 781–802.

Mowlabocus, S. (2010). *Gaydar Culture: Gay Men, Technology and Embodiment in the Digital Age*. Farnham: Ashgate.

Phillips, D. J. (2007). Privacy, Surveillance, or Visibility: New Information Environments in the Light of Queer Theory. In K. G. Barnhurst (Ed.), *Media/Queered: Visibility and Its Discontents* (pp. 231–242). New York: Peter Lang.

Phillips, D. J. & Cunningham, C. (2007). Queering Surveillance Research. In K. O'Riordan & D. J. Phillips (Eds.), *Queer Online: Media Technology & Sexuality* (pp. 31–43). New York: Peter Lang.

Pullen, C. (Ed.) (2012). *LGBT Transnational Identity and the Media*. Basingstoke: Palgrave Macmillan.

Race, K. (2015). Speculative Pragmatism and Intimate Arrangements: Online Hook-Up Devices in Gay Life. *Culture, Health & Sexuality*, 17(4), 496–511.

Rak, J. (2004). The Digital Queer: Weblogs and Internet Identity. *Biography*, 28(1), 166–182.

Roth, Y. (2014). Locating the 'Scruff Guy': Theorizing Body and Space in Gay Geosocial Media. *International Journal of Communication*, 8, 2113–2133.

Shaw, D. F. (1997). Gay Men and Computer Communication: A Discourse of Sex and Identity in Cyberspace. In S. G. Jones (Ed.), *Virtual Culture: Identity and Communication in Cybersociety* (pp. 133–145). London: Sage.

Szulc, L. (2014). The Geography of LGBTQ Internet Studies. *International Journal of Communication*, 8, 2927–2931.

Szulc, L. (2015). Banal Nationalism and Queers Online: Enforcing and Resisting Cultural Meanings of .tr. *New Media & Society*, 17(9), 1530–1546.

Szulc, L. & Dhoest, A. (2013). The Internet and Sexual Identity Formation: Comparing Internet Use Before and After Coming Out. *Communications: The European Journal of Communication Research*, 38(4), 347–365.

Thussu, D. K. (Ed.) (2009a). *Internationalizing Media Studies*. London: Routledge.

Thussu, D. K. (2009b). Why Internationalize Media Studies and How? In D. K. Thussu (Ed.), *Internationalizing Media Studies* (pp. 13–31). London: Routledge.

Turkle, S. (1995). *Life on the Screen: Identity in the Age of the Internet*. New York: Simon & Schuster.

Woodland, R. (2000). Queer Spaces, Modem Boys and Pagan Statues: Gay/Lesbian Identity and the Construction of Cyberspace. In D. Bell & B. Kennedy (Eds.), *The Cybercultures Reader* (pp. 416–431). London: Routledge.

Part I

Histories of Representation in Mass Media and Beyond

1 Respectably Gay

Homodomesticity in Ireland's First Public Broadcast of a Homosexual Couple

Páraic Kerrigan

On New Year's Eve 1961, President Éamon de Valera launched Raidió Telefís Éireann (RTÉ), stating that 'never before was there in the hands of men an instrument so powerful to influence the thoughts and actions of the multitude' (RTÉ, 1961). As broadcast history would now suggest, de Valera's foreboding was not unfounded. With this new medium of television came radical change, bringing 'a new symbolic structure, habitus and practice nightly into people's homes' (Inglis, 1998, p. 138). As alternative conceptions of Irish life were broadcast into people's living rooms, television also served to question the very definition of the Irish home.

This gradual process continued for the following fifty-five years, as was evident with the 27 July 2013 edition of the *RTÉ Guide*. The cover of this edition featured prominent Irish newsreader Aengus MacGrianna with his partner Terry Gill. It marked the first occasion that a gay couple featured as the cover story for the public service broadcaster's publication and was widely welcomed by gay groups in Ireland as 'a symbol of acceptance' (O'Carroll, 2012). The cover story provided an in-depth interview with the couple in their home and included pictures of the two on their alpaca farm, along with questions and answers about Aengus and Terry's engagement. With its focus on the home and wedding plans, the article overtly demonstrated a form of gay domesticity. This moment marked a huge social transformation from the conservative, heteronormative Ireland previously envisaged by de Valera and the Catholic Church. It was not until a television broadcast on 11 February 1980 that Ireland first witnessed an open and self-identifying homosexual couple: on the current affairs programme *Week In*, Laurie Steele and Arthur Leahy discussed their return from London to live as a couple in Ireland. The episode served as one of the first overt challenges to heteronormativity through the deployment of homodomesticity.

By means of an analysis of primary sources drawn from the Irish film and television archives, as well as print media, letters and telephone complaints lodged by RTÉ into the Irish Queer Archives, this chapter illustrates the representation of homodomesticity and reactions to it by the Irish public.[1] Textual analysis is employed to evaluate the programme as it allows us to question and assess ideological and cultural assumptions encoded within it. Additionally, analytical categories of domesticity, heteronormativity and homodomesticity are employed to extract and identify recurring themes.

This chapter argues that the episode of *Week In* signalled a shift in the configuration of gay subjectivity. Many of the early representations on RTÉ were confined to current affairs programming and tended to focus on gay individuals and politics. This predominantly featured the chairman of the Irish Gay Rights Movement, David Norris (*Last House*, 1975; *Tuesday Report*, 1977; *Challenge*, 1977). In contrast to previous discussions of gay liberation politics, the episode with Laurie and Arthur was the first time a programme broadcast a gay couple within the domestic space of their home and provided an alternative to the heterosexual structure of the home dominant within Irish culture. More importantly, the representation of gay and lesbian people tended to have an explicit political valence as they appeared in debates over sexual liberation or acceptance. While gay individuals, presented as eccentric one-offs, were prevalent across the Irish mediascape, gay couples were glaringly absent. Somewhat ironically, during the same-sex marriage referendum 35 years later, in 2015, the couple became the dominant mode of representation, in ways that some argue were too assimilationist.

The early examples of gay visibility in Irish media pertained almost exclusively to gay men, with the exception of RTÉ's *Tuesday Report*, which featured one lesbian with limited screen time. It wasn't until 1980 again, when Joni Crone came out on *The Late Late Show*, that lesbianism in Ireland became visible to the general public. Crone was a lesbian activist and a founding member of the Dublin Lesbian Line and Liberation for Irish Lesbians. Coincidentally, her appearance took place the same week as Laurie and Arthur's on *Week In*.

Irish migration is a recurring theme on television and in the primary sources, in particular the phenomenon of migrating to London. Accordingly, due consideration will be given to such migration as a result of the oppressive social conditions and criminal laws that were in place during the 1970s and 1980s. RTÉ's 1977 documentary *Tuesday Report* highlighted this issue; it followed Irish migrants to London who had emigrated as a result of their homosexuality. I will examine how the episode of *Week In* describes the unsustainability of living a gay life in Ireland and the need to emigrate to form a gay subjectivity. Following this, I will indicate how a return from the diaspora to form a gay domestic or, as I refer to it, homo-domestic space challenges perceived notions of heteronormativity in Ireland in 1980 (this would later become an important part of the rhetoric of the same-sex marriage referendum in 2015). While many gay people emigrated (see Ferriter, 2012, p. 393; Robinson, 1998, p. 18), it is important to note that those who stayed behind in Ireland managed to form a subculture, although an 'out' gay lifestyle as such was not possible for a number of years. The foundation of the Irish Gay Rights Movement in 1974, which found a site on Parnell Square in Dublin to host meetings and discos, helped to establish a gay social consciousness. It enabled gay people to socialise in a public space for the first time in Ireland. With the founding of the

Hirschfeld Centre in 1979, the Irish gay community began to develop social cohesion and embolden a cohesive identity, which perhaps was a contributing factor to Laurie and Arthur's return.[2]

Gay in Ireland

Contemporary Ireland is among the more progressive countries in Europe regarding LGBT rights. On 22 May 2015, a referendum was put to the people of Ireland regarding the Thirty-fourth Amendment of the Constitution which would permit marriage to be contracted by two persons without distinction as to their sex. Subsequently, Ireland became the first country in the world to introduce same-sex marriage by popular vote, with 62.07% of the electorate voting yes to the constitutional amendment (Referendum Ireland, 2015). However, this liberal attitude towards the gay community is of relatively recent origin in Ireland: for much of its history gay sex acts were illegal. For a long time, Ireland's gay history remained invisible, 'simply recorded in police records, prosecutions of men for same-sex activities or medical records of institutional committals of men and women for the mental illness of inversion' (Walshe, 2006, p. 39). In his autobiography, David Norris, Irish gay rights pioneer and Senator, notes this historic culture of invisibility, and explains that gay people in Ireland 'were almost all in hiding [...] There was a hugely active sexual life in Dublin in the 1950s and 60s, but it was concentrated in public lavatories [...] no one could afford to sustain a relationship' (2012, pp. 79–80).

As a result, having a gay relationship was difficult. Being gay in Ireland was recognised in private spaces through sexual acts, which were inadvertently criminal offences under sections of the Offences Against the Person Act 1861 and the Criminal Law Amendment Act 1885 (Ryan, 2014, p. 101). These oppressive laws remained until Norris took a case to the High Court and the Supreme Court to change them. When his attempts failed, Norris was forced to take the case to the European Court of Human Rights in 1988, where he eventually won. Even then, decriminalisation was not enacted until 1993 (Robinson, 2013, p. 122).

Thus the cultural climate of 1980 in which *Week In* was broadcast was a generally oppressive one. Although the Irish Gay Rights Movement had been founded in 1974 and morphed into the National Gay Federation in 1979, there was still a culture of anxiety and a lot of hostility towards gay people. The pressures of being gay have been recounted by Norris (2012), who recalls collapsing in a Dublin restaurant with a suspected heart attack; it was actually a panic attack brought on by his fear of criminal prosecution. After counselling,

> I was referred to a psychiatrist whose advice to me was to leave this country forever and find refuge in a jurisdiction where a more tolerant attitude towards homosexual men prevailed, specifically, the South of France. This well meant advice I found deeply offensive. (p. 113)

The fact that a Catholic ethos was so firmly rooted in Irish culture contributed to this repressive society for gay individuals. The origins of Catholic influence in the legal system of post-independence Ireland lie in the Constitution of 1937, the drafting of which was personally supervised by Éamon de Valera.[3] Article 41.1 'acknowledges that the homage of public worship is due to Almighty God. It shall hold his name in reverence and shall respect and honour religion'.[4] The special position given to the Catholic Church in Irish society by the Constitution reflects the dominance and moral monopoly held by the Church long before 1937, particularly regarding the health and education systems. As Paul Ryan (2012, p. 180) explains, 'the development of the medical profession as a powerful interest group in society was bolstered by close links with the Catholic Church' to such an extent that 'early Free State governments were reluctant to accept venereal diseases as a real public health issue' (Ferriter, 2004, p. 321).

However, during the 1970s this 'moral monopoly' was under threat from groups such as the Irish Women's Liberation Movement, which formed in 1970 (Inglis, 1998). This was closely followed by the Sexual Liberation Movement in 1973, the Irish Gay Rights Movement in 1974 and the Campaign for Homosexual Law Reform in 1975. The pressure from these dissenting groups challenged the hegemonic ethos of the Catholic Church. The visit of Pope John Paul II in 1979 can be read as a necessary move by the Catholic Church in defending its moral monopoly against the threat of the new social movements. The Pope's visit was the biggest national religious event to have occurred since the Eucharistic Congress of Dublin in 1932. At the opening mass in Dublin's Phoenix Park on 29 September 1979, 1,250,000 people – one quarter of the population of Ireland and one third of that of the Republic of Ireland – attended (*The Irish Times*, 2015). The turnout at these events indicates how much of a Catholic ethos still remained in the country.

The devotional practice of Irish Catholics during this period is evident from the National Survey 1973–74. The findings indicate that 90.9% of Irish people attended mass once a week, with 65.6% attending confession once a month (Research and Development Commission, 1985). The mass attendance of Irish Catholics was almost twice the European average (Inglis, 1998, p. 33). These statistics suggest the degree to which Catholic dogma influenced public and private life – including the expression of homosexuality – well into the 1980s. Heather Ingman argues that the Papal visit was pivotal in the Catholic Church's promotion of its traditional ethos, as it 'strengthened conservative opinion, resulting in years of conservative backlash' (Ingman, 2007, p. 21).

Between 1962 and 1972, the Gardaí (the Irish police) reported 455 convictions for crimes of 'indecency with males' or 'gross indecency' (Hug, 1999, p. 211). Against this backdrop, coming out as a gay couple on the public service broadcaster was a political act. The broadcast of two gay men in a domestic space stood in stark contradiction to the surrounding heteronormative society and served to challenge accepted notions of relationships and domesticity in Ireland. *Week In* was part of RTÉ's News and Current Affairs department and the premise of the programme was to engage in a sociological examination of different aspects of Irish life. As a result, the programme took a documentary approach, presenting a wide variety of arguments through rhetorical devices that appealed to 'logics, ethics and emotions' while also 'combining images with verbal testimony' (Pramaggiore & Wallis, 2011, p. 282).

Locating the Homodomestic in Irish Broadcast History

Although the Catholic faith played a significant role in the marginalisation and oppression of gay people in Ireland, the country's pervasive ideology of domesticity was equally influential on the alienating experiences that led many Irish gay people to consider emigrating. The concept of heteronormativity, as it is used in this chapter, refers to the term advanced by Lauren Berlant and Michael Warner (2002); it identifies the way social and political institutions assume the most desirable forms of kinship to be based on a monogamous intimacy between a man and a woman, who in turn reproduce the norm through the regulative institution of the heterosexual family (2002, p. 194).

In an Irish context, concepts of domesticity and heteronormativity are enshrined in the political structures of the State. Article 41.2.1 of the Constitution marks the home as a site of femininity and traditional domesticity: 'as it recognises by her life within the home, woman gives to the State a support without which the common good cannot be achieved'. The designation of the home as the site for Irish women to have and raise children is solidified further when the State 'endeavours to ensure that mothers shall not be obliged by economic necessity to engage in labour to the neglect of their duties in the home'. Constitutionally therefore the Irish home is defined in terms of heteronormativity.

This heteronormative, nuclear family structure circulated massively in the cultural discourses of Irish media in the period prior to the 1980 broadcast of *Week In*, with popular drama series such as *Tolka Row* (1964–1968), *The Riordans* (1965–1979) and *Bracken* (1978–1982) reinforcing domesticity in terms of the heteronormative family unit. These television dramas did not deliberately omit gay domesticity. They did however fail to represent, in overt or open ways, different orientations or family structures. Consequently their silent exclusions reinforced the dominant normative heterosexual structure. Helena Sheehan (1987) argues that RTÉ drama series such as *Tolka Row* presented the heterosexual family as the centre of power relations in an Irish community. Such programmes not only reinforced the desirability of heterosexuality, but also implied that it was key to social organisation and status.

This domestic heteronormativity on national television went unchallenged until the surprising homodomesticity of the 1980 *Week In* episode featuring Laurie and Arthur. The concept of homodomesticity can be traced to photographer Chad Houle's 2009 exhibition entitled *Homodomestic*.

Houle's photographs featured gay men situated in domestic spaces, inspired by the fact that:

> I grew up without any real examples of love. I never was able to make the connection between being gay and the ability to be in a strong, lasting relationship [...] I look back not knowing who I was or how there were so few images of that life I so greatly yearned for [...] With this new 'homo-domesticity' the home plays an important element as a symbol for stability and commitment.
>
> (Houle, 2009)

Although Houle is writing in an American context, it can be argued that his comments are also applicable to Ireland. In a culture notably saturated with depictions of coupled domesticity, there were no representations of gay couples or family structures. When gay people were depicted, they were treated as idiosyncratic individuals or angry activists, confined to current affairs studios where gay liberation politics played out and gay activists fought for equality. But in the case of Laurie and Arthur, homodomesticity becomes a representational strategy.

Houle's concept of homodomesticity helps us revisit representations such as *Week In* to interrogate Laurie and Arthur's lives and to understand the political dimensions of such a representation. Whereas the representation may not have registered as political in comparison to the visibility given to gay activists on broadcast media, its political effects come into view in the context of debates surrounding heteronormativity and theorisations of the homodomestic. Although some scholars suggest that homodomesticity may be depoliticised and assimilationist (see Doran, 2013), I argue that this is not necessarily the case with this particular historic instance of Irish gay domesticity. For one, the representation of Laurie and Arthur was not part of a fictional TV show, but was instead a sociological documentary item as part of a current affairs show aimed at reflecting the realities of being gay in Ireland. It was only the fourth case of gay visibility on Irish television and attempted to highlight that relationships in Ireland were not solely heterosexual. In addition, it became a crucial reference point for the gay community, informing them that it was possible to be gay and stay in Ireland. Thus the programme's representational politics anticipated Houle's idea of homodomesticity as a 'symbol for stability and commitment' (Houle, 2009). This chapter examines how homodomesticity may be used to signal a shift in the configuration of gay subjectivity in 1980, a configuration which was similarly deployed during the same-sex marriage referendum in 2015.

Narratives of Escape and Return

It is important to note that for much of the *Week In* programme the discussion was led by Laurie and Arthur themselves, with some direction from the presenter, Áine O'Connor. This provided the two men with authoritative standing on the topic of homosexuality, rather than what was a common trope in Irish documentary programming of a 'designated off-screen authority to make assertions about the topic' (Pramaggiore & Wallis, 2011, p. 283). The interview first and foremost considered the issues of self-determination and of becoming aware of one's sexuality, as indicated by O'Connor's question to Arthur: 'How did you find out you were actually gay?' To this, Arthur replies, 'it was something I was aware of inside myself causing incredible conflicts and anxiety'. Considering the centrality of the family to Irish culture, it is unsurprising that O'Connor speaks within the frame of family rhetoric when she follows up by asking Arthur about the effects of his sexuality on his family. Arthur replies, 'they were very shocked, they would probably see it in terms of inadequacy'. The response speaks to the attitudes of Irish society towards gay people in the early seventies and the pressure on the formation of heterosexual couples and family ties.

One of the first major issues that the broadcast brings up about being gay in Ireland during the 1980s is that of migrating to find a more accepting society in which to live a homosexual lifestyle. Arthur explains that as a result of the anxiety he felt living in Ireland, he believed he had no option but to migrate to London for the opportunity to form a meaningful relationship with another man. In an essay on diaspora and hybridity, Alan Sinfield (1995) similarly draws attention to how the 'diasporic sense of separation and loss' experienced by gay people often results from being cut off from the heterosexual culture of their childhood, which becomes the site of 'impossible return and impossible memories' (p. 102). What is poignant in Arthur's description of being pushed into a diasporic gay identity is his inability to conform with or assimilate into the social milieu of Irish culture. He hasn't merely lost the culture of his childhood; he faces near-total invisibility and ostracism if he doesn't leave the country. This is specifically linked to how the 1937 Constitution of Ireland inscribes heteronormativity as the basis of the nation-state. Article 41 recognises the family as the 'natural primary and fundamental unit group of society, guaranteeing to protect the family in its constitution and authority, as the necessary basis of social order and its indispensable welfare of the Nation and the State'. Article 41.3.1 galvanises this heteronormativity further by 'guarding with special care the institution of Marriage, on which the family is founded, and to protect it against attack'. Consistent with the importance of the family within the Irish Constitution, the institution of marriage is singled out for discussion in the 1980 broadcast. Gay identities are rendered invisible by the State, as gay people at the time cannot form any recognisable family unit that fits the Constitution's heteronormative definition. With the Church and State advocating marriage as the fabric of society, gay people are rendered invisible by legal means (with the exception of the aforementioned legislation criminalising same-sex acts). Given these constraints, it is hardly surprising that migration played a decisive role in Arthur's coming-out process and 'unsettled the fixities of family and place in Irish culture' (O'Toole, 2013, p. 138).

Because of the centrality of the heterosexual family unit as a means of social organisation and control in twentieth-century Irish society, the *Week In* episode demonstrated how Arthur, even after migrating to London, did not find it easy to take off the shackles of oppression as a result of his upbringing in Ireland. As he explains:

> You're so long oppressed by the society around you that you internalise that oppression and you oppress yourself, so that even if you go to a situation which is free or open, that you still carry that with you, and I think that's the important thing now is that the oppression does damage the sexual development, and you carry that with you for the rest of your life. You carry the oppression with you always and that's part of the gay consciousness.

Arthur's comments illustrate how migrating geographically away from oppression does not necessarily free you from it. Yet the activity of leaving in his case also reminds us that for the queer migrant subject it may be necessary to 'leave to become' – that 'one is forced to leave in order to come out' (Fortier, 2001, p. 404). It also underpins Fortier's description of 'home as not-home' in the narratives of 'gay people who experience estrangement in the original home' and whose migration is thus 'a movement away from being estranged' (2001, p. 403). In discussing the gay scene in London moreover, Arthur describes how he found it difficult to relate to other gay people, to the extent that 'when you actually come to relate to somebody, that you don't have the capacity to do so'. Despite this, he eventually met Laurie in a night club in London, something that, he stresses, would never have happened in Ireland. After living in London for five years, Laurie and Arthur decided to 'come back to Ireland to try make a life for themselves in Cork'.

Arthur and Laurie's return from the diaspora proved to be a transgressive act at the time. First of all, they were a gay couple and as such they were openly confronting an environment that had instituted heterosexual coupling as the fundamental fabric of Irish society. Both their gay identities and, more importantly, their coupling were threats to heteronormativity. Secondly, their relationship could not be validated by marriage, so that in the eyes of the State they were invisible. Arthur explains that his kind of relationship is 'not reinforced by the society around and you are very much on your own... You don't get a sense of identity'. Still, the couple's return from the diaspora and the broadcast of the programme played a significant role in the decision of other gay emigrants to London to return to Ireland as well. Among other examples, gay rights activist Marie Mulholland emphasises this about her return from the diaspora. She recalls of the *Week In* programme:

> I saw that on a visit home to Belfast. I had been living in London at the time. I was seriously thinking about coming home for good and I wanted to know what it would be like to be at home in Ireland

and to be out and his [Arthur's] strength, his energy and his courage, and his boyfriend's, gave me the courage to do it as well.

(in Lynch, 2003)

The visibility provided to a gay couple and their homodomestic space in Ireland indicated to Mulholland that, despite the predominant invisibility of gay people, living an 'out' life might now be possible. As a result of the broadcast, Mulholland moved home and became an integral part of the gay rights movement in Ireland.

The interview takes a characteristic turn as presenter Áine O'Connor starts to speak in the rhetoric of heteronormativity, asking the couple, 'Do you have a sense of husband and wife?' Implied in this question is the expectation that gay men adopt gender stereotypes of dominant and submissive roles, while also having to make attempts to perform identities that enable them to submit to the heteronormative family structure of Irish society. Instead of fulfilling the institutional roles of husband and wife, Laurie explains that he and Arthur have developed a relationship that operates outside of this system and that appeals to the liberal subject: they have decided to put 'the importance on ourselves as individuals living together'. In accordance with the heteronormative logic of the questions, the issue of having children is broached. The couple acknowledges this as impossible, with Laurie explaining that the height of their expectations has been to arrive at a situation 'where there was straight adults and maybe their children'. When asked by O'Connor if people's opinions on 'gays threatening family structure' are valid, Arthur denies this but also notes there is no further possibility of them assimilating into the Irish heteronormative family unit, because the 'family structure just does not accommodate' gay people.

At the time of this broadcast, in 1980, the heteronormative nuclear family structure clearly still dominated the social order and defined the concepts of home and domestic space in Ireland. When Laurie and Arthur decided to leave London for Ireland, they did so with the knowledge that their coupling not only challenged Irish society but made them vulnerable to criminal prosecution. Their example suggests how, historically, Irish people returning from the diaspora have challenged heteronormative society, while it also calls into question the presumption that presenting gay relationships as a non-threatening, alternative form of coupling is necessarily apolitical.[5]

Homodomesticity: Respectably Gay

Writing in 2013, Steven Edward Doran argues that 'for many, the presence of homodomestic representations on mainstream television signals that assimilation and normalisation of gays and lesbians into mainstream culture is complete, that the vision of gay and lesbian activism is realised' (p. 96). However, he argues that homodomesticity does have the potential to marginalise 'gay and lesbian identities, lifestyles and culture through the representational strategies of suppression' to the extent that it may silence and erase 'the possibility of queer alternatives' (p. 97). In the context of Laurie and Arthur's appearance on *Week In*, we might note that in much queer scholarship the domestic depoliticises and demobilises gay populations, promoting heteronormativity in order to tame deviant sexual subjects and render them non-threatening to a straight majority (Gorman-Murray, 2006; Reed, 2007). In this particular historic case, this may be partially true, considering that a respectability politics is employed by Laurie and Arthur to show how some of their social values are continuous and compatible with mainstream Irish values. This respectability politics is conveyed through some of the visual details of the interview.

The interview takes place in the living room of their home in Cork. The room contains a television set and a piano, with pictures decorating the walls – all markers of traditional domesticity. The structure of the interview on camera is also worth considering. Both Laurie and Arthur sit on a couch in the middle of the living room and O'Connor sits on a stool facing them, with her back to a burning fireplace. The fact that the interview is structured in this manner, and not in a studio environment, gives the programme a number of affordances. It makes the gay couple non-threatening, as they have invited the production crew into the private space of their home. It also provides this unusual homodomestic space visibility to the wider Irish public. One particular shot cuts away to Laurie sitting in an armchair reading a newspaper. As it slowly zooms out, it includes a wider shot of the living room within the frame. Arthur enters with a pot of tea and approaches the dining table, which is nicely decorated with cups, saucers and flowers; he beckons Laurie over as he pours him tea. They begin to eat and talk to each other. Other shots included in the interview comprise the couple walking around Cork as city-shoppers.

The homodomestic imagery produced by these visual cues silently promotes the idea of homonormativity. The latter concept refers to 'a politics that does not contest dominant heteronormative assumptions and institutions, but upholds and sustains them, while promising the possibility of a demobilised gay constituency and a privatised, depoliticised gay culture anchored in domesticity' (Duggan, 2002, p. 179). One might certainly argue that the desire to create a domestic space as a gay couple aligns itself, particularly in Irish culture, with heteronormative standards. However, from a historic perspective this was not entirely or necessarily assimilationist. It might also be argued that the selected visual details represent gay men reclaiming the traditional Irish home for themselves.

In one sense, homodomesticity for the couple creates a safe space from the surrounding heteronormative society. Yet although their private home offers a sanctuary of sorts, Laurie points out that there is a 'hassle' being a gay couple 'in terms of your everyday communication with society'. The couple indicates their resistance towards homonormativity and the heteronormative standards set out in the Irish Constitution. Their refusal to conform was significant for the gay audience watching at the time, as was the alternative homodomestic lifestyle presented. Laurie explains that many gay people explore their relationships in 'very furtive fashions' and that some gay individuals would identify as such only fleetingly 'a couple of nights a week' as a result of them being unable to 'tie it in to their work or their families'. He argues that under these circumstances 'most relationships between gays are for a couple of hours [...] there's no possibility of a relationship developing'. This response spoke to the wider gay male culture in Ireland of the 1970s, where a substantial cruising culture existed and gay sexual acts were confined largely to public lavatories. Sociologically speaking, Laurie and Arthur offered an alternative arrangement to the quick and fleeting relationships provided by a cruising culture. They suggested that it was possible to be gay and develop a sustained relationship in a domestic environment, even if this was not reinforced by Irish society. At the same time Laurie was keen to emphasise that he and Arthur were exceptions and that most gay people 'wouldn't be game to set up a situation to encompass both of them in a living situation' as a result of the criminal laws in effect during this period.

The significance of a gay couple on television in Ireland is remembered by civil rights activist Christopher Robson, who recalls watching the broadcast for the first time in the Hirschfeld Centre 'in the company of a lot of other people and the sense of huge pride and delight in seeing a very sensitive programme shown on Irish television' (in Lynch, 2003). As Robson indicates, the programme encouraged gay individuals to gather in the Hirschfeld Centre and watch it collectively, generating a shared sense of pride and the formation of a queer kinship structure, which Judith Butler describes as affective social structures that 'emerge to address fundamental forms of human dependency' (Butler, 2002, p. 15).

As much of an enabling effect as this broadcast had on Ireland's LGBT community, the 'Summary of Telephone Reaction Received on Friday, 8th February 1980' proves to be a barometer for the response of the general public to the broadcast. Perhaps surprisingly, it was quite positive overall, with one of the callers saying, 'I wish to congratulate the *Week In* production team on a really good programme. I feel it gave a very good insight into the problem of homosexuality' (IQA, Box MS 45, 940/4). Although this backhanded compliment indicates the commonly circulating prejudice about homosexuality being a problem in Ireland, it is still largely supportive. The comment was followed by two male callers complimenting the programme and another caller who said he watched it 'with three other homosexuals tonight and thought it was great' (IQA, Box MS 45, 940/4). Here again, it is clear that the broadcast was of significance to the gay community; this is further corroborated by the fact that five callers rang RTÉ requesting the number of the gay rights association in a search for further details.

The generally positive reactions in the telephone summary make for interesting reading when mapped against the broadcast of Joni Crone on *The Late Late Show*, which was shown during the same week. The vehement reactions to her person were marked by comments such as 'I do not want to pay a licence fee to see that filthy person', and callers continued to complain about the subject, referring to what they described as 'last week's prostitute and this week's pervert'. Many of these callers demanded that the subject should not be introduced again on RTÉ because 'RTÉ has a duty to the public not to corrupt them or help sick people corrupt the youth' (IQA, Box MS 45, 940/4). What becomes clear is the contrast between the positive reception of Laurie and Arthur and the hostility displayed towards Joni Crone's appearance as a lesbian. Up to this point in Irish TV history, most of the programming pertained to gay men and their lives; not much attention had been given to lesbians. Joni's appearance on *The Late Late Show* was one of the first cases of lesbian visibility. It may have appeared more threatening to Irish viewers, whereas the homodomestic and gay life of Laurie and Arthur, although a challenge to heteronormative Ireland, gave a form of respectability to homosexuality that had been largely absent from the media.

Some scholars today maintain that the aspect of respectability in homodomestic representations on mainstream television signals that the normalisation of gays and lesbians and their assimilation into heteronormative culture are complete (see Doran, 2013; Gorman-Murray, 2006). Although homodomesticity may indeed provide a way to regulate and sanitise a dissident sexuality, it also has the potential to challenge and subvert the normative heterosexuality of the home. I would prefer to argue then that the homodomestic becomes a symbolic site at the threshold between queerness and normativity – at once gesturing towards an assimilationist conservatism and the domesticated version of gayness it advances, while also serving a progressive purpose in granting visibility to gays in mainstream culture (Doran, 2013; Gorman-Murray, 2006).

Instead of viewing Laurie and Arthur's historic appearance on *Week In* merely through the lenses of assimilation and normalisation, we should understand that the visibility extended to them and their coming out on the public service broadcaster as a gay couple were an achievement in itself for the gay rights movement in Ireland. Because of the centrality of domesticity in Irish society, the presentation of a homodomestic scenario was a political act that challenged hegemonic representations and commonly circulated beliefs about gay people in Ireland. At one level it also represented a queer reclamation of the home and family. It served as a template to configure 'good' gay subjects for the heterosexual audience watching as well as a template for the possibility of a stable and committed gay relationship. In Doran's view, homodomesticity 'suggests that any perceived difference between gays and straights is superficial and politically insignificant' (p. 101). As I have shown however, Laurie and Arthur insisted that there was a distinct difference between gay and straight domestic relationships. The former had to operate on the fringes and formulate its own social structure, which challenged the heterosexual privilege endorsed by the Constitution of Ireland. From a historic perspective, Irish homodomesticity should not be equated with simple equality, nor does it automatically mean a lack of attention to the countless ways Irish gay people have experienced violence, marginalisation and discrimination because of their sexuality.

Conclusion

A reconsideration of the 1980 broadcast of the *Week In* episode on Laurie and Arthur shows that television is able to play a significant role not only in representing gay identities but also in providing gay men with materials and spaces for the exploration and expression of identifications and for an engagement in diverse forms of social interaction. Article 41 of the Irish Constitution has been cited as an indication of the strong heteronormativity prevalent in Irish culture. Following the Marriage Equality referendum in May 2015, a new section has been inserted: 'Marriage may be contracted in accordance with law by two persons without distinction as to their sex'. This indicates a loosening of heteronormativity in Irish culture. However, other parts of the Constitution remain unchanged, particularly with regard to the role of women within the home.

So far Houle's concept of homodomesticity has been applied almost exclusively to US and UK contexts. Localising the concept by applying it to an Irish case study enables us to revisit moments of gay visibility and representation in the media and interrogate the political dimensions of such representations. This first broadcast of a gay couple on RTÉ highlights the oppression and anxiety that surrounded being gay in Ireland, which had previously led to a culture of migration. It also indicates that the personal can become political: Laurie and Arthur's relationship conflicted with existing heterosexual models of domesticity in Ireland and suggested that gay people could form their own alternative relationships. The connection between this gay couple and the national Irish media enabled them to become objects of representation, which entailed a form of agency and empowerment that spoke out against the repressive wider society in Ireland. Television in this context is a significant medium in bringing 'a new symbolic structure, habitus and practice to Irish homes [...] The alternative conceptions of self [...] began to broadcast nightly directly into people's homes' (Inglis, 1998, p. 232). Because alternative conceptions of kinship and domesticity were broadcast into people's homes, the symbolic structure of gay relationships started to change the heteronormative idea of home and the family in Ireland.

Notes

1. I would like to express my deepest thanks to the Irish Queer Archive and, in particular, Tonie Walsh, who provided me with numerous interesting insights into queer Irish history.
2. In 1979, David Norris, Edmund Lynch, Bernard Keogh, Tom McClean, Brian Murray, Joni Crone and Tony O'Shea founded the National Gay Federation (NGF). The NGF leased a building, which it called the Hirschfeld Centre, named

after the German sexologist Magnus Hirschfeld, in the then underdeveloped Temple Bar area of Dublin. The community centre was the first full-time lesbian and gay venue in Ireland. It housed a meeting space, a youth café, ran discos and a small cinema.

3. Éamon de Valera was a prominent political figure in twentieth-century Ireland, serving as Taoiseach (Prime Minister) intermittently from 1932 to 1959, when he resigned after being elected President of Ireland. The presidency is largely a ceremonial office, but the President does exercise some limited powers with absolute discretion.

4. The special position of the Catholic Church in Ireland was recognised until the Fifth Amendment of the Constitution of Ireland. Approved by referendum on 7 December 1972, the Fifth Amendment deleted the section recognising the special position of the Catholic Church.

5. The importance of Irish people returning from the diaspora to challenge hetero-normative society was clear during the same-sex marriage referendum in May 2015. The day prior to the Irish casting a ballot in the referendum, emigrants from Canada, Australia, Africa, Asia and the United Kingdom returned from the diaspora in order to vote yes. This was made evident through the #HomeToVote hashtag, where over 48,000 tweets were made by returning emigrants. See http://www.irishtimes.com/life-and-style/generation-emigration/emigrants-take-planes-trains-and-automobiles-hometovote-1.2222151 and http://www.irishexaminer.com/ireland/referendum-thousands-make-the-journey-home-to-vote-332464.html (accessed 22 July 2016).

References

Berlant, L. & Warner, M. (2002). Sex in Public. In M. Warner (Ed.), *Publics and Counterpublics* (pp. 187–208). New York: Zone Books.

Butler, J. (2002). Is Kinship Always Already Heterosexual? *Differences: A Journal of Feminist Cultural Studies, 13*(1), 14–44.

Doran, S. (2013). Housebroken: Homodomesticity and the Normalization of Queerness in Modern Family. In P. Demory & C. Pullen (Eds.), *Queer Love in Film and Television: Critical Essays* (pp. 95–104). New York: Palgrave Macmillan.

Duggan, L. (2002). *The Incredible Shrinking Public: Sexual Politics and the Decline of Democracy.* Boston: Beacon Press.

Ferriter, D. (2004). *The Transformation of Ireland, 1900–2000.* London: Profile Books.

Ferriter, D. (2012). *Occasions of Sin: Sex & Society in Modern Ireland.* London: Profile Books.

Fortier, A. M. (2001). 'Coming Home': Queer Migrations and Multiple Evocations of Home. *European Journal of Cultural Studies, 4*(4), 405–424.

Gorman-Murray, A. (2006). Queering Home or Domesticating Deviance? Interrogating Gay Domesticity Through Lifestyle Television. *International Journal of Cultural Studies, 9*(2), 227–247.

Houle, C. (2009). Homodomestic. *Artist Statement: The Portfolio of Chad Houle.* Retrieved from http://www.splicetoday.com/pop-culture/homodomestic.

Hug, C. (1999). *The Politics of Sexual Morality in Ireland.* Basingstoke: Palgrave Macmillan.

Inglis, T. (1998). *Moral Monopoly: The Rise and Fall of the Catholic Church in Modern Ireland*. Dublin: UCD Press.

Ingman, H. (2007). *Twentieth-Century Fiction by Irish Women: Nation and Gender*. Hampshire: Ashgate.

Lynch, E. (2003). *Did Anyone Notice Us? Gay Visibility in the Irish Media, 1973–1993*. Dublin: It's a Wrap Productions.

National Library of Ireland, Irish Queer Archives, Box MS 45, 940/4, 'Summary of Telephone Reaction Received on Friday, 8th February, 1980'.

Norris, D. (2012). *David Norris – A Kick Against the Pricks: The Autobiography*. Dublin: Transworld Ireland.

O'Carroll, S. (2012). RTÉ Guide cover 'a symbol of acceptance', *TheJournal.ie* [online]. Retrieved from http://www.thejournal.ie/rte-guide-cover-a-symbol-of-acceptance-1003955-Jul2013/.

O'Toole, T. (2013). Cé Leis Tú? Queering Irish Migrant Literature. *Irish University Review 43*(1), 131–145.

Pramaggiore, M. & Wallis, T. (2011). *Film: A Critical Introduction, Third Edition*. London: Laurence King Publishing.

Reed, J. (2007). The Three Phases of Ellen: From Queer to Gay to Postgay. In Thomas Peele (Ed.), *Queer Popular Culture: Literature, Media, Film and Television*. New York: Palgrave.

Referendum Ireland (2015). Results received at the Central Count Centre for the referendum on the Thirty-fourth Amendment of the Constitution (Marriage Equality) Bill 2015, *Referendum Ireland* [online]. Retrieved from http://www.referendum.ie/results.php?ref=10.

Research and Development Commission (1985). Report No. 21, Religious Beliefs, Practice and Moral Attitudes: A Comparison of Two Irish Surveys 1974–1984. Maynooth: Research and Development Commission.

Robinson, M. (2013). *Everybody Matters: A Memoir*. Dublin: Hodder.

Robinson, S. (1998). Bringing It All Back Home. *Gay Community News*, p. 18.

RTÉ (31/12/1961). President Éamon de Valera's Opening Address. Dublin: RTÉ Productions.

RTÉ (11/02/1980). *Week In…* (RTÉ Archive Reference TY0104171). Dublin: RTÉ Productions.

Ryan, P. (2012). *Asking Angela Macnamara: An Intimate History of Irish Lives*. Dublin: Irish Academic Press.

Ryan, P. (2014). The Pursuit of Gay and Lesbian Sexual Citizenship Rights, 1980–2011. In M. Leane and E. Kiely (Eds.), *Sexualities and Irish Society: A Reader*. Dublin: Orpen Press.

Sheehan, H. (1987). *Irish Television Drama: A Society and Its Stories*. Dublin: RTÉ.

Sinfield, A. (1995). Diaspora and Hybridity: Queer Identity and the Ethnicity Model. In N. Mirzoeff (Ed.), *Diaspora and Visual Culture: Representing Africans and Jews* (pp. 95–114). London: Routledge.

The Irish Times (2015). Pope John Paul II's Irish visit. Retrieved from http://www.irishtimes.com/pope-john-paul-ii-s-irish-visit-1.1454069.

Walshe, E. (2006). Invisible Irelands: Kate O'Brien's Lesbian and Gay Social Formations in London and Ireland in the Twentieth Century. *Queerscope Articles, 1*(6), 39–48.

2 Breaking the Silence

The Early Portuguese Lesbian Press

Ana Maria Brandão, Tânia Cristina Machado and Joana Afonso

Written media have an important role in the development and consolidation of gay and lesbian communities and subcultures. Creating a space where gays and lesbians are able to share, discuss and value their experiences, the gay and lesbian press has also been instrumental in their political consciousness (Hanson, 2011; Howes, 2004; Streitmatter, 1995). As such, it represents an implicated vision of the world that is characteristic of alternative media (Atton, 2003, 2006) and its changes over time reflect the living conditions and fundamental concerns of gays and lesbians in the face of the wider social and political context.

Van der Veen's (1988) and Streitmatter's (1995) typologies of development of the Western gay and lesbian press show its progression from amateur, non-commercial publications aimed at reducing isolation to publications with a clearly political focus on consciousness raising and, more recently, a professional turn towards lifestyles, culture and entertainment.[1] Against this backdrop, the lesbian press shows some specificity linked to the double situation of lesbians as women *and* as lesbians, which raises additional obstacles in terms of access to public space and sometimes contributes to editorial dissension about whether or not to provide support and protection in a heteronormative social context, to raise awareness and mobilise and/or fight male domination and/or heteronormativity (Cutler, 2003; Murray, 2007; Streitmatter, 1995; Whitt, 2008a, 2008b). As a result, lesbian publications are usually more ephemeral and financially less viable, and face additional production and distribution problems (Cutler, 2003; Erickson, 2010; Koller, 2008; Murray, 2007; Streitmatter, 1995; Turner, 2009; Whitt, 2008a, 2008b).

This chapter focuses on the early Portuguese lesbian press and explores its contribution to the development of national lesbian communities and activism. It also contributes to the history of alternative press publications in Portugal, from which the specific case of the gay and lesbian press has been practically absent. Finally, it expands our understanding of the history of the Western gay and lesbian press by highlighting the distinctiveness of the Portuguese case.

The discussion combines data derived from a content analysis of the first three known Portuguese lesbian magazines – *Organa* (1990–1992),

Lilás (1993–2002) and *Zona Livre* (since 1997) – and semi-structured interviews with Portuguese lesbian activists and/or collaborators in those publications. The interviews were conducted between 7 May 2003 and 16 May 2012. The interviewees were all graduates and one of them held a PhD degree by the time they were interviewed.[2] The selection of the magazines' issues obeyed to slightly different criteria.[3] All nine issues of *Organa* were analysed. In the case of *Lilás* the first four, last four and intermediate four issues available were analysed.[4] In the case of *Zona Livre* the first two issues published by each editorial team were analysed.[5]

This chapter is divided into three parts, following the chronological order of emergence of the publications. The early Portuguese lesbian press combined approaches and concerns that can be found also in its Western counterparts, but it obeyed neither the same timeline nor the same time lapse. Compared to what Kulpa and Mizielińska (2011, p. 15) have called the 'Western "time of sequence"', it emerged later, changed faster and often combined characteristics of different historical moments in the same issues. This also suggests the presence of a 'time of coincidence', a 'temporal disjunction' (Kulpa & Mizielińska, 2011, p. 12) in the Portuguese case, which is intimately linked to the historical particularities and semi-peripheral characteristics of Portuguese society. Changes in the magazines' contents illustrate the transformations undergone by Portuguese society in general, as well as the gay and lesbian community in particular. Because this press was born from the lesbian community's need to be heard, it also reveals the process of consolidation of Portuguese gay and lesbian activism and its internal tensions, which mainly revolved around a divide between the purposes of identification and political mobilisation.

Organa's Seminal Work

Organa is the first Portuguese lesbian magazine of which we are aware. It appeared in 1990, almost a decade after the emergence of AIDS and nearly two decades after Stonewall. This time lapse clearly signals the contrast between the situation of Portuguese lesbians and that of many of their Western counterparts.

In Portugal, the phenomenon of geographical concentration found in the major European and North-American metropolises in the beginning of the twentieth century (Chauncey, 1998; Faderman, 1992; Garber, 1990) never had the same importance, being practically circumscribed to Lisbon (Gameiro, 1998). Moreover, from the beginning of the 1930s to the middle of the 1970s the country lived under the ideological hold of the *Estado Novo*, a dictatorship that systematically promoted the 'advantages' of an idealised, stylised rural life as opposed to the (mainly, though not exclusively, sexual) 'decadence' of urban lifestyles (Alão, 1989). This was in line with the regime's aversion to capitalist industrialisation and added to the country's developmental fragilities.

A late industrialisation phase during the 1950s and 1960s would nevertheless bear fruit in the 1970s and 1980s, when a gay subculture linked to the expansion of the new urban middle classes emerged (Gameiro, 1998). Cumulative economic, social and political changes during this period dramatically contributed to the materialisation of an institutional form of gay and lesbian activism whose 'embryonic' stage is situated by Cascais (2006) between 1974, the year of the democratic Revolution, and 1990.

The Revolution and the suppression of censorship led to the first few mobilisation attempts, which were however cut short by an unstable political climate and an overall lack of receptivity to gay and lesbian or even gender equality issues (Amaral & Moita, 2004; Cascais, 2006; Oliveira, Pena & Nogueira, 2011). As a result, the first enduring gay and lesbian organisations were able to emerge only during the 1990s. Their activism was built out of friendship networks forged inside the first AIDS NGOs (Cascais, 2006; Santos, 2005).

In the particular case of lesbians, many of those who had emigrated during the dictatorship returned to the country after the regime's fall. Some had been in touch with organised feminist and/or lesbian groups abroad. Their experience and political maturity were in sharp contrast with the country's overall situation and the personal experience of most Portuguese lesbians. This was the case with *Organa*'s founders, who

> had privileged contacts with foreign organisations; they'd lived abroad and when they returned [...] they were stunned by the existing lethargy and lack of organisation [...]. They'd also been rather influenced [...] by women's and lesbian movements, and they founded a magazine that was meant to be more than simply a magazine; it was meant to be a space of thought, of debate and intervention too.
>
> (Fabíola Cardoso, *Clube Safo*, Porto, 7 May 2004)

The gap between the experience of *Organa*'s first editors and that of its audiences helps to explain the miscellany of politicised militant and non-politicised, sometimes even naïve, texts included in most of the magazine's issues. The editors were trying to reconcile the needs of disparate audiences, a large part of which were still undergoing a process of self-definition. But the disparity was also in keeping with an enduring feature of Portuguese society: the distance between its elites and the majority of the population both in terms of cultural and economic resources and in terms of the co-existence of modern and traditional sectors and lifestyles (Nunes, 1964; Santos, 1985, 1992).

Organa was a hand-crafted magazine, typewritten, photocopied, hand-folded and stapled in the middle. The cover and inside pages contained images, often with poor resolution. The publication was delivered by mail to ensure protection both for its readers and editors. According to Adelaide Costa, the concern with anonymity, which was explicitly mentioned on the

Figure 2.1 Cover and back pages of issue no. 1 of *Organa*, published in 1990.

back cover, was the reason why 'most people would simply use a pseud-onym' or their 'second or first Christian names' (*Organa* and *Lilás* collaborator, Sintra, 16 May 2012).

The magazine was published on an irregular basis. Promotion was sparse and dependent on word of mouth. As a result, the magazine had a small number of subscribers, though the exact number of actual readers is hard to estimate since 'people passed it on' (Adelaide Costa, *Organa* and *Lilás* collaborator, Sintra, 16 May 2012). The low subscription numbers limited the economic viability of the magazine, which was largely supported by the women who produced it.

Organa's specific purposes were announced in the second issue: 'to disseminate positive news of interest to lesbians'; 'to promote mutual tolerance and respect'; 'to encourage the discussion of lesbian issues'; and 'to share communication codes' (*Organa*, 1990, no. 2, p. 3). In this sense *Organa* shared with the first Western lesbian publications an attempt to build a community through the valorisation of lesbian identity and experience, to fight social isolation and to offer emotional support (Bourque, 1996; Cutler, 2003; Streitmatter, 1995; Turner, 2009; Whitt, 2008a). Still, building a community also meant gathering its readership around a common set of values, norms and cultural references. It meant construing a common history (Hanson, 2011; Howes, 2004). Considering the virtual absence of an autonomous production of systematic knowledge about the history, experiences and living conditions of Portuguese lesbians (Santos, 2006), the editors resorted to the few references they had at the time.

One of the features of *Organa* is a characteristic set of editorial contents that the Western gay and lesbian press gradually took on between the end of the 1940s and the beginning of the 1990s (Adams, 2008; Bourque, 1996; Geiger & Hauser, 2010; Howes, 2004; Murray, 2007; Streitmatter, 1995; Whitt, 2008a). The magazine lacked a clear editorial line and seems to have been, in this sense, closer to the Spanish lesbian press at the time, where disparate ideological perspectives, purposes, editorial approaches and contents could also be found (Celaya, 1998). Thus it comprised excerpts of non-fiction works, including some fundamental feminist texts; translated and original fiction; literature and film reviews; recommended 'lesbian tours', including pubs, bookshops, shops, restaurants and hotels; news about relevant gay and lesbian events, legal achievements and public demonstrations; conference announcements; educational contents ranging from references to historical events such as the Stonewall riots to explanations about the origin and meaning of symbols of the lesbian subculture; the prevention of sexually transmitted infections, especially HIV; and exercises to enhance sexual pleasure.

Authors, places and events referred to were almost invariably from, or located in, major US or Western European metropolises, and many of the books and films could not be found in Portugal. Excluding the readers' original contributions, few texts were by Portuguese authors or referred to Portuguese realities, and there was a clear preponderance of Anglo-American references. Considering the generally low incomes and educational levels of the Portuguese population at the time (Barreto, 2000), this must have strongly limited both access and effectiveness. Thus, in the Portuguese case, it is possible to talk about the adoption of heteronomous models and categories (Kulpa & Mizielińska, 2011, p. 14), which simultaneously highlights another attribute of the emerging lesbian activism: the relatively exceptional nature of the women who edited the magazine in terms of their social origins and biographical trajectories.

Despite all this, *Organa*'s ground-breaking work quickly paid off. During its second year, a first meeting brought together about twenty women for three days and led to the creation of the first telephone helpline on homosexuality in Portugal (Marinho, 2001). The meeting had an important additional consequence: four women joined the editorial team and others would follow. This would in turn lead to internal dissension, since 'these other women [...] were essentially feminists [...] influenced by academic thought, who wanted quite different things for the magazine' (Fabíola Cardoso, *Clube Safo*, Porto, 7 May 2004).

The strategy adopted by *Organa* during most of its existence rested on an assimilationist position. This was largely achieved through a 'rhetoric of normalization' (Cutler, 2003, pp. 236, 240) which downplayed the differences between lesbians and heterosexual women in order to maximise social acceptance. Such a rhetoric was apparent in the denunciation of the submission of both lesbians and heterosexual women to a 'sexist education', gender inequality and violence (*Organa*, 1992, no. 8, p. 34); in the portrayal of lesbian relationships as essentially monogamous and consistent with a 'feminine vocation' (*Organa*, 1990, no. 1, p. 3); in references to the importance of physical beauty or in the publication of culinary recipes, both central aspects of normative femininity; and in the explicit accusation of those lesbians who 'due to an extravagant and ambiguous behaviour' contributed to homophobia (*Organa*, 1990, no. 2, p. 3). The charge had a particular target – the 'mannish' lesbian, the unmistakable object of the plea for 'a more liberated expression of each one's sexual preference without enduring the virago-dyke clichés' (*Organa*, 1990, no. 2, p. 14).

From the fifth issue onwards, however, it was possible to sense a turn in *Organa*'s editorial policy. Calls for political mobilisation became more common and were accompanied by a feminist drive. In issue number six, lesbianism was already portrayed as a sort of pinnacle of feminism – a line of thought typical of some debates in second-wave feminism (Faderman, 1992; Golden, 1994; Phelan, 1993; Stein, 1997). It was also argued that lesbians should not 'even dream [...] of mimicking heterosexuals' (*Organa*, 1992, no. 6, p. 32); they should instead create their own culture. Criticism of middle-class lesbians and their alleged attempts to enforce the idea of the 'commendable and respectable lesbian' (*Organa*, 1992, no. 8, p. 46) began to appear as well.

The weakening of the assimilationist strategy is also visible in the use of 'emphatic individualism', which constructs the lesbian as an 'ideal citizen' and focuses on (her) individual responsibility for social change (Cutler, 2003, p. 247). The initially cautious incitements to self-disclosure, seen as 'our most effective educational tool [...] to change [...] prejudiced attitudes regarding homosexuality' (*Organa*, 1990, no. 1, p. 24), gave way to appeals to active political engagement, since 'to have [...] rights [...] one must fight' (*Organa*, 1992, no. 8, p. 5). But internal editorial dissent became most obvious in the last issue, which included a 'farewell text' signed by one of the magazine's founders. She believed that the new editorial policy jeopardised the original idea of an open forum:

> Since its onset the magazine has been intended for all lesbians, whether they do or do not want to come out; whether they do or do not want to mingle; whether they do or do not want to state their opinions [...] for me, a lesbian magazine [...] had to give voice to all lesbians' opinions and [...] nobody was excluded for lack of literary skills or an academic degree.
>
> (*Organa*, 1992, no. 9, pp. 2–3)

The definition of *Organa*'s audience had been changed from 'lesbians and all women interested in lesbianism' to 'all lesbians interested in breaking the silence'. Apparently, differences became irreconcilable at this point, for the magazine ceased to be published. Paradoxically, *Organa*'s success also dictated its fall.

Lilás: The 'Militant' Turn

Lilás appeared in 1993 by the hand of four women who had joined *Organa*'s editorial team. Its publication occurred during the 'maturation phase' of Portuguese gay and lesbian activism (Cascais, 2006). As Cascais (2006, p. 121) claims, by the time the struggle for sexual citizenship in other Western countries began to focus on the rights of same-sex couples, Portugal witnessed a transition from an essentialist to a constructivist view of identities, the splitting between gay and lesbian activism, and a shift from a logic of difference to one of assimilation.

Lilás also combined characteristics of the Anglo-American press of the 1950s and especially from the mid-1960s to the mid-1970s (Streitmatter, 1995). Its most recurrent contents included personal – especially biographical – essays; interviews with lesbians and lesbian activists; book and film reviews; academic, frequently feminist texts; news; and fiction. Occasionally the magazine included health information and analyses of the shortcomings of the Portuguese law regarding gay and lesbian rights.

In spite of its amateur character, *Lilás* shows some material improvements compared to *Organa*. It was typed on a computer and the quality of the images was better, though it continued to be photocopied, folded and stapled. Subscriptions granted some revenue, but this still had to be complemented by the editors' own money. Distribution by mail continued to be a way of safeguarding anonymity. This and the editors' sustained use either of pseudonyms or of Christian names offers a curious contrast with the ideological and rhetorical shift announced in the last issues of *Organa*.

Publicação lésbica
Nº 17, Março 97

Apartado 6104
2700 Amadora

Figure 2.2 Cover of *Lilás* no. 17, published in March 1997.

Textos do Lesbianismo

De *A Nação Lésbica* (1973)

Um pequeno mas significativo grupo de mulheres movidas pela ira e pelo interesse pela História compreendem a revolução das mulheres no sentido visionário do fim da irmandade patriarcal catastrófica e um regresso à antiga glória e sábia equanimidade dos matriarcados. Não sabemos exactamente como é que isto acontecerá, como não sabemos a natureza das novas formas sociais daí resultantes, sabemos que *acontecerá*, e que efectivamente o processo do seu desenvolvimento está já a decorrer irreversivelmente. De suprema importância neste processo é a recuperação por parte da mulher moderna da sua mitologia como modelos para a teoria, consciência e acção. Sabemos que a História masculina suprimiu rigorosamente e distorceu os grandes modelos femininos, do mesmo modo que o homem branco americano separou os pretos das suas origens e distorceu a sua imagem com o intuito de satisfazer a versão da História americana do homem branco. Para as mulheres, que talvez tenham atingido o auge da sua degradação e destituição na época vitoriana, foi a investigação de alguns estudiosos e antropólogos masculinos, no fim dessa época, que iniciou o momento de viragem em todas essas épocas negras de História patriarcal. O suíço Jacob Bachofen foi um dos primeiros a descobrir "a época feminina na costura inferior da História, com o seu domínio feminino sacerdotal, político e económico". Os frutos desta investigação eram, até recentemente, acessíveis apenas a alguns iniciados e agora formam um dos alicerces da segunda vaga da revolução feminista. Sabemos agora que o matriarcado dominava nas culturas das cidades mais avançadas e mais antigas. Sabemos que todas as formas de matriarcado foram,

15

Figure 2.3 Inside page of *Lilás* no. 17, showing a free translation of *Lesbian Nation: The Feminist Solution* by Jill Johnston, first published in 1973.

The editors of *Lilás* were determined to strengthen the political consciousness of the lesbian community. In this respect, the disappearance of personal ads to facilitate affective/sexual encounters, which could still be found in *Organa*, is probably as informative as the magazine's explicit editorial purposes: 'to produce [...] a knowledge community' (*Lilás*, 1993, no. 2, p. 1); 'to think and share lesbianism'; and 'to know [...] who we are and how it was to be a lesbian years ago' (*Lilás*, 1993, no. 1, p. 1). To achieve these purposes, the editors published biographies of well-known women, especially novelists and artists who had same-sex relationships and/or somehow challenged normative gender. Only a few of them were Portuguese. The editors also published excerpts from historical research on female homo-eroticism, none of it referring to Portuguese history and society. The attempt to 'elevate the status' of lesbians (Cutler, 2003, p. 243) by valuing their experience ran parallel to the nurturing of a sentiment of personal belonging to a community and to the (re)creation of its historical continuity – a dominant strategy of the Western gay and lesbian movements of the 1960s and 1970s (Epstein, 1992).

But the key contrast between *Organa* and *Lilás* lies in the militant rhetoric of the latter and in the preponderance of contents clearly shaped by radical and lesbian feminisms. This is obvious when 'the class of men' is defined as 'our chief enemy' and 'hetero-sociality' as the 'most effective strategy [...] to lead women to submission and dependence'; or when lesbianism is pictured not as 'a "harmless" form of desire', but as 'a life practice, a political choice, a form of resisting a relationship of power and appropriation not only in the "private" [...] domain, but also in the "collective" one' (*Lilás*, 1993, no. 4, p. 39). Constructivist approaches to gender and sexuality were also championed, and examples of the 'gross essentialism' that assumes that 'All men would thus be the same Thing and [...] all women would be the same Thing' were criticised (*Lilás*, 1993, no. 2, p. 38).

As these citations suggest, a difficult balance was often the result, since a feminist approach constantly emphasises gender differences whereas a strictly constructivist view of gender subverts those very same categories on which the struggle against male domination and patriarchy rests. A similar difficulty explains why, despite losing strength, the rhetoric of normalisation continued to be implicitly present. It was manifest in (feminist) contents that depicted the lesbian primarily as a woman who, like heterosexual women, is similarly subject to male domination. In a country where feminism got little public attention and proved rarely favourable to lesbian claims (Amaral & Moita, 2004; Brandão, 2011; Marinho, 2001; Oliveira, Pena & Nogueira, 2011; Tavares, 2010) the choice for this sort of text can be explained only by the social origin and personal trajectories of the editors.

Lilás in fact displayed a clearly exclusive character that is apparent in the academic nature of many texts and in the sort of interaction it encouraged with readers. A relatively common practice it engaged in was to ask the latter to comment on some texts (for example Lorde, 1984) whose phrasing and conceptual complexity would represent a difficult exercise for those who did not own the necessary educational credentials or class dispositions (Bourdieu & Passeron, 1999). In this sense *Organa* targeted a broader audience. This is manifest in the simpler texts it also included, which did not rest on grand theoretical ideas. Equally symptomatic of the class component of *Lilás* was a noticeable reduction of information about lesbian hubs, which as Murray (2007) and Stein (1997) have noticed, were not only central to the feminist politics of the 1970s, but also more characteristic of working-class lesbianism.

The clear inspiration that *Lilás'* editors drew from heteronomous models of lesbian activism was obvious furthermore in the multiple references to lesbian separatism. This was understood in relatively broad terms, encompassing criticisms of male domination, the vindication of exclusively lesbian communities and the promotion of autonomous activism. By the time these texts were published, Portuguese gay and lesbian activism had not yet gained prominence; its single recognisable organisation was the *Grupo de Trabalho Homossexual* [Taskforce on Homosexuality] of the Socialist Revolutionary Party, founded in 1991 as a mixed (that is, lesbian *and* gay) organisation. The appeals to separatism indicate rather an import of the Anglo-American model from the mid-1960s and 1970s (Castells, 1998; Streitmatter, 1995; Weeks, 1990), even though it might also have resulted from some lesbians' discomfort with some AIDS-activist gays who were the very few known faces of the Portuguese gay and lesbian community.

In fact, in 1996, one year before the foundation of mixed organisations such as *ILGA-Portugal* or *OpusGay*, the first and so far only exclusively lesbian Portuguese organisation, *Clube Safo*, was born. The internal dissension that led to the end of *Organa* seems to have mirrored the fragmentation of the gay and lesbian community and its leaders. Whereas some lesbians favoured joint efforts with gay men, others seemed more interested in either full or partial separatism. The former could be achieved by creating autonomous organisations, the latter by setting up lesbian 'interest groups' inside mixed organisations. Fabíola Cardoso elucidates this:

> one of the women who founded *Organa* was very important in the foundation of *ILGA[-Portugal]*, namely in terms of the bureaucratic and administrative procedures [...] and then [...] a Group of Women emerges inside *ILGA* [...] and [...] the women who promoted the Group [...] were those who'd left *Lilás* [...] and [they] [...] ended up founding the *GIRL*[6] [...] and continue to have a leading role [...] namely in [...] *ILGA*'s Group of Political Intervention[7]; so these women were indirectly inspired by *Organa* too. [...] *Clube Safo* is also almost genealogically related to *Organa* and *Lilás*. The women who [...] founded *Clube Safo* met via *Lilás*; [...] I was even involved in some of *Organa*'s activities and kept in touch with the group of women who [...] formed *Lilás*.
>
> (Fabíola Cardoso, *Clube Safo*, Porto, 7 May 2004)

From 1996–1997 onwards, when Portuguese gay and lesbian activism entered its 'emancipating' phase (Cascais, 2006), there was a significant change in the contents of *Lilás*. News reports grew in importance and the magazine focused more on the Portuguese reality as a result of the proliferation of organisations and events, such as the Lisbon Gay and Lesbian Festival or the Pride Parties. By the end of the 1990s, personal ads reappeared.

This interesting shift seems to imply several things. First, it affirms the social and cultural distance between lesbian feminists, who stood for a militant and politically active attitude, and a large part of the Portuguese lesbians, who have been typically disinclined both to public intervention and exposure (Brandão, 2011). A second aspect was the still timid and gradual consolidation of a community which expressed in the magazine's pages its discontent with the scarcity of meeting places. This suggests that at least a part of the readership was more interested in social networking and entertainment than in political action. It is possible that these interests were linked not only to class differences but also to overall changes in lifestyles among the Portuguese, which had moved closer to those of their European counterparts (Barreto, 2000; Mateus, 2015). By then the international gay and lesbian press was similarly shifting its focus to consumption and leisure at the expense of militancy (Geiger & Hauser, 2010; Streitmatter, 1995).

The women who founded *Lilás* gradually began to leave the project. Some devoted themselves to the creation and stimulation of lesbian organisations or groups. Editorial changes were symptomatic of their departure and resembled a return to *Organa*'s original project: their aim was a more inclusive media focused on sociability. The emergence of *Zona Livre*, roughly at the same time, was also representative of some activists' perception of the distance between their own world and that of many Portuguese lesbians. The fact that *Zona Livre* competed for the same market segment contributed to the extinction of *Lilás* in 2002.

Zona Livre: A 'Multi-Speed' Job

More than an example of an alternative press, *Lilás* was close to what Fuchs (2010, pp. 181–182) calls 'critical media' – media that encourage the development of a critical, participatory mass attentive to the 'suppressed possibilities of societal development' and politically engaged in its realisation. This ambition however seems to have resulted in the alienation of at least part of the lesbian community. The emergence of *Zona Livre* in this context represents an acknowledgement of the need to work at 'multiple speeds' (Fabíola Cardoso, *Clube Safo*, Porto, 7 May 2004) to meet the different needs of different publics.

Zona Livre appeared as the official newsletter of *Clube Safo* in 1997. By then Portuguese gay and lesbian activism entered a period of great vigour and prominence. According to Cascais (2006, pp. 118–122) the fight against AIDS in Portugal had been 'detached from a gay emancipating discourse', was 'led by third parties not linked to the gay community, namely the medical profession' and 'highlighted the common good'; this in turn offered gay and lesbian organisations a 'respectability capital' that turned them into socially and politically 'credible interlocutor[s]', supported by at least part of the Left and enjoying the sympathy of the media. The struggle to offer legal protection to same-sex relationships entered the political agenda

(Cascais, 2006; Santos, 2005; Vale de Almeida, 2009) and was a subject in *Zona Livre*'s first issue.

Zona Livre combined information and entertainment; its character was still more social than political. Defined as a publication 'of and for lesbians' (*Zona Livre*, 1997, no. 1, p. 1) it was exclusively based on voluntary work. The way it was managed and the strategies used to ensure member involvement reveal its founders' earlier experience in *Organa* and *Lilás* and a certain 'professionalisation' of their work both as editors and activists. Because *Zona Livre* was a strategic instrument of the *Clube*, its production was carefully planned. It was published every two months, alternating with and promoting participation in the *Clube*'s meetings. Each issue had

> a theme proposed in advance so that people [would] write about that theme [...] [which], as a rule, [was] the theme of the next meeting. These meetings [...] usually include[d] [...] a lunch and then a debate. Then, at night, there [were] typically more social activities. This structure [was] not naive at all. [...] A preceding lunch serves [...] as a socialising moment [...] and the debate is usually more productive.
>
> (Fabíola Cardoso, *Clube Safo*, Porto, 7 May 2004)

The newsletter's first issues were printed, photocopied and stapled. They were distributed by mail inside envelopes with no external marks. Anonymity concerns extended to the editors and leaders of the *Clube*, who resorted to pseudonyms in the first issues. This practice was gradually abandoned as the Portuguese gay and lesbian community matured and social acceptance increased.

Figure 2.4 Cover page of issue no. 4 of *Zona Livre*, published in 1998, showing a picture of actual members of *Clube Safo*.

The contents of *Zona Livre* were close to those of the US gay and lesbian press as they developed from the 1950s on. They included national and international news; book and film reviews; original fiction; and comments on legal, political and historical matters of interest to gays and lesbians. Literary writings, especially poetry, were clearly predominant in the first issues and have remained so throughout. These dealt mostly with lesbian identities and lives and were written mainly by the *Clube*'s own members, thereby helping them to value their proper experiences. As Fabíola Cardoso emphasises, when choosing 'between [...] a dreadful love poem we were sent or a wonderful poem written by a foreign author nobody [had] heard of, we [would] publish the dreadful poem' (*Clube Safo*, Porto, 7 May 2004). Attention to national realities was also patent in the book reviews. Although these still referred mostly to foreign literary or academic works, national references became more common as a consequence of the vigour of the Portuguese lesbian community.

Another important difference between *Zona Livre* and its predecessors is the growing significance of advertising. Initially there were only a few small ads from lesbian bars and magazines, as well as from gay, lesbian, bisexual and transsexual publishing houses. By 2011 however, ads had increased exponentially and became more varied, including leisure and cultural services. Unlike the first advertisements, the large majority of the more recent ones do not exclusively target the pink market, which is surely a sign of the growing interest of Portuguese entrepreneurs in the latter niche. The growing commercial appeal might also be a result of the news-letter's increasing attractiveness, especially since it became a digital pub-lication in 2011. Open online access has facilitated anonymous reading, increased dissemination and enlarged its audience, from which advertisers could profit.

From the start, *Zona Livre* also included images. Initially there were photo-graphs or drawings of anonymous female characters, sometimes including nudes and intimate gestures. But in 2003 photographs of real women with their faces uncovered, taken during the *Clube*'s activities or in Pride Parades, began to appear. With the growing politicisation of Portuguese gay and les-bian activism (Santos, 2009), at least a part of its constituency was now more inclined to public disclosure.

From the beginning of the twenty-first century, a number of important changes took place in Portuguese society with the geographical expansion of gay and lesbian organisations and a multiplication of initiatives, including the hosting of international conferences and a more consistent cooperation with the academy (Cascais, 2006; Santos, 2006). A major landmark was the First Portuguese Social Forum in 2003, which brought together gay and lesbian organisations, feminist organisations and unions, creating a dialogue that announced new synergies. Texts about feminism and news about inter-national feminist events pointed to the growing 'cooperation with wom-en's organisations' – 'for example, we always included in our manifesto the matter of abortion and some women's organisations already include[d] lesbian claims in their[s]' (Fabíola Cardoso, *Clube Safo*, Porto, 7 May 2004).

At the same time, Portuguese activists achieved significant legal victories. In 2001 same-sex unions were legally recognised under the regimes of common economy and cohabitation. In 2003 and 2004, respectively, the Labour Code and the Constitution of the Portuguese Republic were amended to prohibit discrimination on the grounds of sexual orientation. The elimination of differences in the age of consent and the approval of same-sex marriage would follow in 2007 and 2010, respectively. The attitudes of the Portuguese people have become more favourable towards homosexuality (Gerhards, 2010; Smith, 2011). But these victories often profited, as Santos (2013, p. 4) contends, from the discursive 'containment' – even '(hetero)normative compliance' – of most of its supporters, including activists themselves.

Throughout its existence, in fact, *Zona Livre* has been marked by a return to a rhetoric of normalisation. Lesbians have come to be depicted once again as women who 'just love differently' (*Zona Livre*, 2011, no. 61, p. 8). The militant rhetoric of *Lilás* gradually faded away, and whenever it reappeared, it was through the voice of the *Clube*'s leaders.

Ten years ago, Cascais (2006, p. 124) already warned against the reversibility of the 'emancipating dynamics' of Portuguese gay and lesbian activism. In the case of *Clube Safo* the prophecy seems to have been fulfilled soon afterwards: in 2008 the *Clube* entered a period of routine administrative management in face of the absence of candidates to its governing bodies. According to one of its last leaders, this reflected 'the deficit of involvement in social organisations, and particularly in LGBT activism in Portugal' (Ferreira, 2012, p. 46). *Zona Livre* ceased to be published. It has reappeared intermittently since 2011, but has never regained its momentum.

Conclusion

This chapter contributes to the history of alternative media in Portugal by focussing on the role of the early Portuguese lesbian press in the creation and consolidation of a lesbian community and the development of lesbian activism. The first lesbian magazines emerged with an eye to informing, bringing closer and mobilising a geographically dispersed and socially isolated audience. But they also mirrored the gap between national realities and the paradigmatic case of the economically developed West.

The editorial policies of *Organa*, *Lilás* and *Zona Livre* shared many features with their Western counterparts. Yet their combination of contents and concerns, and the theoretical, practical and rhetorical instruments they resorted to, provide them with a kind of 'trans-temporal' quality as a result of the compression of several decades of international change within barely twenty years of their existence. If, on the one hand, this could prove to be an advantage due to the authority which certain argumentative resources had already gained in other social contexts, it was also, on the other, a challenge for an emerging lesbian activism, underlying which one finds the social origins and cross-border experiences of editors and their divergence from the socially and historically specific needs of many Portuguese lesbians.

Such a contrast is most obvious in the case of *Lilás* and the militant rhetoric initially adopted by its editors. The persistence of an assimilationist strategy and a rhetoric of normalisation both in *Organa* and *Zona Livre* suggests that their editorial teams acknowledged the Portuguese lesbian community was still in the course of being shaped and that militancy would appeal only to a relatively small group of women. Ideological and editorial disputes, which led to the abandonment of one editorial project in favour of another, are also illustrative of the particular trajectory of Portuguese lesbian activism and its internal tensions.

Eventually, difficulties in defining a coherent editorial policy and/or mobilising audiences led to the disappearance of *Organa* and *Lilás* as well as to periods of suspending *Zona Livre*. However this may be, for over nearly two decades these publications offered Portuguese lesbians a safe haven, a sense of belonging and a forum of ideas. For the women who created and nurtured them, moreover, writing was an act of love and struggle against the blank spaces on the margins of a heteronormative society.

Acknowledgements

The authors made all due efforts to identify and get permission from the authors of the magazines to reproduce the images included in this chapter. *Organa* and *Lilás* however were informal publications whose authors were not mentioned in print. *Zona Livre* is the property of *Clube Safo*, whose current directors were contacted but did not respond, suggesting that the *Clube* is once again inactive.

Notes

1. Throughout this article, references to the Western gay and lesbian press refer essentially to the United States and Western European countries. It should be noted that research on the latter does not usually consider Mediterranean Europe, with the exception of France, which has been considered in van der Veen (1988). This severely limits any comparative analysis between Portugal and other Mediterranean countries.
2. Interview excerpts are followed by the interviewees' real names, the quality in which they were interviewed and the interview's place and date.
3. Since both *Organa* and *Lilás* were informal, unregistered publications, it was necessary to resort to informal channels and to the archives of gay and lesbian organisations to obtain as many of their issues as possible. *Zona Livre* has been registered in the National Library since 1997 with ISSN 2183–0320. Its hyperlink (http://www.clubesafo.com/zona/ZL%2001%20%28Set97%29.pdf) is inactive at the time of writing. In total, 29 issues of the three magazines were analysed. Excerpts were translated into English by the authors.

4. *Lilás* published a total of 27 issues. For this chapter, issues 1 to 4, 8, 9, 16, 17, 22, 23, 25 and 26 were analysed.
5. The publication was suspended between 2008 and 2011. Since 2011 it has reappeared intermittently. The issues analysed in this chapter (1, 2, 34, 35, 46, 47, 61 and 62) refer exclusively to the regular publication period.
6. Acronym for the 'Group of Intervention and Reflexion on Lesbianism', created in 2000.
7. Founded in 1999.

References

Adams, K. (2008). Built Out of Books: Lesbian Energy and Feminist Ideology in Alternative Publishing. *Journal of Homosexuality, 34*(3–4), 113–141.

Alão, A. P. (1989). Amor e Sexualidade: Mudança de Comportamentos. In A. Reis (Ed.), *Portugal Contemporâneo*. Vol. V (pp. 367–380). Lisboa: Alfa.

Amaral, A. L. & Moita, G. (2004). Como se Faz (e se Desfaz) o Armário: Algumas Representações da Homossexualidade no Portugal de Hoje. In A. F. Cascais (Ed.), *Indisciplinar a Teoria: Estudos Gays, Lésbicos e Queer* (pp. 99–115). N.p.: Fenda.

Atton, C. (2003). What is 'Alternative' Journalism? *Journalism, 4*(3), 267–272.

Atton, C. (2006). *Alternative Media*. London: Sage.

Barreto, A. (2000). *A Situação Social em Portugal 1960–1999*, Vol. II. Lisboa: Imprensa de Ciências Sociais.

Bourdieu, P. & Passeron, J.-C. (1999). *La Reproduction: Eléments pour une Théorie du Système d'Enseignement*. Paris: Les Editions de Minuit.

Bourque, D. (1996). Parcours Médias: De l'Importance du Réseau de Communication Créé par les Lesbiennes à Montréal. *Les Cahiers de la Femme, 16*(2), 86–91.

Brandão, A. M. (2011). Not Quite Women: Lesbian Activism in Portugal. In A. Woodward, J. M. Bonvin & M. Renom (Eds.), *Transforming Gendered Well-Being in Europe: The Impact of Social Movements* (pp. 151–168). Farnham: Ashgate.

Cascais, A. (2006). Diferentes Como Só Nós: O Associativismo GLBT Português em Três Andamentos. *Revista Crítica de Ciências Sociais, 76*, 109–126.

Castells, M. (1998). *The Power of Identity: The Information Age: Economy, Society and Culture*, Vol. II. Cornwall: Blackwell Publishers.

Celaya, B. (1998). Identidades Lesbianas en España: Construcción y Articulación de una Identidad Colectiva en Tres Revistas Españolas. *Arizona Journal of Hispanic Cultural Studies, 2*, 63–86.

Chauncey, G. (1998). Gay New York. *Actes de la Recherche en Sciences Sociales, 125*, 9–14.

Cutler, M. (2003). Educating the 'Variant', Educating the Public: Gender and the Rethoric of Legitimation in *The Ladder* Magazine for Lesbians. *Qualitative Sociology, 26*(2), 233–255.

Epstein, S. (1992). Gay Politics, Ethnic Identity: The Limits of Social Constructionism. In E. Stein (Ed.), *Forms of Desire: Sexual Orientation and the Social Constructionist Controversy* (pp. 239–293). New York: Routledge.

Erickson, B. (2010). 'Every Woman Needs Courage': Feminist Periodicals in 1970s West Germany. *Preteritus, 2*, 31–44.

Faderman, L. (1992). *Odd Girls and Twilight Lovers: A History of Lesbian Life in Twentieth-Century America*. New York: Penguin Books.

Ferreira, E. (2012). Movimento Lésbico em Portugal: Uma Reflexão Pessoal. *LES Online, 4*(1), 35–48.

Fuchs, C. (2010). Alternative Media as Critical Media. *European Journal of Social Theory, 13*(2), 173–192.

Gameiro, O. J. C. (1998). *Do Acto à Identidade: Orientação Sexual e Estruturação Social*. Master thesis, Instituto de Ciências Sociais da Universidade de Lisboa, Lisboa, Portugal.

Garber, E. (1990). A Spectacle in Colour: The Gay and Lesbian Subculture of Jazz Age Harlem. In M. Duberman, M. Vicinus & G. Chauncey (Eds.), *Hidden From History: Reclaiming the Gay and Lesbian Past* (pp. 318–331). New York: Meridian.

Geiger, B. & Hauser, M. (2010). Archiving Feminist Grassroots Media. *Interface: A Journal for and about Social Movements, 2*(2), 103–125.

Gerhards, J. (2010). Non-Discrimination Towards Homosexuality: The Union's Policy and Citizens' Attitudes towards Homosexuality in 27 European Countries. *International Sociology, 25*(5): 5–28.

Golden, C. (1994). Our Politics and Choices: The Feminist Movement and Sexual Orientation. In B. Greene & G. M. Herek (Eds.), *Lesbian and Gay Psychology: Theory, Research and Clinical Implications* (pp. 55–70). Thousand Oaks: Sage.

Hanson, J. N. (2011). *Inside the Body Politic: Examining the Birth of Gay Liberation*. Honors Research Thesis, The Ohio State University, Ohio, U.S.A.

Howes, R. (2004). Publicaciones Periódicas Gay, Lésbicas, Travestis y Transexuales en Brasil: Comunidad y Cultura. *Revista Iberoamericana, 70*(208–209), 983–1001.

Koller, V. (2008). *Lesbian Discourses: Images of a Community*. New York: Routledge.

Kulpa, R. & Mizielińska, J. (2011). Contemporary Peripheries: Queer Studies, Circulation of Knowledge and East/West Divide. In R. Kulpa & J. Mizielińska (Eds.), *De-Centering Western Sexualities: Central and Eastern European Perspectives* (pp. 11–26). Farnham: Ashgate.

Lorde, A. (1984). The Uses of the Erotic: The Erotic as Power. In A. Lorde. *Sister Outsider: Essays and Speeches* (pp. 53–59). New York: The Crossing Press Feminist Series.

Marinho, S. (2001). LGBT e Outros Movimentos Sociais. Retrieved from http://www.geocities.com/girl_ilga/intervencaoGTH.htm.

Mateus, A. (Ed.) (2015). *Três Décadas de Portugal Europeu: Balanço e Perspetivas*. Lisboa: Fundação Francisco Manuel dos Santos. Retrieved from https://www.ffms.pt/upload/docs/PortEuroUmBal3Dec.pdf.

Murray, H. (2007). Free for All Lesbians: Lesbian Cultural Production and Consumption in the United States during the 1970s. *Journal of the History of Sexuality, 15*(2), 251–275.

Nunes, A. S. (1964). Portugal, Sociedade Dualista em Evolução. *Análise Social, 2*(7–8), 407–462.

Oliveira, J. M., Pena, C. & Nogueira, C. (2011). Feminist Lesbians or Lesbian Feminists: Portuguese Lesbians Speak Out. *Feminism & Psychology, 2*(2), 228–232.

Phelan, S. (1993). (Be)coming Out: Lesbian Identity and Politics. *Signs: Journal of Women in Culture and Society, 18*(4), 765–790.

Santos, A. C. (2005). *A Lei do Desejo: Direitos Humanos e Minorias Sexuais em Portugal*. Porto: Edições Afrontamento.

Santos, A. C. (2006). Entre a Academia e o Activismo. *Revista Crítica de Ciências Sociais, 76*, 91–108.

Santos, A. C. (2009). Um Nome Que Seja Só Seu: Para uma Cartografia da (In)visibilidade Política Lésbica. *LES Online, 1*(1), 21–28.

Santos, A. C. (2013). Are We There Yet? Queer Sexual Encounters, Legal Recognition and Homonormativity. *Journal of Gender Studies, 22*(1), 54–64.

Santos, B. S. (1985). Estado e Sociedade na Semiperiferia do Sistema Mundial: O Caso Português. *Análise Social, 21*(87-88-89), 869–901.

Santos, B. S. (1992). *O Estado e a Sociedade em Portugal (1974–1988)*. Porto: Afrontamento.

Smith, T. W. (2011). Cross-National Differences in Attitudes towards Homosexuality. *GSS Cross-National Report, 31*, 1–33.

Stein, A. (1997). *Sex and Sensibility: Stories of a Lesbian Generation*. Berkeley: University of California Press.

Streitmatter, R. (1995). *Unspeakable: The Rise of the Gay and Lesbian Press in America*. Winchester: Faber and Faber.

Tavares, M. (2010). Feminismos e Lesbianismo: Derrubando o Mito da *Lavender Menace*. *LES Online, 2*(1), 33–46.

Turner, G. (2009). Catching the Wave: Britain's Lesbian Publishing Goes Commercial. *Journalism Studies, 10*(6), 769–788.

Vale de Almeida, M. (2009). *A Chave do Armário: Homossexualidade, Casamento, Família*. Lisboa: Imprensa de Ciências Sociais.

Veen, E. van der (1988). A Global View of the Gay and Lesbian Press. In International Lesbian and Gay Association (Ed.), *Second ILGA Pink Book: A Global View of the Lesbian and Gay Liberation and Oppression* (pp. 15–32). Utrecht: Interfacultaire Werkgroep Homostudies, Rijksuniversiteit Utrecht.

Weeks, J. (1990). *Coming Out: Homosexual Politics in Britain from the Nineteenth Century to the Present*. London: Quartet Books.

Whitt, J. (2008a). A 'Labour from the Heart': Lesbian Magazines from 1947–1994. *Journal of Lesbian Studies, 5*(1–2), 229–251.

Whitt, J. (2008b). *Women in American Journalism: A New History*. Urbana: University of Illinois Press.

3 'I Am My Own Special Creation'

Sexual and Gender Differences in the Music Performances of an Antwerp Drag Show Company

Robbe Herreman and Alexander Dhoest

Studies on men who appear as women but are still known to be men, whether they are called drag queens, show queens or female impersonators, have revealed that drag and drag performances play a significant role in twentieth-century sexual cultures.[1] One of the first profound studies on the topic, Esther Newton's *Mother Camp* (1972/1979), demonstrated that female impersonators in the 1960s acted as spokespersons for the American LGBT community in general, and gay men in particular, by representing the stigma of the gay world. Newton considered drag queens as gay culture's 'heroes' at a time when homosexuality was still recovering from active oppression under the McCarthy regime while facing new threats by outspoken opponents of LGBT rights such as Anita Bryant.

Yet more recent work has accused Newton of addressing drag queens too much as failed men carrying the dual stigma of homosexuality and effeminacy (Schacht & Underwood, 2004, p. 8). In contrast, research has contributed to the reconfiguration of the academic view of female impersonators by portraying them as crucial agents in the creation and development of alternative embodied forms of gender and sexuality, as well as important interrogators of what no longer may be considered as homophobic, but rather heteronormative and to some extent, homonormative societies. Indeed, the concepts of heteronormativity, criticising the self-evidence of heterosexuality as a social norm (Warner, 1991), and more recently homonormativity, criticising the assimilation of heteronormative values and norms by the LGBT community (Duggan, 2002), have been used to underscore the subversive nature of drag culture, which exposes the performativity of gender and sexuality (Butler, 1991, p. 21).

Despite these differences in interpretation, academic writing consistently identifies a close connection between drag culture and sexual minorities in general, and gay male culture in particular. In this chapter we will focus on gay male culture and use the term 'gay' instead of 'LGBT', which we will use to refer only to broader issues and groups. Research has demonstrated that the majority of drag queens identify as gay (Newton,

1972/1979; Schacht & Underwood, 2004, p. 6) whereas cross-dressing may be understood as a historic means to explore and embody homosexuality (Lapovsky, Kennedy & Davis, 1993). Thus, writing about the construction of gay culture in New York between 1890 and 1940, George Chauncey (1994) states that both cross-dressing and camp were common among men to express and cope with their difference at a time when homosexuality still depended much upon sexual desire, sensibilities and subjectivities rather than upon the later, 'morally neutral' (Halperin, 2012, p. 70) category of sexual identity. From the 1960s onwards, the political category of sexual identity has been promulgated in Western societies by the emerging LGBT movement, and academics have largely made use of this category to investigate homosexuality. However, as argued by Halperin (2012, p. 75), such an approach presents sexuality as an identity rather than an erotic subjectivity or sexual behaviour. As a counterweight he proposes to return to the study of 'gay culture', based in a distinctive sensibility and 'dissident' subjectivity, and apparent in a cultural orientation as well as social and cultural practices such as camp, diva-worship and drag (ibid., pp. 5–7).

In this chapter we will build upon Halperin's work to investigate drag shows in Antwerp, the largest city and gay capital of Flanders, the northern, Dutch-language part of Belgium. In our analysis we will focus in particular on music and music performance. Most drag performances rely on music, mainly covers, either sung live or lip-synched, in their original form or revised. Curiously, few researchers have concentrated on the role of music in drag performance, let alone on its potential role in expressing gay culture or as a mode of subcultural symbolic resistance. In her PhD dissertation on the role of music in drag performances at the 801 Cabaret in Key West, Florida, however, Elisabeth Kaminski (2003) has demonstrated that drag queen performers may strategically use popular songs affiliated with gay culture to build solidarity, to evoke a sense of injustice and to enhance feelings of agency among audience members. We want to explore this repertoire and these functions in a Flemish context by focusing on the Antwerps Travestie Theater (ATT), a drag theatre company based in Antwerp. The group started performing in the late 1970s, for mixed audiences, and became quite successful in the following years with shows in Flanders as well as the Netherlands. In 1984 the ATT changed its traditional concept of drag shows consisting of individual musical acts into a format similar to the musical. While these productions retained the core characteristics of the drag show, including the imitation of women by men and a humorous tone, they added an overarching storyline, thus creating a more local, culturally specific inflection of international drag culture. In this paper we will focus on nine of these 'musicals', exploring the use of music as a form of shared 'gay culture' as well as of symbolic resistance challenging dominant structures of gender and sexuality.

'Gay Music', Camp and Symbolic Resistance

Before exploring the concrete use of music in drag shows, it is worth reflecting on the broader connections between music and gay culture. Several scholars have discussed the key importance of music in LGBT culture as a tool of collective and individual identity building (e.g. Valentine, 1995). Others have discussed the existence of a corpus of 'gay music', music strongly associated with gay culture. In their seminal musicological contribution on the issue, Philip Brett and Elisabeth Wood (2002) have demonstrated that gay music is diverse and contextual, as it is partly in the eye – or rather, ear – of the beholder. Indeed all gay music is somehow coded and needs to be decoded, as its meanings can be rather explicit but also more implicit. Brett and Wood demonstrate that at least three elements play a role in the constitution of what may be perceived as gay music. Firstly, some music is recognised as gay because of explicit references or implicit allusions to homosexuality in the lyrics. Secondly, the label may be used because of the creation and performance of music by LGBT artists. Some of these artists have been called 'gay icons', not least because they have been adopted as models in the politics of LGBT emancipation (Dhoest, Herreman & Wasserbauer, 2015). Thirdly, Brett and Wood discuss music connected to practices and styles associated with 'older' gay culture, especially camp and the diva phenomenon. Other authors confirm this, adding that these connections still matter in contemporary Western gay culture (e.g. Amico, 2009; Kates, 1997).

Clearly then music can be connected to homosexuality on different levels, including those of the lyrics, the artist's biography and the performance style. In relation to the latter, the concept of 'camp' is often used to define the specific stylistic practices in gay music and broader culture, including drag. As explored by Susan Sontag (1964), one of the first to pay attention to the phenomenon, camp involves love for the unnatural, artifice and exaggeration; it is linked to aestheticism and stylisation; it entails a strong affinity for clothes, furniture and visual décor; it has a preference for attenuated (androgynous) or exaggerated gender roles; and it is extravagant, outrageous, playful and frivolous. Sontag identifies a connection between camp and homosexuality, which is further explored by Babuscio (1977). To him, camp has four key characteristics: irony; the importance of aesthetics and style; theatricality; and humour. These theories closely connect camp to American, pre-gay-liberation homosexual and drag culture. Some authors suggest that camp has been relegated to the background since 'Stonewall' (the 1969 Stonewall riots, considered as the symbolic starting point of US gay liberation), when the gay community aimed to downsize feminine subjectivities in favour of a more 'neutral' gay identity (Halperin, 2012; Harris, 1997). Yet according to Campbell (2006) camp is still around and 'it shows no signs of durable crisis' (123). Indeed it continues 'to produce social visibility challenging the normative praxis of everyday life' (Waitt, 2012, p. 85), whether through new forms of activism like prides (Waitt, 2005), in local drag shows (Kaminski, 2003) and drag culture in general

(Halberstam, 2005, p. 129) or in national and international media like movies and TV shows (e.g. Padva, 2000). Therefore, as a concept referring to the theatrical and not overtly political subversion of social and gender norms, camp can still be useful to analyse contemporary drag performances, also outside of the Anglophone world, as we will demonstrate below.

In this chapter we want to argue that drag, in its 'campness' and its subversion of sexual and gender roles, can be conceived as a form of 'symbolic resistance'. This concept, drawn from cultural studies, seems particularly suited to refer to drag's capacity to symbolise otherness as well as subversion in daily life settings (Hall & Jefferson, 1976/2006). It is drawn from the analysis of subcultures, i.e. cultures which take an opposite stance to mainstream culture, which is appropriate as both drag and gay culture have been conceived in such terms (Chauncey, 1994; Halberstam, 2005). 'Symbolic resistance' refers to subtle and non-violent modes of action, for instance through style (Hebdige, 1991), which are not inevitably perceived as deviant (Herreman, Dhoest & Eeckhout, 2015). As a result, this term is particularly fitting for the analysis of practices and styles in drag shows. Concretely, we will use the term to refer to representations and performances subverting dominant heteronormative and homonormative expressions of gender and sexuality.

Methodology

This research draws primarily on the analysis of recorded performances of the Antwerps Travestie Theater in Antwerp. Besides being one of the oldest and longest-operating drag companies in Flanders, the company was selected because it created a unique genre in the Low Countries (Belgium and the Netherlands) by combining the drag show with comic theatre and musical. In this sense it is an exceptional company, although it may be regarded as part of a broader tradition of Belgian drag performances and companies, as will be developed below. Information on the group was initially collected from folders, flyers and local, national and international LGBT magazines, retrieved in the gay/lesbian archives and documentation centre Fonds Suzan Daniel located in Ghent. Subsequently recordings of the performances were tracked down, which was not evident as the company split up after the last production in 2006. We eventually found the former secretary, Herta Krieger, who owned the recordings and agreed to release them for academic purposes. The ATT wrote, produced, directed and performed twelve musicals between 1984 and 2006. We obtained and analysed the video recordings of nine productions, each lasting between two and three hours. Three plays, *Wiener Blut* (1984), *Sweet Travesty* (1986–1987) and *De Dames van Nostra* (*The Ladies of Nostra*, 2000–2001), were not included, either because they were not recorded or because we could not locate the recordings.[2]

In a first analytical step, we created a detailed description of each production to get a clear view of its overall storyline and characteristics, as well as its use of music. This led to a 'script' for every show, containing a summary of the storyline and of each scene, as well as an overview of the characters and the music performed. We then aimed our attention at moments of sexual and gender subversion as well as references to homosexuality, whether spoken, sung or suggested through plot elements. We also tried to identify all musical numbers, which was again something of a challenge because of the poor audiovisual quality of the recordings. Every show contained more than ten musical numbers, whether complete or fragmented, with a maximum of forty. After an extensive search using Shazam and SoundHound, by googling parts of the lyrics and then checking the songs via music databases like YouTube or Spotify, over 95% of the music could be identified. The next analytical phase involved the examination of the functions and meanings of music during the shows. We wanted to verify how music was applied in terms of genre, how music structured the story and whether the music used was 'gay'-related, be it in the lyrics or otherwise. In what follows we will first discuss the overall evolution and characteristics of the ATT shows, while the next part of our analysis will focus on the uses of gay music as well as on explicit and implicit moments of symbolic resistance.

General Overview and Core Characteristics

The ATT originally started in 1979 as an Antwerp-based drag company called *Antwerp Follies*. Although the topic has not been studied to date, our own exploratory research discloses that drag and drag venues were common in Belgium, at least in Antwerp, from the beginning of the twentieth century onwards. As in many other Western cities, moreover, Flemish drag culture developed partly within private and partly within semi-public spaces like bars which were known to offer the freedom to explore non-heteronormative forms of sexual desire and subjectivities (Chauncey, 1994; Kegels, 2009; Lapovsky, Kennedy & Davis, 1993). Flemish drag culture slowly became part of public entertainment in the second half of the twentieth century with the efforts of LGBT organisations, politicians and the media, among others, to make homosexuality more visible. We would argue that drag performances also played a meaningful role in this process.

The Dutch-Flemish drag company The Golden Rainbows was one of the first semi-professional ensembles to perform for mixed audiences in both the Netherlands and Flanders during the 1960s. The group continued to perform at the time the ATT was founded, yet mostly in the Netherlands (Deetman, 1981). This decision may have been a reason why the ATT was established, as there seems to have been a lack of public drag performances in this period in Flanders. In an interview with the Antwerp gay magazine *Link* ('Groots travestiespektakel', 1980) the founders of the ATT explained that they wanted to re-introduce drag shows in Flanders while aiming to bring them on a higher level by combining them with other genres like revue and cabaret.

The first ATT production, *Happy Times*, premiered in 1980 and already contained the main ingredients of what would subsequently become a unique genre combining drag shows with comic theatre and musical. An overarching storyline was introduced in 1984 with the second play, *Wiener Blut*, a drag adaptation of Johann Strauss the Younger's famous operetta. Other crucial changes in the evolution of the ATT plays include the introduction of the Antwerp dialect and lip-synched covers, respectively from 1993 and 1997 onwards. The Antwerp dialect was originally employed to intensify the frequently strong, self-assured personalities and verbal wit of the characters, and it reflected the drag queen persona very well. All musical numbers from the productions until 1997 were conventionally lip-synched original versions of songs. However, *Theater Chagrijn* (Theatre Grouch, 1997) introduced the lip-synched cover, which in this context means that performers covered and recorded an existing song in advance while lip-synching it on stage. This new approach gave the non-professional members of the cast the opportunity to focus on acting rather than on singing live on stage (H. Krieger, personal communication, 13 September 2015), yet it also facilitated the quest for suitable music, as the company was previously forced to interfere in the story, for instance by adapting the names of characters to the names mentioned in the lyrics. All subsequent productions, namely *Rimpels in de Rimboe* (Wrinkles in the Jungle, 1998), *Er Wordt Weer Gelachen* (Time to Laugh Again, 2001) and *1001 Nichten* (1001 Faggots, 2002), combined traditional lip-synching and lip-synched covers with instrumental music. The last musical play, *Caffé Coiffée* (a name for a barbershop) from 2006, only contained lip-synched covers. Together with the previously noted addition of an overarching storyline and the switch to Antwerp dialect, these changes indicate a growing sense of agency, the company increasingly taking the freedom to create its own world.

As indicated, the ATT drag shows analysed here follow a central storyline, in line with the broader genre of the musical. All shows share a humorous tone and can be described as 'comic musicals'. The nine productions contain typical comic elements like absurd storylines (which all have a happy ending), actions and settings, stereotypical characters and the use of verbal wit. All ATT members were non-professional actors and the recordings demonstrate that the audiences are aware of this as they often laugh when characters forget their lines or start to stutter. The actors generally deal with these shortcomings by addressing the audience explicitly to make fun of themselves or the spectators. A final core characteristic of the shows discussed here concerns the use of costumes and props. Most costumes are extremely elaborate and the actors regularly change clothes during the play.

By and large, the ATT musicals illustrate several elements of drag culture, where female impersonators elaborate upon – but simultaneously ridicule and subvert – the image of women by enlarging gendered expressions through practices and styles. The presentation of exaggerated images of conventional femininity combined with self-conscious irony through verbal wit are crucial in this matter. The practice is reminiscent of the drag performances in the cult comedy *The Adventures of Priscilla, Queen of the Desert* (1994, S. Elliott), and a clear illustration of the core characteristics of camp as discussed above: stylisation and theatricality, irony and humour. Moreover, these theatrical representations clearly demonstrate a sense of symbolic resistance, which we have defined above as a deliberate desire not to adjust to dominant heteronormative and homonormative expressions of sexuality and gender.

Music, Gender and Sexual Difference

As there is no space here to elaborate upon the musical repertoire of each show, nor upon the specific ways in which music is used to structure the story and enhance the drama,[3] we will focus on one specific aspect: the use of music to express gender and sexual difference and as a form of symbolic resistance. To do this, we will not discuss the meanings and possible effects of the performative act of being in drag (Butler, 1997; Moreman & McIntosh, 2010; Sieg, 2002) but focus on the different ways in which music refers to sexual and gender difference.

Gender and particularly sexual difference are explicitly referenced in seven of the nine productions. In terms of gender performance, the female impersonators generally act as women without revealing that they are in fact men, but in *(B)engelen in 't Vagevuur* (Angels/Smart Asses in Purgatory, 1995), *Het Verdwenen Schaakstuk* (The Missing Chess Piece, 1996) and *Er Wordt Weer Gelachen*, transvestism is explicitly mentioned. As we will develop further on, it is either considered as an anomaly or presented as an alternative lifestyle. In terms of sexual orientation, five productions contain overtly gay characters, mostly conforming to stereotypical representations of gay men. Almost all gay characters are feminine, some with a high libido and verging on the sexually promiscuous. There is a strong diversity in the number of gay characters, ranging from one in *Theater Chagrijn*, two in *Cabaret Paradiso* (1993) and *Café Coiffée*, three in *1001 Nichten* and an indeterminate number in *Er Wordt Weer Gelachen* because the sexual orientation of the characters in drag is never revealed in this production, despite their roles as male transvestite prostitutes having sex with other men but acting as women.

These representations of gender and sexual difference are clearly connected to feelings of pride or shame. For instance, the characters Jeanne d'Arc in *(B)engelen in 't Vagevuur* and Georgette in *Het Verdwenen Schaakstuk* respond differently after being accused of being a transvestite: the first character denies this while the second is proud of it. Overall, the gay male characters are portrayed as proud, self-confident men, except in the last production, *Caffé Coiffée*, which explicitly deals with the problems gay men face in their environment and where this topic is one of the central themes. The overarching storyline about a family owning a successful barbershop deals with the positive effects of change, and the meaning of one of the characters' coming out needs to be understood in this specific context. Pride and shame are crucial to understand how sexual and gender difference has been experienced historically and expressed in social settings – not only the pride promulgated by the LGBT movement, but also older and persistent affects of shame and pain (Love, 2007; Halperin, 2012). Still, it is striking that the ATT's last production in 2006 still focuses on shame, as by then homosexuality was widely accepted in a city such as Antwerp, and LGBT rights (including gay marriage and adoption) had become legally protected in Belgium (Borghs & Eeckhout, 2010). This may indicate that there is still a gap between political rights and the social experience of everyday lives, notably for people who wish to express their sexual identities in non-normative ways. Indeed the representation of sexual identity in nearly all the productions depends very much upon the embodiment of sexual desire and subjectivity, which in most cases deals with cross-gender practices and expressions.

Homosexual subjectivities and identities are not only explicitly addressed but also evoked through songs, often in combination with feelings of pride and shame, thereby again illustrating the affective power of music. Audiences clearly picked up on this, the video recordings showing how such songs were often awarded with applause. This is the case for instance when Georgette confidently admits that she is a transvestite by singing *I Am What I Am* in *Het Verdwenen Schaakstuk*. The song was originally written for the Broadway production *La Cage aux Folles* (1983), a musical about two openly gay men, Georges and Albin, who own a night club featuring drag entertainment in Saint-Tropez, France. Issues of gender and sexuality are at the heart of the latter play, which revolves around the question whether gay men should act in a more masculine – and hence a heteronormative/homonormative – manner. Albin, who is more feminine than his partner, ultimately rejects this stance ('I am what I am / I am my own special creation') while claiming that his world of 'feathers and bangles' may be different but is not therefore harmful. The song has often been covered by well-known and lesser-known male and female artists such as Shirley Bassey and Gloria Gaynor. However, the ATT preferred a man's voice in the play and opted for the original performance as featured in the Broadway musical. This decision is all the more remarkable because up to this point in the play all 'female' and male characters had been lip-synching songs performed respectively by women and men. The choice not to accord the sex of the character with the proper voice is a means for Georgette to come out explicitly as a transvestite, but it may also signal the ATT members' desire to inform audiences that they are proud to be drag queens, no matter what society thinks of them.

Shame and pride are also the subject in songs performed by gay characters. Thus at the end of *Theater Chagrijn* a lip-synched cover of ABBA's *Gimme Gimme Gimme* is used to inform audiences about the impressions of a gay theatre actor after performing in a story on a family feud. The character reveals he is glad not to have a family life with children because he is gay: 'Fami-fami-familiale problemen / Een familieleven is geen leven voor mij' ('Fami-fami-family problems / I'm not a family man'). Opposite feelings are expressed in a lip-synched cover of Queen's *Bohemian Rhapsody* in *Caffé Coiffée*, where the character is sad after his father has rejected him for being gay. No songs about homosexuality were found in the other productions, except if we were to interpret the characters in *Er Wordt Weer Gelachen* as gay men. And even then, they sing about their life as prostitutes, not about their sexual orientations or the problems they might encounter as homosexuals. As in *Café Coiffée* however, the necessity of being able to choose who you want to be and the possibility to change your future are discussed in the play and some of the songs. These and other plays moreover express a sense of oppression, which may be seen as a form of implicit, symbolical resistance to heteronormative norms, values and ideas.

In our theoretical framework, drawing on Brett and Wood (2002), we raised the concept of gay music, which is to be seen not as music that is 'essentially' gay but rather as music that is in some way associated with gay culture. From this perspective the above-mentioned songs whose lyrics explicitly refer or implicitly allude to homosexuality can be defined as gay music. Other songs may also be labelled as such when connecting them for instance to LGBT artists, divas and camp. The latter examples in particular illustrate how gay music is very much in the eye (or ear) of the beholder: it has to be interpreted and appropriated in this way, and connotations have to be picked up by the listener. Based on a close analysis of the repertoire, it seems that the company did purposefully choose music with 'gay' connotations, at least in the first five productions up to *Theater Chagrijn* in 1997. We discovered that all the songs which did not conform to the dominant genre of the shows and which thus disrupted their musical coherence were quite easy to frame as gay music.

In *Cabaret Paradiso* two songs are not linked to the dominant genres of the American musical and Dutch and German cabaret and revue. *Etienne* and *I Will Always Love You* are pop hits sung by Guesch Patti and Whitney Houston, respectively, two artists who have been perceived as 'gay icons' or 'divas' in gay culture (Gonzales, 2002; Lister, 2001). Both these terms refer to people who are embraced by the LGBT community. Divas are usually depicted as self-assured women who represent themselves or are portrayed as 'larger than life' (Koestenbaum, 1993). Musically there are various reasons why particular artists are called divas, but celebrities like Houston, as well as some of the other women performers we will discuss hereafter, can be included as divas because they have been recognised as being exceptionally good at their genre.

Trobbels at Sea (Troubles at Sea, 1994) contains three songs which stand out stylistically: *Jacky*, originally performed by the gay male artist Marc Almond; *Bandido* performed by Azucar Moreno at the 1990 edition of the Eurovision Song Contest, a show which has been acknowledged to be highly popular among gay men (Lemish, 2004); and a mix of the British boy band Take That and Donna Summer's performance of *Could It Be Magic.* Summer, like Patti and Houston, has also been embraced by the LGBT community as a gay icon (Guilbert, 2002, p. 70) and appraised as a disco diva (Kutulas, 2003), while boy bands have attracted gay male fans because of their girlish masculinity (Wald, 2002). The same applies to the pop songs in *(B)engelen in 't Vagevuur*, where many are performed by artists considered as gay icons and/or rock/dance divas, like Tina Turner (Bego, 2003), Grace Jones (Weidhase, 2015), Dalbello (Brisebois, n.d.), Crystal Waters (Amico, 2001, p. 366) and the aforementioned Guesch Patti. The songs are also connected to the (perceived) collective music preferences within gay culture as they belong to specific subgenres of dance music such as disco and house (Currid, 1995; Dyer, 1998).

Het Verdwenen Schaakstuk contains six songs which are not part of the shows *Chess* and *EFX* or not written by Andrew Lloyd Webber, unlike the rest of the show. All these songs are in some way affiliated again with homosexuality. *Gimme Love* is drawn from the musical *Kiss of the Spider Woman*, in which a homosexual character fantasises about a diva called Aurora. *Come A-Wandering with Me* derives from the musical play *The Gay Life.* The main title of this production originally referred to 'a happy life' yet acquired a homosexual connotation afterwards. *Black Cat, Keep Young and Beautiful* and *Sisters Are Doing It for Themselves* are pop songs performed by Janet Jackson, Annie Lennox and Lennox in a duet with Aretha Franklin, respectively. All these artists are considered to be divas and/or gay icons once again (Geczy & Karaminas, 2013, p. 40; Nathan, 1999). Furthermore, *I Am What I Am* is known as a gay anthem (Hubbs, 2007, p. 242).

Theater Chagrijn is the last production where we noticed an attempt at musical coherence but where some songs did not match the overall genre of the show. These are the lip-synched covers of *I Want to Break Free* by Queen and *Gimme Gimme Gimme* by ABBA, and the traditional playback of *De Aanhouder Wint (It's Dogged That Does It)*, a cabaret-like song originally performed by the Dutch artist Liesbeth List. The first two songs are strongly connected to gay culture, as the lead singer of Queen, Freddie Mercury, was gay while the music of Swedish pop band ABBA has been appropriated as camp (Burnett, 1992). Moreover, the ABBA song is about someone who is desperately looking for a man, probably to have sex with. The final song, *De Aanhouder Wint*, is harder to interpret, as it is stylistically affiliated with 'kleinkunst', a genre which is not generally associated with gay culture in the Low Countries.[4] While the performer, Liesbeth List, is known to be straight and there is no clear evidence that she is perceived as a gay icon, she is somehow connected to gay culture through her collaboration with the gay singer Ramses Shaffy, who was closeted at the time. Also, she is regarded as the leading lady of 'kleinkunst', which makes her a diva in a musical sense.

Conclusion

Drawing on Halperin (2012), in this chapter we studied the historical construction of a shared 'gay culture', based in a distinctive sensibility and apparent in cultural practices such as camp, diva worship and drag. More concretely, we raised the question how Antwerp drag queens used music to construct a sense of gay culture and as a form of symbolic resistance challenging dominant structures of gender and sexuality. We focused on a unique genre in the Low Countries, namely drag musicals, produced and performed by the ATT, an Antwerp-based drag company. As our analysis shows, the nine investigated productions abound with representations of, and allusions to, gender and sexual deviance. As in drag culture in general, in these musicals gender roles are (literally) performed and exaggerated, thereby creating an ironical and theatrical critique of normative masculinity and femininity. The musicals also explicitly refer to homosexuality and transvestism, whether through their characters, storylines or songs. In the process they evoke feelings of pride and shame, so that they may be said to deal with common experiences, desires and affects related to homosexuality in twentieth-century Europe. Furthermore, these musicals clearly reference a corpus of 'gay music', understood here as music with coded gay connotations or associations, whether through the lyrics, the original performer's sexual orientation or their status as a diva or gay icon.

Through all these processes we would argue that the ATT's drag shows contributed to the establishment and spreading of a gay culture in Flanders, in the process challenging dominant structures of gender and sexuality. Besides including more overtly politicised forms of LGBT emancipation, from the 1970s onwards the drag shows studied here offered a more subtle 'symbolic' form of subversion and resistance, using the codes of camp and stylistic excess as well as representations of and allusions to homosexuality to introduce the topic to a broad audience. As in the study of Kaminski (2003) on the politics of music in contemporary American drag performances, the accessibility and emotional appeal of music helped to make potentially alienating statements about gender and sexuality palatable to a mainstream audience. Into the early 2000s, these musicals offered a subtle yet effective way of subverting dominant heteronormative and homonormative expressions of sexuality and gender.

Acknowledgements

This research was supported by the Research Programme of the Research Foundation – Flanders (FWO). We would like to express our sincere gratitude to Herta Krieger, the former secretary of the Antwerps Travestie Theater, who provided us with the necessary materials, in particular recordings of performances, to conduct this research.

Notes

1. 'Drag queens', 'show queens' and 'female impersonators' have been used inter-changeably in literature. However, some scholars have opted to focus on one term either to explain differences in performance or by preferring one over the other in specific historical contexts, as explained by Schacht & Underwood (2004, p. 13). We have applied these terms as synonyms throughout the text.
2. The shows were multilingual, often combining Dutch titles and spoken dialogue with songs in Dutch, English, French or German. All titles are given in their original language with an English translation where necessary.
3. This more extensive analysis is developed in the PhD dissertation of co-author Robbe Herreman, a broader investigation of the role of music in Antwerp's LGBT culture, from which this chapter is drawn.
4. 'Kleinkunst' literally means 'small art' and refers to the simply arranged, soberly accompanied narrative ballad format by one performer or small group in a musical style untouched by international commercial pop.

References

Amico, S. (2001). 'I Want Muscles': House Music, Homosexuality and Masculine Signification. *Popular Music, 20*(3), 359–378.

Amico, S. (2009). Visible Difference, Audible Difference: Female Singers and Gay Male Fans in Russian Popular Music. *Popular Music and Society, 32*(3), 351–370.

Babuscio, J. (1977). Camp and the Gay Sensibility. In R. Dyer (Ed.), *Gays and Film* (pp. 40–57). London: British Film Institute.

Bego, M. (2003). *Tina Turner: Break Every Rule*. Lanham, Md: Taylor Trade Pub.

Borghs, P. & Eeckhout, B. (2010). LGB Rights in Belgium, 1999–2007: A Historical Survey of a Velvet Revolution. *International Journal of Law, Policy and the Family, 24*(1), 1–28.

Brett, P. & Wood, E. (2002). Lesbian and Gay Music. *Electronic Musicological Review, 7*. Retrieved from http://www.rem.ufpr.br/_REM/REMv7/Brett_Wood/Brett_and_Wood.html.

Brisebois, D. (n.d.). *Dalbello*. Retrieved from http://www.canadianbands.com/home.html.

Burnett, R. (1992). Dressed for Success: Sweden from Abba to Roxette. *Popular Music, 11*(2), 141–150.

Butler, J. (1991). Imitation and Gender Insubordination. In D. Fuss (Ed.), *Inside/Out: Lesbian Theories, Gay Theories* (pp. 13–31). New York: Routledge.

Butler, J. (1997). Gender Is Burning: Questions of Appropriation and Subversion. *Cultural Politics, 11*, 381–395.

Campbell, C. (2006). Camp. In D. A. Gerstner (Ed.), *Routledge International Encyclopedia of Queer Culture* (pp. 121–124). London/New York: Routledge.

Chauncey, G. (1994). *Gay New York: Gender, Urban Culture, and the Making of the Gay Male World, 1890–1940*. New York: Basic Books.

Currid, B. (1995). 'We Are Family': House Music and Queer Performativity. In S. E. Case, P. Brett & S. Foster (Eds.), *Cruising the Performative: Interventions into the Repression of Ethnicity, Nationality and Sexuality* (pp. 165–196). Bloomington, IN: Indiana University Press.

Deetman, J. W. (1981). Flor van Noolen 20 Jaar Topamusement. *Gay Krant, 2*, 5–7.

Dhoest, A., Herreman, R. & Wasserbauer, M. (2015). Into the Groove: Exploring Lesbian and Gay Musical Preferences and 'LGB Music' in Flanders. *Observatorio (OBS*), 9*(2), 207–223.

Duggan, L. (2002). *The New Homonormativity: The Sexual Politics of Neoliberalism.* Durham, NC: Duke University Press.

Dyer, R. (1998). In Defense of Disco. In C. K. Creekmur & A. Doty (Eds.), *Out in Culture: Gay, Lesbian, and Queer Essays on Popular Culture* (pp. 407–415). Durham/London: Duke University Press.

Geczy, A. & Karaminas, V. (2013). *Queer Style.* London: Bloomsbury.

Gonzales, C. (2002). Dans les Yeux de Guesch Patti. *CitéGAY.* Retrieved from http://www.citegay.fr/interviews/228184@dans-les-yeux-de-guesch-patti.htm.

Groots Travestiespektakel: Antwerp Follies. (1980, February). *Link, 2*, 36–37.

Guilbert, G.-C. (2002). *Madonna as Postmodern Myth: How One Star's Self-Construction Rewrites Sex, Gender, Hollywood, and the American Dream.* Jefferson, N.C: McFarland & Co.

Halberstam, J. (2005). *In a Queer Time and Place: Transgender Bodies, Subcultural Lives.* London/New York: New York University Press.

Hall, S. & Jefferson, T. (Eds.) (1976/2006). *Resistance Through Rituals: Youth Subcultures in Post-War Britain.* London: Hutchinson.

Halperin, D. (2012). *How to Be Gay.* Cambridge/London: The Belknap Press of Harvard University Press.

Harris, D. (1997). *The Rise and Fall of Gay Culture.* New York: Ballantine Books.

Hebdige, D. (1991). *Subculture: The Meaning of Style.* London: Routledge.

Herreman, R., Dhoest, A. & Eeckhout, B. (2015). 'Fed Up with Men': Music as Symbolic Resistance in the Flemish Lesbian and Women's Movement. In A. Dhoest, S. Malliet, B. Segaert & J. Haers (Eds.), *The Borders of Subculture: Resistance and the Mainstream* (pp. 70–86). London & New York: Routledge.

Hubbs, N. (2007). 'I Will Survive': Musical Mappings of Queer Social Space in a Disco Anthem. *Popular Music, 26*(2), 231–244.

Kaminski, E. (2003). *Listening to Drag: Music, Performance and the Construction of Oppositional Culture* (Unpublished doctoral thesis). Columbus: Ohio State University.

Kates, S. M. (1997). Sense vs. Sensibility: An Exploration of the Lived Experience of Camp. *Advances in Consumer Research, 24*, 132–137.

Kegels, H. (2009). *De Flierefluiter.* Utrecht: Gopher Publishers.

Koestenbaum, W. (1993). *The Queen's Throat: Opera, Homosexuality, and the Mystery of Desire.* New York: Poseidon Press.

Kutulas, J. (2003). You Probably Think This Song Is About You: 1970s Women's Music from Carole King to the Disco Divas. In S. A. Inness (Ed.), *Disco Divas: Women and Popular Culture in the 1970s* (pp. 172–194). Philadelphia: University of Pennsylvania Press.

Lapovsky Kennedy, E. & Davis, M. D. (1993). *Boots of Leather, Slippers of Gold: The History of a Lesbian Community.* Routledge: New York.

Lemish, D. (2004). 'My Kind of Campfire': The Eurovision Song Contest and Israeli Gay Men. *Popular Communication, 2*(1), 41–63.

Lister, L. (2001). Divafication: The Deification of Modern Female Pop Stars. *Popular Music & Society, 25*(3–4), 1–10.

Love, H. (2007). *Feeling Backward: Loss and the Politics of Queer History.* Cambridge: Harvard UP.

Moreman, S. T. & McIntosh, D. M. (2010). Brown Scriptings and Rescriptings: A Critical Performance Ethnography of Latina Drag Queens. *Communication & Critical/Cultural Studies, 7*(2), 115–135.

Nathan, D. (1999). *The Soulful Divas: Personal Portraits of Over a Dozen Divine Divas, from Nina Simone, Aretha Franklin & Diana Ross to Patti LaBelle, Whitney Houston & Janet Jackson.* New York: Billboard Books.

Newton, E. (1972/1979). *Mother Camp: Female Impersonators in America.* Chicago/London: The University of Chicago Press.

Padva, G. (2000). Priscilla Fights Back: The Politicization of Camp Subculture. *Journal of Communication Inquiry, 24*(2), 216–243.

Schacht, S. P. & Underwood, L. (2004). The Absolutely Fabulous but Flawlessly Customary World of Female Impersonators. *Journal of Homosexuality, 46*(3–4), 1–17.

Sieg, K. (2002). *Ethnic Drag: Performing Race, Nation, Sexuality in West Germany.* Ann Arbor: University of Michigan Press.

Sontag, S. (1964). Notes on 'Camp'. *Partisan Review, 31*(4), 515–530.

Valentine, G. (1995). Creating Transgressive Space: The Music of kd lang. *Transactions of the Institute of British Geographers,* 474–485.

Waitt, G. (2005). The Sydney 2002 Gay Games and Querying Australian National Space. *Environment and Planning D: Society and Space, 23,* 435–452.

Waitt, G. (2012). Queer Perspectives on Tourism Geographies. In J. Wilson (Ed.), *The Routledge Handbook of Tourism Geographies* (pp. 82–89). Abingdon: Routledge.

Wald, G. (2002). 'I Want It That Way': Teenybopper Music and the Girling of Boy Bands. *Genders, 35,* 1–39.

Warner, M. (1991). Fear of a Queer Planet, *Social Text, 29,* 3–17.

Weidhase, N. (2015). Ageing Grace/Fully: Grace Jones and the Queering of the Diva Myth. In Jermyn, D. & Holmes, S. (Eds.), *Women, Celebrity and Cultures of Ageing* (pp. 97–111). London/New York: Palgrave Macmillan.

Part II

Media Consumption, Identification and Role Models

4 Coming Out in the Digital Age

The Opportunities and Limitations of Internet Use in Queer-Lesbian Coming-Out Experiences in Germany

Ulrike Roth

In Germany, queer-lesbian[1] ways of living remain stigmatised, while heterosexuality is assumed and encouraged as the norm (Lenz et al., 2012). As a result, the process of coming out remains a defining experience in queer-lesbian biographies and is often tied to feelings of discomfort, fear or even crisis (Butler, 1993a; Wolf, 2004). Access to information about queer-lesbian cultures and lives, as well as contacts with other queer-lesbian women, can be invaluable resources during the process of coming out (Hänsch, 2003; Wolf, 2004; Zuehlke, 2004). The internet, as a platform for both informational and social exchange, is generally assumed to facilitate this process.

Indeed, previous research has highlighted the advantages of the internet for sexual minorities and for their coming-out experiences in general (for an overview see Szulc & Dhoest, 2013). This also applies to the few studies on queer-lesbian girls and women and the internet (Driver, 2007), as well as on lesbian girls and women, coming out and the internet (Munt, Bassett & O'Riordan, 2002). Susan Driver (2007) sees online communities as realms where 'queer youth are active makers and facilitators of provisional and fluid spaces of dialogue, sharing experiences from their life worlds and creating imagined social worlds'. She states that 'it is online that young people find ways to safely and creatively explore their queer difference as lesbian and bisexual girls, transyouth, genderqueers, and birls' (p. 192). Similarly, in their analysis of a self-described lesbian online forum, Munt, Bassett and O'Riordan (2002) argue that 'the circulation of practical information and advice in the site prior to disclosure allows participants to prepare, discuss, and shape their material or lived identities in advance of off-line affiliation' (p. 136). But the forum is not only preparatory as participants return to the site and 'renegotiate their identity' (ibid.). The dialogues that emerge between newly engaged participants and participants who describe themselves as 'older lesbians' function as a transfer of knowledge and '(sub)cultural capital' (p. 130).

Likewise, research on coming out and Lesbians, Gays, Bisexuals, Trans* and Queers (LGBTQ) generally upholds that the internet facilitates coming out. It is used 'to find general information about topics such as homo- and bisexuality or gay sex as well as to contact other LGBs whom they could consult for advice or share their experiences with' (Szulc & Dhoest, 2013, p. 361). The sizable number of videos on coming out (Wuest, 2014) as well as on the experiences of transgender youth (O'Neill, 2014) on *YouTube* indicate the increased accessibility of LGBTQ-related content online.

In her ethnographic study about digital media use among rural queer-identifying and questioning youth in the United States, Mary Gray (2009) notes that especially content which is by and about LGBTQs and which is particularly authentic (a feature she describes as 'queer realness') plays a crucial role in coming-out experiences: 'Internet-based personals, search-engine results, coming-out stories, and chat rooms as genres of queer realness provide moments of storytelling that transform the ways rural youth think and talk about their identities' (Gray, 2014, p. 179). In contrast to these findings, few studies address how marginalisation and power relations in online spaces can limit the ways in which the internet is used as a coming-out resource (Bromseth & Sundén, 2011; Gosine, 2007; Gray, 2014).

In the tradition of Cultural Studies, qualitative audience studies have long called for media users to be understood as active subjects who utilise media and produce meaning dependent on the context of their everyday lives as well as the power relations within their society (e.g. Gray, 1992; Gray, 2014; Hall, 1980; Livingstone, 2002; Morley, 1992). Furthermore, scholars such as Nancy Baym (2010) remark that online and offline worlds are highly intertwined and cannot be understood as separate from each other. Internet use and media engagement have to be seen as 'part of a broader social terrain of experience' (Gray, 2014, p. 173).

From this perspective, I argue for the importance of avoiding generalisations that focus too narrowly on the advantages of internet usage in coming-out experiences. It is essential, rather, to examine the ways in which the internet is actually used and perceived, as well as the ways it is *not* used. From this vantage point, we can gain a deeper understanding of the internet's relevance in coming-out experiences while still remaining aware of its possible constraints. The empirical findings of the present study will show that internet usage is not equally helpful in each coming-out process but depends on the specific context of the coming out and on the circumstances and perspectives of the individual. My data draws on in-depth interviews with eight (former or actual) female-identified individuals or women[2] between 18 and 26 years old who identify as lesbian and/or queer.

In this chapter, I will first briefly explain the term 'queer-lesbian' as it appears throughout the text. Next I will detail the unique challenges of queer-lesbian coming-out processes. My empirical findings, finally, will demonstrate the ways in which the interviewees of my research used the internet during their coming out, as well as the ways in which they did *not* use the internet.

Terminology: Queer, Lesbian and Queer-Lesbian

Researching and discussing the coming-out experiences of female-socialised queers, lesbians and bisexuals poses a challenge in regards to terminology. Since different designations carry their own political implications, I asked my interviewees about their own practices of self-description.[3]

Upon inspection, it appeared that even within my small sample of interviewees self-descriptions were not fixed but varied over time and across contexts. In some situations, participants preferred to describe themselves as 'lesbian' while in others 'queer' was the favoured term. Some interviewees described themselves as lesbian in the past, yet today would not even describe themselves as women. So for all the participants both terms were relevant at some time. Therefore using only a single term would not suffice.

The terms 'lesbian' and 'queer' nevertheless have very divergent historical origins and are connected to different and even contradictory political claims. 'Queer' arose in the late 1980s as a result of political struggles in the United States, serving as a reaction and explicit critique of (gay and) lesbian identity politics (Jagose, 1996). Since queer activism and theory attest that identities are always constituted on the basis of exclusion and of 'what they are not', the term 'queer' tries to be inclusive of future meanings. It is about 'avowing the sign's strategic provisionality' (Butler, 1993b, p. 312). In German queer communities today, it is used for all kinds of gender non-conforming practices, lives and identities.

It should be noted that 'queer' never carried a negative connotation in the German context. This made it possible to substitute – at least in part – the stigmatised label 'lesbian' with a hipper, sexier and therefore more economically exploitable term (Jagose, 2001, p. 188). 'Queer' came to be used simply as a synonym and umbrella term for gay and lesbian (Degele, 2008, p. 53). At the same time, lesbian lives and cultures have seemed to lose visibility under the queer umbrella. This was reflected in the remarks of one interviewee (Chantal), who stated that in her search for queer content online she found only gay men's content.

Even though using the term 'queer' involves an attempt to think and live beyond the narrow boundaries of identity, there have been discussions about the disappearance of lesbians from within the queer community itself.[4] These discussions address two concerns. Firstly, there is the concern that 'queer' tends to mask power relations and thereby erases the experiences of the less privileged – yet again. Secondly, some queers display little appreciation of lesbians, for instance by denying the role of lesbians' historical feminist struggles as a precondition for queerness. Looking closely at the lesbian lives and cultures of the past, we can see that much of what was lived and practised then could now be described as queer, while back then it was described as lesbian (see e.g. Nestle, 1992) – simply because queer was not yet available as a term of collective self-identification. As Jagose puts it, 'queer marks both a continuity and a break with previous gay liberationist and lesbian feminist models' (Jagose, 1996, p. 75), which is also echoed in the self-descriptions of this study's interviewees. Therefore, my use of the term 'queer-lesbian' is an attempt to make these contradictions visible instead of denying them.[5]

Queer-Lesbian Coming Out

The term 'coming out' has been subject to wide discussions of its meaning and of methods to research it. Many coming-out models have been developed, criticised and modified (Wolf, 2004, pp. 126–134; for an overview see Manning, 2014; for a critical discussion of models see Rust, 2003 and Zuehlke, 2004). Generally we might say that coming out is necessary only because society is structured around heterosexuality and assumes and encourages a heterosexual orientation (Adams, 2011; Butler, 1993a; Hänsch, 2003; Wolf, 2004). As long as heterosexuality remains the hegemonic way of living and as long as gender (both lived and desired) requires differentiation between men and women, it will remain necessary to come out as queer-lesbian (Wolf, 2004, p. 59; see also Butler, 1990). Contrary to queer and gay men, moreover, queer-lesbian women face the additional issues of invisibility and discrimination as women, which calls for a specific investigation of internet use and queer-lesbian coming-out experiences (Wolf, 2004, p. 59; Zuehlke, 2004, p. 124).

With her concept of the heterosexual matrix, Judith Butler provides a theoretical explanation of the feelings of anxiety and threat which are directed towards identities and lives beyond heterosexuality. She asserts that becoming a subject and a human being is indivisibly connected to being marked as man or woman, while being a man or a woman is itself constituted by heterosexual desire (Butler, 1990 & 1993a). Whenever someone deviates from this heterosexual desire, their gender identity, and thus their status as a subject, is being challenged. As a result, queer-lesbian desire is perceived as something threatening and 'monstrous' (Butler, 1997, p. 136). Following Butler, the constitution of the subject demands the rejection of homosexual desire. This rejection and exclusion establishes 'the abject' and the '"unlivable" and "uninhabitable" zones of social life', which are 'required to circumscribe the domain of the subject' (Butler, 1993a, p. 3). Queer-lesbian lives are part of these zones of the 'unlivable'. They are perceived as sites of 'dreaded identifications' or as a 'threatening spectre' (Butler, 1993a, p. 3).

Furthermore, Butler's work and the heterosexual matrix address how discourse affects the intelligibility of queer-lesbian lives. What is possible to imagine, articulate and think is produced by

> a set of foreclosures, radical erasures, that are [...] refused the possibility of cultural articulation. Hence, [...] the construction of the human is a differential operation that produces the more and the less 'human', the inhuman, the humanly unthinkable.
>
> (Butler, 1993a, p. 8)

Due to these heteronormative subjectivations, the adoption of queer and/or lesbian lives and of same-sex desires is a process that lies beyond the reach of what Butler calls an 'intelligible subject'. The crucial challenge within this process is to question and positively reframe the devaluation and stigmatisation of queer-lesbian lives and identities (Wolf, 2004). It is not only about presuming the 'unthinkable' and expanding the 'thinkable', but also about gaining resources to engage a life within this realm of the 'unlivable'.

In this context and with reference to Zuehlke (2004) and Rust (2003), coming out can be described as the process of

—sensing and realising romantic or sexual feelings for members of one's own gender;
—different ways of exploring and accepting these feelings;
—sharing these feelings with others and acting on them;
—establishing a queer-lesbian life.

These aspects interact with each other and do not occur in a fixed order. From a queer perspective there cannot be an exact model for queer-lesbian life, nor can one's coming out be seen as a process culminating in a fixed identity (Gray, 2014). Rather, coming out must be seen as an ongoing process in which queer-lesbian individuals continually negotiate their ways of living and practices of disclosure in a heteronormative society.

Negotiations of identities and coming-out experiences are always contextual, interacting with life's other challenges and struggles. These challenges can be personal or familial and can also include other forms of discrimination. In general, the coming-out process is highly influenced by one's personal experiences with support, recognition or rejection, but also by the wider social context in which such experiences occur (Wolf, 2004; Zuehlke, 2004). Coming out is especially challenging for people who expect massive opposition from their social environment while lacking access to information about queer-lesbian lives and communities (Wolf, 2004). As Wolf notes, this is particularly true for queer-lesbians who are very young or very old, from rural areas, grow up in very religious or homophobic social contexts and have disabilities or limited financial or temporal resources. Similarly, Holmes (2000) states that coming-out experiences are dependent on 'gender, geographical and social community, race, class, age, ethnicity, religious beliefs, and political allegiances' (p. 151).

The two main factors that are generally perceived as supportive of queer-lesbian coming-out processes are knowledge about queer-lesbian lives and contact with other queer-lesbian people, as well as with a wider queer-lesbian community (Hänsch, 2003). However, as Wolf (2004) notes, making contact with other queer-lesbians can be an obstacle for many girls and women, since they do not necessarily know where or how to reach out.

As already mentioned, previous research has shown that the internet is frequently used to gain access to these two resources during the coming-out process. Yet these findings remain mostly detached from individual coming-out experiences and their contexts. As a result, research tends to lose sight of the situations in which the internet is *not* used and also ignores the interconnection of offline and online experiences.

General coming-out experiences lie at the core of the present study, flanked by questions regarding the various ways in which the internet both is and is not used throughout the process. This chapter aims to identify the capabilities of the internet as a coming-out resource while remaining open to its limitations.

Coming-Out Experiences and Internet Use

Although the interviews were conducted with eight different people, each with their own unique story, they all occurred in the context of a hetero-normative society. The interviewees grew up in urban, suburban or rural areas and were attending university or higher secondary education at the time of the interview. Two of the interviewees have a history of migration in their families and one is a person of colour.[6] They were recruited online as well as offline via an open call for lesbian- and/or queer-identified people. The interviews took place in the summer of 2011.

Altogether I identified four key experiences within these different coming-out stories: coming to terms in isolation; quick action; the inability to imagine a queer-lesbian life; secrecy and the impossibility of coming out. In each coming-out story one of these experiences seemed to provide an over-arching frame for participants' internet usage. In the following paragraphs I will describe these four key experiences and the features of their corresponding internet usage, addressing these two questions: how is the internet used (or not used) in response to different kinds of coming-out experiences? And to what extent does the internet offer (or not offer) ways to imagine, accept and establish a queer-lesbian life within a heteronormative society?

Coming to Terms in Isolation

Micha (24), Annika (24) and Iris (21)[7] all experienced a long period of questioning and coming to terms with their sexuality. They first recognised their feelings for other girls as a result of various events in their teenage years, but then 'suppressed' their feelings (Iris, Annika) or 'fled into heterosexual life' (Micha). They felt that their feelings for girls were 'somehow really bad and dangerous and just weren't allowed to happen' (Annika) or that they were 'somehow weird' (Micha). As Micha recounts: 'I didn't want it, because none of my friends were like that – or ever said anything like that'.

During this initial period, which lasted between one and three years, these three participants hardly spoke to anyone about their thoughts and feelings for girls and women[8] – whether offline or online. Iris explained that she had to come to terms with it on her own before talking to anyone else.

Annika said that she did not begin talking to other people about her feelings until she herself was 'relatively sure'.

During this time of isolation, the internet[9] became an important resource for all of them. They all looked up information about queer-lesbian life online. They read about it on websites written by individuals and social service centres, through social media conversations, on forums and personal blogs and watched movies online. However, they did not use the internet to get in touch with other queer-lesbian girls or women.

However, after they had come out to (at least some of) their friends, were relatively self-assured about their sexuality and had had their first girl-friends, Annika and Micha started to get in touch with other queer-lesbian women online. But since Micha's group of friends was almost 'entirely heterosexual', she used the popular German social network *Lesarion*[10] in order to get to know other queer-lesbians in the cities around her small hometown. She made friends with someone with whom she discussed 'all this coming-out stuff and this feeling of discomfort' online. When she later moved to a bigger city, she used *Lesarion* again in order to get in touch with local queer-lesbian people. Similarly, when Annika moved to a bigger city, she also used the internet to find out about queer-lesbian spots and wrote to others on *Lesarion* to find people with whom she could attend a lesbian party.

Compared to Annika and Micha, at the time of the interview Iris was not in the least interested in online interactions. She explained that after watching numerous movies online and reading about queer-lesbian women on her computer screen, she 'just had read enough' and wanted to 'talk to someone face to face'. Online she found a queer-lesbian youth group in her city, where she went in order to meet other queer-lesbian women. She valued the internet mostly as a tool for finding information anonymously:

> Basically everything that I've done in this realm I found on the inter-net first and afterwards put into practice. You're in a very anonymous place when you're Googling behind your computer. I think it's quite intimidating to just go somewhere. It's a lot easier when you can Google it beforehand and then prepare yourself.

For Micha, Annika and Iris, information accessed online served as both an emotional and a practical resource during their coming-out process. Micha explained that reading about queer-lesbian women online made her feel less strange and alone: 'All of this reading kind of led to a normal-isation. I no longer thought, "Damn, this is something really weird, really bad". But that there were others'. Iris noted similar effects: 'It definitely made me feel more self-confident, because now I realised that I am not the only one who feels that way'. Meanwhile Annika claimed that her anxiety restricted her use of the internet and other media during her coming out on a fundamental level. In her view, it is important to distinguish 'between different periods' because in the beginning you might not even 'dare to look it up on the internet'.

As a whole, Annika's, Micha's and Iris's deep-seated fears and feelings of discomfort affected their offline as well as online activities. Even online they continued to experience negative feelings, and contrary to the suggestions by Munt, Bassett and O'Riordan (2002) their sense of social isolation was not mitigated by the availability of online communication. Only after they were mostly out of the closet and relatively confident about their desires did Micha and Annika begin contacting other queer-lesbian women online.

Quick Action

After initially realising their feelings for women, neither Chantal (24) nor Toni (18) took long before acting out on their desires and telling their family and friends about them. Chantal had an older sister who had already had a relationship with a woman. This had not been a problem for her parents. So she grew up having a queer-lesbian role model while also being assured of her parents' generally accepting attitude towards same-sex relationships. Once she realised her own interest in girls, she started using her sister's account on *Lesarion*. There she read what the other users were writing about, but never wrote to them herself. She stated that the ability to read about queer-lesbian lives online made her feel 'more confident' because now she knew that 'there are thousands of other people'. Shortly thereafter she began a long-term relationship with a female classmate and lost interest in the social network site. Instead she used the internet to find out about queer-lesbian parties and spaces in her area and also looked up questions regarding sex.

At the age of 16, Toni met an old friend from elementary school who fell in love with her. At first she was 'overwhelmed' but then they started dating. Although Toni did not harbour any negative feelings about homosexuality, she simply 'didn't know that something like this was possible'. After two months of dating her friend, Toni told her mother (a sexual therapist) about it, who reacted very 'positively'. She also came out at school without any particularly negative reactions. Toni saw her father only on weekends and waited two years to tell him. His reaction, while reserved, was not negative either.

After three months Toni's relationship was over and she explained that she needed some time to 'process' her experiences. During this time she visited several girls-only online chatrooms that had 'a lesbian tendency'. By then she was mostly out but did not know any other queer-lesbian women. In these chatrooms she felt that she could process her experiences by talking about them with different and often random (queer-lesbian as well as heterosexual) girls. After two months, she stopped chatting and did not go on to strengthen her relationships with any of her contacts, whether on- or offline. Instead she decided to meet other queer-lesbian women in a lesbian youth group in her city, which she found online.[11]

In summary, Chantal and Toni both experienced a rather quick coming out, during which they both used the internet heavily but also differently. While Chantal lurked on *Lesarion* before she was out to anyone, Toni talked to other girls online following the end of her first relationship and after having come out to most of her social circles.

The Inability to Imagine a Queer-Lesbian Life

Until their early twenties, Beate (25) and Katja (24) had hardly experienced any intimate relationships. This was by no means a problem for them. Both felt that relationships 'might just come later' (Katja). Katja sometimes accepted her friends' and family's efforts to set her up with guys by going on a few dates. But even though these dates never led to anything, the possibility that she might be interested in women never occurred to her.

By contrast, Beate had a lesbian friend from school and referred to herself as bisexual after noticing that her first relationship with a guy at age 15 was not what she wanted. In a way, she said, she had already had her coming out during this time. Still, she never felt the urge to actively pursue her feelings and engage with other girls – whether online or offline. She explained that she 'didn't *really* get it until last year [2010]'. While queer-lesbian desire was simply absent from Katja's consciousness, Beate could not (or did not want to) picture a concrete queer-lesbian life for herself.

Katja's and Beate's inability to imagine a queer-lesbian life for themselves is probably connected to the fact that they both grew up in environments which shunned homosexuality. Katja noticed this in her parents' general attitudes and Beate's single mother even changed churches when they were supposed to get a gay priest. Both Katja and Beate also expressed strong prejudices towards queer-lesbians themselves. They imagined queer-lesbian women to be very dominant and masculine. Beate described the image she had in mind: 'A bull dyke, dressed very masculine, with a buzz cut, acting like a man. That's not my thing. Neither is it the type of woman I'm attracted to'. Katja explained how her assumptions about queer-lesbian women prevented her from imagining herself as a lesbian:

> [Femininity] wasn't part of how I originally imagined a lesbian woman. This prevented me from realising that I am myself a lesbian, since [...] I'm very feminine.

The internet played a key role in reducing the prejudices that discouraged both women from acting out on their feelings. Beate explained she never thought of getting in touch with other queer-lesbian people (offline or online) because she was simply not interested in meeting people who embodied her stereotypes. Neither did she look up any queer-lesbian-related content online, because she felt that it just 'didn't concern' her. However, she did have several online friends on a fan-fiction platform. During her conversations with some of these friends, she incidentally found out about their same-sex relationships and their interest in BDSM sex practices and started talking to them about it online. She explained that this helped her understand that their sexualities were 'just a small part of their identities, because I think I was a bit afraid of being totally defined by it'.

In this way her fears of 'being totally reduced' to her sexuality as a lesbian were diminished and she slowly adopted the idea 'that you can do it [...] without it being something really bad'. In retrospect, she also believes that one reason why she never considered acting on her interest in women was her mother's openly homophobic attitude. 'It would have meant something if I had said, "Mom, I'm a lesbian"'. In order to protect the relationship with her mother, she did not act out on her feelings. In this instance, Beate's offline circumstances prevented her from acting out on her desires – both on- and offline. Even though she could have got in touch with others online without her mother (or anyone else) knowing about it, she refrained from doing so.

When she later wanted to meet other queer-lesbian women and actively pursue her desires, she asked herself: 'So, how am I gonna get to know them?' In this situation, the internet was a practical resource. When she went online and did some research, she found a coming-out group in the city where she lived. Here she met other queer-lesbian women, made friends and began to discover the queer-lesbian community.

Katja described an 'insight-like' realisation of her desires when at 21 years old her friend asked her whether she was in love with their professor. After this revelation, Katja (just like Micha, Annika and Iris) endured a long period of not talking to anyone about her feelings. During this period she spent a lot of time online reading about queer-lesbian women on websites, blogs, social networks and discussion forums. She pointed out the importance of seeing 'that this exists, and that somewhere there are lesbian women who are putting all this information online'. Reading blogs about feminine lesbians impressed her: 'Beforehand it never crossed my mind that a lesbian woman can be feminine as well'.

Katja explained that in school all she had learnt was that 'lesbian' means 'a woman loves a woman', while the knowledge she obtained through the internet made her understand 'that a woman can not only love a woman, but also have sex with her or have kids [...] like my mom and dad. That it is kind of like an equal form of life'. This is how she began to consider a queer-lesbian life as an alternative to the heterosexual model. Her reading experiences on the internet enabled her to develop a desire towards women which she did not previously imagine as possible. She explains that reading about queer-lesbian women online made her

> have the desire to cuddle with my girlfriend or lean against her [...] and kind of wanting this in the first place. That this is possible. Or to have a partnership or a really close relationship with a woman. [...] All this

kind of made me more confident in my way of living and also helped me accept it.

For Beate and Katja then a queer-lesbian lifestyle was not imaginable for a long time. Even though the internet provided all kinds of resources, hetero-normative discourses prevented them from making use of them. While Beate's attitudes towards queer-lesbian women were changed by conversations with online friends, Katja confronted her prejudices by accessing queer-lesbian-related content online.

Secrecy and the Impossibility of Coming Out

Talking about her coming-out experience, Sasha (26) explained that 'this whole I-don't-like-boys story never had anything to do with a crisis'. At the same time, she knew that her family and social circles (she spent a lot of time at a Jewish community centre) harboured negative attitudes towards homosexuality and that she would have to 'wait until I moved out to live it'. While Sasha still lived with her parents, she read a lot of books and also searched the internet for information about queer-lesbians.[12] She found an online magazine which listed gay TV programmes, which she videotaped and watched secretly by herself. In general, she carefully concealed all of her activities related to queer-lesbian content. Only a few times did she talk to others on chatrooms for lesbian girls.[13] In fact, she was not interested in communicating extensively with others online – most of her conversations, she said, were mainly about 'nonsense'. As with Beate, it appears that the perceived impossibility of living a queer-lesbian life translated into her online activities.

Sasha first spoke to someone about her feelings when she was sixteen years old. Her best friend at the time reacted negatively. This experience may have contributed to the feeling of having to wait to live her desires – online and offline – until she moved out. During a year of voluntary service in the Netherlands after high school, she told her roommates about her feelings. They reacted very 'positively', which she described as a 'great' experience. After this she went to college, where she quickly made queer friends. Later she came out to her family, who spurned her, as expected.

Several years later, Sasha came out as 'genderqueer' (and is there-fore referred to gender-neutrally as 'they' in this paragraph). During this coming-out process, Sasha used the internet even more than the first time.[14] Much like Toni, they took a special liking to *YouTube* videos where gender-queer people talked about themselves. Similar to the experiences of other interviewees and their queer-lesbian coming-out experiences, this made them feel less alone and less weird:

> Well, it wasn't like receiving information 'X' is what made me feel better. It was more that I knew I'm not alone. Especially in this early

stage… I'm not alone and I'm watching stories that other people are watching as well, people who feel and think like me and who have similar interests. And this, I think, was like, everything is okay with me. I'm not weird or abnormal.

In summary, Sasha used the internet to gain access to queer-lesbian (as well as later trans*)-related content and culture. She chatted with other girls a couple of times. Yet she was not interested in deepening these interactions, even though this would have offered an opportunity to meet other queer-lesbian girls and openly talk about her desires. The perceived impossibility of living out her desires seemed to affect her offline as well as online activities.

Discussion and Conclusion

The depiction of these empirical findings, together with the four key experiences (coming to terms in isolation, quick action, the inability to imagine a queer-lesbian life and secrecy and the impossibility of coming out) shows that the internet is clearly used as both an emotional and a practical resource during queer-lesbian coming-out processes. These findings thus corroborate previous research about internet usage in the coming-out processes of queer-lesbian women (Munt, Bassett & O'Riordan, 2002) or LGBs in general (Gray, 2014; Szulc & Dhoest, 2013). However, they also show that internet usage does have its limitations.

Such limitations mostly concern online interactions. Contrary to Munt, Bassett and O'Riordan (2002) as well as to my initial hypothesis, online spaces were not used by the interviewees to connect with other queer-lesbian women or to seek anonymous advice and share experiences before doing so offline. In fact, the interviewees who experienced most difficulties coming to terms with their desires and who experienced social isolation spoke to hardly anyone – whether offline or online. Online communication did not ameliorate their social isolation. Instead their feelings of discomfort and fear as well as prejudices towards queer-lesbian women, which Butler (1990) elucidates in her concept of the heterosexual matrix, seemed to be relevant for interactions in offline as well as online spaces.

Furthermore, those who perceived coming out to be impossible due to their homophobic environment mostly refrained from acting out on their desires – whether on- or offline. This is especially interesting since it is often assumed that online spaces offer the possibility to flee the constraints of the offline world. Instead, the generally perceived impossibility of coming out translated into these participants' online activities as well.[15] In other words, online and offline spaces do not follow different social rules and cannot be understood as separate but rather as highly interconnected (Baym, 2010).

Nevertheless, online interactions can still prepare people for situations of offline disclosure, as Munt, Bassett and O'Riordan (2002) suggest. This is especially true when we acknowledge that coming out is an ongoing process which requires continual renegotiations of identity and disclosure. Once the interviewees were relatively self-assured about their desires and were (at least partly) out in the offline world, a number of them chose to get in touch with other queer-lesbian women online. Even so, interviewees who had yet to meet any other queer-lesbian girls or women preferred to meet them offline. Some openly expressed the need to talk to others face-to-face and felt unease due to the anonymity of online interaction. As Wolf (2004) notes, queer-lesbian girls and women learn to estimate the risks of disclosure in different social situations. So the anonymous nature of online communication with unknown persons might have made it more difficult for participants to estimate the risks of disclosure. Since for queer-lesbian women these risks can include a sexist backlash, this might explain a possible disparity with the coming-out experiences of queer or gay men – a distinction which might get washed away in findings about LGBs in general.

Apart from personal communication, the internet also provided participants with access to information about queer-lesbian experiences and cultures. While trying to make sense of their queer-lesbian desires in a heteronormative society, the interviewees developed a huge craving for information. By engaging with this information, they confronted their feelings of fear and discomfort and positively reframed their stigmatised desires. Reading about queer-lesbian women they felt less alone and odd, and learnt about the different aspects of queer-lesbian lives. A lot of the content accessed by the interviewees was produced by and sometimes explicitly aimed at other queer-lesbian women. It was both fictional and non-fictional. The internet also enabled participants 'passively' to take part in the online conversations of other queer-lesbian women, as well as to look at pictures of parties, thereby giving them insight into what Mary Gray (2014) refers to as 'queer realness'. Additionally, practical information about queer-lesbian spaces, events, parties or coming-out groups were easily accessible online. Checking out these places online reduced some participants' fears of actually visiting them.

The low barriers and well-established practices of creating online (personal) content have led to a diversification of available topics, from which queer-lesbian women (as well as other marginalised groups) benefit. However, it should be noted that this information only becomes accessible when it is actively looked for. For interviewees who felt that queer-lesbian lives did not 'concern' them or who did not dare to search for queer-lesbian content, this knowledge remained invisible. Here again heteronormative discourses and the intelligibility of queer-lesbian desires affected offline as well as online activities.

This study has built upon previous research to produce original findings concerning internet usage as part of queer-lesbian coming-out experiences in Germany. Nevertheless, these findings should be corroborated and expanded upon through further research. Firstly, it should be stressed that this research was conducted in a German context. Although coming-out stories remain very diverse even at the national level, these findings cannot be regarded as universally applicable, or even across all of Europe. For instance, none of the interviewees addressed fears of legal repression when talking about coming-out experiences. Secondly, the internet is continually changing. By now the use of social media has grown exponentially and become far more common than at the time of the interviews in 2011. Still, this study shows the importance of putting users' experiences at the centre of our attention, rather than focussing on the use of the technology itself.

All in all, experiences of queer-lesbian coming out cannot be separated from other processes of marginalisation. Mary Gray (2014, p. 189) shows how the 'politics of LGBTQ visibility' compels two of her interviewees 'to put sexual identity ahead of their familial, racial and queer desires'. Thus in further research the interaction between different forms of discrimination in queer-lesbian coming-out experiences should be addressed more thoroughly. At the same time, the two interviews from this study addressing trans* or genderqueer identities notably highlight the importance of the internet (in particular *YouTube*) for trans* and genderqueer people. These findings necessitate further research on the ways in which marginalised groups utilise the internet in their ongoing negotiations and struggles with self-identification.

Notes

1. This chapter uses the term *queer-lesbian* instead of, for instance, *lesbian and/or queer*. The term will be explained further on in the chapter. If other terms are used, these refer to the literature under discussion.
2. In this chapter 'woman' is not understood as a biological fact but as a category which is assigned at birth and which is continually constructed by a conjunction of discursive acts of attribution and structural conditions within society (Butler, 1993a & 1997; Risman, 2004).
3. Detailed findings on these questions are available in German (Roth, 2015).
4. In Berlin, for instance, on 21 March 2015 there was a roundtable discussion on the topic of 'The Invisible Lesbian: On the Disappearance of an Identity' (Noll, 2015).
5. Whenever I use other terms, these are the terms used by the interviewees or in the academic literature referred to.
6. The interviewees were recruited by the following means: one by an online ad on the highly frequented German webpage www.lesbians.org; one via a mailing list which informs subscribers about events and topics related to gender in general and is associated with a university in a big city; two via the mailing list of a consulting centre for lesbian and trans* people in a big city; two via the mailing list of the lesbian student council of a university in another city; two through the snowball system.
7. All names have been changed. All interviews were translated from German into English by the author.
8. Micha explained that she talked to her boyfriend about it, while the others talked to no one at all.

9. Micha and Annika also read books, which they purchased online. They highlight that getting books online is more anonymous than borrowing them from the library or buying them at a bookstore.

10. On www.lesarion.de the network is described as 'the lesbian community' (February 2016).

11. A few years later Toni had another coming out as trans* and changed her name and pronoun to 'he'. During this process Toni explained that he used the internet, especially *YouTube*, even more intensely than in his first coming out in order to find out more about trans* lives and experiences. He assumes this was because with his queer-lesbian coming out he was very focused on his girlfriend, while with his trans* identity he was generally interested in the topic. But he also points out that trans*-related content was easier to find because the amount of information was smaller.

12. Since Sasha is one of the older interviewees who had her first coming-out experiences at a fairly young age (around the year 2000), the internet was only just becoming mainstream.

13. The interview does not clearly convey whether Sasha used the chats before talking to her best friend about her feelings (see below). Both things happened at about the same time.

14. This can be explained by the fact that Sasha's coming out as queer-lesbian took place in the early 2000s. However, Toni, one of the younger interviewees, also confirms these remarks.

15. I assume this is predominantly true if people have not yet acted out their queer-lesbian desires, since Sasha mentions that she always thought she needed to 'have [sexual] experiences' to be lesbian. It might be different if people have already lived their queer-lesbian desires offline and cannot keep pursuing them any longer due to homophobic attitudes or even legal repression in their surroundings. In this situation internet usage might be a counterspace to secretly connect with other queer-lesbian women.

References

Adams, T. E. (2011). *Narrating the Closet: An Autoethnography of Same-Sex Attraction*. Walnut Creek: Left Coast.

Baym, N. (2010). *Personal Connections in the Digital Age: Digital Media and Society*. Cambridge: Polity Press.

Bromseth, J. & Sundén, J. (2011). Queering Internet Studies: Intersections of Gender and Sexuality. In M. Consalvo & C. Ess (Eds.), *The Handbook of Internet Studies* (pp. 270–299). Chichester: Wiley-Blackwell.

Butler, J. (1990). *Gender Trouble: Feminism and the Subversion of Identity*. New York: Routledge.

Butler, J. (1993a). *Bodies That Matter*. New York: Routledge.

Butler, J. (1993b). Imitation and Gender Insubordination. In H. Abelove, M. A. Barale & D. M. Halperin (Eds.), *The Gay and Lesbian Studies Reader* (pp. 307–318). London & New York: Routledge.

Butler, J. (1997). *The Psychic Life of Power: Theories in Subjection*. Stanford: Stanford University Press.

Degele, N. (2008). *Gender/Queer Studies: Eine Einführung*. Paderborn: UTB.

Driver, S. (2007). *Queer Girls and Popular Culture: Reading, Resisting and Creating Media*. New York: Peter Lang.

Gosine, A. (2007). Brown to Blonde at Gay.com: Passing White in Queer Cyberspace. In K. O'Riordan & D. J. Phillips (Eds.), *Queer Online: Media Technology & Sexuality* (pp. 139–153). New York: Peter Lang.

Gray, A. (1992). *Video Playtime: The Gendering of a Leisure Technology.* London: Routledge.

Gray, M. L. (2009). *Out in the Country: Youth, Media and Queer Visibility in Rural America.* New York: New York University Press.

Gray, M. (2014). Negotiating Identities/Queering Desires: Coming Out Online and Remediation of the Coming-Out Story. In A. Poletti & J. Rak (Eds.), *Identity Technologies: Constructing the Self Online* (pp. 167–197). Madison: University of Wisconsin Press.

Hall, S. (1980). Encoding/Decoding. In S. Hall, D. Hobson, A. Lowe & P. Willis (Eds.), *Culture, Media, Language: Working Papers in Cultural Studies, 1972–1979* (pp. 157–162). London & New York: Routledge.

Hänsch, U. (2003). *Individuelle Freiheiten – Heterosexuelle Normen in Lebensgeschichten Lesbischer Frauen.* Opladen: Leske & Budrich.

Holmes, S. (2000). Coming Out: Psychology. In T. Murphy (Ed.), *A Reader's Guide to Lesbian and Gay Studies* (pp. 151–152). Chicago/London: Fitzroy Dearborn.

Jagose, A. (1996). *Queer Theory: An Introduction.* New York: NYU Press.

Jagose, A. (2001). *Queer Theory: Eine Einführung.* Berlin: Querverlag.

Lenz, I., Sabisch, K. & Wrzesinski, M. (Eds.) (2012). Anders und Gleich in NRW – Gleichstellung Akzeptanz Sexueller und Geschlechtlicher Vielfalt: Forschungsstand, Tagungsdokumentation, Praxisprojekte. *Studien Netzwerk Frauen- und Geschlechterforschung NRW, 15.*

Livingstone, S. (2002). *Young People and New Media: Childhood and the Changing Media Environment.* Thousand Oaks: Sage.

Manning, J. (2014). Communicating Sexual Identities: A Typology of Coming Out. *Sexuality & Culture, 19*(1), 122–138.

Morley, D. (1992). *Television, Audiences and Cultural Studies.* London: Routledge.

Munt, S., Bassett, E. & O'Riordan, K. (2002). Virtually Belonging: Risk, Connectivity and Coming Out On-Line. *International Journal of Sexuality and Gender Studies, 7*(2/3), 125–137.

Nestle, J. (1992). *The Persistent Desire: A Femme-Butch Reader.* Boston: Alyson Publications.

Noll, J. (2015). *Wo Sind Nur die Lesben Hin? Podiumsdiskussion am 21.3. im SchwuZ, Berlin.* Retrieved from http://www.siegessaeule.de/no_cache/newscomments/article/1853-wo-sind-nur-die-lesben-hin-podiumsdiskussion-am-213-im-schwuz.html.

O'Neill, M. G. (2014). Transgender Youth and YouTube Videos: Self Representation and Five Identifiable Trans Youth Narratives. In C. Pullen (Ed.), *Queer Youth and Media Cultures* (pp. 34–45). London: Palgrave.

Risman, B. (2004). Gender as a Social Category: Theory Wrestling with Activism. *Gender & Society, 18*(4), 429–450.

Roth, U. (2015). *Coming-Out im Netz!? Die Bedeutung des Internet im Coming-Out von Queer-Lesbischen Frauen.* Essen & Düsseldorf: Netzwerk Frauen- und Geschlechterforschung NRW/LAG Lesben in NRW.

Rust, P. R. (2003). Finding a Sexual Identity and Community: Therapeutic Implications and Cultural Assumptions in Scientific Models of Coming Out. In L. D. Garnets & D. C. Kimmel (Eds.), *Psychological Perspectives on Lesbian, Gay and Bisexual Experiences* (pp. 227–269). New York: Columbia University Press.

Szulc, Ł. & Dhoest, A. (2013). The Internet and Sexual Identity Formation: Comparing Internet Use Before and After Coming Out. *Communications, 38*(4), 347–365.

Wolf, G. (2004). Erfahrungen und Gesundheitliche Entwicklungen Lesbischer Frauen im Coming-Out-Prozess. Herbholzheim: Centaurus.

Wuest, B. (2014). Stories Like Mine: Coming Out Videos and Queer Identities on YouTube. In C. Pullen (Ed.), *Queer Youth and Media Cultures* (pp. 19–33). London: Palgrave.

Zuehlke, R. (2004). *'Nichts an Mir Ist Anders, Eigentlich …': Becoming-Out – Die Verwirklichung Lesbischer Selbst- und Lebenskonzepte im Postmodernen Spannungsfeld von Individuum, Subkultur und Gesellschaft.* Herbolzheim: Centaurus.

5 'I Think I'm Quite Fluid with Those Kinds of Things'

Exploring Music and Non-Heterosexual Women's Identities

Marion Wasserbauer

In a 2014 interview with *Rolling Stone*, Indie-Rock star Annie Clark (St. Vincent) was asked whether she identifies as gay or straight, to which Clark replied, 'I don't think about those words. I believe in gender fluidity and sexual fluidity. I don't really identify as anything'. She added, 'I think you can fall in love with anybody', and 'I don't have anything to hide, but I'd rather the emphasis be on music' (Weiner, 2014). The musician summarises what many non-heterosexual women feel, namely that simple labels do not suffice in order to comprise the complexity of sexual orientation and gender identity. Sexual fluidity in recent years has received quite some media attention, with stars like Miley Cyrus showcasing a no-label sexual attitude in front of a large audience.

Sexual fluidity, though, is by no means a new or VIP-only phenomenon, as various studies have shown. As Lisa Diamond observes, when it comes to sexual fluidity in women '[q]uestions of causation typically receive the most debate and attention, but questions about expression are equally important' (Diamond, 2008, p. 11). This chapter focuses exactly on the expression of sexuality and sexual fluidity through music, rather than on questions of causation.

The region of Flanders in the north of Belgium is an intriguing geopolitical area in which to inquire into these topics. ILGA-Europe's annual Rainbow Europe review ranked Belgium second best concerning LGBTQ rights for two consecutive years in 2014 and 2015, with the country dropping to third place in October 2015 (ILGA-Europe, 2015). LGB individuals are largely visible and included in society; more recently, focus has shifted to the rights of and care for transgender individuals. The social and legal situation for LGBTs in Belgium is thus a relatively comfortable and safe one, and plenty of cultural and community facilities are available. Yet there are still numerous non-normative persons who remain invisible, in particular those who do not identify as heterosexual but would also not describe themselves as simply 'lesbian', 'gay' or 'bisexual'.

Within the larger oral history project on the role of music in the lives of LGBTQ individuals from which this case study derives (see www. queervoices.be), the self-identification of several female narrators strikingly transcends clear-cut definitions: descriptions such as 'queer/lesbian', 'fluid', 'lesbian but …' and 'pan' were used by them. By contrast, most of the male narrators intuitively use the clear-cut label 'gay'. Based on theories of music and identity and notions of female sexual fluidity, this chapter investigates how non-heterosexual women make sense of their sexual and gender identities and how these are linked to music in their lives.

First of all, the women's narratives demonstrate the complexity of situating themselves as non-heterosexual and non-gender-normative women. Secondly, it is worth looking more closely into music's role in the coming of age and identification of these women. Moreover, music as facilitator, reflection and expression of female same-sex sexualities will be discussed. A special focus on Flemish musicians mentioned by several narrators stresses the importance of non-heterosexual role models.

Women and Non-Normative Sexualities

'Lesbian' and 'bisexual' are, certainly in Belgium, widely recognized identity concepts, understood to signify, respectively, a woman being romantically and/or sexually attracted to other women and 'feeling romantically and/or sexually attracted to men and women' (çavaria, 2015). Yet, there are plenty of other terms of sexual and gender identification women employ; and identifying themselves is not as straightforward as these two common identity labels would suggest.

In research involving sexual orientation, meaning 'sexual attraction, identity, arousals, fantasies and behaviours individuals have for one sex, the other sex, or both sexes' (Vrangalova & Savin-Williams, 2012, p. 85), those who identify as 'other' than heterosexual or homosexual are often excluded from the analysis, as they do not fit into neat categories, are not commonly recognised and are difficult to account for. Alison Better proposes that

> there is more queerness and alternative expressions of sexuality and sexual behavior than we know to look for and […] our lack of both language to describe it and the taboo on its discourse hinders our true understandings of the depths of the pervasiveness of these behaviors. (2014, p. 29)

Drawing on empirical research, she suggests that we look beyond lesbian and bisexual identities. Self-identification of sexual orientation, independent of scales or pre-defined answers, is essential in studying sexualities. Similarly, an understanding of gender as a socially constructed and performative phenomenon (Butler, 1990) requires a focus on self-definition, which in turn implies that the use of 'woman' should be taken to signify 'female identified individual' (Tate, 2012, p. 19). Accordingly, whenever the word 'woman' is used in this chapter it should be read as 'self-identified female individual'.

Fluidity is a useful concept when thinking about female non-heterosexuality, as research shows. A survey by Ross, Daneback and Månsson (2012) measures sexual fluidity by looking at the gender of the object of sexual fantasies. This study shows that sexual fluidity is more common in women (49.8%) than in men (15.4%) and that education, religiosity, living situation and sexual activity are relevant factors linked to sexual fluidity (2012, p. 456f). Lisa Diamond's longitudinal research into sexual fluidity in women shows that 'the notion of female sexual fluidity suggests not that women possess no generalized sexual predispositions but that these predispositions will prove less of a constraint on their desires and behaviours than is the case for men' (2008, p. 24). This statement is confirmed by the fact that most of the female narrators in the current chapter do identify as 'lesbian' to some extent, but have the urge to refine, alter and add to this basic definition, as discussed below.

Music and Identity

Whereas research of the sort proposed in this volume believes that media are important in LGBTQ identifications, the focus of media research often lies on internet or film studies rather than on music. Yet music's role in LGBTQ identifications should not be underestimated: whether a non-heterosexual orientation serves as the foundation of one's identity or merely as a peripheral part of it, music may facilitate non-heterosexual identifications. As sociomusicologist Simon Frith claims, music can be seen almost as a metaphor for identity: it is both performance and story, ethic and aesthetic; it is a simultaneous projecting and dissolving of the self in performance (Frith, 1996, pp. 109–110). Thus music not only tells things about people but also creates them 'as a web of identities' (Frith, 1996, p. 121).

Similarly, Tia DeNora investigates music as a resource in and through which agency and identity are produced (2000). The power of music derives not only from the musical stimulus but also from the ways in which the listener appropriates the music (DeNora, 2000, p. 42). As a result, music's role in social life cannot be merely theorised but needs to be explored *in situ*. DeNora notes that music is used as self-care, to shift moods and energies: '[m]usic is not simply used to express some internal emotional state. Indeed, [...] music is part of the reflexive constitution of that state, it is a resource for the identification work of "knowing how one feels" – and building material of "subjectivity"' (DeNora, 2000, p. 57). From her in-depth interviews on women's use of music in everyday life DeNora concludes that music provides a map for making sense of the thing to which it is attached; seemingly trivial things in life, emotional stability or social relationships may all be linked with music (1999).

The connection between LGBTQs and music as subcultural or group phenomena has been researched in various ways: on a theoretical level (Brett & Wood, 2002) or more concretely with respect to gay fans of stars like Lady Gaga (e.g. Jennex, 2013), the Eurovision Song Contest (e.g. Lemish, 2004) or gay fans in specific music genres (Amico, 2001). Halberstam (2005), Leibetseder (2012), Driver (2008) and Taylor (2012) all investigate queer dimensions in music and music audiences. The role of music in individual LGBTQ lives and identities however has not yet been explored in-depth.

Methodology

The narrators for the larger project on 'Queer Voices'[1] that underlies this chapter were recruited online, with posters at LGBTQ venues and through the researcher's activist networks in 2014 and 2015. All narrators identify as LGBTQ, find music very important and are above the age of 18. Informed by the traditions of oral history, feminist research methods and the notion of the queer archive, a collaborative and reflexive interview approach was employed, aiming to acknowledge the narrators' agency. The narrators were encouraged to tell their stories any way they wanted; no fixed set of questions was asked, but an openly visible sheet with keywords connected to identity and music proved helpful to facilitate some interviews. I asked the narrators to think about music and LGBTQ identity beforehand and to take a look at old photographs, diaries, CDs, playlists and so on in order to remember certain periods or events in their lives. As carriers of memories, music and musical memorabilia are structuring elements within this project. During the interviews we created and discussed field notes, which helped to visualise the narrators' stories. In some interviews we also listened to music and, with the narrators' permission, I took photographs of memorabilia.

The interviews typically lasted 90 to 180 minutes, and each narrator either provided their first name or chose a pseudonym. All interviews were transcribed literally and relevant sections were translated from Flemish Dutch into English by the author. With the consent of the narrators, parts of the stories and the playlists accompanying the interviews are publicly accessible on the project home page, www.queervoices.be.[2]

In this chapter, the oral histories of six women between the ages of 23 and 51 were analysed for narratives on the above-mentioned topics. This subset of interviews is striking because of the narrators' fluid gender identifications and sexual orientations and the focus on these topics. All narrators are Belgian natives, with one of them having other Western European roots. Nikki, Laura and Roxy were students at the time of the interview; Anna is an artist; Nina and Patricia had regular jobs. It should be noted that all narrators either already had a diploma in higher education or were about to finish their studies, which reflects the general tendency of highly educated persons participating in my research.

Situating the Sexual Self in a Musical Landscape: Cases

Most interviews start with a conversation on sex, gender and sexual orientation,[3] in which the narrators situate themselves. Same-sex sexualities are in reality not as straightforward as labels like 'lesbian' and 'bisexual' might lead one to assume; neither is it easy to put these sexualities into words. Several women narrate anecdotes in order to frame their sexual orientations; others struggle to find the right words to express themselves, reflected in silences and abrupt turns within sentences. Some women focus on their current identity, but most also tell coming-of-age stories covering various stages of their life. Two salient and interrelated topics within the narratives are 'coming of age as non-heterosexual women and music' and 'music as reflection and expression of female same-sex identities'. Diverse personalities as well as gender and sexual identities of the narrators are connected to and reflected through music.

Nina

32-year-old riot grrrl and zinester Nina explains that she fancies 'just women'. She identifies as 'lesbian slash queer or so [laughs]', elaborating this as follows:

N: I find the queer movement quite interesting [...] I think I do criticise it somewhat, some aspects of it, but... I don't know. It's a broader term maybe. Or uhm, well it also implies some links with transgender for me, and I appreciate that ...

M: An openness concerning gender or something ...

N: Yes. [Silence] Although I don't find it necessary to identify as trans or genderqueer in order to deviate from 'the norm', well, the usual gender expression-like things.[4]

Nina's critical position may be linked to her feminist commitment, her activities in the queercore and Riot Grrrl scenes as well as her academic training in women's studies. Diamond (2008) found that such academic studies are likely to provoke (more nuanced) thinking about one's own gender and sexuality and a tendency to deviate from binary thinking about gender. However, Nina's personal interest in and self-study of feminism started much earlier and she already recognised her attraction towards women as a teenager. Thinking of this now, Nina reflects that discovering her sexuality at age fourteen or fifteen in the mid-nineties is directly related to music:

> I think that my first realisation of being lesbian/queer actually started with music [laughs]. [...] It was in a small record shop [...] and I think that she was a lesbian as well, the shop assistant who worked there, and uhm, who thought that I had good taste because I bought those CDs [laughter]. So yes, someone who likes the combination of Ani DiFranco and Skunk Anansie, I don't think they are straight.

Singer-songwriter Ani DiFranco and Skunk Anansie's lead singer, Skin, have been lesbian idols since the 1990s, and Nina decided to buy their music which she intuitively liked. When asked if she could specify what exactly makes their music so attractive to lesbians, Nina raised a number of features:

> It's acoustic, like folksy music opposed to metal/rock-like music, so... that combination: most people will rather like one [style] than both. [...] But both are bi as well, so I don't know [laughs]. [...] They are very clear in their opinions and don't let anybody mess about with them and they are very vocal and assertive or yes... loud, actually, both in their own way. [...] It's not really hard music, but it is kind of strong.

Not only their music but also the empowering appearance and messages of both singers attracted Nina: 'I found both of them extremely cool, and I think that I had a bit of a crush on both. I think that came hand in hand, somehow'. With this formulation Nina pinpoints a feeling towards female musicians that various narrators describe: a combination between having a crush on them and wanting to be them or strongly identifying with what they express. Similarly, Nina felt as if she wanted to become friends with the lesbian CD shop assistant, as she was one of the few lesbians Nina knew at that time in rural Flanders. Music is thus in many ways deeply connected with Nina's coming of age as a feminist lesbian/queer woman. She emphasises that her identity is inextricably connected to music:

N: I think the music I mostly listen to is very strongly connected to my identity. Because a lot of it is feminist music, queer music and DIY music... yes. I don't know, politically inspired things... [...]

M: And would you say it is also somehow connected to your sexual orientation?

N: Yes, I think so, to some extent. Actually, I ask myself sometimes, had I been straight, I would probably still... to a large extent still listen to the same music, I guess! Because then I would search for it, or would still want to listen to it because it's women, and you want to see women on stage.

Although Nina does enjoy that some of her favourite musicians are queer, her statement clarifies that gender is a more important aspect than sexuality in the music she listens to, but also in the music she makes. She actively supports female artists organising and visiting Ladyfests, and is a member of an all-female crust[5] band. In her experience the dynamics within a band change if there is a male member in it. The feminist concept of an all-female band is inspired by the Riot Grrrl movement, which seeks to draw attention to the fact that the punk and grunge scenes were male-dominated and misogynist. Music is a medium in which Nina (at first intuitively and later on actively) searches and finds a reflection of her ideas about gender and her larger worldview.

Patricia

Patricia (51) identifies as pansexual. For her 'it means that you can fall in love with everyone, with men, women, bi, but also transgender, or with people who are androgynous or... everybody, really'. This fluid approach to sexual orientation is paralleled by Patricia's fluidity in gender and gender roles. She notes that her gender also feels rather mixed, observing that 'I am not able to say "I am lesbian" or "I am bi" or "I feel like I'm a man" or "I feel like I'm a woman"'. These feelings and identifications shift:

> When I'm in a relationship with a woman, my manliness actually comes more to the foreground [...] A tougher side. And that becomes more prominent, like – also the protective, the more attentive and gallant, opening the door, going to fetch something in the shop – such things. [...] And when I'm with a man, I feel actually more woman. And actually I find it regrettable that I have to suppress that male part in me.

Recently, Patricia got involved with transgender communities: 'It's not that I want an operation or anything like that, or that I want to take hormones, I actually just want to... be... be who I am without being judged for it'. She has experienced social exclusion in some of Antwerp's traditional lesbian groups and links not feeling welcome to class differences and gendered expectations: 'Actually, I find that there is little tolerance within the lesbian milieu towards lesbians who are bi, or who look a bit masculine, or who have slightly rougher hobbies or listen to rougher music'. Patricia has also experienced such attitudes in her private life with partners who expected her to behave in stereotypically feminine ways she is not comfortable with.

Until the age of eighteen Patricia did not have the opportunity to listen to any music of her own, since she grew up in a children's home due to a difficult family situation. Then the contact with her family was restored and her siblings introduced her to various music scenes. She recalls encountering gays, lesbians and transgender persons for the first time in the music club *Cinderella's Ballroom* in Antwerp, a legendary dance hall in the punk scene of the late 1970s and '80s. In *Cinderella*, underground music and punk rock brought together open-minded people, and everybody was welcome (Aerts, 2013). Patricia's first big crush on a woman is also closely related to music, as she fell in love with a fellow street musician in her twenties. Within these alternative and underground music scenes she felt at home and discovered an openness towards gender and sexuality which fitted her own views.

The music Patricia mentions mirrors her life story. Throughout her life she has listened to numerous styles and each change in style reflects a new phase or different aspect in her life: punk and hard rock as she started going out in her late teens, pop songs like Simon and Garfunkel's repertoire which she sang as a street musician, traditional music from Ireland as she spent some time there and played the guitar in a band, African and Latin American music that she got to know in clubs, jazz and Chinese opera because of the many influences and stimuli they contain, ABBA and the Bee Gees as companions when she takes a walk. Patricia certainly does not listen only to specifically gay or lesbian music, although she connects a gay or lesbian fan base to artists like Prince or Tracy Chapman. In fact, Patricia's playlist is the most diverse of all narrators, which forms a conspicuous parallel with her pansexual identity, within which anything is possible.

Anna

Actress Anna, 27, describes herself as 'lesbian a priori', but then goes on to add elaborate modifications:

> I think it was a long path for me, like for anyone, and by now I just know for sure that the thing I want is being with a woman, living with a woman, spending my life with a woman. [...] Concerning pure sexuality, that is something quite complex for me. Uh, ever since I was young, I've always had this thing, like more a sort of courtly love, towards women, so [...] they always were a bit 'holy'. And thus untouchable with regard to sexuality: it didn't even cross my mind, because it almost seemed like blasphemy to me. [...] I think that it is by now regulated better with growing older, in the sense that I am able to see my partners as sexual as well [...]. Uh, concerning men it's kind of the other way round, I have always felt that I could not be with them, I don't want any intimacy and daily life and affection with them, I have little complicity with them [...] but I have... I could always, and actually still can, get aroused by simply the male sex.

For Anna, then, there is a clear difference between her attraction to women and men. While she may be attracted to male bodies as sexual objects, Anna can make emotional connections only with women.

Although Anna looks very feminine and has learnt from an early age onwards to make use of that femininity, she feels strong feminine as well as masculine energies inside of her:

> In my body the masculine feeling is like... is faster [snaps her fingers], is straightforward [...] I feel more grounded and less emotional, less nebulous, less, uh, receptive and sensitive and transparent in the world; then I am more active in the world. I am more sun then and less moon, *voilà*.

Anna tries to find a balance between both energies as much as possible. The (translated and digitalised) interview notes showcase the complexity of her gender and sexual orientation.

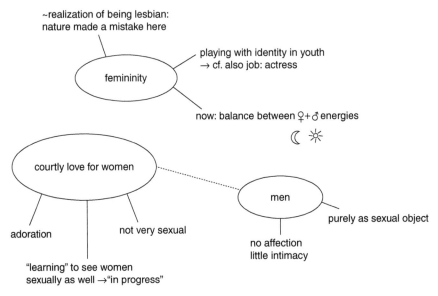

Figure 5.1 A sketch accompanying Anna's narrative.

For Anna music has been an essential companion ever since her adolescence. Unlike most of her peers, she did not listen to popular but to classical music, French chansons and feminist and political music of the Weimar Republic. Anna went through a phase of great loneliness and isolation, as 'any adolescent [does]: you think… that nobody in the world is as sad as you are. And that you are completely alone'. The biggest factor causing Anna's loneliness was her realisation that she was attracted to girls and not boys. She started to find comfort in music and other arts, and recalls thinking, 'thank you that there will always be music, that I will always have that. Luckily, because otherwise I probably might not want to live anymore'. Renowned soprano Maria Callas started to play an important role in her life: Anna fell for her beauty and recognised herself in the drama of Callas' love life.

In a similar manner, actress and performer Greta Garbo played an important role in Anna's identification as a lesbian. Not only did Anna know hardly any lesbians at the time, but

> the ones I knew, they didn't look anything like me. […] I looked in the mirror and really felt, […] 'nature made a mistake here or so', because either I had to get this package and just be straight or I had to be lesbian but just look differently. And I really thought that I was the only lesbian […] who looks feminine, like me, and feeling super feminine too […] until I discovered Greta Garbo. […] I found her so transcendentally beautiful, and so attractive and magnetic and… and absolutely unbelievably fascinating. When I discovered that Greta Garbo

most probably was a lesbian... that was huge, huge, HUGE! [...]
I thought, 'Aaah, I'm not alone!' [we laugh]

Because there were no real-life examples available to Anna, the comfort of
knowing that she was not alone in being a very feminine lesbian came from
music and popular culture.

Similar to Patricia, Anna's sexual identification is connected to gender in
various ways; both of them experienced the pressure of gendered expectations and learnt to navigate those as non-stereotypical lesbians.

Nikki

23-year-old student Nikki's narrative shows an ambiguous approach
towards her lesbian identity. Although she notes that 'I've always been that
way', at the same time she describes that it was a long and hard struggle
to come to terms with being different and attracted to the same sex. This
ambiguous feeling is paralleled by the mixed reactions she received from
her parents to her coming out as a teenager. Her father fully embraced the
diversity Nikki brought to the family, whereas her mother was concerned
about questions of normality, 'decency' and 'what will other people think?'

Nikki listens to a great diversity of musical genres and artists, most of
whom are female. In her life story a parallel between liking women and
female musicians shows up. When asked to describe the difference between
liking guys and girls, she answers that she does not find men attractive at
all; to her mind,

> girls are much more beautiful, and... I can really feel attracted to them,
> while a bloke, that's like – okay. [...] I enjoy being intrigued by things.
> If I'm fascinated by something, I can find it the most amazing thing
> on earth. And a woman or a girl can fascinate me, intrigue me, but a
> man, seriously, no.

She refers back to this description when we look through a pile of CDs,
discussing the music she used to listen and still listens to, remarking that she
prefers women's voices and has only recently started to listen to male singers
voluntarily. When I ask her whether she connects this to her sexuality, she
answers:

> Ha, now it seems as if I hate men – that's not the case at all, but... well,
> as I already said: I can be interested in something only if I am intrigued
> by it. And yes, with a guy, it's gonna cost a lot of effort until I'm inter-
> ested, and with women... well.

When we look at Nikki's musical tastes, the prevailing stereotypes about
lesbian preferences are confirmed (Sarah Bettens, Tegan and Sara, P!nk,

Melissa Etheridge, Tracy Chapman are all mentioned) but they are also diversified. Nikki remarks that she does not think of music in terms of good and bad, and neither does she like to put people into boxes:

> I try to be a little different in my own way, and my music – I don't know. On the one hand, I think things touch you unconsciously, and on the other, well, the way you want to identify. And how you identify is also strongly connected to your environment [...] but I think I'm quite fluid with those kinds of things, compared to other people who are like 'I listen to this and it's the best music'. I'm totally not like that, no. It probably says something about me... but I'm not sure what.

Nikki identifies as fluid in her musical taste and in doing so introduces a new meaning of fluidity into this research. Her question suggests she sees a connection between her identity and the music she listens to; only, it is not easy to make sense of these connections and put them into words.

Roxy

A common theme among the various stories is that the women-narrators prefer female singers. This is confirmed again by Roxy, who notes that she has never been a fan of a male musician or a boy band. Roxy is 25 and identifies as queer/lesbian. She emphasises that at the time of the conversation her queer identity is very important to her. This was different in the past, though: at first, after realising she liked women, Roxy was convinced that everything would be very difficult for her because of her being a lesbian; yet she calls this

> an idea I don't agree with any more. But just, the first years after my coming out I was like... yes, I'm into women and I am lesbian, but that doesn't necessarily have to be such a big deal [...] I was very much against these movements and parties in which LGBTQs separated themselves from others. I don't agree with that stance anymore at all, because now I see where that comes from and that it really is necessary and that you need this sort of collectivity and space [...] There were some years when I was not an activist and just was myself who also liked women, whereas now I am Roxy, and lesbian, and very openly feminist, and yes, well, that's a transformation which also found expression in my musical taste.

The change in Roxy's identity is paralleled by a similar change in her appreciation of lesbian music. Browsing CDs in a media store, Roxy discovered a CD by Lesbians on Ecstasy, which Roxy describes as 'extreme lesbo-music', a genre and attitude she came to embrace.

> It was a hot pink case with triangles and weird lesbians, gays, poodles [...] Then I opened it and it said BUTCH LESBO in the middle;

that was also very intriguing. [...] I was a little scared of it. [...] You know, I just wasn't ready for it. Now I find it awesome!

Roxy's friends have come to project her outspoken queer/lesbian identity onto her music and to associate her taste in women with her taste in music. For example, they expect that one of her favourite musicians, St. Vincent's front woman, Annie Clark, is lesbian, too: 'It's funny, [...] people think that if I like her music so much there must be something gay to it'. Roxy's story shows that music does not only serve to find self-affirmation (DeNora 2000); it can also become a social property with which others identify a listener. She says she has something like a 'queer taste', or a taste for anything queer:

> I always look for queer aspects in books; it's just to identify with it, because that's what art is, and what literature is and what music is: you listen to it and it strikes a chord. And purely straight things don't do the trick for me, especially not in music.

Accordingly, Roxy likes to discover music off the beaten track. Talking about her taste in music stimulates her to reflect on her personality and sexual orientation as well:

> Maybe I'm trying to be different in that... although I don't have to try to be different, as I am already different through my orientation... but I've always searched more in the periphery, and that's what appeals to me. Like pure mainstream is something I can enjoy, for example something like Lady Gaga or so [...], but that is never anything that captures my interest completely – except for Madonna!

A fascination with strong and androgynous women has always been part of Roxy's musical appreciation. Madonna is one of these women, and from a young age onwards Roxy preferred her to other music her peers listened to. As a girl she was also fascinated by Annie Lennox's androgynous appearance and she now describes Lennox's music as feminist and strong.

Laura

Laura, 24, describes her sexuality as fluid:

> I feel female... and my sexual orientation: I find that more difficult. They call that [...] sexual fluidity? A little bit, well, I'm not a hundred per cent sure... well, actually I think I am, but because at the moment I don't have a girlfriend... I don't think men are repulsive either. [...] I didn't fall in love with any, but I can find men interesting. Yes, I find it a bit difficult to say, 'I am a hundred per cent lesbian'. I never say that to others either because then you're pushed into a box...

Revealing her sexual orientation as lesbian is an ambiguous task for Laura. She could also imagine being with a man and wants to avoid the label 'uninteresting except for threesomes', which men in her experience attach to lesbians. Her family might have influenced this position:

> I said sexually fluid or so… because I don't really know for sure. This label thing. By now they seem to understand more that you don't exclusively like women, or exclusively men, but still. But that is also something that they instilled in us at home, like, 'wait with telling everybody', because I think they secretly hoped that I would still fall for a guy, and telling everybody I preferred women would have disturbed that process.

The notion of non-exclusivity Laura introduces is a central point in Lisa Diamond's conception of sexual fluidity. Diamond makes a distinction between 'lesbians who had been exclusively attracted to and involved with women throughout the study and who are least likely to change their identities' and 'everyone else' (2008, p. 68). Strikingly, non-exclusivity in attraction is the norm rather than the exception among women (Diamond, 2008, p. 83). As Laura's story shows, non-exclusivity involves a constant gauging of her own feelings and her environment. Having a girlfriend makes her sexuality clearer for herself and for her environment, while being single makes her more aware of other options and of what people may associate with the label 'lesbian'.

The list of songs Laura prepared for our interview clearly connects music to experiences, feelings and persons. Although music is not essential to Laura's identity, she connects certain musical choices to being a fluid lesbian. Thus, P!nk was very important at a certain stage of her life because her lyrics were very recognisable and her tough attitude attracted Laura. Likewise, the voice of Tracy Chapman intrigued Laura at one point; this is an artist she spontaneously connects with lesbians: '[laughs] a lot of other lesbians are also going to mention her'. Most importantly however, she strongly identifies with lesbian or queer Flemish or Dutch singers, as elaborated below.

Local Heroines

A topic specific to the Flemish cultural context deserves special attention on this occasion: throughout the interviews the discussion of local lesbian heroines stands out. Most musicians discussed by the narrators are international stars singing in English; after all, the general knowledge of English is relatively high in Flanders, and according to the 'European Survey on Language Competences' the English knowledge of Flemish youth is one of the best in Europe (Vlaams Ministerie van Onderwijs & Vorming, 2012, p. 34ff). However, a special bond with Flemish (lesbian) musicians and role models emerges from various stories, and it appears to be stronger than with international stars. Accessibility of the singers, the language advantage and recognisability are three important characteristics of these local heroines.

Roxy brought a CD of the Flemish rock band K's Choice to our interview – 'obviously', she added. She characterises its lesbian frontwoman, Sarah Bettens, along with Flemish singer Yasmine, as the 'archetypical Flemish things of lesbo-music', with Bettens being the first person to come up in many people's minds when thinking 'gay and Flemish'. Despite the fact that her lyrics are in English, Sarah Bettens is a very relatable and proximate idol as she grew up in Flanders. In Roxy's opinion, her band offers 'explicitly lesbian music' with a lesbian story behind it, namely 'that the singer first tried very hard to hide [her homosexuality] from herself, and that she actually knew for a long time that she fancied women, and everyone else knew for a long time' before she came out. Roxy further acknowledges that she is not a diehard fan of the music itself, which she describes as 'all very similar [...] very calm in the beginning with then a sudden rock-ish outburst', but nevertheless she and her lesbian best friend have a strong bond with it.

Roxy's contemporary Laura uses exactly the same words when she talks about her CD of K's Choice: 'Yes of course, obviously, K's Choice'. Laura met Sarah Bettens backstage after a concert and took a photograph with her: 'That was cool. Especially back then, I was crazy about it because it's the same thing as with Yasmine: the lyrics were super recognisable, and I almost felt that I knew her in person [laughs]'. Bettens clearly was an important person she identified with as a young lesbian. Laura explains that when she came out in 2003, not a lot of role models were around and the visibility of the LGBTQ community was low. Laura sums up by saying that listening to K's Choice is mostly linked to the lesbian characteristics of the music:

L: I think you look for that much more. Because, actually, there are other lyrics which are just as recognisable, but that was a nice extra or so, because you know that that person is also writing for a woman [...]
M: So there's a certain bond or what?
L: Yes, I think so. That's so cheesy, but yes [laughs].

Nikki's story bears many similarities with this. At one of the few occasions when she went out with an LGBTQ youth organisation, her peers were 'astonished about my "unknowingness of gay people"' and told her to look up Sarah Bettens. Nikki did this and I asked her whether she liked her mainly because she is lesbian: 'Originally, yes, I think so, but actually, I really found it a good CD'. She also met K's Choice for an interview as an adolescent.

Another Flemish lesbian idol is Yasmine, a TV host and singer who died by suicide in 2009. Yasmine was an out lesbian public figure who also wrote lyrics with lesbian topics. Roxy only briefly mentions her and one specific song, but Laura elaborates on Yasmine's status as a crucial lesbian role model:

> I found it great that she was a woman who came out to all of Flanders, as she was a famous person, but that she also was someone who did not fit the clichés or stereotypes. She was not a masculine – well, you didn't have to guess whether she was a man or a woman, and she was very witty and funny.

Again the need for a feminine, non-stereotypical lesbian role model becomes clear. Laura listened to Yasmine as a teenager and remembers that '[h]er lyrics fit with what happened at that time [...] I was able to identify with it a lot because it was just so recognisable. [...] she was a bit of a role model, yes'.

Finally, two narrators talked about their admiration for 'kleinkunst', a form of cabaret or floor show popular in Flanders. For both Laura and Nikki the choice of (Flemish) Dutch as a language is an important feature because they find lyrics very important. Laura explains that Flemish singer Mira sings about everyday life, but 'often with an ironic touch to it'. She likes the recognisability of the songs and admires that Mira sings in Dutch: 'It's great when you're able to do that in your mother tongue. English is always easier; well, it's not easier, but you often hear that people prefer singing in English rather than in Dutch, because it sounds so weird'. Nikki expresses similar feelings about Mira: 'I find it beautiful how people are able to express their emotions well in words and such – most people suck at that'. Mira's strong and explicitly Flemish accent in her songs is possibly one of the reasons why she and her music prove to be especially relatable.

Conclusion

> I am a bit of a strange gay, [...] I am maybe not totally representative [laughs] and [...] my musical tastes are just a little bit different too... I'm just a bit of a weirdo. (Anna)

With this statement Anna is actually very representative: in the life stories discussed in this chapter there is no such thing as a 'typical lesbian'. There are many different lesbian, fluid or female same-sex identities. As the interviews show, identifying and describing sexual orientation is not a straightforward act. For some women sexual orientation is a primary feature of their identities which is strongly connected to feminist or queer politics, while for others it is primarily a gut feeling. Thus not only the kind of identification but also the strength of identification based on sexual orientation differs among the narrators.

On the one hand, Belgium is an ideal playground to explore sexual identity and its fluidity because it offers a comfortable and safe place for LGBTQs. On the other, there is but little attention to such diversity in everyday life, and non-heterosexual and non-exclusive sexualities are often conflated and reduced to fit the stereotypical boxes of lesbian, gay and bisexual. To some, music affords a possibility to discover fluid and non-normative sexualities.

Although the narratives presented here are very diverse in style and subject, it is clear that female musicians and their music function as building blocks of the respective women's subjectivities, thereby supporting DeNora's findings (2000). Both Nina and Roxy see a clear connection between the music they like, the way they appreciate and read it and their queer/lesbian sexuality. Their queer/feminist activist view of the world clearly extends into their musical preferences and enthusiasms. Queer music and musicians seem to attract them, with a focus on (androgynous) female artists, even if these work in rather different genres. In fact, most of the narrators consider it self-evident to prefer listening to female musicians. They connect this preference to feminist and political attitudes, identification with the music and musician and a stronger general interest in women. The diversity of motivations behind this commonly observable phenomenon related to lesbian women highlights the multiplicity of lesbian or queer interpretations. Thus Roxy and Nikki both express how they feel different and know they are different through their sexuality, and at the same time also enjoy and long to be different. Both express this difference in their musical styles, wandering off the beaten track and exploring musical margins. Patricia compares her eclectic taste in music to her pansexuality, stating that everything is possible.

Several narrators connect music to first getting in touch with LGBTQ individuals and exploring their own sexualities: in a club (Patricia), finding idols functioning as soulmates (Anna) or through the CDs the lesbian shop assistant sold them (Nina). Lesbian musicians also function as role models to the extent that their music is very relatable, as the stories of Nikki and Laura show. The focus on local heroines in several interviews points to the fact that non-heterosexual women need role models who are able to represent them in public, especially during the stage of their coming out. In sum, music definitely reflects the women's sexual identifications on various levels and for some women contributes to their coming of age.

As the anecdotal style of the interview excerpts conveys, gender identification, sexual orientation and musical preference do not only come from within, but are strongly connected to environments and social interactions. Music simultaneously serves as an expression of identity and affords a connection to the community; as such, it is an important medium in LGBTQ lives.

Notes

1. The project is approved by the Ethical Committee of the University of Antwerp (reference: SHW_14_11_02).
2. An extensive discussion of the methodology of this research can be found in Wasserbauer (2016).
3. This is a section in my identification form which is most of the time filled in before the actual interview starts, thereby providing a good conversation starter.

4. A note on the transcriptions: '[…]' = omission of words; '…' = a short silence; 'M' = the interviewer.
5. A genre linked to punk, metal, hardcore and music with political lyrics.

References

Aerts, R. (2013). Weekendpunks, Travestieten, Discotenuekes: Iedereen Welkom! *Gazet van Antwerpen*. Retrieved from http://www.gva.be/cnt/aid1471306/weekendpunks-travestieten-discotenuekes-iedereen-welkom.

Amico, S. (2001). 'I Want Muscles': House Music, Homosexuality and Masculine Signification. *Popular Music, 20*(3), 359–378.

Better, A. (2014). Redefining Queer: Women's Relationships and Identity in an Age of Sexual Fluidity. *Sexuality & Culture, 18*(1), 16.

Brett, P. & Wood, E. (2002). Lesbian and Gay Music. *Electronic Musicological Review, VII.*

Butler, J. (1999). *Gender Trouble: Feminism and the Subversion of Identity.* New York & London: Routledge.

çavaria (2015). *Woordenlijst – Holebi.* Retrieved from http://cavaria.be/begrippen/holebi.

DeNora, T. (1999). Music as a Technology of the Self. *Poetics, 27,* 31–56.

DeNora, T. (2000). *Music in Everyday Life.* Cambridge: Cambridge University Press.

Diamond, L. (2008). *Sexual Fluidity: Understanding Women's Love and Desire.* Cambridge & London: Harvard University Press.

Driver, S. (2008). Introducing Queer Youth Cultures. In S. Driver (Ed.), *Queer Youth Cultures* (pp. 1–26). New York: State University of New York Press.

Frith, S. (1996). Music and Identity. In S. Hall & P. Du Gay (Eds.), *Questions of Cultural Identity* (pp. 108–127). London: Sage.

Halberstam, J. (2005). *In a Queer Time and Place: Transgender Bodies, Subcultural Lives.* New York, London: New York University Press.

ILGA-Europe (2015). *Annual Review of the Human Rights Situation of Lesbian, Gay, Bisexual, Trans and Intersex People in Europe 2015.* Brussels: ILGA Europe.

Jennex, C. (2013). Diva Worship and the Sonic Search for Queer Utopia. *Popular Music and Society, 36*(3), 343–359.

Leibetseder, D. (2012). *Queer Tracks: Subversive Strategies in Rock and Pop Music.* Farnham: Ashgate.

Lemish, D. (2004). 'My Kind of Campfire': The Eurovision Song Contest and Israeli Gay Men. *Popular Communication, 2*(1), 41–63.

Ross, M. W., Daneback, K. & Månsson, S.-A. (2012). Fluid Versus Fixed: A New Perspective on Bisexuality as a Fluid Sexual Orientation Beyond Gender. *Journal of Bisexuality, 12*(4), 449–460.

Tate, C. C. (2012). Considering Lesbian Identity from a Social-Psychological Perspective: Two Different Models of 'Being a Lesbian'. *Journal of Lesbian Studies, 16*(1), 17.

Taylor, J. (2012). *Playing it Queer: Popular Music, Identity and Queer World-Making.* Bern: Peter Lang.

Vlaams Ministerie van Onderwijs & Vorming (2012). *Vlaamse Vreemdetalenkennis in Europees Perspectief. Balans van het ESLC-onderzoek.* Brussels: Vlaamse Overheid.

Vrangalova, Z. & Savin-Williams, R. C. (2012). Mostly Heterosexual and Mostly Gay/Lesbian: Evidence for New Sexual Orientation Identities. *Arch Sex Behav, 41*, 85–101.

Wasserbauer, M. (2016). 'That's What Music Is About—It Strikes a Chord': Proposing a Queer Method of Listening to the Lives and Music of LGBTQs. *Oral History Review*. doi: 10.1093/ohr/ohw021.

Weiner, J. (2014). The Dream World of St.Vincent. *Rolling Stone,* 1212. Retrieved from http://www.rollingstone.com/music/news/the-dream-world-of-st-vincent-20140623#ixzz3pcIiUegn.

6 'I Worry That They'll Pick on Someone I Care About'

Trans People's Perceptions of the British Mass Media and Its Impact on Their Mental Health and Well-Being

Louis Bailey, Jay McNeil and Sonja J. Ellis

In 2010, the UK campaign group Trans Media Watch ran an online survey looking at 'How Transgender People Experience the Media'.[1] The subsequent report (Kermode, 2010) found that 78% of respondents felt that the media portrayals were either inaccurate or highly inaccurate (n=256) whilst 70% felt that, on the whole, representations were negative or very negative (n=249). A further 21.5% had experienced verbal abuse and 8% physical abuse that they believed was associated with representations of trans people in the media. Others (numbers not indicated) felt that media attitudes in general may have contributed to the social climate that led to them being assaulted. The findings of the report fed into a submission to the Leveson Inquiry into the culture, practice and ethics of the press, compiled by Trans Media Watch in December 2011.[2] Titled 'The British Press and the Transgender Community', the submission provided examples of prejudicial treatment of trans people by the press and case studies highlighting the impact of press intrusion on individuals and families. The report called for, among other things, greater protection for vulnerable groups (acknowledging the effect of prejudicial or inaccurate reporting on wider communities, not just the individuals directly affected); greater privacy for an individual both in life and after death; the inclusion of the protected characteristic of 'gender identity' in the Press Complaints Commission code of practice; and penalties for press found to be in breach of the press regulators code.

The report by Trans Media Watch was significant and marked a key starting point for public discussions around the British media's representation of trans people. It provided an important evidence base around trans people's perceptions of media representation and subsequent perceived impact of media representation on any verbal and/or physical abuse that they had experienced. Following on from this, in 2012 the authors of this chapter were involved in the 'Trans Mental Health Study' (McNeil et al., 2012). The study was the first to examine mental health and well-being in the UK trans population, and looked at a range of topics including mental health status/behaviours, experiences of healthcare services, perceptions of life and bodily satisfaction and daily experiences (social support, discrimination and harassment). The findings presented in this chapter pertain to one section of the survey which, building on the baseline data from the Trans Media Watch report, asked trans people about their views about the British mass media (broadcast and printed media). In addition, it presents new data about the influence of the media on trans people's mental health and well-being via self-reporting. The resulting dataset (n=528) is discussed here.

Whilst there is a growing body of work around media representations of sexuality and, in particular, the portrayal of lesbian, gay and bisexual people within the mainstream media (as highlighted elsewhere in this volume), there has been very little that focuses solely on media portrayals of gender identity and trans people's experiences. To date, existing work focuses on media representations in the aftermath of a transphobic murder, such as that of young trans teen Brandon Teena (Halberstam, 2005; Willox, 2003) and young trans woman Gwen Araujo (Barker-Plummer, 2013). Elsewhere, there has been some discussion around the filmic representation of trans characters (such as Abbott, 2013 and Ryan, 2009) and the representation of trans issues within daytime TV (Cavalcante, 2011; Kalter, 2008; Morrison, 2010). Outside of mainstream representation, a few authors are beginning to analyse trans people's self-representations within online and social media (such as Heinz, 2011 and Riggs, 2013). Much of this body of work as a whole is focused on the North American context. In addition, research around the impact of media representations on the daily lives of trans people is lacking.

Background

'Trans' is an umbrella term which includes a diverse range of identities and personal experiences of gender. As a convenient shorthand, trans refers to those whose gender identity differs from their assigned sex at birth. It includes those who have a binary identity as a man or a woman (who may identify as 'trans men' or 'trans women') as well as those who do not define their gender in binary terms ('non-binary'). Due to the growth of social and support networks and legal advancements, trans people are more visible than ever before and this is set to increase over the coming years. According to the Gender Identity and Research Education Society (GIRES), the UK trans population is growing exponentially, resulting in a doubling of this population every six and a half years (Reed et al., 2009). For every one person who is undergoing gender reassignment interventions, there may be up to forty others unaccounted for (ibid.). Trans visibility has increased significantly in recent years and trans issues are now regularly part of the media, with mixed results.

Methods

Ethical approval for the study was granted by Sheffield Hallam University. The survey, carried out online, totalled 89 pages and comprised 187 questions. It was promoted via over 70 voluntary and community sector groups, organisations and networks which included 'trans' as part of their remit. Over 1,000 respondents initially accessed the survey, but the total dataset was reduced to 889 after ineligible participants were removed (those under the age of 18, non-UK residents and those answering only the first survey question). For the purposes of this chapter, only those who answered the questions on media representation and impact are included. The resultant sample comprises 528 participants. Participants had a range of gender identities – clear and constant gender identity as male or female, a non-binary gender identity or no gender identity – and were at various stages of transition. Ages ranged from 18 to 71 years old. Responses to the following questions are analysed in full:

—How do you think trans people are represented in the media generally?
—Does the way trans people are generally represented in the media affect your emotional well-being or mental health?
—Please describe the most significant impact on you that viewing a trans media representation has had.

Media here included TV programmes (from chat shows to soap operas), documentaries, newspaper and magazine articles and advertising features. Whilst the survey as a whole utilised a range of question formats, including standardised scales and rating scales, the items analysed here comprise fixed-response and open-ended questions. Qualitative sections of data were analysed thematically via NVivo.

Negative Perceptions of Representation in the Media

An overwhelming majority of respondents (83% in total) felt that the media represented trans people negatively. This perception was borne out by the sheer amount of transphobia witnessed in the mainstream media and reported in participants' written responses. Four main forms of negative media representation were observed: sensationalism, ridicule, erasure of selfhood and invasion of privacy.

Table 6.1 Perceptions of trans representations

	Very negatively	Somewhat negatively	Neutrally	Somewhat positively	Very positively
How do you think trans people are represented in the media (e.g. newspapers, TV, radio) generally?	31% (n=162)	52% (n=275)	9% (n=48)	7% (n=38)	1% (n=5)

Sensationalism

Many respondents discussed the media's tendency to sensationalise trans issues and trans people's everyday lives. A handful of respondents commented on the slurs used by the media when talking about trans people; words such as 'tranny', 'she-male' and 'gender bender', derogatory headlines which served to objectify and de-humanise trans people. Respondents felt that they were treated like 'circus freaks' by the media and they consequently felt exploited and ashamed of being trans. One respondent claimed that 'grabby' headlines such as 'SEX CHANGE SOLDIER GENDER BENDS IN SEXY HEELS' contributed in part to their desire to 'stay 100% stealthy[3] as possible'. The comments received were mainly in relation to newspapers, such as *The Daily Mail* and *The Sun*, which often relied on provocative wording and cynical framing in order to provoke a reaction from readers and, by turns, reduce trans people's identities and bodies to titillating titbits.

The media's use of seemingly innocuous slogans such as 'sex change', 'woman trapped in man's body', 'born in the wrong body' were widely criticised by respondents on the basis that they were inaccurate and misleading.[4] The term 'sex change' has become a convenient shorthand to describe the experience of going through gender transition as facilitated through medical processes of gender confirmation (also known as gender reassignment or gender affirmation). However, the phrase simplifies what is otherwise a holistic and lengthy process, distilling years of subtle and nuanced social, psychological, emotional and medical changes into a single medical procedure: genital reconstructive surgery. Trans people are subsequently reduced to the sum of their parts – their genitals – often in order to 'prove' or 'disprove' their gender identity. The trope of the 'wrong body' is widely used by media and public alike in order to attempt to convey the experience of gender dysphoria, which refers to the symptoms of discomfort and disembodiment felt by some, but by no means all, trans people. Whilst some trans people may use the term to describe their relationship to their body, the problem occurs when it is overly used in order to describe all experiences of being trans. Many of the nuances of trans embodiment are lost in the process and such descriptions set up a dominant and sensationalist narrative of embodiment.

The morbid curiosity with and subsequent scapegoating of trans people by the media was noted by a large number of respondents: 'We are seen as having sex swaps and mutilating our genitals or we are sexual deviants, we are never just seen as us, the trans angle is always there for titillation'; 'Always seem to be portrayed as sad and strange. Always has to include something about genital surgery. Wish we could get away from this kind of curiosity'. Respondents went on to list the range of derogatory comments that are used by the media to describe trans people: 'objects', 'novelties', 'liars', 'fake', 'less of a man or a woman', a 'sexualised fetish', 'sexually perverse', 'bizarre' or 'freakish'. One respondent highlighted the cumulative effect of this: 'It makes me feel less human'.

As well as language, some respondents also took issue with the media's framing of trans people's lives and, in particular, the media's questioning of their motivations and life decisions, particularly regarding gender affirmation surgeries:

> Local news broadcasts on trans people have often been negative, condescending, labelled trans people as 'controversial' and accused them of stealing taxpayer's money to fund their 'sex changes'.

> I remember being enraged and upset for days by a ludicrous Daily Mail claim that a transman's surgeries would typically cost the NHS £100,000, which was lapped up by commentators arguing that the NHS should not be funding 'lifestyle choices' or 'pandering to perverts' delusions'.

One person highlighted the ways in which the media's obsession with trans people's body parts, medical status and genitals played out in their own encounters with uninformed cisgender people: 'on a number of occasions people I do not know have felt entitled to ask about the status of my genitals. They feel like they own you because you are getting treatment'.[5] There was a sense, according to several respondents' views of media and public reporting, that trans people who obtained gender affirmation surgeries via the NHS were a drain on resources.

A number of respondents described the way in which the media's obsession with sensationalising trans issues has meant that the trans status of an individual is always highlighted, even when it has no relevance to the story being reported. In the words of one respondent, 'It is *never* "incidental" to the media's description of a person, always something to be pointed out (and usually made fun of)'. A case in point is the coverage of an incident in 2013 during which a woman was severely injured by a deer whilst on a walking holiday in Scotland. Most national news coverage of the event focused on the woman's trans status, with the main tabloids running titles such as: 'Deer spears sex-swap Kate'; 'Sex swap scientist in fight for life'; and 'Sex-swap scientist gored by stag'.[6]

Ridicule

A number of respondents discussed the ways in which the humour employed by the media served to reduce trans people to caricatures and objects of derision and ridicule. Within these accounts, trans women, in particular, were used as props for comedy and subsequently mocked.

Numerous comments were received in relation to the British comedy series *Little Britain* and, more particularly, its portrayal of trans women through its fictional characters Emily Howard and Florence (who are played by the programme's creators, David Walliams and Matt Lucas). The humour hinges on the alleged disjunction between how the characters present themselves – as ultra-feminine ladies who are out of touch with modern life – and the 'knowingness' of the audience, which serves to undermine their projected identities. Continual references to their male genitalia and their slippage into 'old masculine habits' supposedly enforce the notion that they are not 'real' women but simply men who are deluding themselves and deceiving others. The transphobia is clear and a handful of respondents highlighted the consequences of such depictions in their everyday lives. The following respondent feared that the comedy show's catch phrase 'I'm a lay-dee!' would undermine their identities as a woman: 'When I watched *Little Britain*'s Emily Howard character, I expected people would use her catchphrases against me'; whilst three respondents had actually experienced ongoing abuse from members of the public. According to one, 'Having "oooh a laaaaaydeeeeee" shouted at you on an almost daily basis [...] tends to be a bit socially and emotionally crippling'.

Another respondent noted the impact that both the *Little Britain* programme and an advert created by the Irish bookmaker Paddy Power had on their everyday lives:

> I have experienced harassment directly related to media events, 'tranny spotters' during the Paddy Power advertising campaign, and 'I'm a lady' calls when *Little Britain* was on TV regularly.

The advert asked viewers to guess if race goers at the Cheltenham races were 'stallions or mares', drawing particular attention to trans women in attendance. One respondent highlighted the impact of the advert (since banned after a number of complaints and a ruling by Ofcom, the regulator for the UK communications industries) on her planned social trip: 'Paddy Power's recent misogynistic and transphobic Lady's Day ad stopped me going to the gold cup event in Cheltenham'.

Discussing the wider impact of these kinds of media representation, one respondent observed that they 'demean trans people and make them a valid target of amusement for many people. This fuels my fears of being humiliated and mocked in public'. Respondents demonstrated the ways in which the media shapes people's attitudes and opinions, which, in turn, affect how they treat trans people within society. One respondent described how such jokes '[give] phobic people a means of expression towards other people who are specifically targeted by these jokes'. Another respondent said that it 'affects the way general public think/react to me. Makes me feel like a freak and that is how "we" are portrayed...' The drip effect of such humour creates a culture which normalises and promotes the mocking of trans people. Life mirrors 'art' in the routine ridicule and humiliation of trans women in particular, especially those who are more visibly gender variant, serving to feed into a culture whereby trans women are, at best, viewed with pity and, at worst, seen as tricksters and consequently punished, often through violence (McNeil et al., 2012).

Elsewhere, British comedian Russell Howard was also cited for, according to one respondent, his 'lazy transphobic' lady-boy sketch, the premise of which was that the airline company EasyJet, in its bid to further reduce costs, hired 'lady boys' instead of cis women; the company's cheapness inferred by the reference to the fact that the women portrayed still had their male genitalia intact. The use of 'cocks in frocks' humour is not new and was highlighted as unacceptable by a number of respondents.

The device of men dressing up as women for the purpose of comedy has been a mainstay of British comedic culture, but has become problematic in recent years when such representations – increasingly considered to be misogynistic – are used to depict trans women. Trans women are often conflated with men who cross-dress and subsequently used for humorous effect, the result being, as one respondent notes, that people are 'sensitised to believing that all cross-gender activity is humorous'. The end result, according to respondents, is 'belittling' and 'demeaning' humour at the expense of trans women.

Many respondents felt that trans people had become acceptable targets of media scorn and that the media, as dictated by society's mores, has free reign to make trans people objects of ridicule and hatred:

> It's disgusting and I know if those jokes were racist or homophobic, it wouldn't be allowed, so the fact transphobic media isn't prohibited in the same way makes me extremely uncomfortable.

Several respondents shared the sense that there would be an outcry if other minority groups were subjected to the same degree of ridicule as that directed against trans people, and that, even though there has been a clampdown on racist and sexist jokes within the media, trans people were still considered to be 'fair game'.

Erasure of Selfhood

Many respondents discuss the ways in which they felt that trans people were misrepresented by the media: 'Any time a trans person is in the media, the most important part of the article is always emphasizing how they're not *really* a girl/boy... Sigh'. This respondent alludes to the manifold ways in which the media misgenders trans people by using an incorrect name or pronoun or by using someone's past gender history in order to invalidate their current identity and selfhood. Examples of this would be the reporting of a trans woman by using the male pronoun or by hinging correct pronoun usage (she) on genital surgical attainment; or the peppering of an article about a trans man with references to him 'being born a woman' or being a 'woman who is now a man', the emphasis on birth sex serving to undermine their gender identity (as a man). One respondent describes how such experiences led to self-harm: 'Upset me to cutting, left me depressed at mispronouncing a friend who was murdered'. Most of the deaths of trans people that feature in the news are the result of suicide or transphobic hate crime and the misgendering by the media serves as the final act of injustice and disrespect to a life cruelly taken, to a person who cannot answer back, and to an identity that has been doubly erased – in life, and now in death.

Invasion of Privacy

In February 2012, immediately before the survey was launched, *The Sun* newspaper ran the following article: 'Man becomes first in the UK to give birth to baby: Born a woman, now HE is a mum' (Sales, 2012). The newspaper had received a tip-off about a pregnant trans man, falsely believed to be the first British trans man to give birth, and subsequently issued a hotline number for readers to call if they knew the man in question. The incident was later declared by former Green party leader Caroline Lucas as a 'transphobic witch-hunt' and was subsequently brought to the attention of Parliament. The following statements capture something of the distress and fear felt within the UK trans male community at the time, as reported via the survey:

> The recent story of 'trans man gives birth' (sold to the paper by the ex-partner) resulted in the newspaper encouraging people to hunt down the man in question, who I know. It made me feel physically sick that he would be targeted that way.

> I got very anxious when the newspapers were hounding that poor man for having a baby – in a few years' time that could be me.

One respondent described their reaction to the way in which the story was reported: 'I get very angry when I see things like a person being portrayed as some kind of freak for a simple human desire like wanting children'. Online comments received in relation to an article by *The Telegraph* at the same time reveal something of the reception that such news got: 'She chose to become a man and in so doing should have been stripped of the right to have a child. Sick and twisted doesn't even cover it. That poor, poor baby...'; 'This is not a MAN giving birth! This is a woman who has had her breasts removed and who is taking hormones to give the APPEARANCE of being a man' (Alleyne, 2012). The man's decision to retain his reproductive system so that he could give birth to his own child was too much for these commentators, who subsequently conflated biological sex with gender identity, prioritising the former over the latter as a means of undermining his identity as male and, in so doing, maintaining cisnormative assumptions of embodiment.[7]

Respondents went on to discuss the limitations they placed on their lives, curtailing their ambitions and missing opportunities, because they feared being targeted by the media and, as a result, losing everything dear to them: family, relationship, friends, work, home. According to one respondent, 'It [...] denies me my civic rights. I would never DARE to stand for election, either to the parish, borough or county council, much less to parliament as I would be sure to be "outed" and made to look stupid by the gutter press'. This sentiment was echoed by other respondents who were worried that, should they become famous, they had no doubt that the press would disclose their trans status.

Elsewhere, respondents feared being 'outed' by the press simply because of their trans status: 'Negative portrayals actively make me more scared to be out (in the sense of out as trans*, and in the sense of outside)'; 'Fear that some of the viewers will take the negativity on board and attack a trans person'. The threat of media invasion, and subsequent public reprisals, loomed large in the minds of many trans people:

> Generally concerns me that witch hunts and exposure can manifest at the drop of a hat with seemingly no oversight.

> Because we are made out to be freak shows and I am scared that they may come after me or my friends next.

The knock-on consequences of this fear were expanded on elsewhere, with some respondents stating that fear of media reprisals made them guarded about who they disclosed their trans status to. These fears were not unfounded. One respondent described being 'outed' by the media after a tip-off received from a colleague: 'I was outed by a red top newspaper after I had told my staff of my impending transition. It destroyed my marriage within days'. Another respondent describes not giving their consent for an article that was published about them simply because they were going through transition (it is not clear who sold the story to the newspaper): 'See myself featured in a newspaper when I transitioned. Article not so bad but inaccurate, sub-editing (titling) awful. Didn't get consent for article or photo'. In both cases, these were ordinary trans people who were targeted simply because they were going through transition. Such instances contribute to a climate of fear within the trans community whereby anyone can be 'outed' at any time against their will, with potentially severe consequences.

In response to media actions like this, journalists and editors of red-top newspapers were described by one respondent as 'parasites only interested in making money out of salacious stories' and having 'no real regard for the dignity or privacy of the individual'. Elsewhere, newspapers were described as 'gutter rags' whose sole purpose was 'muck-slinging' at the expense of marginalised people.

The Impact of Negative Representation in the Media on Mental Health

The Price of Media (Mis)Representation

Just over half of respondents (50.5%) felt that the way trans people were represented in the media had a negative effect on their mental health and well-being.

Table 6.2 Perceived impact on mental health

	Yes, negatively	Yes, positively	No	Unsure
Does the way trans people are generally represented in the media affect your emotional well-being or mental health?	50.5% (n=265)	4% (n=20)	31% (n=163)	14.5% (n=80)

The following keywords came up in relation to the negative emotional impact reported: 'wearing', 'hurtful', 'insulting', 'demeaning', with respondents stating how angry, sad, scared or frustrated they felt. Some respondents felt that media representations were degrading or de-humanising whilst others emphasised the consequences for their mental health: 'I have felt depressed and nauseous following reading some newspaper articles'; 'Just generally contributing to underlying stress and anxiety that these views are being propounded about us'; 'Made me cry and feel depressed for days'. Some described feeling fearful and wary of interacting with other people, especially strangers, and the sense of paranoia that they felt: 'Occasionally causes panic attacks. They want to hurt us, they lie about us, they draw people's attention, they point out how to identify us'. Others discussed the impact on their self-worth and confidence: 'It made me hate myself. I thought I was a freak'. One respondent self-harmed after being exposed to some media portrayals: 'the most horrible ones usually leave me shaking, crying, or unable to sleep. A few years ago, even hearing about poor media representations of trans people would sometimes provoke cutting'. Another respondent felt suicidal, citing '*Daily Mail* hate stories and attacks about wasting NHS budget' as being responsible.

Some respondents detailed how each media attack against a trans person felt like a personal attack and affected them emotionally: 'I feel that when a trans person is portrayed negatively, they are also criticising me'. A few respondents discussed the ways in which media ignorance shaped the attitudes of family and friends, which, in turn, impacted their relationships: 'My parents read into the news too much and think being trans is wrong, this affects their treatment to me'. Respondents discussed how negative media stories hindered their ability to come out and get support, serving to delay their transition and, subsequently, their lives. They describe the costs associated with denying their identity:

> Spent years in closet for fear of being the freak the papers made me out to be.

> Dissuaded me from seeking the help and support I needed because I didn't want to be [seen] as 'one of them!'

Reading poorly informed and sensationalist articles had a particularly detrimental impact on some respondents when they were younger or at the early stages of transition, as the following example demonstrates: 'When I was a teenager, and struggling to understand why I felt the way that I did, the typical media story of the "sad, pathetic tranny" made me feel like a freak, like no one would ever understand me, that I would have no life if I chose to be open about being trans'. Elsewhere, a few respondents discussed the ways in which they internalised the negative messages issued from the media, resulting in a sense of detachment from mainstream society and a feeling of defeatism about their situation: 'It is upsetting and just reinforces the feeling of isolation and being "different"'; 'It adds to the negative feelings I already possess about myself, and almost confirms them in a way'. This respondent highlighted how seemingly innocuous and well-intentioned reports and documentaries carry misinformation about trans people's lives, which can be difficult to reverse: 'I feel like it perpetuates inaccurate ideas about what it means to be trans, which makes it harder for me to explain to uninformed people what it means to me'.

Avoiding the Media

Where respondents felt that the media represented trans people negatively but that this had no impact on their mental health, this was in large part because they claimed not to watch much TV or did not regularly buy newspapers, thereby limiting the impact of the media. There was also a sense of respondents not relying on the media for accurate reporting and therefore, when they did come across it, of not taking media stories too seriously: 'It's annoying to have to correct media stories, generally though I just don't place any stock in their authority on trans issues'. A handful of respondents described how they made complaints against the media or found other ways to highlight prejudice, such as boycotts, as a means of finding their voice and fighting back. Distrust of the media was prevalent across respondents' narratives.

Mixed Perceptions of Representation in the Media

Several respondents had mixed views about the media's handling of trans people and trans issues, largely based on the varying quality of subsequent representations:

> Depends on the feature; documentaries have me either smiling or nodding in agreement, but stories in papers like the *Daily Mail* make my blood boil.

This respondent expanded on the impact that both positive and negative examples served to have: 'The negative portrayals of trans people contribute to a culture of transphobia. On the other hand, when I see a positive representation it is so important for me to see people who are "like" me or are representing different experiences of trans which are so important to discuss'.

Along the same lines, a handful of respondents discussed the ways in which, on the whole, media representations of trans people have progressed over the years: 'The presentation of trans people now seems generally to be more positive than previously'. Although respondents acknowledged that the media's treatment of trans people is changing, they nonetheless felt that the media had a long way to go before the representations accurately reflected trans people's own realities and lived experiences.

A few participants also emphasised the downside of documentaries featuring transition-related surgery: 'I am worried that showing transmen's surgery scars on TV will out me to the general public who otherwise would not have recognized my scars for what they were'. Because of an overemphasis on surgery status by (even well-intentioned) documentaries, such programmes had the unintended consequence of revealing what to look for to the otherwise uninitiated, thereby outing people who might not otherwise wish to be 'outed'. The double-edged sword of trans visibility means that recognition is gained at the cost of disclosure (and its risks).

Lack of Representation

A handful of respondents lamented the lack of representation of certain subgroups of the trans community, such as trans men and non-binary people:

> What representation!? Trans men were almost entirely absent until very recently with My Transsexual Summer and before that Make Me a Man. Two documentaries in how many decades of broadcasting!

A few respondents subsequently discussed how the lack of trans male representation within the media and the absence of positive role models whilst they were growing up negatively impacted their mental health: 'I am sure that not seeing any representations of trans men was not good for my knowledge about trans men, sense of self and self esteem'. One respondent expressed relief that visibility of trans men was non-existent because, he said, 'other types of trans people don't have a good representation, so a part of me is kinda glad. I think it would just depress me'.

Elsewhere, a number of non-binary and genderqueer respondents did not see themselves represented in the media either by way of role models or by narratives that they could identify with. One respondent described initially identifying with Frankie, a character from British teen drama *Skins*, who 'was so obviously androgynous and clearly didn't identify as female', but goes on to describe their disappointment when the character becomes 'more feminine'. They say, 'seeing the one androgynous person I knew of in the media being invalidated and changed really hurt me. I wanted Frankie to succeed as a gender-neutral person and to be accepted as such because that is what I want for myself, and having any kind of example to which I can refer other people to is better than none at all'.

Some respondents critiqued the media's promotion of certain identities and bodies over others, and the emphasis on a youthful, cisnormative ideal of attractiveness. One of them wrote: 'We are not all the perfect 10. Passable, convincing, hour glass figure. Some women are tall and big boned'. Another expanded on the repercussions of promoting the body beautiful ideal as the only example of 'success': 'When there is a success story, the person's trans status is usually presented as having been a real obstacle to that success. Furthermore, those success stories involve younger, able-bodied, usually non-minority people who are attractive in a mainstream sense, which I don't think is helpful because it suggests that conformity and invisibility are the only ways to being happy'. In order to be considered 'successful' by the media, a trans person must 'pass' as non-trans, tuck all aspects of their gender variance away and adhere to a cisnormative ideal of gender conformity.

Positive Perceptions of Representation in the Media and Its Impact

Overall, 8% of respondents felt that media representations of trans people were positive, and a further 4% stated that it had a positive impact on their mental health. Where respondents discussed the positive aspects of media coverage of trans people and trans issues, this was mainly around the generation of information and support, which served to reduce any isolation or marginalisation they might have otherwise felt. The minority of respondents who felt that media representations were positive, with beneficial mental health outcomes, highlighted how media can raise awareness, therefore serving as an educational mechanism for the wider public:

> It has helped a lot as generally articles are intelligent and provide a positive image of trans people as being just like anyone else, but also

point out the struggles and the emotional difficulties etc. Makes me feel heard as it's also my fears and concerns being raised.

Elsewhere, respondents stated that finding out that trans people existed helped them to feel less alone: 'Seeing that there are not just other trans people out there, but other trans people like me'; 'That others have gone through very similar thoughts and doubts as me'. Linked to this, some respondents felt that seeing other trans people in the media helped them to realise that transition was possible: 'Seeing other transpeople has helped me come to terms with what is "wrong" with me, and it has given me hope that something can be done to improve my life'. Respondents discussed how media coverage gave them the necessary language to communicate their feelings and referred to magazine articles or documentaries which had been formative in helping them to accept their identity during their childhood or adolescence.

Some media sources that provided information about transgenderism and links to support networks and organisations were cited by respondents as being particularly helpful during the early stages of 'coming out'. Two respondents felt that media that was made for and by trans people was particularly positive – such as web comics, videos and blogs, detailing people's gender-related stories and transition experiences. Similarly, some respondents noted the importance of role models who were trans being given a platform in the mainstream media. However, in both cases, the impact of these positive influences was not described, the examples were merely listed.

Twenty-six comments were received in relation to the British documentary series *My Transsexual Summer* (Channel 4), which was aired immediately prior to the launch of the survey in November 2011, the majority positive: '*My Transsexual Summer* really helped. It showed trans people as people first'. The show followed seven trans people who spent a summer sharing a house. The documentary broke away from tradition to highlight the mainly social and emotional aspects of transition and revolved around the participants' relationships with each other, with friends, employers and family members. Respondents described how the show helped them seek help with their transition and educate family members about their experiences: 'Watching *My Transgender Summer* made me contact and attend a local group. I was very isolated at the time'; '*My Trans Summer* really helped my mum and dad deal with me being trans'. If well made, documentaries in particular provided an important resource for raising awareness and understanding of otherwise hidden and stigmatised lives and experiences.

Some respondents hoped that raising the visibility of trans people/issues in the media would have a knock-on effect for increasing the acceptance of transgenderism within mainstream society, 'helping it become less of a taboo subject'. A few respondents discussed the educational properties of the media, but only if they felt that representations were presented accurately and realistically.

Conclusion

In the survey results we have been presenting in this chapter, there was clearly a feeling of injustice from respondents, a sense that the media were targeting a minority and marginalised population. Many respondents felt that the media portrayed trans people in a particularly negative light, perpetrating lazy stereotypes and misinformation in order to shock and titillate a largely cisgender readership. Respondents pointed to the damaging impact that resulted, and the damningly real consequences of off-key 'humour' and vitriol in their everyday lives. Tabloid witch hunts, triggered by disgruntled ex-partners or co-workers, led many respondents to feel apprehensive and fearful that they could be targeted next.

Whilst documentaries were, in the main, better received than other forms of mass media, reception depended on how accurate and realistic the representations were. The particular value of documentaries, amongst other genres of media where the emphasis is on self-narration and validation, has been discussed elsewhere (see Gray, 2009). Programmes like *My Transsexual Summer*, which allowed participants more control over the telling of their stories, were favourably received by respondents, and respondents highlighted the ways in which these representations provided a source of information and support. This was particularly helpful for respondents at the early stages of questioning their gender who might be especially isolated and vulnerable. Media portrayals, if done well, served as a valuable educational mechanism for family and friends of trans people as well as the wider public (for more on this, see Cavalcante, 2014 and Sender, 2014).

There was a sense from some respondents that the media's representation of trans people and trans issues had steadily progressed over the years, but also that the media still had a long way to go. Whilst there has been an explosion in trans visibility within the mass media and a drastic increase in trans people playing trans roles since 2012 (the US series *Orange Is the New Black* started the trend, followed by two UK shows, *Boy Meets Girl* and *Cucumber, Banana, Tofu*), news reportage remains mixed. In the same year as the survey, a British teacher committed suicide. The coroner's report subsequently found the *Daily Mail* partly accountable for her death (Pidd, 2013). The inquest heard that, in the period leading up to her death, the teacher, Lucy Meadows, had complained to the Press Complaints Commission about 'harassment from the press'. In particular, there was a column written by Richard Littlejohn titled 'He's not only in the wrong body... he's in the wrong job' (url now removed). The event coincided with the Leveson Inquiry (2012) and demonstrated the need for tighter regulations within the media, an outstanding issue which remains unaddressed.

As well as tighter press regulations, the next important step now remains to move away from representations of trans people which are made by cisgender people for cisgender people. It is time for trans people to set their own agenda, to lead debates based on issues which are pertinent to them and to have greater control over the telling of their stories in order to accurately represent the realities of their lives, identities and experiences. It is crucial that media representations move away from a cisnormative framework which sensationalises and objectifies, which reduces trans people to medical curiosities or cautionary tales, and which picks through trans bodies in order to celebrate some (the bodies beautiful) at the expense of others. It is imperative that we move away from cis-centric narratives about 'wrong bodies' and 'sex changes' to highlight instead the nuances of trans embodiment. The future of trans media representation lies in more equal collaborations between trans people and the media and, ultimately, in the hands of trans people themselves.

Notes

1. Trans Media Watch was founded in 2009 in order to ensure 'that trans and intersex people are treated with accuracy, dignity and respect by media organisations in the UK'. In September 2011, Trans Media Watch, along with On Road Media, launched the Trans Media Action initiative, which is today known as All About Trans, http://www.allabouttrans.org.uk/.
2. The Leveson Inquiry, chaired by Lord Justice Leveson, was a public inquiry which ran during 2011 and 2012 into the culture, practices and ethics of the British press following the 'phone-hacking scandal'.
3. The term 'stealth' refers to trans people who do not reveal their gender history and are subsequently assumed to be non-trans.
4. Barker-Plummer (2013) draws attention to the utilisation of the 'wrong body' narrative as a problematic explanation for gender nonconformity in her discourse analysis of reports in the aftermath of the death of Gwen Araujo, a trans teen who was murdered in 2002.
5. The term 'cisgender' refers to the majority of the population whose gender identity matches the sex assigned to them at birth; people who are also referred to as non-trans.
6. As a result of a landmark negotiation with the Press Complaints Commission, the newspapers responsible acknowledged that this was in breach of the PCC editors' code, which states that details of someone's trans status 'must be avoided unless genuinely relevant to the story'. All references were subsequently removed.
7. This incident followed in the wake of publicity surrounding 'pregnant man' Thomas Beatie in 2007. Riggs (2013) draws on the media publicity surrounding Beatie to consider the visibility of trans men having children post-transition. The root of the ensuing moral panic, he argues, centres on traditional concepts of child-bearing and hegemonic attributes of masculinity, which have culturally been set in opposition. The reproductive options for trans men, therefore, deconstruct these tensions.

References

Abbott, T. (2013). The Trans/Romance Dilemma in *Transamerica* and Other Films. *The Journal of American Culture, 36*(1), 32–41.

Alleyne, R. (2012/12/02). Sex Change British Man Gives Birth to Son. *The Telegraph*. Retrieved from http://www.telegraph.co.uk/news/health/news/9077506/Sex-change-British-man-gives-birth-to-son.html.

Barker-Plummer, B. (2013). Fixing Gwen: News and the Mediation of (Trans)gender Challenges. *Feminist Media Studies, 13*(4), 710–724.

Cavalcante, A. (2011). From the 'Jerry Springer Smackdown' to the 'Oprah Winfrey Sitdown': Paradigmatic Shifts in Transgender Visibility. *Paper presented at the annual meeting of the International Communication Association.* Boston, MA.

Cavalcante, A. (2014). Shifting from Resistance to Resilience: Articulating Resiliency as an LGBTQ Audience Practice. *Paper presented at the annual meeting of the International Communication Association.* Seattle, WA.

Gray, M. (2009). *Out in the Country: Youth, Media, and Queer Visibility in Rural America.* New York: NYU Press.

Halberstam, J. (2005). *In a Queer Time and Place: Transgender Bodies, Subcultural Lives.* New York: NYU Press.

Heinz, M. (2011). Transmen on the Web: Inscribing Multiple Discourses. In K. Ross (Ed.), *The Handbook of Gender, Sex and Media.* New Jersey: Wiley-Blackwell.

Kalter, L. (2008). Catching Up: Although They Have a Long Way to Go, News Organizations Are Beginning to Report with More Sophistication about Transgender Issues. *American Journalism Review, 30*(5), 10–11.

Kermode, J. (2010). *How Transgender People Experience the Media: Conclusions from Research, November 2009 – February 2010.* Trans Media Watch. Retrieved from http://www.transmediawatch.org/Documents/How%20Transgender%20 People%20Experience%20the%20Media.pdf.

Leveson, Lord Justice (2012). *The Leveson Inquiry: Culture, Practices and Ethics of the Press Report.* Retrieved from https://www.gov.uk/government/uploads/ system/uploads/attachment_data/file/270943/0780_iv.pdf.

McNeil, J., Bailey, L., Ellis, S., Morton, J. & Regan, M. (2012). *Trans Mental Health Study. Equality Network.* Retrieved from http://www.gires.org.uk/assets/Medpro-Assets/trans_mh_study.pdf.

Morrison, E. G. (2010). Transgender as Ingroup or Outgroup? Lesbian, Gay, and Bisexual Viewers Respond to a Transgender Character in Daytime Television. *Journal of Homosexuality, 57*(5), 650–665.

Pidd, H. (2013/05/28). Lucy Meadows Coroner Tells Press 'Shame on You'. *The Guardian.* Retrieved from http://www.theguardian.com/uk/2013/may/28/lucy-meadows-coroner-press-shame.

Reed, B., Rhodes, S., Schofield, P. & Wylie, K. (2009). *Gender Variance in the UK: Prevalence, Incidence, Growth and Geographic Distribution. Gender Identity Research and Education Society.* Retrieved from http://www.gires.org.uk/assets/ Medpro-Assets/GenderVarianceUK-report.pdf.

Riggs, D. W. (2013). Transgender Men's Self-Representations of Bearing Children Post-Transition. In F. Green & M. Friedman (Eds.), *Chasing Rainbows: Exploring Gender Fluid Parenting Practices* (pp. 62–71). Toronto: Demeter Press.

Ryan, J. R. (2009). *Reel Gender: Examining the Politics of Trans Images in Film and Media.* (Unpublished doctoral dissertation). Ohio: Bowling Green State University.

Sales, D. (2012/02/13) Man Becomes First in the UK to Give Birth to Baby: Born a Woman, Now HE Is a Mum. *The Sun.* Retrieved from http://www.thesun.co.uk/ sol/homepage/news/4124499/Man-becomes-the-first-ever-in-the-UK-to-give-birth-to-baby.html.

Sender, K. (2014). Transgender, Transmedia, Transnationality: Chaz Bono in Documentary and Dancing with the Stars. In L. McLaughlin, L. Steiner & C. Carter (Eds.), *The Routledge Companion to Media and Gender* (pp. 300–310). London: Routledge.

Trans Media Watch (2011). The British Press and the Transgender Community: Submission to the Leveson Inquiry into the Culture, Practice and Ethics of the Press. Retrieved from http://webarchive.nationalarchives.gov.uk/20140122145147/ http:/www.levesoninquiry.org.uk/wp-content/uploads/2012/02/Submission-by-Trans-Media-Watch.pdf.

Willox, A. (2003). Branding Teena: (Mis)Representations in the Media. *Sexualities*, 6(3–4), 407–425.

Part III

LGBTQs as Producers in the Digital Age: Blogging

7 Safe Space, Dangerous Space

Counterpublic Discourses in the Russian LGBT Blogging Community

Evgeniya Boklage

Ever since male same-sex acts were decriminalised in Russia in 1993, Russian politicians have been trying to keep the LGBT community within the 'zones of internet and commerce' and away from the political debate (Healey, 2008, p. 175). In many ways, the community remains marginalised and strongly surrounded by an aura of depravity and illegality; an open public discourse about LGBT issues remains virtually non-existent.

The political climate in Russia has changed considerably since the rise to power of Vladimir Putin in 2000. The new conservative developments have negatively influenced LGBT people, with homophobia and discrimination being on the rise (Poushter, 2014). More deliberate attempts to restrain sexual minorities from entering the realm of public debate evolved into a 'new politics of homophobia' (Healey, 2008, p. 175). Mainstream media portray LGBTs as dangerous invaders aggressively trying to 'LGBT-ise' the heterosexual majority (Lenskyj, 2014). Most importantly, on 11 June 2013 the Russian parliament passed a bill which prohibited 'propaganda for non-traditional sexuality', sparking worldwide protests. In practice this legal initiative, which consolidated previous regional-level initiatives, criminalised any public expression of LGBT identities and thus proscribed the public association and assembly of sexual minorities (Persson, 2015).

Today the Russian LGBT community faces a number of challenges with regard to its meaningful involvement in the public sphere, which Habermas (1962) describes as a communicative space where members of civil society come together in order to deliberate issues of public concern so as to shape public opinion through critical reasoning. For a public sphere to function well, it has to treat all participants equally, focus on the matters of public concern and be open to a variety of social groups and opinions. In modern Western democracies, traditional mass media and online communicative spaces form the main venues for the public sphere.

The Russian mass media system has a number of features which prevent it from sustaining an open public debate. A complex infrastructure of formal and informal regulations and censorship secures the boundaries of the public sphere and keeps unwanted voices away (Simons, 2015). In such a context, citizen initiatives facilitated by the internet are important instruments of citizen inclusion in an exchange of socially relevant information and opinion. The work presented in this chapter turns to the concept of the counterpublic as an alternative to the classical critical-rational public sphere. It offers the case study of a Russian LGBT blogging community as an example of such a counterpublic space.

Theorising Counterpublics

In her critique of the historical public sphere outlined by Habermas (1962), Fraser (1992) proposes the concept of counterpublic. For Habermas the singularity of the public sphere was associated with better democracy, while fragmentation would result in the ineffectiveness and dissolution of public debate. More recent reflections on the public sphere however indicate that the social structures of the modern world facilitate and demand a departure from the idea of a unified public towards a pluralistic model with a multiplicity of publics (Verstraeten, 1996). Alternative communicative arenas encompass a variety of communicative modes beyond critical-rational debate, media forms and organisational structures as well as inter-public relations of domination and contestation.

Fraser (1992) describes subaltern counterpublics as parallel discursive spaces where the members of subordinated social groups can come together to participate in public debate. Historically, members of 'subordinated social groups – women, workers, peoples of colour, and gays and lesbians – have repeatedly found it advantageous to constitute alternative publics' (Fraser, 1997, p. 81). Counterpublics give these groups an opportunity to 'invent and circulate counter-discourses to formulate oppositional interpretations of their identities, interests, and needs' (ibid., p. 123). Their political and social struggles, which often take place outside the traditional public sphere, could thus be recognised (Squires, 2002). Multiple publics emerge to uncover and possibly resolve the existing imbalance in power between the mainstream discourse of dominant social groups and relatively powerless marginalised groups with a lack of economic, political or social resources (Cohen, 1999).

In a society with pronounced inequality in access to the dominant public sphere, counterpublics play a double role. Firstly, they act as 'spaces of withdrawal and regroupment' (Fraser, 1992, p. 124) where members of a group work out their own forms of public debate and use them to articulate their own group identity, needs and interests. Communities alienated from the mainstream public sphere use the arena of counter-publicity to create the language which can later be used in a broader public debate. In this sense, counter-publicity becomes the field of identity work for the members of subordinated groups. Secondly, the counterpublic sphere is a venue of agitation, activism and contestation. Its members try to reach the wider public and make society outside of the oppressed group aware of their presence. Challenging a group's invisibility in the mainstream discourse and the negative representations which often prevail in the dominant public sphere are among the central tasks of counter-publicity in its relation to the dominant public. Counterpublics question not only the ideas and policies circulating in the dominant space but also the speech genres, modes of address and hierarchy among the media (Warner, 2002).

Although they exist in opposition to the dominant public sphere, counterpublics are never isolated from the dominant discourse (Asen & Brouwer, 2001). They are influenced by it and their discursive horizons are determined by the excluding structure of the public sphere with its high-handed dynamics. They appear to 'oscillate between the protected enclaves' and the more hostile environments of the wider public (Mansbridge, 1994, p. 63). This liaison is necessary for counterpublics to prevent group polarisation, detachment from constructive criticism and cultivation of narrow-mindedness, extreme views or intolerance. As Warner (2002) observes, counterpublics are also publics and follow the same circular postulates the dominant publics do.

Counterpublics are arenas for formulating alternative discourses, that is, for debating a different set of topics and speaking them differently. They find themselves in an antagonistic relationship with the dominant public and arise as a response to the pressure of the dominant order. Therefore, counter-publicity also means a radicalisation of the dominant public sphere (Dahlberg, 2007). It expands the discourse of the general public sphere as normalised through rationality and universalism and critically approaches what, until then, has stayed outside the limits of rational debate. A discursive radicalism is cultivated through an inter-discursive contestation between inside and outside, rational and irrational, dominant and subordinate. By constantly elaborating on existing issues and bringing up new ones, counterpublics transform the nature of public debate, which becomes a process of perpetual deliberative contestation.

Counterpublics Online

Today the existence of counterpublics is almost inseparable from internet technologies. Technological affordances of the web quickly made it into a communicative space where those groups who are excluded from the mainstream public discourse could form their own discursive spheres and pursue their contestation activities. As Wimmer (2009, p. 37) articulates it:

> The Internet has helped to realize the idea of a decentralized communication network, maintained by civil society and understood as a medium that provides for self-organization. Critical counter-public spheres can no longer be conceptualized without these new technical possibilities.

Counterpublic spheres have their organisational basis in communication which increasingly takes place online. The centrality of the web infrastructure to counterpublics associated with social movements and causes becomes apparent as the web intertwines 'different aspects of the democratic public life' (Milioni, 2009, p. 413). It provides information, assists in the mobilisation of action and generation of resources and facilitates dialogue (Stein, 2009).

Counterpublics depend on common identities shared by their participants. Experiences of oppression and discrimination inform these identities and group solidarity, which are developed internally. The internet provides a multitude of communicative possibilities for people to share knowledge, personal stories and life events with each other. This allows for the location of common experiences and values which constitute the foundation for a larger social group. Social media are particularly convenient in this sense as they offer simple tools for the political positioning of individual users and online communities through shared profiles and interaction.

In this respect, blogs have been invaluable as they allow users to publish different kinds of content and interact with each other, forming online communities around the practice of blogging. In a study of digital activism by a group of Muslim women, Echchaibi (2013, p. 852) observes how blogging technology was used to discursively 'influence an ongoing and contested process of social change in Islam'. The author finds that the outlet launched by one Muslim-American woman rapidly grew into a blogging community of 21 women of different nationalities who took it as their mission to contest the ongoing debate of women in Islam, which has been steeped in prejudice, misogyny and sexism. The same study finds that counterpublics benefit from the intersection between various digital channels. After operating solo for about a year, the blogger turned to Facebook to recruit writers from a Muslim feminist group. The text-based communication allowed for a careful selection of skilful writers who demonstrated their desire to contest dominant discourse in the counterpublic arena.

The external function of a counterpublic consists in communicating the group's views and interests to a wider audience, including that of the dominant public sphere. Social media have been used by citizen activist groups to articulate counterpublic discourses and bring them into a broader public sphere. Popular social media platforms assist the signalling of counterpublic positions and facilitate interaction with established mass media organisations (Neumayer & Valtysson, 2013). Thus they become an instrument of visibility for a counterpublic in the public sphere.

It seems that online communication is better suited to support the development of multiple counterpublics than the singular public sphere of Habermas (Zhang, 2006). It can also be beneficial in resolving the disputes emerging from democratic pluralism (Laclau & Mouffe, 1985). With its multimodal structure, the internet can unite different counterpublics into a heterogeneous yet interlinked communicative space. The Russian blogosphere under discussion, which is primarily based in the LiveJournal (LJ) blogging platform, is an example of such a formation. The affordances of LiveJournal are several (Cover & Lockridge, 2009): the platform allocates every user an individual space in the form of a personal diary and simultaneously offers a social network-like function of connectivity when users become members of various interest groups and blogging communities.

AntiDogma as an Online Counterpublic

This case study is based on qualitative content analysis of a selection of blogposts and comments from the LiveJournal-based blogging community called *AntiDogma*. The community describes itself as '[t]he largest independent community of LGBTs (lesbians, gays, bisexuals, transgenders [sic]) and their friends in ZheZhe [the Russian equivalent for LJ]' and displays no formal ties to any official organisation, thus emphasising its grassroots, bottom-up structure. In February 2014, it totalled 2,532 members (the number of users eligible to post blog entries and see protected posts) and was watched by 3,178 LJ users. These are overlapping groups, meaning that the members are also listed as watchers. In order to become a member, one has to have an LJ account and send a request to join the community. The first blog entry – its mission statement – was posted in April 2006 by one of its moderators. The blog posts are publicly accessible with or without an LJ account.

The analysis was conducted in early 2014, when the blogging community had been active for nearly seven years and contained 7,322 journal entries which received 180,261 user comments. From this number, a smaller primary sample of 212 blog entries together with their 2,203 comments was selected for closer examination. These were all the posts which appeared in four 15-day periods. Two of these periods were chosen intentionally: 29 February–14 March 2012 was approximately one week before and one week after the passing of the 'homosexual propaganda' law in Saint Petersburg; 23 June–7 July 2013 were the days soon after President Putin signed the nationwide ban. Two further periods, 8–22 January 2013 and 20 August–3 September 2013, were picked randomly. Some additional materials, such as the community's organisational documents, were considered when necessary. Textual analysis of selected material included the technique of multiple close reading. Selected blog entries with commentaries were studied to identify the central discourses which reflected the process of identity building within a community. This was achieved by locating specific passages which indicated the meanings of LGBT identity expressed by community members as well as the construction of an 'us'/'them' dichotomy.

The aim of this study is to investigate the counterpublic discourses which take place within the *AntiDogma* community. In particular, my research interest lies in the realm of discursive activism defined as texts contesting the existing dominant discourse, revealing the underlying power relations and denaturalising what appears as natural (Fine, 1992, p. 221). With its focus on the Russian LGBT community, this study hypothesises that *AntiDogma* uses the discursive affordances of the blogosphere to challenge the existing negative image of the LGBT community fostered by the Russian mainstream media and to offer alternative meanings to people defined or self-defining as LGBT. This work examines selected blog posts with a special focus on the comments written by *AntiDogma* users.

Rules of Commentary: In Search of Ideal Deliberation

Assessing a discourse within a given communicative space requires a closer look at formal rules regulating it. In *AntiDogma*, this is regulated by a set of commenting rules published in an entry called 'Let's live together amicably'. The title demonstrates the prominence of politeness as a central principle of interaction among community members so as to guarantee an 'amicable' atmosphere. The guidelines ban obscene language and personal insults, and explicitly call upon users to be respectful towards each other by using the formal address 'Vi' (a formal version of the pronoun *you* in Russian). They prohibit calls for violence, hate speech, intolerance and propaganda of homophobia 'in accordance with the Criminal Code of Russia', which outlaws the promotion of hatred against any group of people.

Lakoff (1979, p. 64) defines politeness as 'a device used in order to reduce friction in personal interaction'. Polite communication allows individuals to engage in a verbal exchange while avoiding the escalation of interpersonal conflicts and inflamed speeches. *AntiDogma*'s community moderators are clearly inspired by the ideal concept of public deliberation, which favours mutual respect among participants. They also adhere to the norm of critical-rational debate based on reason-giving and objectivity (Mansbridge et al., 2010), as the following instruction demonstrates:

> Try to be objective. In order to have a constructive dialogue it is recommended that you support your conclusions with references to the studies and documents in psychology, sexology, medicine, law, sociology, demography etc. which are generally acknowledged by the scientific community.

In other words, the statements posted in the discussion section must be dispassionate and non-partisan. Participants are explicitly encouraged to engage in reason-giving and use rational argumentation, which includes providing references to 'studies and documents'. Personal statements are expected to be supported by facts 'generally acknowledged by the scientific community'. The obvious ramification of such a rule is the possibility of exclusion of participants who may be unable or unwilling to offer such judicious arguments.

Another rule unequivocally excludes potentially irrational statements. It advises against involvement in the debate in case participants lack understanding of the topic:

> It is earnestly requested that you refrain from commenting if the topic under discussion seems to you absurd, confusing or meaningless [...] Systematic

unmotivated statements (except personal opinions) which claim to be scientific and have a persistent negative connotation can be regarded as offensive and deleted by moderators.

The passage does not directly refer to homophobic speech, but it is apparently this type of rhetoric the moderators want to prevent. MacDonald (1976, p. 23) defines homophobia as 'an irrational, persistent fear or dread of homosexuals'. Homophobic rhetoric does not always appear in the form of extreme demonisation through strong language. Some anti-gay groups adopt a more reserved approach, which allows for biased opinions to be disguised, by using rationalised language and a scientifically sounding, albeit pseudo-scientific, argumentation (Irvine, 2005). It is this kind of communication the rule aims to impede.

Rules also demarcate what is perceived as rational argumentation (based on authoritative sources) from reasonings viewed as irrational (personal opinions): 'it is recommended that you accompany personal opinions with a clear indication that this is a personal opinion'. Thus a connection is made between posters' personal opinions and the irrational, the subjective and the emotional, as opposed to more substantiated arguments.

This set of regulatory statements attempts to prevent any confrontation which could develop into a heated debate whenever strong language is used by participants. It proves that, regardless of the actual climate of the debate, the community is at least aspiring towards the ideal public sphere reigned by rational-critical argumentation. The ban on inflammatory statements and the option of reporting them protect community members from personal insults and homophobic attacks. Yet the regulation to appeal to scientific sources and develop a rational objective argumentation can privilege some users and disadvantage others, especially those whose style of communication might not follow the standards of a rational debate.

A Balancing Act: How Counter Is a Counterpublic?

LJ defines itself as 'a journal where many users post entries about a similar topic. Users who are interested in a particular subject can find or create a community for this subject'. This definition emphasises the importance of shared interests as a core aspect of community building. Knowing that others share similar interests improves the relationship of trust among users. The widespread homophobia and repressive legislation concretised in the ban on 'propaganda of homosexuality' turns any public initiative of a conversation about LGBTs in Russian society into an endeavour fraught with risk. Homosexuality in Russia is still strongly surrounded by an aura of illegality and marginalisation, and 'the silence and secrecy surrounding it for so long means that Russian has never developed a gay vocabulary' (Kondakov, 2013, para. 15). In this sense, *AntiDogma* accentuates its orientation towards sustaining a community and challenging the silence of the dominant public sphere. Its members are expected to abide by the mission statement in order to be included in the community. In exchange, they are offered a safe space to discuss matters relevant to LGBT people with a reduced risk of verbal attacks.

The formation of a counterpublic does not mean it ceases all contact with discourses in the dominant public sphere. The interactions between the two publics 'are usually highly scripted, and members of marginal groups are compelled to conform to a "public transcript" which reinforces unequal social positions and frustrates natural impulses to perform reciprocal actions on the oppressor' (Squires, 2002, p. 458). The influence of the dominant public discourse about sexual minorities is visible in a preventive twist within *AntiDogma*'s mission statement, which stipulates that the community does not 'recruit or propagandise our beliefs and lifestyle', neither does it assume 'that same-sex relationships are acceptable, desirable or preferable for everybody'. The passages are easily read as a response to the 'propaganda ban', which has legally fortified the idea that both sexual identity and sexual orientation originate in an exposure to certain information. On the one hand, the statement seems to submit to the propaganda ban: it affirms that the community does not breach it, which simultaneously implies that it is in fact possible to propagandise sexuality. On the other hand, the mission statement reinstates the essentialist position that the 'predisposition to one sexual orientation and gender identity or another, according to scientific research, is first and foremost innate'. Communication within a counterpublic sphere becomes a balancing act between compliance and resistance, which in this case results in a discursive ambiguity in its stance towards sexual identity and orientation.

Likewise, a counterpublic typically balances between openness and seclusion. It is meant to be a protected space for the marginalised group but is never fully isolated from the dominant public sphere. Although a relatively safe venue for like-minded people, *AntiDogma* is not completely isolated from the larger network and is accessible to all LJ users. The availability of completely anonymous communication leads to openness, which increases the risk that participants will be exposed to homophobic verbal assaults from unidentified internet users. Discursive safety is maintained by means of the relative seclusion of the community: its moderators keep the right to ban users and certain posts can be 'locked' from the LJ users who are not *AntiDogma* members.

Safe Space, Dangerous Space

As a counterpublic, a blogging community should provide a safe space for a marginalised group to speak their mind openly. However, the relatively open structure of *AntiDogma* makes it permeable for anyone, which brings an element of risk into the communication flow. There are no formal mechanisms to verify the identities of users or their attitudes towards LGBTs, and therefore no guarantee against prejudice and hate speech. The internal organisation of the community, which insists on ideas of politeness and civility, may do a disservice to the practice of discursive resistance. These ideas arguably benefit whoever is in the dominant position because it is they who set the rules (Mayo, 2002). Abiding by these rules, the marginalised group can end up being an accomplice in silencing its own resistant voices. The payback for the comfort of having an 'amicable' conversation is the relinquished 'opportunity to display our own self-righteous anger' (Carter, 1998, p. 35).

The interplay of safety and danger turns an online counterpublic into a zone of ambiguity in which participants use the discussion to 'establish and challenge the lines of power among themselves' as members of a marginal-ised or dominant social group (Atkinson & DePalma, 2008, p. 188). The structural inequalities ingrained in relationships of sex and gender offline are easily translated into online discussions. When we consider an online counterpublic to be a safe space, the question remains 'for whom [...] [it is] safe and why' (Mayo, 2002, p. 185). An example is a blog entry posted on 9 March 2013, which generated a total of 224 comments:

> What you may be disliked for.
> And not just by some unbridled homophobes, but by ordinary peo-ple who normally regard you neutrally. Very simple: for the efforts to impose your own opinion. Here is a topic about the [gender-]neutral pronoun [link provided]. For what reason can somebody dictate to someone else how to address strangers? Note that the question is not about an insult, but simply about an indication of sex. Or about an indication of age: woman, girl. This is how people normally address each other, but there are some people who begin to resent such an innocent address. As someone in the comments said: 'Such bastards. Should be punched in the muzzle for this'. Excuse me but for such a reaction someone himself will get punched in the muzzle, and in the eyes of the majority of people, with a neutral attitude towards LGBTs, it will be quite deserved. The person was addressed the way it is accepted in society and he starts scuffling. And it is easy to extend this attitude to all of you. Roughly speaking. When you say that you want to integrate in society so that you're not alienated, that's OK. But when you start dictating things to society, which is in majority hetero-sexual, then you won't be understood, to put it mildly.

The text was posted by a member of *AntiDogma*. As may be derived from the text, the user is a heterosexual man who, after reading another *AntiDogma* post about the Swedish initiative to introduce gender-neutral pronouns, became indignant about what he saw as LGBT people dictating to the rest of society how to speak. The presumptuous tone of the post can be inter-preted as an appeal to LGBT members of *AntiDogma* to respond to it, but is also charged with conflict. The language of the author is antagonistic in the way he bluntly accuses the LGBT community of alienating the heterosexual majority, which, according to the blogger, is not homophobic but becomes it as a justified reaction to the unreasonable demands of LGBTs. His resentment is intensified by a comment made elsewhere in the blogosphere: that those who fail to use gender-neutral pronouns are 'bastards' who need to be 'punched in the muzzle'.

The author tries to show if not his solidarity with, then at least his sympathy for, the struggle of the LGBT community for rights: 'When you say that you want to integrate in society so that you're not alienated, that's OK'. While such a statement expresses approval outwardly, the overtone of condescension in the passage crystallised in numerous references to the universalising claims of the dominant discourse both in the blog post and in subsequent comments. The author frequently spoke of the majority, referring to heterosexual people and to their perception of gender-neutral pronouns as being enforced by a few. The implication was that the LGBT community has the right to demand better treatment, but it must be aware that some demands are simply unacceptable in the eyes of the dominant society and cannot be imposed upon it.

The post restores the power of the dominant group over the minority by trying to stipulate the conditions of resistance and its boundaries. Without regard to the needs of LGBT people and their right independently to determine such needs, it dictates what the author believes to be 'reasonable' demands. The numerous references he made to the notions of majority, normality and tradition – specifically the tradition of language use – indicate an attempt to speak on behalf of the heterosexual cisgender majority.

A short exchange with another *AntiDogma* member demonstrates how civility can be used to repressive ends, which Mayo (2002, p. 185) describes as 'practices [...] that constrain and impede nascent justice claims'. Out of more than 200 comments posted to the cited blog entry, only one contained strong language and was explicitly 'uncivil'. In the comments, the author had continued to defend his position that people who requested that they be addressed with a pronoun opposed to their biological sex were 'abnormal' and 'most likely will be avoided'. The deprecating nature of these statements produced a legitimate expression of discontent on the part of one respondent, who decided to protest in the most straightforward, though not the most cordial, manner by writing: 'Aren't you being fucking saucy to judge who is normal and who is not?' This coarse comment unveiled that the original post was a thinly disguised effort to reinstate the hegemonic order and police others by determining what is accepted by the majority as normal and what is not. It delineated the boundaries of resistance and demonstrated the power position of the dominant group, which would remain an authorising body to decide on the course of LGBT protests. In the end, civility was used as a tool to power down the counter-hegemonic attempt when the author replied: 'You are indeed abnormal'.

Thus, the author dodged the challenge by using anger directed at him to his own advantage. He likened what he saw as preposterous demands of LGBTs to the explicitly uncivil communication of a single reader, branding them both 'abnormal' and therefore unfit for mainstream society. Coincidentally or not, the same user stopped posting any further replies after this statement. Either this was out of a desire to avoid further confrontation or for other reasons, but the respondent was effectively silenced and the question remains whether in this instance the counterpublic failed to provide a safe haven for the marginalised opinion it was expected to encourage.

From Individual to Collective Self

As a counterpublic, *AntiDogma* becomes a space where community members and other readers come together to speak to and be heard by each other. This process of being heard is a crucial aspect of the human condition (Arendt, 1958). The users who engage in conversations on the blog use language to project themselves and elucidate who they are and what they do (Gee, 1999). They use language to construct their identities, which consist of 'multiple facets', are 'subject to tensions and contradictions' and are 'in a constant state of flux' (Burgess & Ivanič, 2010, p. 232). The participants of *AntiDogma* illuminate their identities for others and for themselves through the practice of writing affected by the 'accumulation of life experiences' (Ivanič, 1998, p. 181). They also discursively inscribe themselves into a larger community unified by a shared collective identity. To this effect, the discursive space of *AntiDogma* serves as a point of intersection between users' individual and collective selves (Simon, 1999).

One of the common practices to be found in *AntiDogma* discussions is the sharing of personal stories and experiences with other users. One analysed entry asked readers to share the 'rubber stamp questions' they have heard after coming out. The conversation took a humorous turn and commenters tried to deride the narrow-minded stereotypes about sexual identity and orientation with irony and sarcasm. One user however took it more personally as she wrote:

> It's not even funny to me :(all my life I was hiding, because I wanted a 'classical family', and now I have mutual love and want to build a family with her. And what will I be told? Until the age of 35 you didn't find a normal man and then you switched to women. But in reality it's only at the age of 35 that I found a normal woman, but you can't explain that :).

The sincerity of this passage reveals a lot about its author as she chose to disclose intimate details. Yet by telling her tale she could also show the commonality of experience with others (Alexander, 2002). Her posting demonstrates a spectrum of sexist prejudice which could be encountered by any lesbian in Russian society. The stereotype frames lesbians as heterosexual women who simply failed at heterosexual relationships and depicts female singlehood as a pathology and a personal failure to be overcome at any cost. According to this stereotype, the transition to lesbianism is a radical measure to solve the situation. To respond to these prejudices, the author reinstated her agency by telling that 'it's only at the age of 35 that I found a normal woman'.

Another user provided an example which illuminated the prevalence of what Rosenthal (1990, p. 1) calls a devastating 'intersection of ageism with sexism' against women:

> I was asked probably twice in one week how I am going to live with a beloved woman when we grow old. I flat-out don't understand why these lovely ladies seem to think that an old husband is more attractive than an old wife...

These questions illustrate the hegemonic value placed on young women, who are the only people to be considered sexually desirable (Montemurro & Gillen, 2013). The esteem of older women is diminished to the point that they are not worth living with later in life. Interestingly, the author made it clear that those who asked her the question were other women, thereby demonstrating signs of internalised ageism (Gerike, 1990). As with the previous quotation, the implication that such a prejudice could target any lesbian, and in fact any woman, appeared to deepen the sense of collective identity. The user shared her experience with other community members but also used a counterpublic sphere to contest the rhetoric of the stereotype by asking whether an old husband 'is more attractive than an old wife'. The blogger benefited from her confession in a counterpublic by receiving support from fellow members.

Finally, written elaborations on the individual self can become a vehicle for an activist message when concerned users share their personal experiences to encourage others and provide them with a sense of community. Shortly after the ban on the 'propaganda of homosexuality' was passed in Saint Petersburg, one user posted a protest video discouraging foreigners from visiting the city as long as the ban stood and asked users to sign an online petition to the city's governor. The first comment on the clip was a pessimistic statement saying that 'nothing will come of it. No one will pay attention... So much has been signed already. Was there any use of it?' The author then tried to encourage the reader by using an activist argumentation and some personal background. He explained that the goal was resonance and that the motivation was not to 'bring to reason fucking stupid officials [...] We attract the attention of the public', he wrote.

Another reader, a Russian expat living in Western Europe, acknowledged the effect the video had on people abroad, citing his British friends who cancelled a trip to Saint Petersburg. He also implied that new legislation would force gays back into the closet: 'In general I'm infinitely happy not to be in Russia now [...] Cannot imagine not being able to hold hands with a person you love or flirt a little...' Yet this was the author's reply: 'None of us, not a single activist I know, will get back into the closet – neither in Saint Petersburg nor anywhere else. And those who think they can shut our mouths with such laws are naïve'. In this reply, the blogger reaffirmed his position as an LGBT activist. He referred to a community he identified with and emphasised his connection with others through an assertion that 'not a single activist I know will get back into the closet'. He also used a personal reference, the intimate concept of the closet, which he immediately conveyed in the domain of the public. He represented being and living outside the closet simultaneously as an act of personal courage and as an activist statement. For the blogger, the act of coming out was not only a personal step but a matter of civic responsibility (Oesterreich, 2002).

Conclusion

The concept of the counterpublic encompasses deliberative spaces which exist in relative opposition to the dominant public sphere. Counterpublics are crucial for marginalised minorities because they offer a public venue to discuss their issues without the interference of an oppressive majority and its social order. This study examined a Russian LGBT blogging community called *AntiDogma* as an instance of an online-based counterpublic.

One challenge to *AntiDogma*'s development into an effective counterpublic was the need to balance discursive openness with safety of debate for its members. The key task of a counterpublic is to provide a safe space for the members of an oppressed community, who join it to deliberate relevant matters, articulate community concerns and elaborate the tactics and practices for contesting discrimination. While *AntiDogma* offers an exclusive discussion area for LGBT people and their supporters, it also aspires to foster an inclusive environment for opinion exchange characterised by high degrees of discursive openness. Anyone can access *AntiDogma*'s conversations, also anonymously. In effect however community members can become exposed to explicit and implicit verbal assaults that are difficult to prevent in such an open space.

The way in which the rules of commentary adhere to norms of politeness and civility of conversation can work as a mechanism of exclusion for individuals who follow different conversational standards – for instance, those favouring emotions and passionate language. *AntiDogma*'s rules explicitly prohibit strong language, encourage readers to use rational argumentation, cite scientific publications and abstain from discussing subjects about which users do not have sufficient understanding. As a result, the counterpublic discourse is set to follow the same rigid structures of the dominant public sphere which work to exclude minority voices as irrational, emotional, ridiculous or absurd.

Despite these limitations, the blog entries on *AntiDogma* have produced a substantial number of comments, as community members and unaffiliated readers appear to be enthusiastic about the opportunity to engage in conversation. The authors have asked their readers for feedback, demonstrating their inclination for deliberation. Using the commentary sections provided below every blog entry, bloggers and their readers have shared personal stories and opinions on a variety of subjects, generating a vibrant counterpublic which is essential for the creation and maintenance of a sense of belonging and collective identity of LGBT people in Russia.

References

Alexander, J. (2002). Homo-Pages and Queer Sites: Studying the Construction and Representation of Queer Identities on the World Wide Web. *International Journal of Sexuality and Gender Studies*, 7(2–3), 85–106.

Arendt, H. (1958). *The Human Condition*. Chicago: University of Chicago Press.

Asen, R. & Brouwer, D. (2001). Introduction: Reconfigurations of the Public Sphere. In R. Asen & D. Brouwer (Eds.), *Counterpublics and the State* (pp. 1–32). Albany, NY: SUNY.

Atkinson, E. & DePalma, R. (2008). Dangerous Spaces: Constructing and Contesting Sexual Identities in an Online Discussion Forum. *Gender and Education*, 20(2), 183–194.

Burgess, A. & Ivanič, R. (2010). Writing and Being Written: Issues of Identity Across Timescales. *Written Communication*, 27(2), 228–255.

Carter, S. L. (1998). *Civility: Manner, Morals, and the Etiquette of Democracy*. New York: Basic Books.

Cohen, C. J. (1999). *The Boundaries of Blackness: AIDS and the Breakdown of Black Politics*. Chicago: University of Chicago Press.

Cover, J. G. & Lockridge, T. (2009). Icons and Genre: The Affordances of LiveJournal. com. *Reconstruction*, 9(3). Retrieved from http://reconstruction.eserver.org/Issues/093/cover_lockridge.shtml.

Dahlberg, L. (2007). The Internet, Deliberative Democracy, and Power: Radicalizing the Public Sphere. *International Journal of Media and Cultural Politics*, 3(1), 47–64.

Echchaibi, N. (2013). Muslimah Media Watch: Media Activism and Muslim Choreographies of Social Change. *Journalism*, 14(7), 852–867.

Fine, M. (1992). Passions, Politics, and Power: Feminist Research Possibilities. In M. Fine (Ed.), *Disruptive Voices: The Possibilities of Feminist Research* (pp. 205–232). Ann Arbor, MI: University of Michigan Press.

Fraser, N. (1992). Rethinking the Public Sphere: A Contribution to the Critique of Actually Existing Democracy. In C. Calhoun (Ed.), *Habermas and the Public Sphere* (pp. 109–142). Cambridge, MA: MIT.

Fraser, N. (1997). *Justice Interruptus: Critical Reflections on the 'Postsocialist' Condition*. New York: Routledge.

Gee, J. P. (1999). *An Introduction to Discourse Analysis: Theory and Method*. London: Routledge.

Gerike, A. E. (1990). On Gray Hair and Oppressed Brains. *Journal of Women and Aging*, 2(2), 35–46.

Habermas, J. (1962 [1989]). *The Structural Transformation of the Public Sphere: An Inquiry into a Category of Bourgeois Society*. Cambridge, MA: MIT.

Healey, D. (2008). 'Untraditional Sex' and the 'Simple Russian': Nostalgia for Soviet Innocence in the Polemics of Dilia Enikeeva. In T. Lahusen & P. H. Solomon, Jr. (Eds.), *What Is Soviet Now? Identities, Legacies, Memories* (pp. 173–191). Berlin: LIT Verlag.

Irvine, J. M. (2005). Anti-Gay Politics Online: A Study of Sexuality and Stigma on National Websites. *Sexual Research & Social Policy*, 2(1), 3–21.

Ivanič, R. (1998). *Writing and Identity: The Discoursal Construction of Identity in Academic Writing*. Philadelphia: John Benjamins.

Kondakov, A. (2013, June 20). Do Russians Give a Damn about Homosexuality? *Open Democracy*. Retrieved from http://opendemocracy.net/od-russia/ alexander-kondakov/do-russians-give-damn-about-homosexuality.

Laclau, E. & Mouffe, C. (1985). *Hegemony and Socialist Strategy*. London: Verso.

Lakoff, R. (1979). Stylistic Strategies within a Grammar of Style. In J. Orasanu, M. Slater & L. Adler (Eds.), *Language, Sex, and Gender* (pp. 53–80). New York: New York Academy of Sciences.

Lenskyj, H. J. (2014). *Sexual Diversity and the Sochi 2014 Olympics: No More Rainbows*. Basingstoke: Palgrave Macmillan.

MacDonald, A. P. (1976). Homophobia: Its Roots and Meanings. *Homosexual Counseling Journal*, 3, 23–33.

Mansbridge, J. (1994). Using Power/Fighting Power. *Constellations*, 1(1): 53–73.

Mansbridge, J., Bohman, J., Chambers, S., Estlund, D., Føllesdal, A., Fung, A., Lafont, C., Manin, B. & Martí, J. L. (2010). The Place of Self-Interest and the Role of Power in Deliberative Democracy. *The Journal of Political Philosophy*, 18(1), 64–100.

Mayo, C. (2002). The Binds That Tie: Civility and Social Difference. *Educational Theory*, 52(2), 169–186.

Milioni, D. L. (2009). Probing the Online Counterpublic Sphere: The Case of Indymedia Athens. *Media, Culture & Society*, 31(3), 409–431.

Montemurro, B. & Gillen, M. M. (2013). Wrinkles and Sagging Flesh: Exploring Transformations in Women's Sexual Body Image. *Journal of Women and Aging*, 25(1), 3–23.

Neumayer, C. & Valtysson, B. (2013). Tweet against Nazi? Twitter, Power, and Networked Publics in Anti-Fascist Protests. *Mediekultur*, 29(55), 3–20.

Oesterreich, H. (2002). 'Outing' Social Justice: Transforming Civic Education within the Challenges of Heteronormativity, Heterosexism, and Homophobia. *Theory & Research in Social Education*, 30(2), 287–301.

Persson, E. (2015). Banning 'Homosexual Propaganda': Belonging and Visibility in Contemporary Russian Media. *Sexuality & Culture*, 19(2), 256–274.

Poushter, J. (2014). Russia's Moral Barometer: Homosexuality Unacceptable, but Drinking, Less So. *Pew Research Center*. Retrieved from http://pewrsr.ch/ 1fWnAVU.

Rosenthal, E. R. (1990). Women and Varieties of Ageism. *Journal of Women and Aging*, 2(2), 1–6.

Simon, B. (1999). A Place in the World: Self and Social Categorization. In T. R. Tyler, R. M. Kramer & O. P. John (Eds.), *The Psychology of the Social Self* (pp. 47–69). Mahwah, NJ: Erlbaum.

Simons, G. (2015). Russian Media and Censorship: A Means or an End? *Russian Journal of Communication*, 7(3), 300–312.

Squires, C. R. (2002). Rethinking the Black Public Sphere: An Alternative Vocabulary for Multiple Public Spheres. *Communication Theory*, *12*(4), 446–468.

Stein, L. (2009). Social Movement Web Use in Theory and Practice: A Content Analysis of US Movement Websites. *New Media & Society*, *11*(5), 749–771.

Verstraeten, H. (1996). The Media and the Transformation of the Public Sphere: A Contribution for a Critical Political Economy of the Public Sphere. *European Journal of Communication*, *11*(3), 347–370.

Warner, M. (2002). Publics and Counterpublics. *Public Culture*, *14*(1), 49–90.

Wimmer, J. (2009). The Publics behind Political Web Campaigning: The Digital Transformation of 'Classic' Counter-Public Sphere. In S. Baringhorst, V. Kneip & J. Niesyto (Eds.), *Political Campaigning on the Web* (pp. 31–51). Bielefeld: Transcript Verlag.

Zhang, W. (2006). Constructing and Disseminating Subaltern Public Discourses in China. *Javnost – The Public*, *13*(2), 41–64.

8 Is the Pope Judging You?

Digital Narratives on Religion and Homosexuality in Italy

Giulia Evolvi

'If someone is gay and searches for the Lord and has good will, who am I to judge?' (Donadio, 2013). With these words, pronounced on the plane back from Brazil a few months after his election, Pope Francis addressed the problem of gay clergy within the Roman Catholic Church. The words were considered by many as an innovation for the Church since Jorge Mario Bergoglio has been the first Pope to publicly use the word 'gay'. His rhetorical question 'who am I to judge?' kindled debates worldwide, especially in countries which are traditionally and majoritarian Catholic, such as Italy. A number of media outlets interpreted the sentence as an attitude change of the Church towards homosexuality. The Italian version of the *Huffington Post* for instance titled an article 'Pope Francis opened to homosexuals: "God made us free"' (*L'Huffington Post*, 2013).

However, the statements Pope Francis made about homosexuality are ambiguous enough to produce different interpretations within religious and non-religious groups: is he favourable to same-sex unions or is he against homosexuality? Sceptics point out that the Pope opposed same-sex unions when he was the Archbishop of Buenos Aires, and that he has not shown any intention of changing the Church doctrine on the matter so far. Furthermore, there are discrepancies between the allegedly open attitude of Pope Francis and the rise of a number of Catholic-inspired movements against LGBTQ rights in Europe (Paternotte, 2014).

This ambiguity evoked a number of discourses and interpretations within religious and non-religious groups in Italy. The Italian UAAR, the Union of Rationalist Atheists and Agnostics,[1] for example, published a number of articles on its blog that are suspicious of the allegedly 'gay-friendly attitude' struck by Pope Francis. UAAR criticises the Pope and the Catholic Church for accepting homosexuals only on the condition that they do not openly live their sexuality. This attitude may make homosexuals feel 'inadequate', as explained in the following quote on the UAAR's blog:

> For Bergoglio, as well as for his predecessor Ratzinger, when homosexuals feel inadequate, fragile and uneasy, they don't pose a problem for the Church... When homosexuals are proud, organised and claim

their rights, then they pose a problem. They are portrayed as people who provoke and 'parade' their homosexuality.

(*A Ragion Veduta*, 23 September 2013)

Similarly, Italian Catholics who support traditional family values negate that the Pope's words meant an effective acceptance of marriage equality. Rather, they stress the need to accept homosexuals in order to help them. This attitude results in discourses which consider homosexuality as problematic and define it as a 'cross to bear' or a 'disorder', as the following quote about Pope Francis's words exemplifies:

[Christian] People who accept homosexuals without exploiting them are people who do not judge them but give a name to their suffering, their 'cross' to bear, and help them by showing a way to overcome their uneasiness. But accepting means also being aware that this cross is the result of a disorder.

(Invernizzi & Marchesini, *Il Blog di Costanza Miriano*, 18 September 2013)

In Italy there are no same-sex marriage or laws against hate speech based on sexual orientation; civil unions for same-sex couples were introduced only in 2016. Religion is a central element in debates about LGBTQ rights in Italy, where the presence of the Vatican creates a peculiar intertwinement between religion and politics. Catholics and atheists articulate a number of different discourses around LGBTQ issues, both in support of and against LGBTQ rights. Certain atheist groups, such as UAAR, strongly support LGBTQ rights; by contrast, some Catholic groups, such as the organisation *Sentinelle in Piedi* (Standing Sentinels), are strongly adverse to them. These specific discourses are more often articulated on the internet than in national mainstream media.

By performing a critical discourse analysis of atheist and Catholic blogs in Italy, the present study explores attitudes towards homosexuals and their rights in the country, especially in relation to religion. The chapter starts by investigating the current situation of LGBTQs in Italy, considering the Catholic background of the country, and analysing the literature on media use by LGBTQs. It then compares and contrasts antithetical positions about homosexuality in Italy, analysing atheist blogs which support LGBTQ rights and Catholic blogs which oppose them. In addition, the chapter explores Catholic conversion therapies for homosexuals and their articulations on the internet. In conclusion, the chapter offers some reflections on the current debate on LGBTQ rights in Italy from religious and non-religious viewpoints and discusses the potential of the internet for articulating counterpublics.

Homosexuality in Catholic Italy: Don't Ask, Don't Tell

In Italy there are around one million people that self-identify either as homosexual or bisexual, according to a 2012 survey conducted by the Italian National Institute of Statistics (ISTAT, 2012). The current Italian attitude towards homosexuality could be defined as 'don't ask, don't tell' (Capozzi & Lingiardi, 2003; Lingiardi et al., 2015; Prati, Pietrantoni & D'augelli, 2011): homosexuals in Italy do not constitute a problem as long as they remain outside of the public domain. The ISTAT data confirms the 'don't ask, don't tell' attitude. More than half of the Italian population supports civil unions and other rights for homosexuals. 74.8% of Italians disagree that 'homosexuality is a sickness'[2] and 62.8% agree that a homosexual couple should have the same rights as a heterosexual one. However, the survey reveals that at the same time 55.9% of respondents agree that 'homosexuals should be more discrete' and only 20% of Italian homosexuals and bisexuals disclose their sexual orientation to their parents. Moreover, a number of studies show a low level of acceptance of homosexuality in Italy: 'Italians have one of the highest scores [in the European Union] in negative attitudes towards homosexuality' (Prati, Pietrantoni & D'augelli, 2011, p. 2603). Italy indeed holds a 'peripheral' position on the European map of liberal sexual politics (Colpani & Habed, 2014).

I argue that religion also influences this 'don't ask, don't tell' attitude: on the one hand, the Catholic Church formally prohibits same-sex relationships; on the other, it tries to include homosexuals, as the words of the Pope exemplify. As a result, there are a number of different negotiations of religious values in relation to homosexuality. Conservative Catholic values also figure prominently among the predictors for acceptance (or non-acceptance) of homosexuality in Italy, next to a number of other social predictors such as political ideology, age, gender and education (Baiocco et al., 2013; Hichy, Gerges et al., 2015; Lingiardi et al., 2015). The pervasive character of Catholicism in Italy has been analysed as a cause of negative attitudes towards LGBTQ rights: 'Italy is now one of the few European countries where same-sex marriage or civil unions are not allowed, mostly because of the strong influence of the Roman Catholic Church and more conservative religious attitudes of Italians' (Antonelli et al., 2014, p. 704).

The Vatican played a central role in Italy's transition to a republic in the postwar period, and the 1947 Republican Constitution recognised the privileged position of the Catholic Church (Diamanti & Ceccarini, 2007; Domenico, 2005; Salvati, 2003; Samuels, 1997). While the State renegotiated its relationship with the Vatican in 1984, formally recognising the secular character of the State, the Catholic Church has maintained a privileged position to this very day, exemplified by its role in civil society (Garelli, 2007) and education (Frisina, 2011). Statistics show that the majority of the population (more than three-quarters) self-identify as Catholic and close to 98% of the population has been baptised.[3] This predominance of Catholics in the country makes the Catholic Church the main and almost exclusive religious commentator on social and political issues in Italy.[4]

The Vatican has repeatedly displayed a negative attitude towards homosexuals, exemplified by the 2003 publication of the *Lexicon*, a dictionary of terms such as homosexuality and homophobia which the Vatican finds problematic (De Pittà & De Santis, 2005). The Vatican indeed openly supports the traditional heterosexual family as the only cultural and social model. This model influences law-making processes in Italy when it comes to issues such as same-sex partnerships (Crowhurst & Bertone, 2012). Furthermore, the Vatican's opposition to a so-called 'gender ideology'[5] has inspired a number of movements in support of traditional family values in different European countries, including the group *Sentinelle in Piedi* in Italy (Paternotte, 2015).

However, a recent study conducted in Italy by Hichy, Coen and Di Marco (2015) takes into account religious orientations more than religiosity or religious affiliation *per se*. 'Orientation' indicates the degree to which people question religious beliefs and employ them to make sense of social norms. Religious orientations can result in greater or lesser support of homosexuality. Catholicism is heterogeneous in the matter of religious orientations. Italian Catholicism has indeed been described as an instance of 'belonging without believing': Italians belong to the Catholic Church because they perform religious rituals, such as weddings and baptisms, but they do not always believe in all the values promoted by the Vatican (Marchisio & Pisati, 1999). As a result, many Italian Catholics renegotiate religious values and articulate alternative positions in regards to social matters, including homosexuality. An example of the heterogeneity within Italian Catholicism with regard to homosexuality is found in the study of Bertone and Franchi (2014) on parents of gay men and lesbians. Catholic parents often find strategies to accept their children's sexuality and make sense of it within their religiosity. According to the authors, some parents frame homosexuality in terms of suffering and love and accept it in the private sphere without openly challenging the doctrine of the Church.

Bertone and Franchi's study focuses on believers whose religious orientation is flexible in accepting homosexuality. In fact, many Catholics accept homosexuality and, in case they identify as homosexuals themselves, are able to reconcile their sexual identity with their faith. Other Catholics are less flexible and do not accept same-sex relations within the Catholic Church. Similarly, some homosexuals are not able to make sense of their faith in relation to their sexual orientation and choose to distance themselves from the Church, for example by embracing atheism. These different religious orientations result in a number of divergent approaches to same-sex unions. The 'don't ask, don't tell' attitude of the country creates a national context which tends to overlook issues around LGBTQs, but it can be challenged by alternative media discourses which draw on religion to deploy their arguments.

LGBTQs and Media Use

Media are important venues to address LGBTQ issues and they have a potential to create a space to challenge the hegemonic 'don't ask, don't tell' attitude. Warner (2005) studies the formation of queer counterpublics in relation to mass media consumption. For him a public is formed by virtue of the reflexive circulation of media texts; therefore it is constituted by strangers that are addressed by the same media content. A public is a social entity that can be related to either mainstream or subcultural social values. Non-mainstream publics are identified by Warner as counterpublics: 'some publics are defined by their tension with a larger public' (2005, p. 56). Counterpublics compel a re-thinking of participation within democracy and address the exclusion of certain groups from the public sphere. The interplay between public and private is central in the formation of queer counterpublics: they are, after all, concerned with the formation of public spaces where it is possible to enact a performance of the 'private self'. The notion of the counterpublic helps to explain how LGBTQ communities in Italy employ media to become more vocal about their issues. By bringing their private narratives into the public sphere, certain groups try to challenge the 'don't ask, don't tell' attitude and seek visibility for issues often overlooked by mainstream media.

The creation of counterpublics is often connected with the articulation of narratives about private experiences. Couldry (2010) analyses how voices can create social awareness and kindle public debate through narratives. With the term 'voices' Couldry indicates the process of recognition of certain social matters and values which are relevant for a community or an individual, and the consequent discussion of such matters in public debates. LGBTQ counterpublics often employ alternative narratives to challenge mainstream media discourses and find a space in the public sphere. Nonetheless, according to Couldry, in a neoliberal context certain voices are listened to and privileged while others are silenced; as a result, the latter need to find spaces of expression other than mainstream media.

The internet often becomes a space for articulation of LGBTQ counterpublics. A number of studies focus on the importance of the internet for LGBTQs to negotiate their identities and define their cultures and subcultures, as well as to get in touch with other LGBTQs (De Ridder & Van Bauwel, 2015; Gray, 2009; Mowlabocus, 2010; Potârcă, Mills & Neberich, 2015). Szulc and Dhoest's study (2013) reveals that the internet is important for the exploration and articulation of sexual identity, especially before and during coming out, and Penney's research (2015) shows how LGBTQs use the internet to challenge stereotypes of mainstream media representations, for example through the creation of memes and satirical images.

I argue that the digital space is important for Italian LGBTQs because of their underrepresentation or misrepresentation in mainstream media. With the term 'mainstream media' I intend national television, radio and newspapers which target a general audience rather than specific groups. Italian mainstream media, and television in particular, have been strongly influenced by Catholic political parties (Padovani, 2007) and rely on Catholicism to construct the Italian identity (Ardizzoni, 2007). As a result, Italian mainstream media tend to portray Catholicism in a hegemonic and non-problematic way. They mirror dominant Catholic discourses and often overlook potentially controversial topics, such as LGBTQ issues. The internet then can provide a space where LGBTQs create counterpublics and articulate private narratives of the self, mirroring offline movements and discourses which have difficulty finding a space within mainstream media. In addition, the internet allows for the articulation of discourses around LGBTQ rights, so different groups can create different online counterpublics, both in support of and against controversial issues such as same-sex unions.

Previous academic scholarship on LGBTQs and media in Italy mainly focused on cinema representations (Baldo, 2014; Bolongaro, 2010; Dunkan, 2005; Watson, 1992). The present chapter, by contrast, aims at understanding how homosexuality is discussed within online media in Italy. It focuses on religion by taking into account the perspectives of both Italian atheist activists for LGBTQ rights and certain Italian Catholic groups against LGBTQ rights. As I have shown in the previous part, religion is an important social element in connection with LGBTQs. In Italy, a country with a unique religious context because of the presence of the Vatican, religion is more relevant in public debates than in many other European countries. Thus through my analysis I aim to explore two research questions. How does the internet allow for the articulation of atheist and Catholic positions overlooked by mainstream media representations in Italy? And how do specific religious orientations affect online discourses about homosexuality?

Method and Sample

In order to answer my research questions, I focus on the role of digital media, particularly blogs, in creating pro- and anti-LGBTQ-rights narratives. I analyse the official blog of UAAR (www.uaar.it) as well as an additional atheist blog written by an anonymous member of the association (*Dalla Parte di Alice*, www.dallapartedialice.wordpress.com). The UAAR includes people who self-identify in various ways, such as 'atheists', 'secular' and 'laic'. The majority of blog posts employ the term 'atheists' to include all the association's members and therefore I use the same term in this chapter as an umbrella word. Besides these atheist blogs I also analyse Catholic blogs, with a particular focus on the anti-LGBTQ-rights group *Sentinelle in Piedi* (www.sentinelleinpiedi.it) and the blog of the Catholic journalist Costanza Miriano (www.costanzamiriano.com), who is a prominent member of the group. I chose these blogs because I found them to be currently the most vocal and radical about LGBTQ issues in Italy, and they often address each other in their discourses. The blogs focus on homosexuality more than on the entire LGBTQ community, which is why in my analysis

I refer only to the former, mirroring the blogs' discourses and terminology. The blogs do not encompass the totality of atheist and Catholic discourses because in Italy there are also atheists who do not support LGBTQ rights and Catholics who freely live their LGBTQ identities or advocate for LGBTQ rights. The discourses included in the analysis express antithetical and non-flexible religious orientations and are therefore useful to explore specific positions on homosexuality.

I performed a critical discourse analysis (CDA; Wodak & Bush, 2004) of blog discourses from 2011 up to the present, having found that the debate around LGBTQ rights intensified in Italy during this period, most likely because of a number of Western countries legalising civil unions or same-sex marriages. Drawing from critical linguistics, CDA takes into account ideology, power and social hierarchies, considering language in relation to social practices. Thus it is a useful approach for the analysis of discourses on non-mainstream groups which constitute social 'others', such as LGBTQs. CDA gives special attention to the context of production of media texts, which in the case of the internet means the acknowledgement of the connection between online and offline spaces. While I employed CDA to analyse the creation of online discourses, I drew on Warner's (2005) idea of counterpublics to contextualise the formation of non-mainstream communities on the internet.

In addition, I performed semi-structured face-to-face interviews with the two main authors of the UAAR blog, Raffaele Carcano and Massimo Maiurana, who are respectively the president and treasurer of the association. I also interviewed Massimo Introvigne and Marco Invernizzi, prominent figures within the Catholic pro-family movement as well as guest writers for the blog of Costanza Miriano. I observed an anti-LGBTQ-rights protest by the group *Sentinelle in Piedi*, during which I met Giorgio Ponte, a self-identified Catholic homosexual with a strong online presence. The interviews were performed in Italian. All quotes presented in this chapter, either from the interviews or from the blogs, are my own translations. I personally do not belong to any of these groups. I do however share the UAAR's effort in support of LGBTQ rights and do not agree with *Sentinelle in Piedi*, but I tried to suspend my personal judgment while conducting interviews and performing analysis.

Atheist and Catholic Digital Debates

The analysis of the blogs reveals that the internet allows for the articulation of narratives which either strongly support or strongly oppose LGBTQ rights. First of all, I will present atheist discourses that frame the LGBTQ question as a matter of equality and civil rights. Secondly, I will describe anti-LGBTQ Catholic blogs that describe homosexuality as a condition of uneasiness. Thirdly, I will analyse two specific narratives of Catholic homosexuals who either refuse or try to change their sexual orientation.

Atheist Blogs: Homosexuals Should Reject Religion

> Not only the Catholic Church is today the principal agent of homopho-
> bia in Italy, but the adorable Pope Francis is firmly leading the Church's
> battles against the rights of homosexuals.
>
> (*Dalla Parte di Alice*, 15 April 2015)

Atheist movements in Italy often engage in information practices and activities to promote LGBTQ rights. The UAAR's blog *A Ragion Veduta* (With
Hindsight) actively promotes anti-homophobia laws and marriage equality.
The UAAR's website dedicates an entire section to the definition and history
of homosexuality, arguing that '[d]iscriminations that homosexuals suffer
almost always have a religious origin. The UAAR, ever since its creation
(and with great visibility in the "famous" Gay Pride in Rome in 2000), has
supported their battles' (*A Ragion Veduta*, homepage, retrieved on 11 April
2016). From the perspective of UAAR, it is natural for Italian homosexuals
to embrace atheism – or at least to refuse the Papal authority – because
of the hostility of the Church against LGBTQ rights. This point of view
is exemplified by the opening quote, retrieved from an atheist blog that is
connected with the UAAR, which identifies Pope Francis as one of the major
opponents to LGBTQ rights in Italy. The blog ironically describes the Pope
as 'adorable' because of his popularity among believers and non-believers.

The blog of UAAR often articulates discourses in support of homosexuals for two main reasons. Firstly, UAAR wants to oppose the hegemonic
position of the Catholic Church within Italian society, and it does so by challenging traditional Catholic values. The association proposes a re-thinking
of the Catholic model of the family:

> This type of family [the Catholic one] is not unchangeable... Obviously
> traditionalists, especially Catholic traditionalists, do not agree. They
> feel betrayed every time anybody dares to propose any form of sup-
> port for other families, which will certainly not result in less support
> for their own families. The traditional family has become another tool
> to impose a certain worldview, a culture, a religious faith.
>
> (*A Ragion Veduta*, 12 February 2014)

UAAR criticises the Catholic Church for discriminating against all individuals who do not conform to its religious worldview. As exemplified by the
quote, the association considers the institution of the family as disconnected
from religious principles, since the Catholic model of the family represents
only a 'small percentage of families' (ibid.). UAAR denounces the attempt of
the Catholic Church to impose this model on others because it is not only a
way to maintain a hegemonic position but also to deny civil rights to a part
of the population. A re-thinking of the dominant model of the family will
result in a public sphere which could be more inclusive, granting equality to
homosexuals and more visibility to atheist positions.

Secondly, UAAR considers rights as a moral and ethical resource for atheists' lives, as well as the basis for a democratic and non-religious society. For this reason the organisation is involved in a number of campaigns which support civil and human rights, even if these are not immediately related to atheism. The advocacy for LGBTQ rights is part of a bigger effort which sees UAAR engaged in struggles for gender equality and reproductive rights. A democratic and secular state, according to UAAR, needs to grant its citizens freedom and equality, as the blogger and association's treasurer Massimo Maiurana articulated:

> As an association we are absolutely favourable to homosexual marriage, because we believe in the principle that every human being has the right to self-determine. Until the rights of one human being do not damage other people's rights, they need to be protected.
>
> (personal communication, 30 July 2015)

In an interview Maiurana explained that the association supports the LGBTQ cause in Italy because it is an example of unjust discrimination. UAAR believes that recognising LGBTQ rights will create greater equality without damaging other citizens' rights, including the rights of Catholic believers.

From the analysis of these atheist digital discourses it emerges that the internet offers a useful space to articulate certain non-mainstream voices. Atheists are a minority in Catholic Italy and they often support other groups whom they perceive as minorities, such as homosexuals. The internet plays an important role for these minorities, allowing them to form a counterpublic which challenges dominant Catholic-inspired representations in society and mainstream media. This counterpublic is characterised by their advocacy for equality and civil rights. At the same time however certain Catholic blogs also use the internet to advocate strongly against LGBTQ rights.

Catholic Blogs: Homosexuals Need No Rights

> [A] few weeks ago the Juvenile Court of Rome recognised the adoption of a child by the [female] partner of her mother, creating a dangerous precedent: it is the first Italian case of *stepchild adoption*... Today opposing all this is considered 'homophobia'... **For this reason, Sentinelle in Piedi will protest in squares all across Italy.**
>
> (*Il Blog di Costanza Miriano*, 3 October 2014, emphasis in original)

A number of Catholic-inspired groups and writers in Italy recently became vocal against LGBTQ rights. An example is the group *Sentinelle in Piedi*, founded in 2013 to protect traditional family values against same-sex unions. Inspired in their practices and name by the French *Veilleurs Debout*, the group conducts protests in public squares, where people remain silent for an hour reading a book. *Sentinelle in Piedi* is formally apolitical and are-ligious. However many of its members come from Catholic movements and find an intellectual inspiration with Catholic journalists and bloggers, such as Costanza Miriano. According to the group, same-sex marriage would be a threat to traditional Catholic values; therefore *Sentinelle in Piedi* wants to preserve the right to criticise homosexuality, as exemplified by the opening quotation.

It is important to note that groups such as *Sentinelle in Piedi* do not represent the totality of Italian Catholics; on the contrary, they are a minority which recently became vocal against LGBTQ rights, and they are not officially recognised by the Vatican.[6] Being a minority these groups employ the internet to form a counterpublic where they can be vocal in their fight against homosexuality, gaining the attention they do not enjoy in mainstream media.

The main values of *Sentinelle in Piedi* and similar groups are traditional Catholic ones, specifically those linked to the conservative model of the Christian family. In addition, they reject feminism and often advocate against gender equality, as exemplified by a quote from Miriano: 'Many wise persons suggested to me to practise submission… Submission is the honest and truthful desire to serve one's husband […] It means that we are able to understand his inclinations' (*Il Blog di Costanza Miriano*, homepage, retrieved on 11 April 2016). Miriano considers women's fulfilment as dependent on assuming the roles of mother and wife, and on 'submitting' to their husbands. She argues for the importance of maintaining strict gender roles, because men and women are allegedly different and cannot aspire to the same achievements. As a result, she strongly opposes the 'gender ideology' that would grant gender equality within the family. Catholic groups which are inspired by such principles cannot accept the subversion enacted by same-sex couples, which form families that are not based on traditional feminine and masculine gender roles.

Despite their advocacy against LGBTQ rights, these groups do not self-identify as homophobic: they do not criticise homosexuality *per se* but only the fact of granting homosexuals what these groups consider to be 'special' rights. Differently from the atheist positions analysed above, these Catholic discourses often insist on the fact that homosexuals in Italy are not weak or discriminated against. For example, in the blog post 'Letter to a homosexual friend' Miriano writes: 'Why do you think we need a law against homophobia? Italy is already one of the most tolerant countries in the world' (23 July 2013). Ignoring the lack of LGBTQ rights in Italy described above, Miriano argues against the idea that homosexuals, or LGBTQs, are discriminated against in Italy. In another blog post (11 June 2015) she argues that same-sex marriage should be prohibited both for symbolic and practical reasons. According to Miriano homosexuals cannot aspire to marriage in a Catholic sense, because their unions are against the principles of the Church. Furthermore, they should not aspire to marriage in a civil sense, because the right they demand 'already exists': co-habitants who are not civilly married, Miriano explains, do not suffer from any lack of civil recognition compared to civilly married couples. With this post, which contains a number of juridical inaccuracies,[7] Miriano seeks to argue that LGBTQs' battles are unjustified.

Homosexuals, and LGBTQs more generally, are framed in the analysed Catholic blogs as a powerful lobby. *Sentinelle in Piedi* identifies itself as a marginalised group which stands against the 'gay lobby', mentioned as such by Pope Francis as well (Magister, 2013). *Sentinelle in Piedi* claims that, because of the power of this lobby, freedom of expression is limited and Italians are prevented from criticising homosexuality:

> With a law [against homophobia] everyone who says that a family should be constituted by a man and a woman, everyone who is against adoption by homosexual couples, would be denounced and risk from six months to one year in prison. We don't accept that we cannot express our opinion and that's why we protest.
> (*Sentinelle in Piedi*, homepage, retrieved on 16 April 2016)

Through its internet discourses, *Sentinelle in Piedi* subverts traditional narratives of civil rights, explaining that LGBTQs not only are a 'powerful lobby' but also aim at limiting other people's rights. As exemplified by the quote, the group organises protests to protect their right to 'express their opinion' against homosexuality. Furthermore, these Catholic groups present LGBTQ rights as damaging to children's rights:

> 'Gay marriage' means that one violates the fundamental right of every child to have a father and a mother. A person who believes in this right does not discriminate. On the contrary, it is an adult who employs power to deprive an innocent and weak creature of its natural rights who practises discrimination.
> (*Il Blog di Costanza Miriano*, 13 January 2013)

In this quote Miriano turns common LGBTQ narratives upside down by framing children of homosexual couples as 'discriminated' against, and refusing to consider homosexuals as a marginalised group. She considers homosexuals as 'discriminating' because, not recognising children's rights to have a mother and a father, they damage 'innocent and weak creatures'.

Although bloggers such as Costanza Miriano and groups such as *Sentinelle in Piedi* frame LGBTQs as a 'powerful lobby', they do occasionally recognise the negative social consequences of being homosexual. However they negate that the cause for this is a lack of civil rights. Instead they argue that homosexuals are unhappy because of the intrinsic condition of their sexual orientation, which does not lead to procreation and hence is 'unnatural'. These Catholic opinion-makers insist on the fact that homosexuals, as well as other LGBTQs, suffer because of spiritual and psychological shortcomings.

Digital Narratives of Catholic Conversion Therapies

> Breathe, relax, be happy: the Church doesn't hate you. God doesn't hate you and neither does the world... If indeed one says that homosexuality is not a fixed condition, that only a man and a woman can have children, this is not an instance of hate, nor a threat to people who cannot live this love. It is only evidence.
>
> (Giorgio Ponte, *Tempi,*[8] 13 May 2015)

While Catholic-inspired activists and bloggers advocate against LGBTQ rights, they often articulate the need for the Church to help homosexuals. To their mind Catholic homosexuals can achieve happiness in two main ways: either by living their lives in chastity or by going through a psychological process to become heterosexual. A number of Catholic groups consider spiritual and psychological practices of 'healing' homosexuality as the most effective way to help homosexuals. The inclination to repress or change one's sexual desires does not characterise all Catholic homosexuals but only a small minority. Advocates of this inclination can however gain a special prominence on the internet in the form of conversion stories, according to which the unhappiness of homosexuals, supposedly caused by psychological traumas such as the absence of a father, is overcome thanks to an encounter with religion or an experience of faith. Recently, two Catholic homosexuals in Italy became popular online because of their conversion stories: Giorgio Ponte and Luca di Tolve.

Ponte is a writer and a religion teacher, as well as a member of *Sentinelle in Piedi,* who decided to come out as a Catholic homosexual. He does not write his own blog but offered his testimonies to Miriano's blog and Catholic online magazines. According to Ponte, the Church and groups such as *Sentinelle in Piedi* are not homophobic. To the contrary, they spiritually help homosexuals accept the limits of their 'condition'. Ponte believes that homosexuality is a sexual desire that can be changed into heterosexuality or repressed through the choice of chastity. As exemplified by the opening quote in this section, Ponte feels accepted by the Catholic Church and identifies religion as the only way to achieve true happiness. He explains that he does not identify with the LGBTQ community because he refuses to be judged by a 'single aspect' of his personality, meaning his sexual orientation. He rather self-identifies as someone with 'homosexual tendencies' and accepts the impossibility of his marrying and procreating, instead celebrating the importance of chastity within Catholicism.

Di Tolve is another example of a Catholic homosexual who became famous for offering his testimony. After being active in the LGBTQ community, Di Tolve discovered that he was HIV-positive and had a religious awakening. His encounter with Catholicism made him start a process which led to heterosexuality; he is presently married to a woman. Di Tolve explains his experiences in the form of a printed autobiography and on his blog (www.lucaditolve.it). He talks about his religious awakening as a 'complete inner rebirth' and advocates for spiritual and psychological therapies aimed at changing the sexual orientation of homosexuals. For example, Di Tolve published on his blog an interview with the psychologist Gerard van den Aardweg, who helps homosexuals change their orientation:

> There are people who suffer alone and in silence. 50% of young people who discover they have this kind of feeling [homosexual desire] do not want to fall into a homosexual life. They would like to change, but everything seems to make this impossible for them because LGBTQ activists and politicians discriminate against them. (19 February 2015)

In the same post, Di Tolve criticises LGBTQ groups as promiscuous and unable to offer their members true support. Instead of helping members, he claims, the LGBTQ community 'discriminates' against homosexuals when they try to change their sexual orientation. Both Ponte and Di Tolve criticise the LGBTQ movement for considering homosexuality as an unchangeable identity. They present a viewpoint which is not usually found in mainstream media and is antithetical to the UAAR's stance: instead of self-identifying as being discriminated against because they are homosexuals, both these men claim that LGBTQ groups discriminate against them for not conforming to a specific set of atheist values. Atheist blogs, in the meantime, strongly reject religious-inspired 'healing' practices. According to UAAR such practices are both ineffective, because homosexuality is not a disease, and problematic, because they consider LGBTQ people as deviant and unable to create normal affective relationships (24 December 2007).

Conclusion

The ambiguity surrounding Pope Francis's question 'who am I to judge?' has produced a number of different interpretations of the position of the Church on homosexuality. However, the two groups in this analysis seem to have no doubts about Pope Francis's attitude towards homosexuality. Both pro-LGBTQ-rights atheists and anti-LGBTQ-rights Catholics believe that the Pope does not approve of homosexual unions. While they agree on this interpretation, the blogs frame it in diametrically opposed ways: for atheists this is an instance of the backwardness of the Catholic Church while for Catholics it is a positive defence of traditional values.

The presence of the Vatican makes Catholicism a central element in public debates about LGBTQs in Italy. The blogs selected for analysis underscore the centrality of religion when debating LGBTQ issues. Constituting themselves as counterpublics, they express what could be considered in the Italian context as radical opinions: either they advocate for total support of LGBTQ rights or they ask for a complete rejection of these rights. The internet allows for voices and narratives which are more extreme than the ones generally covered in the mainstream media. These are not therefore disconnected from the reality of the country but rather express positions which exist in society and are articulated through a set of offline practices, such as the Gay Pride movement, supported by UAAR, or the public protests of *Sentinelle in Piedi*.

When we compare the discourses on atheist and Catholic blogs, two main results emerge. Firstly, the two groups frame LGBTQ issues in an antithetical way and use different resources and styles to defend their ideas. Atheist groups focus on the support of civil rights and equality. They do not discuss whether homosexuality is natural or induced, nor do they frame it in a positive or negative manner. Their discourses do not focus on private narrations of members of the LGBTQ community but rather articulate collective voices opposed to the lack of civil rights. By contrast, Catholic blogs counterpose family values to civil rights. For these groups homosexuality is a negative condition because it is unnatural and against the principles of the Catholic Church. They focus only on specific Catholic experiences, such as those by Ponte and Di Tolve, instead of addressing the whole LGBTQ community. These narratives are examples of 'voices' as defined by Couldry (2010).

Secondly, there is more complexity in Catholic voices than in the atheist ones. For atheists the principle of equality, including marriage equality, is not a matter of discussion: UAAR expects all its members to share this view. Certainly there are atheists who are against LGBTQ rights, but these positions are rarely found in atheist blogs. By contrast, groups such as *Sentinelle in Piedi* represent only a part of the multitude of Catholic voices – a specific orientation, as described by Hichy, Coen and Di Marco (2015). Digital narratives show that there are multiple ways of negotiating religion and homosexuality. Stories such as those by Ponte and Di Tolve exemplify an alternative to the negotiation of religious meanings analysed by Bertone and Franchi (2014). Their testimonies are examples of the heterogeneity and broad bandwidth of Catholic positions in relation to homosexuality. As a result, Catholic blogs continuously articulate and defend their ideas.

It would seem that no dialogue is possible between these two positions: the Catholic idea of the traditional family cannot accept equality in civil rights and the atheist blogs do not take into account religious feelings. The discourses the blogs reproduce or create are also antithetical because UAAR frames homosexuals as marginalised while Catholic blogs subvert this narrative by portraying a powerful 'gay lobby'.

As the analysis of the blogs focused on certain 'radical' voices, an avenue for future research would be to undertake a comparison with mainstream media discourses as well as other websites and blogs about homosexuality. However, exploring radical voices on the topic in itself helps to understand the complexity of the Italian debate on LGBTQ issues, which goes beyond the perceived 'don't ask, don't tell' attitude. The conspicuously divergent opinions of the two groups under investigation mirror a general Italian problem: institutional decisions on civil rights are hard to reconcile with religious positions. Pope Francis does not want to judge homosexuals, but the debate around LGBTQ rights in Italy often includes such judgments. Atheist groups judge homosexuals as marginalised because of their lack of civil rights. Certain Catholic groups judge them to be unhappy because they cannot conform to the principles of the traditional family. The LGBTQ debate in Italy is often intertwined with the rejection or endorsement of Catholic values, which inevitably leads to people passing judgment.

Notes

1. In Italian, Unione Atei e Agnostici Razionalisti.
2. The survey questions are translated from the Italian by the author.
3. According to the research centre CESNUR (http://www.cesnur.com/la-chiesa-cattolica/), in 2009 the number of Italians that had received Catholic baptism was close to 59 million, which corresponds to 97.9% of the population. However, there is a common practice of baptising children even within non-Catholic families. The statistic institute Doxa (http://www.doxa.it/news/religiosita-e-ateismo-in-italia-nel-2014/) published the results of a 2011 survey which shows that 75% of Italians self-identify as Catholics, and an additional 10% consider themselves religious but do not belong to any church.
4. Other Christian denominations and non-Christian religions in Italy, while sometimes engaged in social and political issues, have an influence that is not comparable with that of the Roman Catholic Church, which is often considered as holding the Italian religious monopoly.
5. The term 'gender ideology' is extensively employed by *Sentinelle in Piedi* and Costanza Miriano. Neither of these provide a clear definition of the term, but it generally refers to the effort to erase gender differences and promote same-sex unions. In the blogs analysed here, a Papal speech against gender ideology is frequently cited: http://it.radiovaticana.va/news/2015/01/19/papa,_aereo_trascrizione_integrale_del_testo/1119009.
6. When referring to 'Catholic blogs' in the present chapter, I include only this minority.
7. The claim by Costanza Miriano is inaccurate because, while the Italian State recognises some civil rights for couples who live together without being married, such couples are not granted the same benefits as legally married couples. A homosexual for example cannot adopt the child of his or her partner even if the couple lives together.
8. *Tempi* is a Catholic online magazine available at http://www.tempi.it.

References

Antonelli, P., Dèttore, D., Lasagni, I., Snyder, D. K. & Balderrama-Durbin, C. (2014). Gay and Lesbian Couples in Italy: Comparisons with Heterosexual Couples. *Family Process*, 53(4), 702–716.

Ardizzoni, M. (2007). *North/South, East/West: Mapping Italianness on Television*. Lanham: Lexington Books.

Baiocco, R., Nardelli, N., Pezzuti, L. & Lingiardi, V. (2013). Attitudes of Italian Heterosexual Older Adults Towards Lesbian and Gay Parenting. *Sexuality Research and Social Policy*, 10(4), 285–292.

Baldo, M. (2014). Familiarising the Gay, Queering the Family: Coming Out and Resilience in *Mambo italiano*. *Journal of GLBT Family Studies*, 10(1–2), 168–187.

Bertone, C. & Franchi, M. (2014). Suffering as the Path to Acceptance: Parents of Gay and Lesbian Young People Negotiating Catholicism in Italy. *Journal of GLBT Family Studies*, 10(1–2), 58–78.

Bolongaro, E. (2010). Representing the Un(re)presentable: Homosexuality in Luchino Visconti's *Rocco and His Brothers*. *Studies in European Cinema*, 7(3), 221–234.

Capozzi, P. & Lingiardi, V. (2003). Happy Italy? The Mediterranean Experience of Homosexuality, Psychoanalysis, and the Mental Health Professions. *Journal of Gay & Lesbian Psychotherapy*, 7(1–2), 93–116.

Colpani, G. & Habed, A. J. (2014). 'In Europe It's Different': Homonationalism and Peripheral Desires for Europe. In P. M. Ayoub & D. Paternotte (Eds.), *LGBT Activism and the Making of Europe: A Rainbow Europe?* (pp. 73–93). Basingstoke: Palgrave Macmillan.

Couldry, N. (2010). *Why Voice Matters: Culture and Politics after Neoliberalism*. Los Angeles: Sage.

Crowhurst, I. & Bertone, C. (2012). Introduction: The Politics of Sexuality in Contemporary Italy. *Modern Italy*, 17(4), 413–418.

De Pittà, M. & De Santis, R. (2005). Rome, Italy: The Lexicon – An Italian Dictionary of Homophobia Spurs Gay Activism. *Journal of Gay & Lesbian Issues in Education*, 2(3), 99–105.

De Ridder, S. & Van Bauwel, S. (2015). The Discursive Construction of Gay Teenagers in Times of Mediatization: Youth's Reflections on Intimate Storytelling, Queer Shame and Realness in Popular Social Media Places. *Journal of Youth Studies*, 18(6), 777–793.

Diamanti, I. & Ceccarini, L. (2007). Catholics and Politics after the Christian Democrats: The Influential Minority. *Journal of Modern Italian Studies*, 12(1), 37–59.

Domenico, R. P. (2005). 'For the Cause of Christ Here in Italy': America's Protestant Challenge in Italy and the Cultural Ambiguity of the Cold War. *Diplomatic History*, 29(4), 625–654.

Donadio, R. (2013, July 29). On Gay Priests, Pope Francis Asks, 'Who Am I to Judge?'. *New York Times*. Retrieved from http://www.nytimes.com/2013/07/30/world/europe/pope-francis-gay-priests.html?_r=1.

Duncan, D. (2005). Stairway to Heaven: Ferzan Özpetek and the Revision of Italy. *New Cinemas: Journal of Contemporary Film*, 3(2), 101–113.

Frisina, A. (2011). The Making of Religious Pluralism in Italy: Discussing Religious Education from a New Generational Perspective. *Social Compass*, 58(2), 271–284.

Garelli, F. (2007). The Public Relevance of the Church and Catholicism in Italy. *Journal of Modern Italian Studies*, 12(1), 8–36.

Gray, M. L. (2009). Negotiating Identities/Queering Desires: Coming Out Online and the Remediation of the Coming-Out Story. *Journal of Computer-Mediated Communication*, 14(4), 1162–1189.

Hichy, Z., Coen, S. & Di Marco, G. (2015). The Interplay Between Religious Orientations, State Secularism, and Gay Rights Issues. *Journal of GLBT Family Studies*, 11(1), 82–101.

Hichy, Z., Gerges, M. H. H., Platania, S. & Santisi, G. (2015). The Role of Secularism of State on the Relationship Between Catholic Identity, Political Orientation, and Gay Rights Issues. *Journal of Homosexuality*, 62(10), 1359–1373.

ISTAT (2012). La Popolazione Omosessuale nella Società Italiana. Retrieved from http://www.istat.it/it/archivio/62168.

L'Huffington Post (2013, September 19). Papa Francesco Apre agli Omosessuali: 'Dio Ci Ha Reso Liberi'. 'Non Insistere Troppo su Aborti, Nozze Gay e Condom'. Retrieved from http://www.huffingtonpost.it/2013/09/19/papa-francesco-gay_n_3954780.html.

Lingiardi, V., Nardelli, N., Ioverno, S., Falanga, S., Chiacchio, C. D., Tanzilli, A. & Baiocco, R. (2015). Homonegativity in Italy: Cultural Issues, Personality Characteristics, and Demographic Correlates with Negative Attitudes Toward Lesbians and Gay Men. *Sexuality Research and Social Policy*, 1–14.

Magister, S. (2013, July 18). Papa Francesco e la Lobby Gay in Vaticano. *L'Espresso*. Retrieved from http://espresso.repubblica.it/googlenews/2013/07/18/news/papa-francesco-e-la-lobby-gay-in-vaticano-1.56816.

Marchisio, R. & Pisati, M. (1999). Belonging without Believing: Catholics in Contemporary Italy. *Journal of Modern Italian Studies*, 4(2), 236–255.

Mowlabocus, S. (2010). *Gaydar Culture: Gay Men, Technology and Embodiment in the Digital Age*. Farnham: Ashgate.

Padovani, C. (2007). *A Fatal Attraction: Public Television and Politics in Italy*. Lanham: Rowman & Littlefield.

Paternotte, D. (2014, May 8). Christian Trouble: The Catholic Church and the Subversion of Gender. *Reviews & Critical Commentary*. Retrieved from: http://councilforeuropeanstudies.org/critcom/christian-trouble-the-catholic-church-and-the-subversion-of-gender/.

Paternotte, D. (2015). Blessing the Crowds: Catholic Mobilisations against Gender in Europe. In S. Hark & P.-I. Villa (Eds.), *Anti-Genderismus: Sexualität und Geschlecht als Schauplätze aktueller politischer Auseinandersetzungen* (pp. 129–147). Bielefeld: Transcript.

Penney, J. (2015). Responding to Offending Images in the Digital Age: Censorious and Satirical Discourses in LGBT Media Activism. *Communication, Culture & Critique*, 8(2), 217–234.

Potârcă, G., Mills, M. & Neberich, W. (2015). Relationship Preferences Among Gay and Lesbian Online Daters: Individual and Contextual Influences. *Journal of Marriage and Family*, 77(2), 523–541.

Prati, G., Pietrantoni, L. & D'augelli, A. R. (2011). Aspects of Homophobia in Italian High Schools: Students' Attitudes and Perceptions of School Climate. *Journal of Applied Social Psychology*, 41(11), 2600–2620.

Salvati, M. (2003). Behind the Cold War: Rethinking the Left, the State and Civil Society in Italy (1940s–1970s). *Journal of Modern Italian Studies*, 8(4), 556–577.

Samuels, R. (1997). Tracking Democracies: Italy and Japan in Historical Perspective. *Journal of Modern Italian Studies*, 2(3), 283–320.

Szulc, Ł. & Dhoest, A. (2013). The Internet and Sexual Identity Formation: Comparing Internet Use before and after Coming Out. *Communications: The European Journal of Communication Research*, 38(4), 347–365.

Warner, M. (2005). *Publics and Counterpublics*. New York: Zone Books.

Watson, V. (1992). Shakespeare, Zeffirelli, and the Homosexual Gaze. *Literature Film Quarterly*, 20(4), 308–325.

Wodak, R. & Bush, B. (2004). Approaches to Media Texts. In J. Downing, D. McQuail, P. Schlesinger & E. Wartella (Eds.), *Sage Handbook of Media Studies*. Thousand Oaks: Sage.

9 Contesting Hegemonic Gender and Sexuality Discourses on the Web

A Semiotic Analysis of Latvian and Polish LGBTQ and Feminist Blogs

Joanna Chojnicka

This chapter offers a semiotic analysis of Latvian and Polish LGBTQ and feminist blogs, focusing on the functions of layout, image-text relations and denotative/connotative meanings of images as integral elements of online discourses of gender dissidents. The term *gender dissident discourse* refers to texts by authors who identify as lesbian, gay, bisexual, transgender or queer (LGBTQ) and/or feminist (in these texts). Dissident discourse is all about relating to validity claims (in Habermas's 1998 sense) that have been previously raised (either by mainstream/hegemonic discourses or hearsay). Specifically, the discourse of gender dissidents responds to the validity claim of heteronormativity and/or patriarchy. Some texts accept heteronormative or patriarchal claims to rightness, but also construct sexual/gender dissidents to be as good as the 'normals' (Goffman, 1963) in realising these claims. For example, gays, lesbians and feminists can also be faithful monogamous partners, generous caretakers, amazing parents and so forth. Other texts deny the heteronormative/patriarchal claims, e.g. by glorifying dissident lifestyles or rejecting the very gender (masculine/feminine) and sexual (hetero/homo) distinctions as artificial, unnecessary and restrictive social constructs (Chojnicka, 2015). This chapter explores the role played by visual elements – either independently or together with texts – in constructing these dissident positions.

Social Context of the Study

Latvian and Polish societies are traditional, characterised in part by ultra-conservative resistance to gender equality and fervent anti-feminist attitudes. Women receive lower salaries and do most domestic labour, and many fall victim to (gravely underreported) sexual/domestic violence (Czerwińska & Piotrowska, 2009; Heinrich Böll Stiftung, 2015; van der Molen & Novikova, 2015). Another problem is the predominance of sexualised representations of women in the media and, in Poland, serious restrictions on reproductive rights (Grabowska, 2015); in Latvia the central issue is the lack of a considerable women's movement (Novikova, 1996).

These nation-states are also considered homophobic due to expression/ assembly right limitations, regular cases of hate speech by public figures

(Amnesty International, 2006; O'Dwyer & Schwartz, 2010), high levels of homo- and transphobia-motivated violence, low social levels of tolerance for non-heteronormative behaviours and identities and lack of legislation addressing LGBTQ needs (Abramowicz, 2007; Locmelis, 2002; Śmiszek & Dynarski, 2014).

These conditions make any research on the situation, representations and dissident voices of feminists and LGBTQs in Latvia(n) and Poland/Polish particularly relevant. Another reason for this chapter's choice of countries/languages is the wish to challenge Anglo-American bias in LGBTQ (media) studies (Kulpa & Mizielińska, 2011; Szulc, 2014) and to address the shortage of respective research in LGBTQ and discourse studies. The comparative approach is justified by parallel historical trajectories (the history of state socialism and transition to democracy/westernisation) and similarities in the current socio-political situation of LGBTQs, which however does comprise some important differences in need of explaining (see details further in this section and in Discussion and Conclusions).

At the same time, this chapter considers Latvian and Polish blogs in a linguistic sense (although some of them contain occasional posts in other languages). A blogger's origin (ethnicity), nationality (citizenship) and their blog's language do not necessarily overlap. Among bloggers writing in Latvian for example there may be persons of Russian origin and Latvian nationality. There is a blogger of Polish origin and Dutch citizenship writing in Polish (BPL17). Moreover, it is not always clear whether the bloggers actually live in the respective nation-states. In some cases it is clear that they live abroad (e.g. BPL6, BLV16).

For these reasons, it may be incorrect to assume that the geo-political and cultural context of these blogs is constituted by the nation-states of Latvia and Poland; this context could be irrelevant to the lives of some bloggers. It may thus be appropriate to consider the *media environments* rather than national contexts of the analysed blogs. Media environments are 'defined by the media available to people at a particular place and time and by the properties of these media' (Prior, 2007, p. 9). From a critical perspective, the media affect people's perception and evaluation of the world, other people, groups and communities, situations and events (Fowler, 1991). Thus they participate in the construction of what is perceived as objective reality. Shifts in media environments may, in other words, have political and cultural implications (Prior, 2007).

Global developments of media technologies such as cable or satellite television and the internet mean that media environments no longer overlap with national borders, contributing to the emergence of a global 'public sphere' (Richardson & Meinhof, 1999). Participation in this public sphere is however restricted – in terms of costs and skills required by the technologies as well as linguistically. Some young Latvians and Poles speak English fluently and can afford to read electronic versions of American/British broadsheets more frequently than printed newspapers in their mother tongues, which makes them belong to a completely different media environment than their compatriots who speak only one language or do not use the internet.

Additionally, in Latvia the term *media environment* (*mediju telpa*) has been widely used in social sciences and journalism to refer to the presence of Russian-language media, produced both locally and in Russia, and their political and cultural influence on the country (Muižnieks, 2008). Some residents, especially in the east of the country, receive more information from Russian than from Latvian media (so that they belong to the Russian media environment). This could have important consequences for the attitudes of these residents towards LGBTQs.

For all these reasons, it is necessary to be extremely careful when comparing Latvian and Polish data. Not all differences between blogs in these languages can be traced back to national/cultural differences. A previous study (Chojnicka, 2015) based on the same corpus identified some such (textual) differences. The Latvian blogosphere was described as *gay and lesbian* only; bisexual, transgender, queer or feminist blogs – in terms of content and their authors' self-identification – were not found. Many Latvian blogs tended to accept heteronormative and patriarchal validity claims and focus on the description of suffering and loneliness. Polish blogs were more 'angry', provocative and sarcastic; rights were demanded rather than asked for; feminism was – sometimes enthusiastically – supported rather than ignored or resisted (Chojnicka, 2015, p. 239). These differences were attributed to diverging stages of development of LGBTQ/feminist movements in Latvia and Poland. It may be more accurate however to recognise the impact of bloggers' varying media environments, which is the approach taken here.

Theory and Methodology

Patriarchy and *heteronormativity* are seen as manifestations of the same system whereby women as a group are subordinated to men as a group, and whereby heterosexuality is constructed as a compulsory function of the gender order, with sexual transgressions perceived as gender transgressions (e.g. gay men are read as less masculine and lesbians as less feminine) (Rich, 1980). Furthermore, the position of gay men is directly linked to the status of women: the more powerful the patriarchy, the more men who do not conform to the hegemonic masculinity model are persecuted and degraded (Graff, 2010, p. 108).

This chapter uses a corpus of 48 blogs, 29 in Polish and 19 in Latvian, to study discourses that challenge such patriarchal and heteronormative understandings of gender and sexuality (see the full list at the end of this chapter). The blogs were selected informally, using Google search keywords such as *gay* or *queer blog* and following links provided on the blogs already included (Szulc, 2016). While the Polish selection offers an illustrative fragment of a rich blogosphere, and an attempt to represent all possible voices (gay, lesbian, bisexual, trans- and a-gender, feminist), its Latvian counterpart includes all there was to find (which indicates the first serious difference between Latvian and Polish material).

The internet may be considered a 'safe space', which is especially relevant to those groups marginalised within a society's public space. For LGBTQ individuals it combines the 'connected sociality of public space with the anonymity of the closet' (Woodland, 2000, p. 418). Wakeford notes that 'coming out may be easier on-line' (1997, p. 32) and that the internet 'may compensate for the social or geographical isolation of sexual minorities by operating as a medium through which contacts can be more easily facilitated' (1997, p. 31). Importantly for both LGBTQs and feminists in patriarchal societies, blogs 'are another possibility for expression of those belonging to marginalised groups, whose voice is not always compatible with the politics of mainstream culture' (Gruszczyńska, 2007, p. 104). Blogs in particular allow people to articulate and make sense of their identity and experiences, receive support from the community and raise readers' awareness.

Still, it should be noted that opportunities offered by the internet are not equal for everyone: there are technological and cost restrictions on access, linguistic restrictions on participation (e.g. inclusion in the international LGBTQ-friendly media environment depends on one's English skills), while prejudice and homophobia also exist online (Wakeford, 1997).

In terms of methodology, the chapter uses Kress and van Leeuwen's (1990) image grammar and Barthes's (1977) typology of image-text relations – two approaches to semiotics, the study of 'signs' understood as anything 'that stands for something other than itself' (Danesi, 2004, p. 4). Despite some theoretical differences (e.g. Barthes considers language the 'master code' necessary to articulate and explain meanings of other codes, including images, while Kress and van Leeuwen advocate perceiving visual communication as no less important than language, each realising fundamental functions in the dissemination of meaning), the two approaches offer methodological solutions that can be successfully used in conjunction. These solutions are summarised in the following three subsections.

Layout

Layout refers to the arrangement of visual elements on a page in accordance with its horizontal and vertical axis. Kress and van Leeuwen (1990, p. 104) suggest that there is a certain meaning potential to the composition of vertical and horizontal structures. On the vertical axis, top is the 'space of the ideal' – of goals, promises, abstract and general concepts; bottom is the 'space of the real' – of means, products, empirical and specific concepts. On the horizontal axis, the left-hand side represents what is well established, known, understood, implicitly held – the Given; the right-hand side equals what is still to be established, not yet known, not taken for granted, to be made explicit – the New (see Figure 9.1). This theory is applied here to explain the placement of elements common in blogs, i.e. headers, sidebars and the post body space.

The ideal/most highly valued; *the given*	The ideal/most highly valued; *the new*
The real/less highly valued; *the given*	The real/less highly valued; *the new*

Figure 9.1 The meanings of visual structure (after Kress & van Leeuwen, 1990, p. 108).

Image-Text Relations

Kress and van Leeuwen (1990, following Barthes, 1977) propose two main types of structural connections between images and texts:

1 *incorporation*: the integration of textual information within one cohesive image, clearly divided from the surrounding text;
2 *embedding*: the placement of an image (consisting only of visual or both visual and verbal elements) within the text.

There are also two main types of function of these connections:

1 *relay* – the text extends the meaning of the image or vice versa; new and different meanings are added for a full message (e.g. speech balloons in comic strips);
2 *elaboration* – the text elaborates the image or vice versa; the same meanings are restated in a different, e.g. more definite/precise way:
   a *illustration* – the verbal text comes first;
   b *anchorage* – the image comes first (e.g. captions under photographs).

See discussion of Figures 9.3–5 for more details.

Denotation and Connotation

Images used in blogs, quite trivially, represent; they show something. This is their representational, surface meaning. But there is another, more complex and intricate meaning. There must be a reason for including specific visual materials in certain locations of a dissident blog. Consider for instance a transgender blogger's decision to publish their portrait. The photograph represents them, shows what they look like. But it also serves a political purpose, supporting the blogger's agenda of openness and honesty about their gender identity. It may be argued that the photograph symbolises these values. The question of hidden meanings of images is exactly the question of what ideas and values underlie the surface representations.

Following Barthes (1973, 1977), van Leeuwen (2001) suggests conceptualising surface and hidden meanings in terms of denotation and connotation, respectively. Denotation refers to what the image 'is about', while connotation refers to the deeper layer of meaning, the layer of broader concepts, ideas and values of which the represented people, places and things are signs (van Leeuwen, 2001, p. 94).

It is widely recognised that language is a social practice contributing to the reproduction of specific social relations. Images too do not only represent reality but construct it as well. Journalistic photographs for instance have the power of 'naturalising' cultural associations, myths or ideological contents (van Leeuwen, 2001, p. 97). To give an LGBTQ-related example: the mainstream media of a given country may decide always to use similar visual material – for instance photographs of half-naked participants of a gay pride parade – whenever reporting on a gay-related topic. This way a stereotypical image of a gay person – considered to be threatening by many people – is reinforced, and the association of homosexuality with promiscuity and indecency is strengthened. In a country such as Poland, where only 25% of the population know an openly gay or lesbian person (CBOS, 2013, p. 2), it is relatively easy to sell such stereotypes as objective truth (thus keeping the stereotypes naturalised).

In the following, empirical part of the chapter, this combined framework is applied to study the meanings of 1) the layout, 2) image-text relations and 3) the connotative meanings of images used in blogs.

Layout

The most usual blog layout – the visual arrangement of page elements – consists of 1) a header, 2) one/two sidebar(s), and 3) the body space. Some also have 4) a footer. Figure 9.2 illustrates the positions of these elements. The following three subsections consider elements 1) to 3).

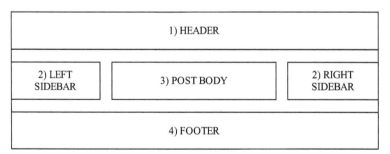

Figure 9.2 Position of blog layout elements.

Header

The header is the most consistent element of blog layout in the corpus (except for the post body space) – 45 blogs have one. Headers function as logos or emblems; their appearance and style are fixed and unchangeable. Thus it is relevant to consider the kind of information about the blog and its author conveyed by headers.

Headers comprise three optional elements – titles, descriptions and illustrations – which can all refer to LGBTQ/feminist issues. When it comes to *titles*, one third of the corpus blogs contain such references. They can be explicit, as in the following examples: *Geju vēstis*, 'Gay news' (BLV5); *Gender.pl* (BPL8); *Les-rodzina*, 'Les-family' (BPL15); *Trans-optymista*, 'Trans-optimist' (BPL25). Titles can also refer to homosexuality through the concept of the closet: *Cilvēks no skapja*, 'Person from the closet' (BLV3); *Wyjdź z szafy razem z nami*, 'Come out of the closet with us' (BPL28). Some titles connect to the topic through names of recognised LGBT organisations or their slogans: *Miłość nie wyklucza*, 'Love does not exclude' (BPL3). Others use terms referring to cast-off/subordinated social groups, re-appropriated from academic discourse – *Subalterns*, 'Subaltern' (BLV17) and *Abiekt*, 'Abject' (BPL2) – or reclaim pejorative words and insults from conservative discourse: *czarownica*, 'witch' (BPL5) and *pedał*, 'fag' (BPL6).

Some titles seem to be intentionally misleading: *Nie-lesbijka*, 'Not-lesbian' (BPL14) conceals a blog by a bisexual, not a heterosexual woman; similarly, the blog *Żona, ja i reszta świata*, 'Wife, me and the rest of the world' (BPL30) is written not by a man but by a woman. Both titles take advantage of prevalent heteronormative binary distinctions – the former between heterosexuality and homosexuality (excluding bisexuality), the latter between gender roles (only a man can have a wife) – challenging them at the same time in a jocular and slightly provocative way. Most titles however are unrevealing, e.g. *Melleņu nakts*, 'Blueberry night' (BLV9) or *Vecā vilka piezīmes*, 'Old wolf's notes' (BLV19).

References to LGBTQs/feminism may also be included in the blog's *description*, e.g. *Katram vajadzīgs savs skapis*, 'Everyone needs their closet' (BLV7). A popular strategy for descriptions is to reclaim terms from conservative discourse, e.g. *Jankas dienasgrāmta, LGBT ziņas, homoseksualitātes propaganda*, 'Janka's diary, LGBT news, homosexual propaganda' (BLV5); *Bo Polska jest lesbą, a ja jej synem pedałem!*, 'Because Poland is a lesbian, and I [am] her son the fag!' (BPL6, fragment); *I'm not feminazi, I just bleed 5 days a month* (BPL22).

Header *illustrations* may work together with titles and descriptions or convey LGBTQ/feminist meanings on their own. Most illustrations are neutral – photographs of landscapes, streets, art reproductions and so on. Only a few seem to support LGBTQ-related titles. For instance, the image in the header of BPL30 used to be[1] a compilation of old-fashioned, black-and-white photographs of women socialising on a beach. Denotatively they show female homosocial friendship networks. Yet in conjunction with the blog title, which already challenges one hetero-norm (heterosexual marriage), they become ambiguous. Connotatively they remind the reader that homosexual fascination is a potential component (though usually taboo stigmatised) of all homosocial relationships, which constitute the very foundation of heteronormative, gender-segregated cultures (hence the [recently abolished] Don't Ask, Don't Tell policy of the American military or marginalisation of homosexuality in male team sports; Graff, 2010).

Interesting are illustrations that convey the blog's topic on their own (no LGBTQ/feminist title/description). To exemplify this, the headers of BLV6 and BLV7 will be considered in more detail. Both blogs have surprisingly similar titles: *Kāda puiša ieraxtu žurnāls, kas **paslēpts** zem matrača*, 'A boy's journal, **hidden** under a mattress' (BLV6); *Kāda puiša **noslēpumu** antresols*, 'A boy's entresol of **secrets**' (BLV7). Note the identical indefinite form of self-reference (*kāds* is a pronoun meaning 'a', 'some'). Its use may indicate the wish to remain anonymous, but it may also serve to universalise and objectify a personal experience. Both titles also convey the meaning of secrecy (the words in bold – a verb and a noun, respectively – have the same root, *-slēp-*).

In contrast to these titles, the headers' illustrations are completely different. BLV6 is a *celebratory* blog – an unapologetic, shameless and frank account of the author's rich, glamorous and carefree sex- and nightlife. Such a construction of the gay lifestyle, not attested in the title, is signified by the header's images: proud, smiling naked men; a disco ball; food (sensual pleasure); a row of naked legs symbolising a promiscuous lifestyle, which may include sex with strangers at a party, and so forth. BLV7, in contrast, is a *normalising* blog, narrating a desexualised, love-based, monogamous gay relationship. Its header consists of images of gay couples at different ages, from childhood to seniority. Their relationships are innocent and pure; all they do is kiss and cuddle. The represented old men do not even touch each other lest they violate two taboos, homosexuality and sexuality among old people.

In BLV6 and BLV7, the header images correspond not to the titles but to the type of discourse each blog represents. Since headers are fixed in position for all posts, they may be interpreted as anchors, guiding the interpretation of all texts. They are visual summaries, reminders of what the given blog is about. And they are normalising (BLV7) and celebratory (BLV6) on their own, independently of texts.

Sidebars

The second element – the sidebar – is only slightly less frequent than the header: 41 blogs have at least one. Sidebars serve the purpose of navigating within the blog (archive, lists of comments, link to a page with information on the author) and outside of it (links to recommended websites, blogs followed by the author, etc.).

Only three blogs in the corpus have images in their sidebars: BPL1, BLV13 and BPL16. In BPL1 the combination of blog title, description and sidebar may be confusing. The title includes one of the most recognisable keywords of liberal discourse (*równość*, 'equality'), suggesting an activist, argumentative blog. The description however insists that the blog should be read as a private journal (references to home, family, privacy). The sidebar, a messy and poorly organised affair, contributes to this confusion. Here some navigational features (recent posts list, pageview counter) alternate with embedded video and audio files, e.g. marriage equality campaign videos.

One of these photographs is from the Warsaw Equality Parade; the presence of the well-known LGBT activist and politician Robert Biedroń and of LGBT symbols make it political. Other photos in turn show same-sex couples with children, in an idealised, romanticised, desexualised manner. They are stylised as private amateur photos taken for a family album, not intended for public viewing. Such a combination of political and intimate, of public and private, sheds some light on the confusing blog description: the connotative message here is that it is impossible to separate the two spheres – they influence each other in essential ways. The private life of same-sex couples in Poland is inextricably linked with politics, as the government refuses to recognise them. Normalising discourse decontextualises representations of this life, ignoring its political dimensions and the whole socio-political framework in which it is immersed; it focuses on daily chores, obligations, joys and little pleasures, ignoring the bigger picture. The strange layout of BPL1 may thus be read as a critique of this normalising, decontextualised discourse. Also, it may justify an assertion that LGBTQ online space is public and private at the same time, not separately and depending on the context (Gruszczyńska, 2007, p. 95).

Images in the right sidebar of BLV13 seem to serve a different function. This blog offers a combination of posts on political and personal topics, all written from the perspective of a confident, assertive lesbian woman with an agenda; this politicised perspective permeates all texts. The sidebar includes, among other things, two image galleries consisting of 1) four photographs of Adèle Exarchopoulos and Léa Seydoux, leading actresses in the film *La Vie d'Adèle*, and 2) fourteen photographs of Erika Linder, an androgynous model. I would argue that these galleries serve a sort of promotional function: they use attractive subjects (actresses/models) to present same-sex love and androgyny or gender ambiguity in a positive light. Such use may pose certain risks, as it perpetuates traditional beauty standards and presents lesbian sex in ways pleasing to heterosexual men. Publishing such images despite these risks may prove that at least some gender dissidents do take the general audience into account as target readers/viewers of their blogs.

Post Body

Only three blogs have no images in their posts: BPL16, BPL19 and BPL28. In the other blogs, two main types of image management may be distinguished. Some posts have images whose function is *supportive* of the text; their embedding seems well motivated and a link between their meanings and textual meanings can easily be established. In other cases, this link is not always obvious and some images give the impression of having been chosen rather randomly, possibly fulfilling a *decorative* function.

In some blogs, an image always precedes the post text, functioning as a kind of emblem distinguishing one post from another – each post has at least one unique, unrepeated 'logo' (e.g. BLV4, BLV12, BPL25, BPL26). Most of the time an effort to link the image's meaning with the post topic is evident. To illustrate this, a post entitled *Par ātru?* ('Too fast?') in BLV4 is accompanied by a picture of a clock with blurred hands, suggesting that they are moving at a (too) high speed.[2] This symbolises moving too fast, which in turn is a metaphor for certain behaviour in a new relationship (being too demanding, too close, etc.) and also the topic of the post.

Other blogs give preference to images of a certain style, creating a kind of image continuity or coherence. For instance, most posts in BLV12 are preceded by photographs of attractive women or lesbian couples engaged in a loving embrace or in sexual activity. In the majority of cases, the photograph matches the post topic: for instance, a photograph of a woman kissing another woman accompanies a post about kissing one's partner before leaving for work in the morning.[3] But the principle of image coherence means that an image matching other images on the blog is more important than an image matching the post text, which may lead to confusing discrepancies. For example, a photograph showing a man sitting in an armchair and two women – one completely naked, the other in underwear – which suggests (a fantasy of) a three-way, accompanies a post about the value of long-lasting, monogamous, faithful relationships and the effort they require.[4]

The following sections on image-text relations and connotation are based on the analysis of images found in the post body space only, and extend the description provided above.

Image-Text Relations

Incorporation

Incorporation refers to the use of text within one cohesive image. Such text can serve the functions of relay or anchorage. To illustrate this, consider Figures 9.3 and 9.4.

The third strip (posted in BPL6[5]) in Figure 9.3 shows a pink 'gender monster' and a priest's head threatening misbehaved children that 'the monster will come for them'. The use of text in comic strips is a prototypical case of relay (Barthes, 1977). It provides new information unavailable in the picture, attributing speech acts to represented characters or describing circumstances of represented actions. In Figure 9.3 the fact that the man is a priest is made clear by a symbolic attribute: his clerical collar. The monster however is not such a salient cultural figure, which is why its identity is explicated by verbal means. Note that the word *dżender* (spelled as it is

Figure 9.3 Example of relay (BPL6) (Image by Łukasz Kowalczuk).

Figure 9.4 Example of anchorage (BPL25).[6]

pronounced in Polish) is highlighted through the size and colour of letters, which mark it as a caption for the monster figure.

Figure 9.4 (a 'meme' by an unknown author, included in a no longer available post in BPL25) is a photograph of a conservative Polish MP, Krystyna Pawłowicz, with a moustache photoshopped to her face. In verbal captions all forms of reference to her are grammatically masculine (*pan poseł*, literally 'mister MP'; *Krystyn* instead of *Krystyna*). Here the text exemplifies anchorage, since these masculine forms convey exactly the same meaning as the moustache. In connotative terms the image criticises Pawłowicz's insistence on using masculine forms of nouns to denote professions, positions, titles and so forth (e.g. *profesor*, *poseł*) when referring to women (including herself) instead of feminine forms (e.g. *profesorka*, *posłanka*). On the political right, masculine forms are universal or neutral while feminine forms are considered pejoratives or unacceptable neologisms. The consistent use of feminine forms with reference to women is what gives away Polish feminists or liberals today.

Embedding

Embedding refers to the use of images within post texts, where they serve the functions of relay or illustration.

Relay could be attested in blog posts where the text and image(s) convey different meanings which support each other. A post in BPL6 may serve as an example. In a text on gays and lesbians in armies across the world[7] one finds an embedded image consisting of two main elements: a map and, underneath, a list of countries ordered according to an assessment of LGBT persons' situation in the army. The image itself is an example of anchorage, since the list of countries functions as the map's legend (it is a textual equivalent of the map). With regard to the post text however the image as a whole provides completely new information, adding content to the post which the text itself does not comprise (relay).

Illustration is exemplified by Figure 9.5 (BPL25, no longer available). Here shapes (visual elements) organise information provided in the form of (textual) nominal phrases into a hierarchical structure (categories falling under the trans gender umbrella). This restates, in an abridged, less detailed but more transparent manner, what the post text has to say (in this case what it means to identify as transgender).

Figure 9.5 Trans gender umbrella (BPL25) (Image by Mel Reiff Hill from *The Gender Book*, www.thegenderbook.com).

In linguistic terms, *trans gender/transgender* is a hypernym that encompasses all words referring to people crossing/challenging traditional gender roles. A hypernym can also be called an 'umbrella term', which invokes the metaphorical use of the expression 'to fall under', i.e. 'to be included in', 'to be classified as'. Figure 9.5 makes apt use of this metaphor: here all hyponyms of *trans gender* indeed *fall* under the umbrella.

Connotation

Images fulfilling the functions of relay and illustration (and, marginally, anchorage) are characterised by a close conceptual relationship to the texts they accompany. They are never mere decorations but serve as visual variants of verbal arguments which advance a certain point of view – visual equivalents of argumentative discourse (supportive function). Many of them are charts, schemas, diagrams and so on. The use of such images is always clearly motivated and occasioned. Unsurprisingly, such pictures are mostly found in blogs classified as *argumentative* (politically involved, activist).

On the other hand, images with a less obvious relationship to the text, carrying out the decorative function, are more often found in *narrative* blogs (personal journals telling stories from the blogger's life). This decorative function however does not imply that they are trivial or devoid of deeper meaning. Decorative images are always symbolic, as in the example of a clock with fast-moving hands.

Connotatively both supportive and decorative images may have very similar effects. Two photographs of kissing (gay) couples from BLV17 and BLV18 can serve as examples. One is an image of an Icelandic singer, Jón Þór Birgisson, in an embrace with his partner, Alex Somers.[8] The image is realistic: supposedly taken at a party, with an amateur camera, it depicts a spontaneous, natural action. Taken at close range, it shows the men's faces and the jumpers they are wearing. The other image shows a couple kissing in a garden pavilion at night, illuminated by hundreds of lights.[9] It is carefully staged, probably taken by a professional. Instead of depicting a real, everyday situation, it shows an ideal romantic moment. It is not realistic, showing authentic people in a specific time and space, but fantastic – out of time and space, presenting a possibility rather than an event which has actually happened. The couple is shown from a distance, which makes recognising their faces – their particularity – impossible.

Kress and van Leeuwen's (1990) Ideal/Real distinction, normally applied to the vertical placement of layout elements, could be extended to compare these two types of images. Here the first photograph represents the Real – the concrete, specific, actual, down-to-earth. The other one represents the Ideal – the goal, promise, possibility, something abstract and general. Both images naturalise and normalise gay love in connotative terms; both argue that 'homosexuals love just as heterosexuals do', thereby conforming to the heteronormative ideal of long-lasting monogamous relationships. But they do so in different ways. The first photograph presents real guys, who are friendly, likeable, normal. They may look a bit awkward and wear ridiculous(ly cute) jumpers, but this only makes them more amiable. The image makes the idea of gay love less threatening. The other photograph represents a cliché of a romantic moment – a moment so perfect and pure that it cannot possibly be associated with anything unnatural, abnormal or disgusting. It is also desirable; everyone is supposed to wish they could participate in it.

These pictures have a strong normalising value. Alternatively, some images serve a celebratory function. People represented in celebratory photographs convey for instance an attitude of openness and pride. They do not look into each other's eyes so as to avoid the viewer's gaze; they look into the camera instead, unashamed, demanding attention. While normalising images are desexualised and romanticised, celebratory ones are erotic, sensual, lush. They show that being gay is fun. Who cares about being 'normal' if life can be an endless party?

Discussion and Conclusion

In terms of layout, most blogs in the corpus conform to the schema in Figure 9.2. The vertical arrangement validates Kress and van Leeuwen's (1990) theory (Figure 9.1): blog headers represent the Ideal/Abstract, while the post body and sidebars represent the Real/Particular. By contrast, the horizontal distinction is not validated. As sidebars contain fixed, unchangeable information, they represent the Given (expected on the left) whereas posts, each constituting original, unique information, represent the New (expected on the right). In the corpus however more blogs have sidebars on the right than on the left of the post body.

A somewhat perplexing result is that most headers do not reflect the blogs' LGBTQ/feminist topics very clearly. Only eighteen titles, eight descriptions and seven illustrations mark such references. Sidebars carry dissident meanings even less frequently. It may be assumed that the blogs' fixed elements (headers and sidebars) are supposed to prevent casual readers from making inferences about their content upon first glance. This confirms the claim that the internet is not an entirely safe space, and while blogs offer LGBTQs the opportunity to express their views freely and anonymously, they grant this possibility to haters and homophobes, too (Gruszczyńska, 2007, p. 105).

Images in blogs have been shown to carry out supportive and decorative functions towards post texts. Supportive images reinforce and emphasise dissident messages constructed with textual means within posts of a mostly argumentative nature. Many decorative images (even if they seem to have been chosen randomly or to keep the blog's style consistent) also support the blog's message, but on a more general level, more independently from concrete posts. Decorative images weave their own story, post after post, presenting LGBTQ lifestyles in normalising or celebratory ways. On the connotative level this is a political function, even if political issues are avoided in the blog's texts.

Thus I am proposing that the analysis of a blog's layout (especially headers) and images offers conclusions which are pertinent to the distinction between private and public spheres. Gruszczyńska (2007) writes that the internet functions interchangeably as a private and a public sphere, depending on the context. However, I agree with Rak (2005, p. 173) that the internet – or at least the blogosphere – carries out private and public functions simultaneously, allowing these spheres to permeate and intertwine with each other. An example is the political function of decorative images in personal blogs discussed above. Also the mixture of photographs illustrating events from private and public life in BPL4 indicates their interconnectedness. The use of indefinite pronouns in the titles of BLV6 and BLV7, furthermore, objectifies and universalises a personal experience, exposing what is often perceived as an individual failure or weakness (shame about one's sexuality) to be a social problem (the effects of a society's homophobia).

In spite of the early optimism brought about by the anonymity and disembodiment of the internet experience – suggesting that it would be possible to live full queer lives online, in agreement with one's 'true' identity – blogging is undeniably embedded within offline institutional and cultural practices (Wakeford, 1997, p. 27). It draws from the same social resources as day-to-day interaction and has not effectively challenged the patriarchal gender order, sexism and heterosexism which bloggers encounter offline (Marwick, 2013). This may perhaps explain the state of the Latvian LGBTQ blogosphere as described at the beginning of this chapter.

At the same time, the most interesting finding of this chapter is the lack of any significant differences in layout and use of images between Latvian and Polish blogs. While textually much more careful and restrictive than Polish blogs, visually the Latvian ones are just as explicit and open in normalising/celebrating LGBTQ lifestyles. The above comments about the private/public nature of blogs in conjunction with the proposed media-environment approach could help to explain why.

Latvia and Poland are similar in terms of the social, cultural and political conditions affecting LGBTQ/feminist activism (the tabooing of sexuality during state socialism, the short history of democracy, difficulties associated with the transition, the lack of civil society, etc.), but Latvia additionally suffers from belonging to the expressly homophobic Russian media environment (see Boklage in this volume). Under such hostile conditions, posting normalising/celebratory images rather than texts may feel safer, as images represent phenomena without the need to name or label them.

It is also possible that the Latvian language has not (yet) developed patterns and repertoires for talking about homosexuality and non-heteronormative lifestyles which the bloggers find satisfactory and useful. Some Latvian bloggers may not know English well enough to be inspired by ways of talking about LGBTQs online in English while having access to visual information (images) provided by these media. It is also possible that they actually do not want to be inspired by foreign discourses. Some researchers have suggested that the 'Western' ways of constructing and labelling LGBTQ identities might not match the reality in 'Central and Eastern Europe' – that many people there may perceive them as foreign or imposed, feeling that they have not been given enough time to develop their own identities and ways of talking about these identities after their states' respective transitions to democracy (Kulpa & Mizielińska, 2011). This means that the lack of activist blogging in Latvian may be attributable to something completely different from a lack of tolerance or weak LGBTQ/feminist movements in the nation-state of Latvia. These issues would definitely merit more attention and consideration in future research projects.

Notes

1. It has been changed to an old-style photograph of two women skiing, which could be analysed in similar terms.
2. http://neatkarigais.net/2014/04/par-atru/, last viewed 6 March 2015.
3. http://naktsizkliedzklusumu.blogspot.de/2014/05/rita-skupsts.html, last viewed 30 October 2015.
4. http://naktsizkliedzklusumu.blogspot.de/2014/04/attiecibu-lielveikals.html, last viewed 30 October 2015.
5. http://dopiskipedala.blox.pl/2014/01/Gender-slowem-roku-2013-kosciola-katolickiego-w.html, last viewed 28 January 2016.
6. In spite of undertaking all reasonable attempts to identify the author of this image, I have been unable to do so. For the other pictures authorisation was obtained from the authors.
7. http://dopiskipedala.blox.pl/2014/03/Za-mundurem-chlopcy-sznurem.html, last viewed 30 October 2015.
8. https://subalterns.wordpress.com/2009/08/05/sis-ir-mans-laikam-jau-virs/, last viewed 6 March 2015.
9. http://vejaskrejejs.blogspot.de/2012/12/priecigus.html, last viewed 30 October 2015.

References

Abramowicz, M. (Ed.) (2007). *Situation of Bisexual and Homosexual Persons in Poland: 2005 and 2006 Report*. Warszawa: Kampania Przeciw Homofobii.

Amnesty International. (2006). *Lesbian, Gay, Bisexual and Transgender Rights in Poland and Latvia*. London: Amnesty International.

Barthes, R. (1973). *Mythologies*. London: Paladin.

Barthes, R. (1977). *Image-Music-Text*. London: Fontana.

CBOS. (2013). *Stosunek do Praw Gejów i Lesbijek oraz Związków Partnerskich*. Warszawa: CBOS.

Chojnicka, J. (2015). Contesting Hegemonic Gender and Sexuality Discourses on the Web: Latvian and Polish Discourses of Gender Dissidents. *CADAAD Journal*, 7(2), 222–242.

Czerwińska, A. & Piotrowska, J. (2009). *20 Lat Zmian - Raport. Kobiety w Okresie Transformacji 1989–2009*. Warszawa: Heinrich Böll Stiftung, Fundacja Feminoteka.

Danesi, M. (2004). *Messages, Signs, and Meanings: A Basic Textbook in Semiotics and Communication.* Toronto: Canadian Scholars' Press.

Fowler, R. (1991). *Language in the News: Discourse and Ideology in the Press.* London: Routledge.

Goffman, E. (1963). *Stigma: Notes on the Management of Spoiled Identity.* New York: Prentice Hall.

Grabowska, M. (2015). Cultural War or Business as Usual? Recent Instances and the Historical Origins of the Backlash against Women's Rights and Sexual Rights in Poland. In Heinrich Böll Stiftung (Ed.), *Anti-Gender Movements on the Rise? Strategising for Gender Equality in Central and Eastern Europe* (pp. 54–64). Berlin: Heinrich Böll Stiftung.

Graff, A. (2010). Niebezpieczne Związki, czyli: Gender – Seksualność – Naród. In J. Kochanowski, M. Abramowicz & R. Biedroń (Eds.), *Queer Studies: Podręcznik kursu* (pp. 125–137). Warszawa: Kampania Przeciw Homofobii.

Gruszczyńska, A. (2007). Living 'la vida' Internet: Some Notes on the Cyberization of Polish LGBT Community. In R. Kuhar & J. Takács (Eds.), *Beyond the Pink Curtain: Everyday Life of LGBT People in Eastern Europe* (pp. 95–115). Ljubljana: Mirovni Institut – Peace Institute.

Habermas, J. (1998). *On the Pragmatics of Communication.* Cambridge: The MIT Press.

Heinrich Böll Stiftung. (Ed.) (2015). *Anti-Gender Movements on the Rise? Strategising for Gender Equality in Central and Eastern Europe.* Berlin: Heinrich Böll Stiftung.

Kress, G. & van Leeuwen, T. (1990). *Reading Images.* Victoria: Deakin University Press.

Kulpa, R. & Mizielińska, J. (Eds.) (2011). *De-Centring Western Sexualities: Central and Eastern European Perspectives.* London: Ashgate.

Locmelis, A. (2002). Sexual Orientation Discrimination in Latvia. In *Sexual Orientation Discrimination in Lithuania, Latvia and Estonia* (pp. 26–53). Vilnius: Open Society Institute, Kimeta Society.

Marwick, A. (2013). Gender, Sexuality and Social Media. In T. Senft & J. Hunsinger (Eds.), *The Social Media Handbook* (pp. 59–75). New York: Routledge.

Muižnieks, N. (Ed.) (2008). *Manufacturing Enemy Images? Russian Media Portrayal of Latvia.* Riga: Academic Press of the University of Latvia.

Novikova, I. (1996). Women's Studies in Latvia. *Women's Studies Quarterly, 24*(1/2), 438–448.

O'Dwyer, C. & Schwartz, K. Z. S. (2010). Minority Rights after EU Enlargement: A Comparison of Antigay Politics in Poland and Latvia. *Comparative European Politics, 8*(2), 220–243.

Prior, M. (2007). *Post-Broadcast Democracy: How Media Choice Increases Inequality in Political Involvement and Polarizes Elections.* Cambridge: Cambridge University Press.

Rak, J. (2005). The Digital Queer: Weblogs and Internet Identity. *Biography, 28*(1), 166–182.

Rich, A. (1980). Compulsory Heterosexuality and Lesbian Existence. *Signs, 5*(4), 631–660.

Richardson, K. & Meinhof, U. H. (1999). *Worlds in Common? Television Discourse in a Changing Europe.* London: Routledge.

Śmiszek, K. & Dynarski, W. (Eds.) (2014). *Gender Recognition in Poland: A Report on Court and Administrative Procedures.* Warsaw: Fundacja Trans-Fuzja, Polskie Towarzystwo Prawa Antydyskryminacyjnego.

Szulc, L. (2014). The Geography of LGBTQ Internet Studies. *International Journal of Communication*, *8*, 2927–2931.

Szulc, L. (2016). Domesticating the Nation Online: Banal Nationalism on LGBTQ Websites in Poland and Turkey. *Sexualities*, *19*(3), 304–327.

van der Molen, I. & Novikova, I. (2005). Mainstreaming Gender in the EU-Accession Process: The Case of the Baltic Republics. *Journal of European Social Policy*, *15*(2), 139–156.

van Leeuwen, T. (2001). Semiotics and Iconography. In T. van Leeuwen & C. Jewitt (Eds.), *Handbook of Visual Analysis* (pp. 92–118). London: Sage Publications.

Wakeford, N. (1997). Cyberqueer. In A. Medhurst & S. R. Munt (Eds.), *Lesbian and Gay Studies: A Critical Introduction* (pp. 20–38). London: Cassell.

Woodland, R. (2000). Queer Spaces, Modem Boys and Pagan Statues: Gay/Lesbian Identity and the Construction of Cyberspace. In D. Bell & B. M. Kennedy (Eds.), *The Cybercultures Reader* (pp. 416–431). London: Routledge.

List of analysed blogs

BLV1. *Ar prieku pa(r) dzīvi.* http://klab.lv/users/puisis/.

BLV2. *Baltais Bērns.* http://baltaisberns.blogspot.com/.

BLV3. *Cilvēks no skapja.* http://skapjcilveks.blogspot.com/.

BLV4. *G*blogs.* http://neatkarigais.net/.

BLV5. *Geju vēstis.* http://veestis.wordpress.com/.

BLV6. *Kāda puiša ieraxtu žurnāls, kas paslēpts zem matrača.* http://zemmatraca.blogspot.com/.

BLV7. *Kāda puiša noslēpumu antresols.* http://antresols.com/.

BLV8. *Kārlis Streips: pārdomas par dzīvi.* http://karlisstreips.blogspot.com/.

BLV9. *Melleņu naktis.* http://mellenunaktis.wordpress.com/.

BLV10. *Mozaīka.* http://mozaikasvalde.blogspot.com/.

BLV11. *Par cilvēku ar lāstu.* http://klab.lv/users/exiled/.

BLV12. *Putekļiem noklātā dvēseles iela.* http://naktsizkliedzklusumu.blogspot.com/.

BLV13. *Rendijas blogs.* http://homosexuality.wordpress.com/.

BLV14. *Skaļi nepateiktais.* http://mareksnroses.blogspot.com/.

BLV15. *Skatiens atslēgas caurumā.* http://ziemciete.blogspot.com/.

BLV16. *Smilinglatvian's blog.* http://smilinglatvian.wordpress.com/.

BLV17. *Subalterns.* http://subalterns.wordpress.com/.

BLV18. *Un skrien VējaSkrējējs gar likteņa jūras malu...* http://vejaskrejejs.blogspot.com/.

BLV19. *Vecā vilka piezīmes.* http://vecaisvilks.blogspot.com/.

BPL1. *Aaaaaa właśnie że równość!* http://katarzynaformela.blox.pl/html.

BPL2. *Abiekt – Obcy penetruje (nie tylko) Internet.* (archived blog) http://web.archive.org/web/20120717232823/http://abiekt.blogspot.com/.

BPL3. *Blog Stowarzyszenia Miłość nie wyklucza.* http://miloscniewyklucza.blogspot.com/.

BPL4. *cHyłKiem i dUszKiem.* http://chylkiem-i-duszkiem.blog.onet.pl/.

BPL5. *Czarownica Zła.* http://czarownicazla.blox.pl/.

BPL6. *Dopiski wkurwionego pedała.* http://dopiskipedala.blox.pl/html.

BPL7. *Dynarski.pl.* http://dynarski.pl/.

BPL8. *Gender.blox.pl.* http://gender.blox.pl/html.

BPL9. *Gierki w mówionego.* http://gierkiwmowionego.blogspot.com/.

BPL11. *Hardcore dla myślących*. http://hardkor.wordpress.com/.

BPL12. *Hyakinthos 1978*. http://hyakinthos1978.blogspot.com/.

BPL13. *Hodowla idei*. http://hodowlaidei.blogspot.com/.

BPL14. *Jednak nie lesbijka*. http://nielesbijka.blox.pl/html.

BPL15. *Les-rodzina blog*. http://les-rodzina.blog.pl/.

BPL16. *Lipshit*. http://lipshitblog.blogspot.com/.

BPL17. *Miłość po 30*. http://www.miloscpo30.net/.

BPL18. *Mr. Dobel*. http://mrdobel.blog.onet.pl/.

BPL19. *Nemst powrót*. http://nemst.blogspot.com/.

BPL20. *Queerpop*. http://queerpop.blogspot.com/.

BPL21. *Scenki*. http://scenki.blogspot.com/.

BPL22. *Szprotest*. http://szprotestuje.wordpress.com/.

BPL23. *This is my truth. Tell me yours*. http://gothmucha.blox.pl/html.

BPL24. *Tramwaj zwany podglądaniem*. http://wtramwaju.blox.pl/.

BPL25. *Trans-optymista*. http://transoptymista.pl/.

BPL26. *Trzyczęściowy garnitur*. http://trzyczesciowygarnitur.blogspot.com/.

BPL27. *Widziane z okna na strychu*. http://zoknanastrychu.blox.pl/html.

BPL28. *Wyjdź z szafy razem z nami*. http://comingout.blox.pl/html.

BPL29. *Z życia heteroseksualistów*. http://heteroseksualisci.blox.pl/html.

BPL30. *Żona, ja i reszta świata*. http://dwiepanie.blox.pl/html.

Part IV

Discourses on and by LGBTQs on Social Media

10 Homosexuality on Dutch and Flemish Facebook Pages

Situational Meanings, Situational Attitudes?

Tim Savenije

As the first two countries to legalise same-sex marriage, the Netherlands and Belgium have a reputation for being extraordinarily LGB-friendly.[1] This assumed LGB-friendliness is confirmed by representative studies showing that the overwhelming majority of Dutch (92%) and Belgian (85%) respondents agree with the statement that gay men and lesbians should be free to live their own lives as they wish (Kuyper, 2015, p. 8). Other findings about the Netherlands and Flanders (the Dutch-speaking part of Belgium that I will discuss in this chapter) also corroborate this LGB-friendly reputation. For instance, only eight percent of Flemish people (Pickery & Noppe, 2007) and four to eight percent of Dutch people (Keuzenkamp, 2010; Keuzenkamp & Kuyper, 2013; Kuyper, 2015) would consider it problematic if their child's school teacher were a homosexual man or woman. And only 1% of Dutch people and 4% of Belgian people indicate that they would feel uncomfortable about having gay or lesbian neighbours (Keuzenkamp, 2010).

Unfortunately, these happy facts do not tell the full story. Persistent incidences of anti-homosexual violence in both the Netherlands and Flanders indicate that homonegativity is an issue that both regions continue to struggle with (Buijs, Hekma & Duyvendak, 2011; D'haese, Dewaele & Van Houtte, 2014; Felten & Schuyf, 2011; Schuyf & Felten, 2012). And while equal-treatment rights regarding inheritance and housing can count on the support of approximately 90% of the population in the Netherlands (Adolfsen & Keuzenkamp, 2006), this is not true for an issue like child adoption. Support for equal rights in this area was found to range between 53% and 69% in the Netherlands (Adolfsen & Keuzenkamp, 2006; Keuzenkamp, 2010; Keuzenkamp & Kuyper, 2013; Kuyper, 2015) and between 40% and 47% in Flanders (Pickery & Noppe, 2007).

Moreover, studies show that acceptance of LGBs is often conditional. Dutch studies have repeatedly concluded that for substantial parts of the population homosexuality is acceptable only if LGBs come out of the closet, are discrete about their homosexual orientation and act in accordance with established gender norms (Buijs et al., 2011; Duyvendak, Bos, Hekma, Mans & Tabarki, 2006; Hekma, Keuzenkamp, Bos & Duyvendak, 2006; Van Lisdonk & Kooiman, 2012). Surveys show that many Dutch people express less tolerance for same-sex couples holding hands and kissing in public than for straight couples doing the same (Keuzenkamp, 2010; Keuzenkamp & Kuyper, 2013; Kuyper, 2015). Flemish studies find that at least gender normativity and being discrete are also important demands made to LGBs by many Flemish people (Dewaele & Vincke, 2009; Pickery & Noppe, 2007; Versmissen, 2011).

All in all, Dutch and Flemish attitudes towards homosexuality seem to be somewhat conflicting. How can it be that a substantial number of people express support for the idea that LGBs should be free to live their lives as they wish, while at the same time supporting (some) legal and informal norms that constrain equal participation of LGBs? Why is it that homosexuality (or certain expressions of it) is sometimes regarded as problematic? And why is it sometimes *not* regarded as problematic?

In order to explore such questions, I studied Dutch and Flemish public debates through an analysis of the comments that Facebook users make about homosexuality on the public Facebook pages of Dutch and Flemish news media. But before moving to the empirical research, let us first look at theoretical work on this topic.

Theoretical Framework: Interpreting Homosexuality

Various scholars have explored why people hold certain opinions about homosexuality. They have done so coming from a variety of disciplines and perspectives. Despite notable differences, the theories which have been put forward have in common that at some point in their explanation they emphasise how people conceptualise homosexuality. Some argue, although in different ways, that homonegative attitudes are connected to people's interpretation of homosexuality as a form of gender deviance (Butler, 1988; Connell & Messerschmidt, 2005; Pharr, 1997; Rubin, 1975; Savenije & Duyvendak, 2013) or as a threat to the family, society or the nation (D'Emilio, 1983; Inglehart & Welzel, 2005; Law, 1986; Mole, 2011). Others believe that more positive attitudes towards homosexuality are intertwined with interpretations of homosexuality as an expression of love (Mol, 2005; Schnabel, 1990) or of the authentic self of specific individuals (Inglehart & Welzel, 2005). Still others think that more positive attitudes should be viewed as a product of resistance against the church (Eeckhout & Paternotte, 2011), as based on the idea that LGBs are a vulnerable group in need of protection (Puar, 2006, 2013) or as rooted in people's interpretation of homopositive attitudes as part of their national identity (Mepschen, Duyvendak & Tonkens, 2010; Mepschen, Duyvendak & Uitermark, 2014).

According to such theoretical explanations, interpretations of homosexuality function as the link between broader (material and/or cultural) societal contexts on the one hand and people's (normative) attitudes towards homosexuality on the other. The broader contexts are believed to cause, imply or encourage certain conceptualisations of homosexuality as well as certain attitudes towards it. Tensions around gender norms or gender inequality for example may lead people to see homosexuality in terms of gender – interpreting it as undesirable gender deviance. If such mechanisms are indeed at work, we can learn which contexts play a role by looking closely at how people interpret and judge (certain expressions of) homosexuality: if, for instance, homosexuality is disapproved of and understood as gender-deviant, this indicates that conservative forces regarding gender norms and perhaps gender inequality are influencing people's attitudes towards homosexuality.

So far little empirical research has been directed specifically at discovering people's interpretations of homosexuality. Much quantitative research of the kind mentioned in the introduction to this chapter asks respondents about the extent to which they agree with (normative) statements, indicating their level of acceptance of, say, 'homosexuality' or 'homosexual men and women'. Yet it is unclear how these respondents perceive such concepts when they answer questions of this sort. The starting point for my analysis therefore is to find out how people interpret concepts like homosexuality and LGBs, and to what extent their interpretations are related to their normative positions vis-à-vis homosexuality or LGBs.

Methods: Researching Interpretations and Attitudes

In order to discover people's interpretations of such concepts, I turn to public debates in the Netherlands and Flanders, the two regions that make up Dutch-speaking Europe. As became clear from the introduction to this chapter, the two are similar in that they can be counted among the world's most progressive regions regarding homosexuality and because substantial parts of their populations express similarly paradoxical attitudes towards homosexuality. This makes the Netherlands and Flanders interesting cases for further study: why is it that even in two of the most explicitly accepting regions in the world, substantial parts of the respective populations support informal and legal norms that constrain equal social participation of LGBs?

Of course, studies also find notable differences between both regions. As demonstrated by the statistics mentioned in the introduction, fewer Flemish (or Belgian) than Dutch respondents tend to express accepting attitudes towards homosexuality. Finding such interregional differences is anything but surprising; based on his research on cross-cultural differences, Geert Hofstede even concluded that 'no two countries [...] with a common border and a common language are so far culturally apart [...] as Belgium and the Netherlands' (Hofstede, 2001, p. 63). Studying two regions which share the same language as well as the pressures that come with being an affluent nation in the centre of Western Europe, yet which are also characterised by strikingly different cultural values, stimulates an awareness of not only the commonalities but also the cultural specificities that play a role in each region's attitudes towards homosexuality. Because of these specificities, I first analysed the Dutch and Flemish data separately. As the results for both regions turned out to be largely similar, I synthesised them only afterwards. Wherever I found cross-regional differences, I mention this in my discussion below. Because of the limited size of this study however more research is necessary before definitive conclusions about such differences can be drawn.

In order to study Dutch and Flemish interpretations and attitudes, I turned to discussions on public Facebook pages. Facebook is an interesting site for research because – like other social media – it has made possible an entirely new type of public debate. By commenting on public Facebook pages, without having to pass by gatekeepers such as news media editors, people from a variety of backgrounds can easily enter into a direct discussion (more direct than in any other debate of this scale) with a large number of other people, whether laymen or experts, outsiders or insiders. As a result, a greater variety of perspectives are likely to be voiced in this type of public debate, including opinions that may not be mediagenic or politically correct, than in discussions taking place in traditional media (Papacharissi, 2015).[2]

The exchange of perspectives on homosexuality that may be found on Facebook provides an interesting data source for other reasons as well. Compared to data gathered through interviews or surveys, the strength of Facebook comments lies in the combination of ecological validity and the elaborateness of people's responses. Thus Facebook comments can potentially provide us with a better understanding of the associations and argumentations which inform people's everyday responses to homosexuality. An obvious limitation is the difficulty of determining how representative the data are: although internet access is widespread in both the Netherlands and Belgium (The World Bank, 2015), not everyone actively uses Facebook, and not all who do read or comment on the Facebook pages of news media. This means that I will be studying the comments of samples of the Dutch and Flemish populations that are unlikely to be representative of these societies as a whole. Some current discourses on homosexuality may therefore be absent from this study. A second drawback of the use of Facebook comments is that the identity of authors is impossible to verify with any certainty.

Because I am interested in understanding mainstream – as opposed to particular subcultural – attitudes towards homosexuality, I studied Facebook pages of well-known news media with a reach and scope that includes all of the Netherlands or all of Flanders. Out of an initial selection of nineteen sources I eventually selected eight news media.

Table 10.1 Selected news media

Type	Netherlands	Flanders
Quality newspaper	De Volkskrant	De Standaard
Popular newspaper	Algemeen Dagblad	Het Laatste Nieuws
Niche newspaper	Reformatorisch Dagblad	*Non-existent*
Quality TV news (public broadcaster)	NOS	VRT
Popular TV news	Hart van Nederland	*Non-existent*

An important aim was to keep the sample manageable while maximising variation in the character of the various media, taking into account that different styles of news reporting may elicit different types of responses. More Dutch than Flemish Facebook pages were selected because the Dutch media landscape is more diverse in types of news media and individual Dutch media attract far fewer Facebook followers on average than Flemish media do. The media were also selected because preliminary research showed that more discussion took place on their Facebook pages than on those of other media, and because comments on these pages more frequently contained argumentations instead of brief expressions of support or disapproval.

One way to study people's interpretations of, and attitudes towards, homosexuality is by analysing the comments that people make directly in response to Facebook posts about homosexuality. For the analysis I will undertake here however, I specifically looked at comments in which homosexuality or LGBs are mentioned even though the original Facebook post does *not* mention these themes. By studying in which contexts and ways commenters insert homosexuality into discussions, I explore the ways in which people themselves understand the concepts of homosexuality, gays, lesbians or bisexuals. What kinds of situations or issues are associated with homosexuality? How are these connected to homosexuality? What does this tell us about how people interpret homosexuality?

I gathered Facebook comments over a period of two weeks in early 2015, using the Netvizz application (Rieder, 2013). This application allowed me to download files that contain user comments. I searched through my data for keywords which suggested that a comment discusses homosexuality or LGBs. The comments in which these keywords were mentioned – 89 on Dutch Facebook pages and 73 on Flemish ones – were selected for further analysis.

I then performed a qualitative content analysis in which comments containing any reference to homosexuality were both my sample units and my observational units (Bryman, 2004; Elo & Kyngäs, 2008; Hsieh & Shannon, 2005). This led to eleven clusters of comments that presented similar interpretations of homosexuality or LGBs.

Although I searched for comments that mentioned male and female homosexuality as well as bisexuality, almost all comments that I found referred to either gay men or '*homo's*'[3] – a term that may sometimes include lesbians but has a predominantly male connotation. On the one hand, this is a significant research finding in itself: bisexuality and female homosexuality are apparently much less salient for many commenters than male homosexuality. On the other, it means that below we will learn more about people's ideas about gay men than about lesbian women or bisexual men and women. In the next section I will discuss how homosexuality or LGBs were understood by commenters, illustrating this with quotations.

Findings: Interpretations and Attitudes

The following discussion is structured into three blocks: the first focuses on interpretations of homosexuality that go hand in hand with supportive attitudes towards LGBs and homosexuality; the second discusses interpretations that are characterised by a certain matter-of-factness which does not call for strong, explicit normative statements; whereas in the third block the focus will be on interpretations that tend to be accompanied by disapproval of LGBs.

Interpretations Connected to Supportive Attitudes

As discussed in the introduction, Dutch and Flemish people sometimes express very inclusive attitudes towards homosexuality and LGBs. Examples of such attitudes – expressions of the belief that LGBs should be free to live their lives as they wish – were also present in the Facebook comments. The need for inclusiveness tended to be asserted in contexts where LGBs were perceived to be under threat. In such situations, commenters tended to respond by sticking up for LGBs.

One entity believed to pose a threat to LGBs is society at large: LGBs are portrayed as a group that is facing discrimination in contemporary Dutch or Flemish society. This interpretation of LGBs is invoked in different contexts. Where such a portrayal of LGBs is accompanied by a clear normative position, the position is a supportive one. On a Dutch page for example, a news article is posted which reports about television viewers' disappointment with a not-so-talkative lesbian participant of a televised dating show. One commenter argues that people are overreacting and rushes to the participant's defence:

> homosexuals are probably so reserved when it comes to showing their affection among each other because it is not being tolerated in the Netherlands. Holding hands in the streets: impossible. And especially on TV, in front of so many people, no, they are on their guard...

Religion – both specific religions and religion in general – is a second presumed 'enemy' of LGBs. Various commenters attribute homonegative stances, as well as other conservative ideas, to religion and religious people. In line with the theoretical work of Eeckhout and Paternotte (2011), their comments present these conservative and homonegative ideas as a disqualification of religion: liberal attitudes are equated with qualities such as benevolence, love, respect and mildness, whereas religions or religious interpretations are portrayed as possessing the opposite qualities.

This interpretation of LGBs as suffering from religious homonegativity was invoked in discussions about posts referring to religious extremism or to violence assumed to be religiously motivated. For example, in response to a post about violent religious extremism, one commenter argues that 'religion is a big cause of suffering' for it leads to young girls being abused, mutilated and murdered, and to 'homosexuals hating their own sexual orientation so much that they choose celibacy as a priest (a kind of escape) only to wind up groping 14-year-old altar boys when, after years of self-repression, they can't restrain themselves any longer'.

The idea that LGBs suffer from religious intolerance is so pervasive in the Netherlands and Flanders that even religious commenters seem to feel compelled to deal with it. They do so by distancing their own religion or religious interpretations from homonegative positions. In response to the news about an attack on a synagogue in Copenhagen which presumably was religiously motivated, a commenter on the Facebook page of a Flemish news medium writes:

> I also wish the Jews much strength – they are usually the targets and the victims – because they too are your fellow people. But because I am a Christian I prefer the word 'neighbour'. Love your neighbour like yourself. No distinction: woman, man, child, gay, lesbian or of whatever nationality.

Commenters sometimes refer to religion or religious people in general. At other times they refer specifically to Christianity or Islam. The latter was repeatedly the case following news items discussing Islamic extremism or violence that was known or suspected to be motivated by Islamic beliefs. Here the presumed negative attitudes of the Islamic religion and/or Muslims towards homosexuals, and the presumed attacks of Muslims on homosexuals, were presented as reasons for the exclusion and discrimination of Muslims.

It is important to note that not only homosexuals were perceived as victims of Muslims: they shared this role with other groups featuring in the same comments, such as Christians, Yazidis, Shi'ite Muslims and especially Jews and women. One commenter on the page of a Flemish news medium for example responds to a report about terrorist attacks in Copenhagen by providing a hyperlink to an article in which it is reported that half of the

Belgian Muslims do not want homosexual friends or do not trust Jews. To this hyperlink s/he adds the comment that 'this "half" has to leave the country'. The interpretation of LGBs as a group under threat from Muslims or Islam can be understood as an expression of the homonationalist dynamics which has been described in recent years by various authors (Mepschen et al., 2010; Mepschen et al., 2014; Puar, 2006, 2013).

In what can be seen as a variation on such homonationalism, the role of the inimical Other was not played by Islam or Muslims but by the Russian president, Vladimir Putin. This association occurred only in the Dutch data. Here again homonegativity was presented as a disqualifying feature. And once again homonegativity figured as only one reason among others to condemn the ideological opponent. An example will illustrate this: in a discussion about international politics, a commenter is accused of having a 'Putin obsession'. The commenter inquires what is being meant by this:

> the fact that I disapprove of a country like Russia arming 'separatists' and unthinkingly annexing parts of a sovereign country? Yes, in that respect I am quite anti-Putin. Apparently, right-wing boys like you think his acts towards opposition members, homosexuals, dissidents and the taking down of commercial airplanes are fantastic, don't you?

Interpretations Not Connected to Strong Normative Statements

The interpretations discussed so far go hand in hand with supportive attitudes towards homosexuality and LGBs. A number of other interpretations of homosexuality however do not coincide with any strong and explicit expressions of normativity.

This is for instance the case where homosexuality is understood as a self-evident aspect of variation within the human (and sometimes animal) species. Where this occurs the underlying assumption seems to be that LGBs self-evidently and legitimately have a place in society. Such a conceptualisation of homosexuality can be understood as being in line with Inglehart and Welzel's (2005, p. 7) theory that 'in post-industrial societies with advanced welfare institutions [...] more room is given to individual self-expression', leading to greater acceptance of homosexuality, among other things.

In my data, homosexuality was mentioned as a self-evident aspect of diversity almost solely in contexts where either the focus of the news is on some other type of diversity or a news item is – at least in the eyes of some commenters – heteronormative. An example of the former is found in response to a Dutch report about a trans man who has been ostracised by his son. One commenter responds:

> parents always have to accept their children the way they are, but one cannot ask respect for one's choice the other way round??!! A bit inconsistent, isn't it? Imagine that the son came out as gay: would he have liked to get such responses from his parents??!!!

An example of a news item perceived as heteronormative is a Flemish Facebook post that reads: 'A man does not have to continue providing for his wife after divorce, says British judge'. One commenter points out the heteronormativity of this post by writing: 'We are a married gay couple... uhm... who should pay alimony to whom in our case?? Would love to know that before I run off with "a young thing"... [name] haha'.

Two other interpretations of homosexuality, or specifically of what it means to be a gay man, were not connected to explicit normative positions. The first is the idea that gay men have a well-developed sense of fashion. In response to the news on a Flemish page that Neil Patrick Harris hosted a part of the Academy Awards ceremony in his underwear, one commenter replied that 'one would expect nicer underwear from a gay man'.

The second idea is that gay men have little interest in, or appreciation for, female bodies. This was brought up in cases where (mostly naked) female bodies were discussed. When commenters identify themselves as gay men, they use this conceptualisation to clarify their specific 'gay' perspective on matters. For instance, when a Dutch news medium announces that a cable company has decided to substitute a straight porn channel for foreign public television channels, one commenter responds that it is of no use to him since he is gay.

When presumably straight commenters refer to the idea that gay men have little appreciation for female bodies, they do so by jokingly suggesting that someone must be gay if they fail to appreciate naked or scarcely dressed female bodies. This happened for instance in response to the news that people used tape to hide the breasts of a naked woman who was pictured on a commercial poster in Amsterdam. Commenters jokingly suggested that homosexuals must have done this, or that people from Amsterdam are all gay. Although such remarks are relatively benign, teasing others for supposedly being gay does of course suggest that these commenters value homosexuality at least somewhat less than heterosexuality.

Interpretations Connected to Disapproving Attitudes

This brings us almost automatically to interpretations which coincide with more negative attitudes. One objection that is sometimes raised is not strictly about homosexuality but about sexual orientation in general: the idea seems to be that one's sexual orientation is or should be unchanging. Failure to live up to this demand of a stable sexual orientation can elicit disapproval. This is revealed by comments about the private life of female celebrities who are believed to have 'suddenly' changed their sexual orientation. The direction of the change – whether from a heterosexual relationship to a lesbian one or the other way round – seemed to be less the issue than the change per se. Such disapproval can be regarded as evidence for D'Emilio's (1983) theory that homosexuals are scapegoated for the instability of modern-day family life, even though this instability is in reality caused by the implications of a capitalist economic system.

In various contexts LGBs were understood as a group which demands too much attention. This idea is sometimes raised in a light-hearted manner, for example when a commenter refers to debates about making the world of soccer more inclusive to gay men by wondering whether the pink outfits of a Belgian team were chosen in order to encourage soccer players to come out of the closet.

Other comments however show considerably more irritation. A case in point are some of the comments made in response to a Dutch article about a lonely swan which, after its partner died, is to be coupled with another swan. The Facebook post adds that since both swans are male there is no chance that they will find love again. After a number of commenters express their surprise at people assuming animals cannot be gay or bisexual, other commenters sigh that 'not everyone is gay' and 'not everything and everyone is gay, even in swan land'.

As discussed earlier, Dutch news items about President Putin or Russia sometimes triggered interpretations of homosexuals as a group that was being threatened by the Russian president. Some commenters responded differently though. The posts on a Dutch Facebook page about the murder of Russian politician Boris Nemtsov also led to responses that presented gay men as Putin's 'evil opponents' – either as a group which is running an active and unjustified campaign against Putin or as a group of perverted criminals who would deservedly be punished by Putin but are protected by the Dutch government. The attitude towards gay men expressed in these comments is one of contempt. In response to the accusation from other commenters that Putin is anti-gay, someone for instance replies that Putin 'is no hater of homosexuals. People wake up! Only propaganda from the NATO!! You are really Sandmen and you believe the MSM'. Here MSM (an abbreviation for men who have sex with men) seem to be understood as a group which is spreading false anti-Putin propaganda. In another comment the Dutch mainstream media are accused of spreading such propaganda and Putin's policies are defended, for example by claiming that – unlike the Dutch government – he knows how to handle criminals. The commenter presents a homosexual man as an example of the perverted criminals against whom Putin is fighting a justified battle.[4]

Other comments depict male homosexuality as signifying a cluster of qualities that includes unmanliness, lack of toughness, weakness and whininess. These qualities seem to be referred to whenever male homosexuality is used as an insult. This happened in a variety of contexts. In response to an article about the enormous costs of union strikes that took place in Belgium, one commenter wrote that 'if the government gives in to these ridiculous strikes, then [...] this government is just as ridiculous and faggy as all our previous governments'. And following the news on a Flemish page that a beer brand was changing its name, one commenter wrote that the new name 'does not seem ideal for the real fan: the hard-core boozer, not the festival gay who drinks only two crates per year'.

Insults of this sort also pop up in the context of Dutch and Flemish soccer, a sphere in which virility is celebrated and where it thus makes sense to insult others by calling their virility into question. Many groups, such as football fans, football players and hooligans, were 'accused' of being gay. The accusation of gayness as a 'de-masculinising' insult is made very explicit by a commenter who does not like football and is told by other commenters to shut up if he doesn't see 'the beauty of the game':

> Beauty of the game? Do you mean those 44 naked legs? I decide for myself whether or not I say something about a faggot's game. Ice hockey, that is a men's game. To play it you also don't need a year of drama education in order to fall in the right faggy way to persuade the referee-woman to award you a free kick. If you fall in an ice-hockey match, you get a couple of extra hits. That's how a men's sport rolls. Football is for pussies.

This connotation of male homosexuals with unmanliness can be regarded as evidence for the idea, prominent in many theories, that homonegativity is the result of homosexuality's incompatibility with established gender norms (Butler, 1988; Connell & Messerschmidt, 2005; Demetriou, 2001; Law, 1986; Pharr, 1997; Rubin, 1975; Savenije & Duyvendak, 2013). Some of these theories also emphasise how specifically the idea of homosexual *visibility* is perceived as problematic because of its potential to undermine established gender norms. The conceptualisation of homosexuals as a group that demands too much attention can be seen as further evidence for such a dynamic.

Finally, comments expressing the strongest condemnation of gay men presented a combination of two interpretations of homosexuality discussed earlier: the idea that fashion is the domain of gay men and the idea that gay men have little appreciation for the female body. In isolation these two ideas were not accompanied by very outspoken opinions about LGBs. In combination, however, they sometimes were.

Again context seems to matter. When it was reported on the Facebook page of a Dutch news medium that the fashion model Doutzen Kroes would no longer be working for the brand Victoria's Secret, one commenter jokingly combined both interpretations of homosexuality by suggesting that the creative director of the brand, who announced the news, was probably gay. Other commenters however explicitly combined the two notions into the idea that gay men are imposing an unhealthy beauty ideal on women. This framing of gay men was evoked only by a Flemish news medium reporting on a fashion magazine which had come under fire for displaying an anorectic female model on its cover. Commenters on this news item expressed a strong condemnation of gay men in the fashion industry. One of them writes:

> I have nothing against homosexuals, but I do have something against the fact that they want a woman to look like a man!! They decide what

the models who present their collections on the catwalk should look like! Usually these are girls who don't even need to wear a bra because they don't even have breasts!

These commenters interpret gay men as being in charge of the fashion industry and as disliking female bodies, understood as curvy bodies. Condemnation follows because such gay men are believed to be using their powers to promote an unhealthy female beauty ideal. Some commenters even extended this condemnation to all gay men and their supposed misogyny in general.

Discussion and Conclusion: The Importance of Context?

In order to gain more insight into the backgrounds of Dutch and Flemish people's seemingly paradoxical stances towards homosexuality and LGBs, I assessed how Facebook commenters conceptualise homosexuality and LGBs, and how these conceptualisations are in turn related to the attitudes towards homosexuality that commenters express. Aside from my being able to establish eleven clusters of meaning given to homosexuality, three other findings stand out.

Firstly, my analysis shows that the immediate context (the topic of the news item under discussion) significantly directs which interpretations of homosexuality or LGBs are presented in the comments. News that involves religious extremism or religiously motivated violence tends to lead to comments framing LGBs as a group which is being threatened by religion or religious people. Discussions about soccer tend to evoke comments in which gay men are portrayed as unmanly.

Secondly, people's interpretations are in turn intimately correlated to the normative stances being taken vis-à-vis homosexuality or LGBs. If commenters present LGBs as a group that is being discriminated against, attacked or threatened, then they tend to stick up for LGBs and advocate accepting attitudes towards them. But if commenters interpret gay men as unmanly, disapproving attitudes towards them are expressed.

A third observation is that in many cases the main conflict discussed in the comments was hardly about homosexuality. It was for instance between President Putin and the West, between women and the fashion industry or between people who like soccer and people who don't. These dichotomies constituted the most salient distinctions between what was defined as us and them, and – typically coinciding with this opposition – good and bad. Mentioning homosexuality was in such cases instrumental to building arguments about utterly different issues.

So how did LGBs and homosexuality become involved in such arguments? It would seem that, based on the available associations between LGBs or homosexuality on the one hand and a given topic of discussion on the other, homosexuality or LGBs can become part of all sorts of discussions. This can be as a weapon (e.g. when a homonationalist self-image is utilised to disqualify a presumably homonegative Other), as scapegoats (e.g. when gay men are believed to be responsible for the promotion of unhealthy beauty ideals) or as collateral damage (e.g. when commenters insult football fans by calling their masculinity into question through labelling them as gay). The observation that LGBs in many cases share their 'supporting role' with other groups, such as Jews, women and Russian dissidents, emphasises the instrumentality of the attitudes that people express about LGBs in such instances.

What do these observations tell us about the relationships between the immediate contexts, the ways in which people conceptualise homosexuality or LGBs, and people's attitudes towards homosexuality or LGBs? Do certain contexts trigger certain interpretations, which in turn lead to certain normative stances? Or is it the case rather that people already hold certain relatively stable, if sometimes contradictory, opinions about homosexuality or LGBs, which they tend to express only if the context allows for an interpretation that fits their already existing attitude? Or are not only people's attitudes but also their interpretations of homosexuality stable, and do they comment only in contexts that match their interpretations?

Although the statistics reviewed in the introduction to this chapter suggest that the attitudes of many people are not unambiguous, it is impossible to draw definitive conclusions about these questions based on the current study. After all, we do not know if commenters using a certain interpretation and taking a certain position in one discussion would present different perspectives in discussions about other aspects of homosexuality.

The findings nevertheless suggest an explanation for the apparent contradictions in Dutch and Flemish people's aggregated attitudes towards homosexuality and LGBs: these attitudes might appear to be paradoxical because what people say about homosexuality does not always express stable attitudes towards a coherent concept. Instead the findings suggest that depending on the context various issues or conflicts are of greater importance to commenters than the issue of homosexuality, and that this results in people expressing (and perhaps sincerely embracing) situationally expedient framings of homosexuality.

To be very clear about this, I am not suggesting that the subject of a news message fully determines these interpretations and attitudes. On the contrary, similar contexts sometimes lead to different interpretations of, and very different attitudes towards, homosexuality. A possible explanation is that different commenters have different stakes in the conflicts under discussion; some people may for example feel more loyalty to the West whereas others feel more loyalty to Russia.

Such situational dynamics would not only explain the findings of this study, but could potentially also explain the paradoxical attitudes of Dutch and Flemish people towards homosexuality and LGBs more generally. Similar dynamics could be at work after all in everyday life and when people fill out social-science surveys: survey questions about same-sex couples kissing may make salient different beliefs about LGBs than questions about inheritance rights.

Yet one question still remains: why, out of an infinite number of theoretical options, are certain interpretations of LGBs available to people? Why do people associate gay men with undesirable unmanliness? Why do they view LGBs as a group they should stick up for because of the religious intolerance they face? Are people's distinctions, interpretations and attitudes completely situationally defined? Or are there cultural templates (a repertoire of 'practical schemas', as Bowen et al. (2014) would call them) related to homosexuality, minority groups in general or even broader notions that, depending on the circumstances, they pick from? And if so, how do these cultural templates come about?

In my discussion of findings based on a sample of Facebook comments, I have noted that certain conceptualisations of LGBs can be understood as evidence for dynamics expounded in extant theories. These theories suggest that social processes (although they disagree about *which* social processes) related to gender norms, homonationalism, anti-religious sentiments, the instability of families and the ascendance of self-expression values can help to account for people's attitudes towards homosexuality. Yet my study also found interpretations of LGBs that cannot so easily be connected to extant theories. If we believe that contemporary Dutch and Flemish conceptualisations of homosexuality are not completely situational but are related to the broader societal context, we need both more empirical studies to achieve a fuller picture of how people perceive LGBs and a theoretical model to integrate the various sources of these perceptions.

Notes

1. This chapter focuses on attitudes towards homosexuality. Therefore, I write about the groups that are identified based on their specifically (although not necessarily exclusively) homosexual identities: LGBs.
2. This is not to say that no views might be excluded from such discussions: Facebook can remove content that violates their community standards (Facebook, 2015).
3. Translated in the quotations in this chapter as 'homosexuals'.
4. The pro-Putin comments raise suspicions about the authors of these messages. One reason for this is the use of the abbreviations NATO and MSM in one of the comments. The typical word for NATO in Dutch is NAVO, and the use of the term MSM in the Netherlands is rare outside of sexual health promotion. Moreover, the references in another comment to a variety of issues – to Joris Demmink as a gay man (instead of a suspected paedophile), to the consent Putin has given to the construction of the largest mosque in Europe (presented as evidence that Putin is not anti-Islamic) and to a (presumably fair) deal Putin is said to have offered to Russian oligarchs – seem rather far removed from a typical Dutch frame of reference. These comments in particular remind us of the methodological limitation of a Facebook sample where we do not know who the authors are nor whether comments are personal expressions of opinion or perhaps commissioned by others.

References

Adolfsen, A. & Keuzenkamp, S. (2006). Opinieonderzoek onder de Bevolking. In S. Keuzenkamp, D. Bos, J. W. Duyvendak & G. Hekma (Eds.), *Gewoon Doen: Acceptatie van Homoseksualiteit in Nederland* (pp. 27–56). Den Haag: Sociaal en Cultureel Planbureau.

Bowen, J. R., Bertossi, C., Duyvendak, J. W. & Krook, M. L. (2014). *European States and Their Muslim Citizens: The Impact of Institutions on Perceptions and Boundaries*. New York: Cambridge University Press.

Bryman, A. (2004). *Social Research Methods: Second Edition*. New York: Oxford University Press.

Buijs, L., Hekma, G. & Duyvendak, J. W. (2011). 'As Long as They Keep Away from Me': The Paradox of Antigay Violence in a Gay-Friendly Country. *Sexualities,* 14(6), 632–652. doi:10.1177/1363460711422304.

Butler, J. (1988). Performative Acts and Gender Constitution: An Essay in Phenomenology and Feminist Theory. *Theatre Journal, 40*(4), 519–531. doi:10.2307/3207893.

Connell, R. W. & Messerschmidt, J. W. (2005). Hegemonic Masculinity: Rethinking the Concept. *Gender and Society, 19*(6), 829–859.

D'Emilio, J. (1983). Capitalism and Gay Identity. In A. Snitow, C. Stansell & S. Thompson (Eds.), *Powers of Desire: The Politics of Sexuality* (pp. 100–113). New York: Monthly Review Press.

D'haese, L., Dewaele, A. & Van Houtte, M. (2014). *Geweld tegenover Holebi's– II: Een Online Survey over Ervaringen met Holebigeweld in Vlaanderen en de Nasleep Ervan (Tweede Tussentijds Rapport – Februari 2014)*. Antwerpen: Steunpunt Gelijkekansenbeleid.

Demetriou, D. S. (2001). Connel's Concept of Hegemonic Masculinity: A Critique. *Theory and Society, 30*(3), 337–361.

Dewaele, A. & Vincke, J. (2009). *Het Discours van Jongeren over Man-Vrouw Rolpatronen en Holebiseksualiteit: Over Flexen, Players en Metroseksuelen*. Antwerpen: Steunpunt Gelijkekansenbeleid.

Duyvendak, J. W., Bos, D., Hekma, G., Mans, L. & Tabarki, F. (2006). Van Homo- en Lesbozijde Bekeken: Het Algemene Beeld. In S. Keuzenkamp, D. Bos, J. W. Duyvendak & G. Hekma (Eds.), *Gewoon Doen: Acceptatie van Homoseksualiteit in Nederland* (pp. 80–110). Den Haag: Sociaal en Cultureel Planbureau.

Eeckhout, B. & Paternotte, D. (2011). A Paradise for LGBT Rights? The Paradox of Belgium. *Journal of Homosexuality, 58*(8), 1058–1084. doi:10.1080/00918369. 2011.598414.

Elo, S. & Kyngäs, H. (2008). The Qualitative Content Analysis Process. *Journal of Advanced Nursing, 62*(1), 107–115.

Felten, H. & Schuyf, J. (2011). *Zoenen Is Gevaarlijk: Onderzoek naar Geweld tegen Lesbische Vrouwen*. Utrecht: Movisie.

Hekma, G., Keuzenkamp, S., Bos, D. & Duyvendak, J. W. (2006). Samenvatting en Slotbeschouwing. In S. Keuzenkamp, D. Bos, J. W. Duyvendak & G. Hekma (Eds.), *Gewoon Doen: Acceptatie van Homoseksualiteit in Nederland* (pp. 221–245). Den Haag: Sociaal en Cultureel Planbureau.

Hofstede, G. (2001). *Culture's Consequences: Comparing Values, Behaviors, Institutions and Organizations Across Nations*. London: Sage Publications.

Hsieh, H.-F. & Shannon, S. E. (2005). Three Approaches to Qualitative Content Analysis. *Qualitative Health Research, 15*(9), 2177–2188.

Inglehart, R. & Welzel, C. (2005). *Modernization, Cultural Change, and Democracy: The Human Development Sequence*. Cambridge: Cambridge University Press.

Keuzenkamp, S. (2010). De Houding van Nederlanders tegenover Homoseksualiteit. In S. Keuzenkamp (Ed.), *Steeds Gewoner, Nooit Gewoon: Acceptatie van Homoseksualiteit in Nederland* (pp. 31–53). Den Haag: Sociaal en Cultureel Planbureau.

Keuzenkamp, S. & Kuyper, L. (2013). *Acceptatie van Homoseksuelen, Biseksuelen en Transgenders in Nederland 2013*. Den Haag: Sociaal en Cultureel Planbureau.

Kuyper, L. (2015). *Wel Trouwen, Niet Zoenen: De Houding van de Nederlandse Bevolking tegenover Lesbische, Homoseksuele, Biseksuele en Transgender Personen 2015*. Den Haag: Sociaal en Cultureel Planbureau.

Law, S. A. (1986). Homosexuality and the Social Meaning of Gender. *Wisconsin Law Review*, 187–235.

Mepschen, P., Duyvendak, J. W. & Tonkens, E. H. (2010). Sexual Politics, Orientalism and Multicultural Citizenship in the Netherlands. *Sociology: The Journal of the British Sociological Association, 44*(5), 962–979. doi:10.1177/0038038510375740.

Mepschen, P., Duyvendak, J. W. & Uitermark, J. (2014). Progressive Politics of Exclusion: Dutch Populism, Immigration and Sexuality. *APSA Migration and Citizenship Newsletter*.

Mol, A. (2005). Het Leven met Technieken voorbij de Mythe van de Rationaliteit. *Tijdschrift voor Humanistiek, 6*(23), 70–76.

Mole, R. (2011). Nationality and Sexuality: Homophobic Discourse and the 'National Threat' in Contemporary Latvia. *Nations and Nationalism, 17*(3), 540–560.

Papacharissi, Z. (2015). Toward New Journalism(s). *Journalism Studies, 16*(1), 27–40.

Pharr, S. (1997). *Homophobia: A Weapon of Sexism*. Berkeley: Chardon Press.

Pickery, J. & Noppe, J. (2007). Vlamingen over Homo's: Loopt het Beleid Voorop? Attitudes tegenover Holebi's en Holebiseksualiteit in Vlaanderen. In J. Pickery (Ed.), *Vlaanderen Gepeild! Studiedag 18 September 2007* (pp. 199–224). Brussel: Vlaamse Overheid.

Puar, J. K. (2006). Mapping US Homonormativities. *Gender, Place & Culture: A Journal of Feminist Geography, 13*(1), 67–88.

Puar, J. K. (2013). Rethinking Homonationalism. *International Journal of Middle East Studies, 45*(2), 336–339. doi:10.1017/S002074381300007X.

Rieder, B. (2013). *Studying Facebook via Data Extraction: The Netvizz Application*. Paper presented at the 5th Annual ACM Web Science Conference, New York.

Rubin, G. (1975). The Traffic in Women: Notes on the 'Political Economy' of Sex. In R. R. Reiter (Ed.), *Toward an Anthropology of Women* (pp. 157–210). New York: Monthly Review Press.

Savenije, T. & Duyvendak, J. W. (2013). De Relatie tussen Opvattingen over Gender en Homoseksualiteit: Een Casestudy van *De Groene Amsterdammer* sinds 1911. *Sociologie, 9*(3–4), 317–343.

Schnabel, P. (1990). Het Verlies van de Seksuele Onschuld. *Amsterdams Sociologisch Tijdschrift, 17*(2), 11–50.

Schuyf, J. & Felten, H. (2012). Geweld tegen Lesbische Vrouwen: Een Kwalitatieve Studie. *Tijdschrift voor Seksuologie, 36*(4), 241–249.

Van Lisdonk, J. & Kooiman, N. (2012). Biseksualiteit: Vele Gezichten en Tegelijkertijd Onzichtbaar. In S. Keuzenkamp, N. Kooiman & J. Van Lisdonk (Eds.), *Niet Te Ver uit de Kast. Ervaringen van Homo- en Biseksuelen in Nederland* (pp. 78–99). Den Haag: Sociaal en Cultureel Planbureau.

Versmissen, D. (2011). *Zzzip²: Onderzoek naar de Levenskwaliteit van Vlaamse Holebi's*. Antwerpen: Steunpunt Gelijkekansenbeleid.

The World Bank. (2015). Internet Users (per 100 People). Retrieved from http://data.worldbank.org/indicator/IT.NET.USER.P2?order=wbapi_data_value_2014+wbapi_data_value+wbapi_data_value-last&sort=desc.

11 Gay the Correct Way

Mundane Queer Flaming Practices in Online Discussions of Politics

Jakob Svensson

This chapter focuses on political discussions in an LGTBQ community online. Today at least 100 million people regularly participate in online communities (Kozinets, 2011). LGBTQs were particularly quick to embrace the internet and its affordance of time-space compression and anonymity (Szulc & Dhoest, 2013). Young LGBTQs, often feeling geographically and emotionally isolated, turned to the internet as a somewhat safe space to explore their sexual identities among supportive and like-minded others. Hence researchers have underlined the potential of establishing online spaces of belonging for people identifying as L, G, B, T or Q (see, e.g., Campbell, 2004; Wakeford, 1997). Community, spatiality, identity, structure and agency issues have been discussed in academia (see O'Riordan & Phillips's 2007 anthology *Queer Online*), but also surveillance, gay-bashing, flaming and hate speech (Campbell, 2004; Kuntsman, 2007).[1] Nevertheless, Karl (2007) argues that new media studies show a lack of engagement with non-normative identities. This chapter, and indeed this whole section of the volume, addresses this perceived lack.

My contribution to the study of non-normative identities online has focused on political participation in the Swedish LGBTQ (mainly dating) community Qruiser (see Svensson, 2013, 2014a, 2014b, 2015). These studies have been justified with reference to theories of *cultural participation*, political participation in a *cultural public sphere*, i.e. a site of popular culture becoming a public sphere because it offers images and symbols which evoke emotions and affective investments that constitute reasons for participating politically (see Hermes, 2006). As such, Hermes's account is a critique of Habermas's (1989) more narrow and communicatively oriented norms of participation and public sphere. Dahlgren and Alvares's (2013) delineation between engagement and participation, while it simultaneously underlines their mutual interdependence, can also be understood from a cultural participation perspective. According to these authors, engagement is the *subjective* requirement for participation, a sense of personal involvement in the questions of political life. In relation to Qruiser, I argue that the communicative exploration of sexual identity online may constitute the subjective requirement for political participation, not least since affective communication helps us think reflexively about ourselves, our life situations and how to navigate the society in which we find ourselves (see McGuigan, 2005). Qruiser may thus be understood as a cultural public sphere where political participation and exploration of sexual identities intersect. In other words, identifying as L, G, B, T or Q may constitute the subjective require-ment for engaging in political discussions, making such participation sub-jectively meaningful.

In this chapter, the aim is to understand the role(s) of sexual identity when users participate in political discussion on Qruiser. Perceiving political participation as important, and given arguments within the field of polit-ical communication that we should broaden our scope beyond realms of institutionalised politics when studying political participation (see, e.g., Carpentier, 2011; Wright, 2012), this becomes an important study. As will become apparent in the next section, the political discussions on Qruiser I sampled were conflictual and full of flaming practices. The question this chapter seeks to answer is: what roles, if any, did sexual identity play when engaging in such conflictual participation? In order to answer this, I will propose an analytical framework for identity negotiation, flaming practices as deep play and culturally embedded performances of queerness online. But first I will examine the setting, LGTBQ rights in Sweden, the Qruiser platform and how users discussed politics there.

Setting

This study is set in Sweden and the online community Qruiser. Sweden is currently considered among the most progressive countries in the world regarding LGBTQ rights. Yet it was not until 1944 that sexual intercourse between adults of the same sex was legalised, and the medical classifica-tion of homosexuality as a mental illness lasted until 1979. Discrimination on the basis of sexual orientation, gender identity and expression has been banned since 1987. In 1995, homosexuals received the right to register part-nerships, legislation that was withdrawn in 2009 when the marriage act became (legally) gender-neutral. In 2003, homosexuals were given the right to adopt children and, in 2013, forced sterilisation of transgendered people when undergoing gender reassignment surgery was abolished (for full infor-mation about the legislation, see www.riksdagen.se). The RFSL (the Swedish Federation for Lesbian, Gay, Bisexual and Transgender Rights), formed in 1950, was no doubt a driving force behind these changes.[2]

Qruiser is, in its own words (see www.qruiser.com), the largest online LGBTQ community in Sweden (and in the Nordic region). In addition, it is part of the larger affinity portal QX (Queer Extra), which is also an offline monthly paper and publishing house (see www.qx.se). The core of the study took place during November 2012. According to its statistics, Qruiser had 109,153 active members on 1 November. The majority of the mem-bers were between 20 and 40 years old, with an average age of 33. 72% of the members were based in Sweden and only 17% defined themselves as in a relationship (underlining Qruiser's dating function, which I examine below). 72% defined themselves as gay, lesbian or bisexual and 72% defined themselves as male. In this sense, Qruiser is a gay community (even though a researcher, who interacts with nicknames, cannot be sure whether this person identifies as an L, G, B, T or Q). I would thus also argue that the results of this chapter are indicative of gay men rather than of transgendered people (for a discussion of using all-encompassing terminology, see Sullivan, 2003, p. 45).

Qruiser is primarily used for flirting, dating, finding friends and sexual partners. As such Qruiser has similarities with better-known gay dating sites such as Gaydar and GayRomeo. The name Qruiser refers to cruising – an activity undertaken by homosexual men (mostly in the pre-digital era and before the general acceptance of homosexuality in the West) strolling around in outdoor areas known as a space (often parks) where they can find other homosexual men by checking each other out, looking for – as well as having – casual sex. Qruiser is not only an online space for cruising. Like any community (see Kozinets, 2011), people use it for different purposes, such as interacting with like-minded people, hanging out with friends, establishing social bonds and so on.

On Qruiser there are also possibilities for political discussions in forums and clubs. A club is a gathering of like-minded people supporting everything from a particular music band to a political party, fashion brand, sexual activity and so forth. In the forums, members can start up as well as discuss (already started) threads on various topics. In this chapter, I focus on discussion threads in the forum Politics, Society & the World (my translation of 'Politik, Samhälle & Världen'; for a study of participation in the clubs, see Svensson, 2014a). I have spent time on the forum, observed, participated and interviewed participants there.

In previous research on these discussion threads, I concluded that they were antagonistic (Svensson, 2013), centred on polarising participation frames (Svensson, 2014b), full of trolling and flaming practices and understood as a way for participants to pass time and entertain themselves (Svensson, 2015). Two frames that provided participants with anchoring points for their participation dominated the discussion threads (for an elaboration of this concept of participation frames, see Svensson, 2014b). The first focused on the left versus the right. Since all political parties in the Swedish parliament embrace LGBTQs (some more than others), this frame was largely centred on workers' rights versus facilitating employers (making it cheaper to employ). The second frame focused on xenophobes (especially islamophobes) versus a politically correct multiculturalist elite; in other words, pro or against immigration. This frame can be related to ideas of *homonationalism*. Puar (2007) describes homonationalism as a growing 'global gay Islamophobia' (p. xvi) – how Muslims are articulated as threats to LGTBQ persons, who in turn embrace (and are embraced by) nationalist agendas.

In interviews, the participants revealed that they were generally motivated to debate, to improve their debating skills and to impress an imagined audience of lurkers, rather than to understand, agree with or learn from other active participants in the threads. Interview data suggest that the forum was generally conceived as a place free from political correctness, providing an outlet for political frustration. In this context, the participants talked about their participation as a pastime, verbal fighting as a game which entertained them and was fun (Svensson, 2015). The question I ask in this chapter is: does sexual identity have anything to do with this conflictual participation? In order to answer this, I will first turn to the analytical approach.

Analytical Approach

How are we to understand the political participation taking place in the Qruiser discussion threads? As mentioned above, I position this study within a cultural participation framework. Carpentier (2011) underlines that discussions on an online community provide opportunities for mediated participation in a (semi-)public debate as well as for self-representation in one of the spaces which characterise the social. We are thus talking about a group of individuals interacting socially and negotiating themselves at the same time. They establish social bonds and have a common online arena for interactions (Kozinets, 2011). At the same time, as the Qruiser forum exemplifies, online communities may also be sites of conflict (Carpentier, 2011). In online communities, practices become increasingly fused with existing and new systems of meaning, which in turn contribute to the emergence of a 'net culture' (Kozinets, 2011, p. 23). By starting from such an anthropological approach to culture (as systems of meaning making), we notice how participation in Qruiser forum discussions becomes dialectically intertwined with processes of identity negotiation, self-presentation and meaning making.

The notion of identity, which is at the core of this chapter, can be connected to meaning making and participation. According to Giddens (1991), identity negotiation concerns how we reflexively construct self-made biographies, i.e. our understandings of ourselves and our place in this world. Our overall identity needs a story, a sense of ontological coherence and continuity in our everyday life. To be successful in this reflexively organised endeavour, the individual needs an ability to construct, deconstruct and reconstruct (i.e. negotiate) their own identity (Giddens, 1991). This identity negotiation also becomes a source of meaning and could also be approached from a participatory perspective. The latter is possible because identity expression, as a way of maintaining self-made biographies, can be understood as a rationale behind political participation, which motivates participation and provides it with meaning (as I have argued elsewhere, see Svensson, 2008). Identity should thus not be understood as essentialised but rather as performed (see Butler, 1997). And it is through rhetorical operations that identities are performed (see Laclau, 2005). Inspired by positioning theory (Harré & Moghaddam, 2003), I consider identity as temporary and dependent on individual speech acts and framings, such as the ones seen in the Qruiser discussion forum (the left vs. the right and islamophobes vs. multiculturalists). In this chapter, the online discussion threads in Qruiser's political forum constitute a space where LGTBQ (mostly gay) identities are performed through speech acts. The question is: how is this done and can such performances be related to the conflictual participation on Qruiser?

Studying heated political discussions on the Qruiser forum between what I conclude was mostly (gay) men reminds me of Geertz's famous 1973 essay on Balinese cockfights. Spending time with his wife in a Balinese village, and becoming accepted by the locals by participating in illegal cockfights, Geertz develops a thick description of the practice. He especially draws on Bentham's notion of deep play, defined as a game where the stakes are so high that it becomes irrational to engage in the game (from a utilitarian standpoint): in their search for pleasure, the participants enter into relationships which cause them pain (Geertz, 1973). This resonates with my study of the discussions on the Qruiser forum. While the participants were looking for a pastime and for fun, their discussions became so heated that they actually started labelling each other in unflattering and caricatural ways (see Svensson, 2015).

Apparently, however, being teased was a sign of acceptance. Being attacked was acknowledgement of the person as a player; it was part of the game and much better than being ignored. Likewise, Geertz argues that participating in a cockfight signals a symbolic expression of the ideal self at the same time as it shows a darker side of this ideal self. Status is at stake, but status on a symbolic level, since the outcome of a cockfight only momentarily (while still publicly or semi-publicly) affirmed, or insulted, one's status. By referring to Weber, Geertz (1973, p. 434) explains this seemingly irrational engagement in deep play. The potential access to significance (i.e. meaning) more than compensated for the costs involved. In this way, deep play becomes more than a game in that the cockfight enables the participant to see a dimension of his/her own subjectivity (Geertz, 1973, p. 450).

Geertz's reasoning resonates with Kuntsman (2007) and her chapter on flaming in an online queer migrant community. Similarly to Geertz, she problematises an either/or understanding of flaming (i.e. verbal cockfights). Rather than understanding flaming as either playful ritual or acts of violence, she suggests that flaming is a 'cultural embedded performance of queerness' (p. 101). In her chapter, flaming becomes a performance of mannered and theatrical rudeness which is particularly linked to gay men (through, among other things, the history of drag shows and clichés of gay men in the movies). Kuntsman (2007) describes flaming as the choreography of moves between many topics and genres 'inseparably binding the playful and the hurtful' (p. 104). Flaming can thus simultaneously be aggressive and rude as well as constructive and playful – condemned by some but embraced by others as legitimate and entertaining. This applies very well to the verbal fights on Qruiser.

Following Kuntsman, the verbal fights on the Qruiser forum may be linked to a negotiation of meaning and belonging. In turn, Geertz argues that meaning is negotiated through status, by being acknowledged as a player, being part of the verbal cockfight. The question thus arises: what role does sexual identity play in such verbal cockfights? To answer this, I turn to positioning theory. Harré and Moghaddam (2003) delineate a positioning triangle consisting of speech acts, positions and story lines (framings such as the left vs. the right etc.). This analytical model provides me with an entry point to my material on Qruiser. Given that I want to study the role(s) of sexual identity, I have to identify speech acts in which the participants position themselves (or others) as L, G, B, T or Q in the storylines (or participation frames) of the left versus the right and islamophobes versus multiculturalists.

Method

I chose a netnographic method to gather empirical data because discussion forums are particularly suitable for netnographic research (Kozinets, 2011). Netnography is a form of ethnography adapted to online communities' characteristics. The three main differences between ethno- and netnography are how researchers 1) enter the culture, 2) collect data and 3) the ethical considerations they have to make. The first difference is straightforward: you enter the culture online through the communication platform(s) the community uses. The second difference – collecting data – is possible through a combination of methods. Three types of data can be collected in netnographic research (Kozinets, 2011): 1) archive data (easily selected through copy and paste), 2) elicited data (gathered in interaction with the participants through observations and interviews) and 3) field notations (noted in a reflexive diary, which was not used for this chapter).

Participant observation is of particular importance here. Kozinets (2011) argues that all netnographic research builds on fieldwork, i.e. a researcher spending much time in an online community trying to understand members via an embedded cultural understanding and thick description (see Geertz, 1973). From 1 to 20 November 2012, I conducted participant observations in all the discussion threads in the forum Politics, Society & the World. I collected archive data by downloading all these discussion threads and the posts in them until 25 November 2012. This gave me a corpus of 76 different threads started by 31 different nicknames, containing a total of 2,853 posts. Kozinets (2011, p. 139) argues that about 1,000 pages in double spacing is a suitable amount of archive data from discussion forums. The 76 discussion threads on Qruiser in November 2012 resulted in about 1,700 pages of posts. I went through the material to find speech acts where participants positioned themselves and others as L, G, B, T or Q in order to study the role(s) of sexual identity in these verbal fights.

In addition, all the thread-starters and recurrent posters were invited to participate in online interviews. In total, I conducted interviews with 36 different nicknames on the platform (through the message service). The interviews differed in length, but together I have around 250 pages of interview material. This material also includes interviews, conducted in Swedish, from a pre-study in April 2012. I translated excerpts from the interviews (as well as from the posts). All the interviews started with me presenting myself, my research and noting that my interest focused on their motivation for participating in the discussion threads. Since these interviews continued over a long period, I had the opportunity to adjust my questions to the type of interviewed participant and how they had participated in the discussion threads. I also noted their answers as well as ideas that arose during the course of the analysis. As I did with the posts, I went through the interviews to find speech acts in which the participants positioned themselves and others on the basis of their sexual identity.

The third difference with offline ethnography concerns ethical issues. Qruiser is neither a public nor a private forum. One needs to be a member to access the site, a process which takes only two minutes. All visitors, also non-members, can view member profile pictures on the login page (see www.qruiser.com). Despite this easy access and public display of members' profile pictures, it is doubtful that the participants foresaw that their participation would be part of a research project. I was therefore totally open on Qruiser about my presence and my research aims, not least on my profile page (as advised by Kozinets, 2011, p. 201). On 4 November I changed my nickname to *forskaren* (the researcher). I also contacted the administrators, who gave me permission to conduct research on the forum. I repeatedly attempted to obtain permission from the publisher as well, without any success. However, I did check the terms of use and the different policies on Qruiser to ensure that none of these were violated when I conducted my research. All thread-starters were asked to participate in interviews. Although not all wanted to do so, all those who answered my request gave me permission to study the threads they had started (as advised by Kozinets, 2011, p. 203). In this chapter, no personal information is revealed about any of the participants (such as their nicknames or age). This does not guarantee complete anonymity but something scholars label 'middle masking' (Kozinets, 2011, p. 211). Only interview excerpts are used from participants who gave me permission to do so. Hence the participants were assured a great deal of confidentiality. Furthermore, the data I collected were from a forum in which some of the participants provided a link to their blogs, showing their real names and personal information. Finally, in the forum people confront each other about their opinions (see the results section) and it can thus be argued that the participants did not act as if the communication were private (for a discussion of this, see Andersson, 2013). In conclusion, the risk of harm to the participants is minimal.

Results

Gay the Politically Correct Way

What role did sexual identity play in the verbal cockfights? After a first glance at the 76 discussion threads, the answer seems to be: a very small one. There are some threads about HIV, one thread critiquing RFSL (the main LGBTQ organisation), one about hate crimes, two about male prostitution and two about countries (mainly Muslim) banning same-sex relations. Studying this archive, it is rather the polarising frames of left versus right and islamophobes versus multiculturalists which are highlighted. A closer look reveals that sexual identity is sometimes connected to these frames. For example, there are two threads about the right-wing (and perceived homophobe) EU Commissioner Tonio Borg, and one thread discusses how a 'queer communist' had risen to power in Sicily. Two threads discuss Muslim congregations and their attitudes towards homosexuality. As a response to these threads, there is one discussing nationalist parties and anti-gay sentiments within these. It seems that rather than sexual identity inciting discussions on the forum, this identity was used at a later stage when participants were already arguing from a leftist, right-wing, islamophobic or multiculturalist position to justify their predetermined position within these frames. In other words, sexual identity seldom sparked verbal fights, but polarising participation frames did (see also Svensson, 2014b).

Venturing into the posts themselves, this becomes even more apparent. Sexual identity was referred to quite often when justifying positions *within* the participation frames. In other words, the posters argued that if one of them identified as L, G, B, T or Q, it would be reasonable for them to have a particular opinion on an issue. It was almost as if identifying as L, G, B, T, or Q would *rationally* imply a particular position within these frames. For example, multiculturalist posters would accuse their opponents of lacking 'self-respect' since they, as perceived Sweden Democrats (the name of a populist and nationalist political party), would also implicitly support conservative 'family' ideas. On the other hand, the participants positioned as multiculturalists were accused of having 'insufficient self-respect' since such a position would also imply a 'defence and/or silencing of Muslim homophobia'.

In the interviews, when asked what motivated the interviewees' participation, sexuality was likewise seldom mentioned. The participants mentioned they had previously also been engaged in politics, sometimes even in political parties. One interviewee phrased it as 'I have a political agenda as a member of the Social Democratic Party'. Identifications such as belonging to the working class or an urge to get the right wing to understand things were referred to as the interviewees' motivations for participation, as in the excerpt below:

> What motivates me? Well, to put the idiotic right-wing pack in place. I have quite a long political engagement, mostly IRL. As a member of the working class and as a woman, I fight against the structures

and institutions (capitalism, patriarchy, state, etc.) that oppress me and others in the same situation as me.

Rather than igniting the flames of conflict, sexual identity was used to fuel the fire, i.e. to argue for the political opinions the participants could rationally hold. The role of sexual identity in these discussions was the common denominator of participants across different political positions. Sexual identity could be used therefore when appealing to opponents' common sense. The participants took it for granted that posters were identified as L, G, B, T or Q and this assumption was then used in the argumentation. In other words, LGBTQ identities and experiences were considered as shared among the participants and could thus be invoked to strengthen an argument within the participation frames. In the interview excerpt below for example, the interviewee questions whether it is compatible to simultaneously be LGBT and racist:

> I'm overall very tired of ignorance. And I become even more tired as an LGBT when Qruiser allows faceless trolls to sit here and spread racism and coarse lies... on an LGBT site. It is an insult to us who have fought for our rights. First the right wing work against us, but then we have to put up with them in our community? No!

This suggests that the political discussion threads on Qruiser were, to some extent, spaces for reflecting on identities embedded in the community, but within the frames that sparked participation. It could be argued that LGBTQ identities can provide subjective entry-points to larger political issues, such as immigration. However, having studied the discussion threads on Qruiser, I suggest that the entry-point was identifying with clear positions in the dominant frames provided. Sexual identity was used to justify these positions at a later stage. In other words, the participants argued for one correct way of being gay.

The Political Is Personalised

Feminists in the late 1960s famously argued that the personal should be treated as political (Hanisch, 1970). The Qruiser forum discussion threads are also examples of intersections between the personal and the political. However, in this context I suggest swapping the words in the feminist slogan and instead proclaiming that *the political is personalised*. The personal (here sexual identity) comes second when used to justify and argue for predetermined political positions within the polarising participation frames. Politically engaged people, such as those participating in the Qruiser forum, seem to have extended their political engagement to an affinity community online based on the subjective and emotive (such as sexuality). This is about extending the political to the personal, allowing political engagement to permeate all spaces of the everyday. This argument relates to Bakardjieva's (2012) concept of *mundane citizenship* – how political participation is embedded in the everyday life of citizens. For example, I asked the interviewees why they chose Qruiser for their political engagement instead of other discussion fora. One of them answered: 'I guess that is because I have got to know some of the nicknames here and have private contact with LGBT people on this forum'. In another interview, I asked whether Qruiser, as an LGBTQ community, influenced the discussions in the threads. The interviewee answered that 'sex is no more interesting than politics, but for a single, older and gay man such as myself Qruiser is one of the few venues where one can deal with both at the same time'. This suggests that the political was extended to a space primarily geared towards finding sexual partners (which is also true of the Qruiser political clubs, see Svensson, 2014a). Even though some participants primarily logged in to discuss politics, most of my interviewees stated that their main reason for hanging out on Qruiser was to find a date. This suggests that discussing politics becomes a mundane practice connected to other issues, such as checking updates, looking for dates and sexual encounters.

When the participants were questioned about their engagement in the threads, it was almost as if this were accidental, something that just happened. Since most of the participants were there anyway, they saw no reason not to engage in some political discussions, as the interview excerpt below explains. The interviewee had outlined the political issues in which he was most interested when I asked him why he discussed these on Qruiser:

> Do I regard Qruiser as a forum to push these issues? I cannot say that I use the forum in this way. I'm here to contact other people, perhaps find a date and such things, not to be an activist. But then, it's always fun that these issues are also addressed on this forum.

It became apparent that many of the interviewees were engaged in issues they had previously been interested in. Quite a few of the participants were engaged, or had been engaged, in political parties. Some participants inserted links to their blogs outside the forum. When spending time on Qruiser, it was almost as if they could not help themselves: they had to discuss politics. This further explains why the issues addressed were not immediately related to sexual identities. One interviewee said that 'most issues in the forum do not affect LGBT perspectives, but it can be good to highlight these perspectives in various issues'. And when LGBTQ experiences were highlighted, they were often steered towards one of the dominant participation frames. In the example below, the thread-starter actually begins with the personal, initiating a discussion about hate crime on the basis of a personal experience when leaving a gay club with a sexual partner.

However, this quickly turns into a thread about immigration and Arabs with homophobic attitudes:

> Many politicians and people in the media do not dare to talk about this, that these are people from outside Europe, and I'm not talking about Latin Americans or East Asians here. [...]
>   I have been harassed only once in Malmö during the last 10 years... some youth, most of whom originate from Arab countries... [...]
>   Homophobia is rife in suburbs with a dense immigration population. And we cannot rely on politicians in any case, because they do nothing to change these attitudes. And simultaneously people from these countries with another attitude towards LGBTs are pouring in.

The reason for participants choosing the Qruiser forum to engage in these discussions and not anywhere else seems to be because they were on the platform anyway and felt they belonged to this community. I asked the participants why they chose Qruiser and not a tabloid. One interviewee answered: 'Aftonbladet.se [the biggest tabloid in Sweden] is not as personal and I believe that gaining personal proximity may be a good way to become recognised and gain credibility'. This also resonates in the interview excerpt below:

> It is a question of democracy to have a forum in which gays can debate, also within our little group. I do not believe there are so many other fora in which gays can do this in Sweden. Being in the commentary fields of Aftonbladet or GP [two tabloids] and arguing there has never interested me. What you write here has more impact, even if it is within a considerably smaller group of people.

In conclusion, it seems that most of the participants had previously been politically engaged, and finding themselves on Qruiser anyway (to find a date) they could not see why they should not combine this with discussing politics. This reasoning is about extending the political to domains of the personal, to allow the political to permeate more mundane everyday spaces.

Flaming as a Subgenre of Queer Sarcasm

Another way of studying how sexual identities made participation in the verbal fights on Qruiser meaningful is to pay attention to the genre of flaming. As mentioned before, flaming can be understood as a 'cultural embedded performance of queerness' (Kuntsman, 2007, p. 101). In other words, the style in which the fights on Qruiser played out may connect these verbal fights very well with LGBTQ identities (here mostly gay identities).

In the discussion threads, for instance, more than just opinions along the polarising participation frames were caricaturised and made fun of. Spelling mistakes and nicknames were often picked up as targets for mockery (as also in Kuntsman's study). Thus someone with a nickname alluding to a preference for younger men would be addressed as a paedophile, and on detecting spelling mistakes in posts (which were common) opponents would pick up on this and make references to the author being drunk, 'early on the bottle this morning', and so on. Below is an excerpt from the thread 'failed former politicians on QX':

> The discussion forum on QX seems to have become the resort of failed former politicians. One after another these failed creatures appear and preach the future as if they are the famous oracle of Delphi. The oracle of Delphi sat on a tripod on earth substances, sniffing the toxic fumes that came from the earth. The rambling started right away. What are the QX oracles sniffing?

Bitterness was a sentiment often ascribed to opponents and used in caricaturing them, as in the following interview excerpt: 'There seems to be a lot of bitterness here, probably because many unfortunately live alone – this has become their window to the world'. Thus, while on the one hand the discussion threads were populated with people who already seemed to have a voice, on the other they were later made fun of for being alone, bitter and having nothing else to do with their lives.

In relation to this, Kuntsman (2007) highlights how the genre of the litany becomes connected to that of 'queer flaming'. There are countless examples of complaints being phrased in an ironic tone (e.g. in threads such as 'Pallywood' countering arguments that Palestinians fake Israeli attacks in order to gain international sympathy). This also highlights how litanies become performative speech acts, constructing a collective we, an offended we (though not without humour) weeping about misfortunes from a rather privileged position as an LGBTQ in Sweden. On Qruiser I witnessed discussions about human rights violations in Sweden and elsewhere (as in the threads about Tonio Borg and anti-gay legislation in Uganda) rather than about achievements in the area of LGBTQ rights (which does not mean that LGBTQ rights have been fully established and that there is nothing left to fight for). By engaging in such litanies, a collective we was constructed which went beyond the borders of Sweden. In this sense, litanies may be understood as 'performances of queerness' (Kuntsman, 2007) negotiating a collective we while simultaneously using this to highlight rights violations worldwide.

To understand the negotiation of belonging on the Qruiser forum, we could also conceive of flaming practices as 'performances of queerness' in themselves, a way of being together and thus a basis of collectivity. This might explain why so many of the participants regarded the verbal cockfights as a pastime and as fun. The interview excerpt below explains:

> Most of us in here on the forum enjoy our conflicts and vendettas a little; conflicts can be stimulating and entertaining, especially if you have no

other tasks at the moment. Sometimes it goes too far though; when it turns into bullying and threats, then the fun disappears of course.

This underlines how verbal cockfights can be both fun and hurtful at the same time (see Geertz, 1973). We should remember that to be teased was a sign of acceptance, to be acknowledged as a player, a part of the game. These flaming practices may themselves be connected then to a negotiation of LGBTQ identities and belonging to a general LGBTQ collective. Like affective communication in general, they help us think reflexively about our life situations and how we can navigate society (McGuigan, 2005).

It is in relation to flaming that the medium's affordance is most apparent. The quickness of the digital medium, the possibility of anonymity online and the tendency to interact only with the like-minded (so-called filter bubbles, see Pariser, 2011) allow for attacks in affect, in the heat of the moment. The polarisation of the participation frames on the forum may thus to some extent be explained by their taking place online. You could say that some of the participants behaved like *internet trolls*, using flaming expressions in the hope that opponents would bite and then ignite a verbal cockfight. I argue that the difference between the latter and more common forms of online hatred and cyber-bullying is the more playful 'bitching' tone on Qruiser. This tone makes the particular genre of 'queer flaming' somewhat pleasurable, a way of passing the time and of negotiating LGTBQ belonging.

Conclusion

To conclude, what does this study tell us about LGBTQ identities online? What roles did these identities play when forum participants engaged in such conflictual practices? This study shows that the political is personalised on Qruiser by attaching LGBTQ identities to existing participation frames, which focused on the left versus the right and islamophobes versus multiculturalists. As discussed in the analytical framework, it is through identity negotiation processes that we understand ourselves and our place in this world. On Qruiser such understanding was achieved through participation frames rather than LGBTQ identities. Sexual identities were attached to these frames at a later stage to argue in favour of a particular position in these frames; hence the title of this chapter: gay the correct way. To be acknowledged as a player, as part of the verbal cockfight, participants held a firm position within the polarising frames and used LGBTQ identities to justify their positions.

Dahlgren and Alvares (2013) argue that the subjective (engagement) is a requirement for participation. The study of Qruiser partly reinforces their argument. In this instance however the subjective is used to justify political positions and negotiate a coherent identity in which the personal and political go hand in hand. Invoking that as an L, G, B, T or Q you should take a particular political position is an appeal to the personal to help you navigate the political. The problem (or the good luck) is that, from a political stand-point, LGBTQ identities are vague today (see Laclau, 2005), empty enough to be used to justify many different political positions. In other words, there is no correct way to be gay but many ways we can perform LGTBQ identi-ties in political discussions.

On the Qruiser forum the participants used the subjective to anchor their political standpoints. They brought their political engagement to a personal setting, to the mundane everyday practices of chatting on an LGBTQ dating community. The way this was done, the general bitchiness of these discus-sions, may very well be connected to LGBTQ identities as a 'performance of queerness' (Kuntsman, 2007). In this sense, discussing politics on the Qruiser forum was connected to the negotiation of meaning and of LGBTQ belonging.

This chapter has thus contributed to the area of cultural participation studies, to debates on how the personal is handled in political discussions and to understanding the role of the subjective in the participatory. Above all, it has contributed to an understanding of the role of LGBTQ identi-ties when discussing politics on a cultural, public, online sphere primarily geared towards dating. The chapter is also a contribution to the general study of LGBTQs online and particularly to discussions of flaming in terms of how such practices may be understood as participatory forms of community-building in an LGBTQ setting.

Notes

1. For a broader overview of LGBTQ studies online, see Szulc, 2014.
2. For a broader overview of LGBTQ rights in Sweden, see Dahl, 2011 and for Nordic LGBTQ studies, see *Lambda Nordica* at www.lambdanordica.se/en.

References

Andersson, E. (2013). *Det Politiska Rummet: Villkor för Situationspolitisk Socialisa-tion i en Nätgemenskap av Och för Ungdomar* (Doctoral dissertation). Örebro: Örebro Studies in Education.

Bakardjieva, M. (2012). Mundane Citizenship: New Media and Civil Society in Bulgaria. *Europe-Asia Studies, 64*(8), 1356–1374.

Butler, J. (1997). *Excitable Speech*. London: Routledge.

Campbell, J. E. (2004). *Getting It Online: Cyberspace, Gay Male Sexuality, and Embodied Identity*. Binghamton: Haworth Press.

Carpentier, N. (2011). *Media and Participation: A Site of Ideological-Democratic Struggle*. Bristol: Intellect.

Dahl, U. (2011). Queer in the Nordic Region: Telling Queer (Feminist) Stories. In L. Downing & R. Gillett (Eds.), *Queer in Europe: Contemporary Case Studies* (pp. 143–158). Farnham: Ashgate.

Dahlgren, P. & Alvares, C. (2013). Political Participation in an Age of Mediatisation: Towards a New Research Agenda. *Javnost - the Public, 20*(2), 47–66.

Geertz, C. (1973). *The Interpretation of Cultures*. New York: Basic Books.

Giddens, A. (1991). *Modernity and Self-Identity: Self and Society in the Late Modern Age.* Cambridge: Polity Press.

Habermas, J. (1989). *The Structural Transformation of the Public Sphere: An Inquiry into a Category of Bourgeois Society.* Cambridge, MA: Polity Press. First published in German, 1962.

Hanisch, C. (1970). The Personal Is Political. In S. Firestone & A. Koedt (Eds.), *Notes From the Second Year: Women's Liberation: Major Writings of the Radical Feminists* (pp. 76–78). New York: Radical Feminism.

Harré, R. & Moghaddam, F. (2003). *The Self and Others: Positioning Individuals and Groups in Personal, Political, and Cultural Contexts.* Westport: Praeger Publishers.

Hermes, J. (2006). Hidden Debates: Rethinking the Relationship Between Popular Culture and the Public Sphere. *Javnost - The Public, 13*(4), 27–44.

Karl, I. (2007). On-/Offline: Gender, Sexuality, and the Techno-Politics of Everyday Life. In K. O'Riordan & D. J. Phillips (Eds.), *Queer Online: Media Technology & Sexuality* (pp. 45–65). New York: Peter Lang.

Kozinets, R. V. (2011). *Netnografi.* Lund: Studentlitteratur.

Kuntsman, A. (2007). Belonging Through Violence: Flaming, Erasure, and Performativity in Queer Migrant Community. In K. O'Riordan & D. J. Phillips (Eds.), *Queer Online: Media Technology & Sexuality* (pp. 101–120). New York: Peter Lang.

Laclau, E. (2005). *On Populist Reason.* London: Verso.

McGuigan, J. (2005). The Cultural Public Sphere. *European Journal of Cultural Studies, 8*(4), 427–443.

O'Riordan, K. & Phillips, D. J. (Eds.) (2007). *Queer Online: Media, Technology and Sexuality.* New York, Peter Lang.

Pariser, E. (2011). *The Filter Bubble: What the Internet Is Hiding from You.* London: Penguin.

Puar, J. K. (2007). *Terrorist Assemblages: Homonationalism in Queer Times.* Durham: Duke University Press.

Sullivan, N. (2003). *A Critical Introduction to Queer Theory.* Edinburgh: Edinburgh University Press.

Svensson, J. (2008). Expressive Rationality: A Different Approach for Understanding Participation in Municipal Deliberative Practices. *Communication, Culture and Critique, 1*(2), 203–221.

Svensson, J. (2013). What Kind of Cultural Citizenship? Dissent and Antagonism When Discussing Politics in an Online Gay Community. In W. Casteknovo & E. Ferrari (Eds.), *Proceedings of the 13th European Conference on eGovernment ECEG2013* (pp. 674–680). Reading: Academic Conferences and Publishing International Ltd.

Svensson, J. (2014a). Participation as a Pin: Political Discussions in an Online Swedish LGBT Community. In A. Ionas (Ed.), *Proceedings of the 14th European Conference on eGovernment ECEG 2014* (pp. 235–241). Reading: Academic Conferences and Publishing International Ltd.

Svensson, J. (2014b). Polarizing Participation Frames: A Study of Political Participation in a Gay Community. *JeDEM eJournal of eDemocracy, 6*(2), 166–181.

Svensson, J. (2015). Participation as a Pastime Political: Discussions in a Queer Community Online. *Javnost - the Public, 22*(3), 283–297.

Szulc, L. (2014). The Geography of LGBTQ Internet Studies. *International Journal of Communication, 8*(2014): 2927–2931.

Szulc, L. & Dhoest, A. (2013). Internet and Sexual Identity Formation: Comparing Internet Use Before and After Coming Out. *Communications: The European Journal of Communication Research, 38*(4): 347–365.

Wakeford, N. (1997). Cyberqueer. In A. Medhurst & S. R. Munt (Eds.), *Lesbian and Gay Studies: A Critical Introduction* (pp. 20–38). Washington: Casell.

Wright, S. (2012). From 'Third Place' to 'Third Space': Everyday Political Talk in Non-Political Online Spaces. *Javnost - The Public, 19*(3): 5–20.

12 'I Sort of Knew What I Was, So I Wanted to See What Awaited Me'

Portuguese LGB Youngsters and Their Situated Experiences with New Media

Daniel Cardoso

New media have been fundamental in creating new dynamics for groups and minorities working with intimacy citizenship, 'an array of concerns [...] which extend notions of rights and responsibilities [...] linked to our most intimate desires, pleasures and ways of being in the world' (Plummer, 1994, p. 151).

Assumptions about the nature of new media usually frame them as being 'for porn', even though evidence abounds to the contrary and the data mobilised to explain this assertion is low-quality (Fae, 2015; Ogas & Gaddam, 2012). This comes from a long tradition of judging each new medium as more intense, more loaded with effects and an ability to move people than the ones coming before (Leong, 1991).

This research was conducted in Portugal, with youngsters aged 16–19 at first contact. The research crosses four different areas: accessing information about sexuality and gender; engaging in civic participation; using pornography; and being involved in sexting (the swapping of sexual content through text, voice, image or video messages, online or via cell phone networks). These areas of investigation are intended to illustrate usages of new media for consumption (information seeking and pornography) and production (civic participation and sexting) in normatively non-eroticised and eroticised contexts. The intersection between such activities will show how unstable their definitions are and how youngsters mobilise them differently according to their positioning vis-à-vis societal structures of privilege. It will also serve to inquire into how, from a Foucauldian perspective, youngsters use their access (and lack thereof) to new media as resources which come into play in processes of governmentality and *assujettissement* as technologies of the self (Cruikshank, 1993; Foucault, 2000, 2002, 2005) – how, in other words, through their practices, discourses and moral positioning, youngsters co-produce and shape themselves and each other as sexual(ised) subjects, governing and disciplining their behaviours and others'. Foucault's theoretical corpus is deployed here to frame youngsters' practices as governmentality over their own and others' selves.

This chapter will focus on the roles new media play in the lives of self-identified LGB youths by taking their experiences and contributions and putting their voices at the forefront of the analysis. The experiences they related will be compared to testimonies of straight-presenting youths in order to determine how sexualised experiences with new media and their identities are co-constituted.

Media, Sexualities and Youngsters: Panics, (De)regulations and Rights

References to how specifically sexual the internet is abound in academic literature (Peter & Valkenburg, 2006; Selwyn, 2008). This discourse around the characteristics of the internet exists in the context of a debate about the sexualisation of media in general, or what is sometimes called 'pornographication' (McNair, 2002). While for Brian McNair 'pornographication' had to do with a democratisation of desire which breaks the hegemonic role that heterosexist media representations have, other authors have interpreted the expression negatively. The latter interpretation sees the proliferation of sexual content as loss or corruption, a surplus which taints all other forms of media representation (Hawkes & Dune, 2013; Smith, 2010). Clarissa Smith (2010, p. 105) argues that pornographication, 'even as it claims to trace patterns, processes and trajectories, [...] actually obscures them in order to make discursive assertions of effects and consequences which must be acknowledged as "obvious"'.

When considered as a social group, youngsters occupy a hazy position vis-à-vis sexuality, technology and bodily autonomy. To be a teenager – or an emerging adult (Arnett, 2000) – is to be defined by potentiality and liminality, ruled by a teleological model that ideally leads to an adulthood with a number of culturally relevant markers which supposedly, taken together, are made to signify adulthood (Blatterer, 2010; Castañeda, 2002; Lesko, 1996).

This translates into what Kerry Robinson (2012) calls a 'difficult citizenship' for children and youngsters, regulating their access to knowledge about sexuality and sexuality itself. Concurrently, the fact that sexuality is present in regular experiences of media consumption (Buckingham & Bragg, 2004) means that the way youngsters interact with sexuality is often not critically consensual, leaving them with little power to engage as active participants or to *disengage* autonomously (Fahs, 2014).

Sexualised Usages of New Media

The practices included in this study are investigated in an attempt to capture different dynamics in how the internet and new technologies are used. Calling those usages sexualised does not mean that the intention or content needs to be linked to an erotically charged situation, but rather that they are framed as such.

What follows is a short summary of current literature on the four selected activities, focusing wherever possible on critical overviews which question normative and ontological assumptions about the (always constructed) nature of each of those modes of engagement.

The usage of the internet as a resource to *gather information about sex, sexuality and gender* by youngsters has been increasingly researched: Sung Un Kim and Sue Yeon Syn (2014) have identified over 80 studies conducted between 2000 and 2012 which involved youngsters aged 13–19 years old, with 89% taking into consideration the role of the internet in this context. Laura Simon and Kristian Daneback (2013) have identified four large areas of research and, according to these authors, markers like ethnicity, sexual orientation and gender heavily influence if and how youngsters use the internet to find information about sex and sexuality.

Information found – on and off the internet – is often problematic, incomplete, misleading or of low quality (Eysenbach, Powell, Kuss & Sa, 2002). Youngsters are often met with literacy presuppositions (e.g. the terminology used) which hamper their ability to parse and mobilise what information they find (Hansen, Derry, Resnick & Richardson, 2003).

Although information found online might be more readily available and its access more anonymous to youngsters, they will often compare it to books, information available from other media and from peers or family members; information available online might also feel more personally targeted at the youngsters' experiences and make them empathise with it, as well as endowing them with a sense of self-control over their bodies and intimate experiences (Gray, Klein, Noyce, Sesselberg & Cantrill, 2005). School has been gaining importance as a main referential agent for information about sexuality; gendered and age differences moreover mean that girls will usually have a more diversified range of trusted sources, rely less on the internet and have a specific set of areas of concern when compared to boys (Tanton et al., 2015).

Following Banaji and Buckingham (2013), *civic engagement* in a new media context is employed here in a broad sense, encompassing forums, online groups, social networking activity and participating in non-formal networks. Studies seem to agree that socio-economic inequalities are redeployed online (Sloam, 2014). Against the fear that new technologies re-centre all public discourse on entertainment-as-alienation (Theocharis & Quintelier, 2014) or that they just create homogenous echo chambers (Dumitrica, 2014), other authors focus on how such technologies build a prime area for young citizens to express and perform their identities even when they do not consider themselves to be activists (Neumayer & Svensson, 2014), as evident in Bakardjieva's (2009, p. 96) concept of subactivism: 'small-scale, often individual decisions and actions that have either a political or ethical frame of reference (or both) and remain submerged in everyday life'.

This is particularly relevant to members of stigmatised groups, who can acquire empathy, coping strategies, gains in self-acceptance and self-esteem as well as literacy, and build communities of belonging (Döring, 2009;

Keskenidou, Kyridis, Valsamidou and Soulani, 2014; Kubicek, Beyer, Weiss, Iverson & Kipke, 2010). Lukasz Szulc and Alexander Dhoest (2013) warn that the internet's importance should not be overestimated, as the role it has when youngsters are exploring their identities around sexual orientation is not the same as when they feel they can cope with that part of their lives.

Regarding *pornography*, several authors have commented on how research is often biased towards a positivist model of media effects which assumes a negative effect from exposure to pornography, disregarding other possible outcomes and the voices of consumers themselves (e.g. Attwood, 2002; McKee, 2005, 2009; McNair, 2014). Because of this, results vary wildly: pornography sometimes correlates with less progressive gender attitudes (e.g. Peter & Valkenburg, 2010), sometimes it does not (McKee, 2007), and at other times results are inconclusive (e.g. Malamuth & Donnerstein, 2000; Owens, Behun, Manning & Reid, 2012). Gender plays a role in framing the watching of porn as a masculine activity while also serving to transgress and explore what being a 'girl' can be (Scarcelli, 2015; Smith, 2012). Feona Attwood (2002) asserts that an immanent definition of pornography is impossible since the deploying of the word itself produces a pornographic *corpus*.

There is a crossover between more formal means of education and the way pornography can serve as a learning tool, in ways which make clear that sexual pleasure can be pursued as an end in itself (Gomes, 2015) and in ways which can make youngsters feel wary about what they find online (Jones, Biddlecom, Hebert & Mellor, 2011). Porn seems especially relevant whenever other sources are available, as it draws the focus towards the body as more than a biological system (Scarcelli, 2014). It is also very important for members of sexual minorities, who are often denied any formal and familial sexual education and to whom it may serve to validate their own sexual desires and experiences (Marques, Nogueira & Oliveira, 2014).

In Europe (with Portugal being no exception) self-reported exposure to pornographic material among 9-to-16-year-olds happens more in *offline* contexts (Rovolis & Tsaliki, 2012), something that remains true in more recent data (Livingstone, Mascheroni, Ólafsson & Haddon, 2014).

According to Chalfen (2009), *sexting* is the continuation via new media of the tradition of sharing images between people, where four different cultural tendencies cross with each other: mediatic, technological, visual and adolescent culture. It is important to pay attention to how youngsters construe the phenomenon – for instance as a safer path to sexuality (Chalfen, 2010) or as an expression of their autonomy in relationships with peers and with their own social identity (Campbell & Park, 2014).

A systematic literature review on sexting which encompasses 31 studies published between January 2010 and August 2013 (Klettke, Hallford & Mellor, 2014) found mixed results: prevalence varying between 10–16%; variable correlations with gender; some studies pointing at correlations with ethnicity (more non-white youngsters engaging in the activity) and sexual orientation (more non-straight youngsters engaging in the activity).

Youngsters are aware of the risks, but boys tend to emphasise the positive aspects of sexting while girls emphasise the negative aspects. This is in line with the gender dynamics involved: the photos or videos become a form of surplus value which is extracted from the girls and which feeds into normative and predatory masculinity, while at the same time also being deployed by the girls to construct their own femininity and desirability, within a tense and not wholly consensual social background (Ringrose, Gill, Livingstone & Harvey, 2012; Ringrose & Harvey, 2015). Both engaging and not engaging in sexting can carry negative consequences (Lippman & Campbell, 2014) and regardless of the actual rates of sexting it seems normalised in how youngsters deal with it and talk about it (Ringrose et al., 2012).

Smartphones and the general rise of mobile platforms of almost-always-on communication have been fundamental for shifts in sexting. Most sexting is done between people who know each other (e.g. Temple & Choi, 2014) and most situations of harm seem to come from situations when content is unduly re-shared.

It is of fundamental importance to engage with how youngsters construct their own experiences of what they are doing and being with the media – acknowledging that a youngster might, for example, use a platform to seek out information about sexuality *and* look at sexually explicit material *and* disseminate their self-produced sexually explicit material *and*, through it, raise awareness about non-heterosexualities. I argue that the important aspect is the interconnection between these four elements.

Media in Context: Portugal's Relationship with Sexuality and New Media

Portugal is in a state of late or unfinished modernity (Mattoso, 2011; Ponte, 2012). From early in the twentieth century up until 25 April 1974, Portugal lived under a right-wing fascist and religious dictatorship, where homosexuality was prosecuted and any mention of sexuality in the media was subject to censorship. The 'Estado Novo' regime was traditionalist and issues like education were deprioritised – the results of which are still felt nowadays since Portugal ranks as having the fifth-lowest adult education level of the OECD (2015). Data from the National Statistics Institute (INE) show that the number of enrolled students in 2014 was slightly inferior to the number in 2000. At the same time, a multi-year economic crisis and austeritarian measures from the government have been part and parcel of what the youngsters interviewed for this study have known since their early teens. Recent demographic changes have worked to make this a 'generation stuck between a futureless today and a postponed tomorrow' (Pais, 2012, p. 27).[1]

Attempts to kick-start sexual education in Portugal started in the early 1980s (with heavy resistance from parents, politicians and educators), but in spite of high-quality legislation the results have been lacking. Initiatives are usually medically framed, with little active participation from students and very little consideration for sexual diversity (Marinho, Anastácio & Carvalho, 2011; Matos, Reis, Ramiro, Ribeiro & Leal, 2014). Thus 'victimization, fear and morality' (Nogueira, Saavedra & Costa, 2007, p. 59) seem to drive the practical aspect of sexual education in Portugal, dominated by a 'pedagogy of heterosexuality' (P. C. M. Vieira, 2010, p. 128). At the same time, it became the eighth country in the world to legally allow same-sex marriage, but also the first to do so while explicitly *disallowing* adoption and co-adoption rights to same-sex couples, which has since changed.

Most Portuguese adolescents and young adults do not feel comfortable talking about sexuality with parents and teachers, but they do feel comfortable talking to peers or going online to search for information (Matos, Simões, et al., 2011; Matos, Reis, Ramiro & Equipa Aventura Social, 2011; C. P. Vieira, 2012), making the school and other youth sociality spaces very important in the construction of their own gendered and sexual identities, but also in the reinforcement of hegemonic expressions of gender and sexuality (Pais, 2012; Pereira, 2012).

Portugal has invested in youngsters' access to computers and the internet, most relevantly via the 'e-Escolas' program (2007–2015), which distributed laptops and discounted internet connections to school-aged children; the government distributed almost 1.4 million laptops through this program. Portugal was, by 2010, ahead of most other European countries when it came to children possessing or having access to a laptop at home, facilitating a specific 'bedroom culture' around them (D. Cardoso, 2012; Livingstone, 2002). Ownership of mobile phones is also comparatively high in Portugal; in 2011, about 92% of national residents (16–74 years old) had a cell phone, with Portugal being fourth in terms of mobile penetration rate in Europe (140%); in 2013, about 40% of Portuguese residents used their mobiles to access the internet (G. Cardoso, Mendonça, Lima, Paisana & Neves, 2014; Ponte, 2012); 47% of youngsters did so according to a recent statistically representative study (Simões, Ponte, Ferreira, Doretto & Azevedo, 2014). According to INE, overall internet access for 16-to-24-year-olds was at about 98% in 2014. Portuguese youngsters are then placed in a very specific intersection between low average literacy but high access to new media and the internet.

Methodology

An online-based questionnaire using the LimeSurvey platform on my own commercially hosted website was set up and links were shared on social networks and via co-operating institutions: *rede ex aequo*, the only LGBT NGO in Portugal targeted at youngsters; *Associação para o Planeamento Familiar* (Family Planning Association), a Portuguese institution which focuses on raising sexual, reproductive and overall health literacy; and *Programa Escolhas* (Choices Programme), a governmental initiative aimed at providing support to disadvantaged youths. The questionnaire touched on each of the aforementioned areas plus sociodemographic indicators and, finally, a field where each person could volunteer themselves for a face-to-face interview; 183 valid responses were collected.

26 people volunteered for the interview, but in the end only 11 respondents followed through. The interviews lasted from 45 minutes to an hour and a half and were held in public spaces in several parts of the country (though mostly in Lisbon). Participants' ages ranged from 17 to 20 years old. At the start of the interview, they were asked to write down their gender (no default options given) and to pick an alias for themselves. Youngsters were not asked to self-identify their sexual orientation, as one of the objectives of the interview was to see how or if the issue would arise. Some of the interviewees self-disclosed their sexual orientation.[2]

The interviews were transcribed and sent to the interviewees for comments and clarifications. No relevant changes were made. Afterwards the interviews were thematically coded using NVivo 10, with the themes being derived from what the youngsters mentioned about their experiences through a close reading of the transcripts. Part of the coding was cross-coded by an external researcher and checked for cross-coder reliability, after which the coding was finalised.

With the data from the content coding to serve as framing, the interviews were subjected to Foucauldian Discourse Analysis (FDA), looking into what discourses, practices, rules and models were deployed by youngsters to talk about their experiences, identities and worldviews (Jäger & Maier, 2010).

What follows is a partial presentation of this data, focusing on the intersection between youngsters' narratives and their (stated or perceived) sexual orientation. Although the analysis will focus on non-straight-presenting narratives, straight-presenting respondents serve to put into relief the identitary role of new media in the construction and performing of sexual orientation.

Youngsters Discussing Their Mediated Selves

> You know, there's information that comes to you. And then there's information you have to seek out. (Donald, 20, male, self-identified as gay)

One of the most fundamental ways the internet was framed during the interviews, both by straight- and non-straight-presenting respondents, was as a *compensation system*. For non-straight youngsters, accessing information relevant to their erotic and identitary experiences via the school system or the family presented enormous challenges. The heteronormative knowledge 'comes' to them, but the *rest* needs to be sought out, enmeshing the individual in a network of moral obligations and tasks which allow them to be an autonomous subject possessing a sexuality (Foucault, 1994a, 1994b). Although several respondents point out that information is now more readily available for 'them' (i.e. LGB people), such availability can also be redeployed by straight-presenting youngsters under a rationalist model where being in favour or against LGB people and rights is seen, as Beatriz says, to form 'both sides of the matter […] and I try to see, on each side, what each side says, and try to get to a consensus of sorts'.

The difficulty of talking to family or friends due to one's sexual orientation and of finding resources in mainstream media or within the school places the internet as a prime resource about sexual orientation. The internet is a *safer mechanism*; youngsters mentioned how the anonymity of the internet protected them. This involves the discursive and the non-discursive: the possibility of not having to physically engage with other people (seen as potentially risky) is a condition for being able to access such information.

Which information is sought out also depends on what one associates with sexual orientation. Redgi said that she did not seek information about sexual health: 'It's stupid, I know, but I've always made an association between [having sex with] girls and having less chance to catch [an STD] compared to guys'. By contrast, several non-straight males mentioned their interest in actively seeking out information about HIV and other STDs.

Given the inability of the biomedical discourse to deal with their perceived needs and interests, youngsters diversify their approach to information collection: blogs, forums (especially in Portuguese), Facebook groups and pornography were mentioned. Youngsters recognise that information found in these media might not be '100% accurate', but that is not the point: they are (also) seeking *subjective* experiences that might guide them and help them in their everyday lives, something that is far beyond the purview of the medical discourse on sexuality. Alternate epistemologies are validated and incorporated into the moral construction of a sexualised subject.

These alternative sources are nonetheless framed by the sexuality *dispositif* (Foucault, 1994a), where sexuality is seen as a mode of truth-revealing: 'I found out even more things about myself […] it was my age of self-discovery' (Subject A). This essentialist discourse on sexuality means, as Foucault points out, that the sexualised subject is morally tasked with discovering the truth about their own sexuality, and to govern it in a way which allows them to become what they already are. In this context the media serve as moral technologies of the self.

In the interviews from straight-presenting participants, this issue is conspicuously present by its *absence*. Heterosexuality is alluded to obliquely and the requirements of the constitution of the non-straight sexualised subject are absent – replaced with the seeking out of different ideas for having sex, in a way which does not involve constructing or uncovering one's identity. Likewise, heterosexuality also requires no assurance of validity or concerns about privacy.

Youngsters must also learn to *perform* their identity. Here the use of *pornography* is especially relevant, making the youngsters become acquainted with the *praxis* that will allow them to *be* gay/lesbian/bisexual:

> The first kind of pornography I used was straight pornography [...] to try and understand whether I liked that or not! (Miguel)
> I sort of knew what I was, so I wanted to see what awaited me... But, like, when I saw [lesbian pornography]... I was, like, grossed out... but, like, 'okay, maybe this might feel nice' [*laughs*]. (Redgi)

Pornography functions as a *test* or a *validation* of a given (non-straight) sexual orientation, reaffirming its veridictive power, allowing the subject to attain the *truth* of their desire, and also the how-to that having such a truth as an identity implies. In Redgi's case, this truth overrides even the somatic experience of disgust; the subject must educate/govern their body to fulfil and embody that truth. New media also open up curiosity as a venue for further exploration: according to some of the respondents, porn serves as motivator for youngsters to go and explore related topics.

This moral work has a collaborative and social aspect via *civic participation* as well. 'We don't want to spend our life hiding, being no one', says Maria. Living in a heteronormative society means living as simultaneously invisible and exposed. The internet, cell phones and other communication media allow LGB youngsters to gather information, social resources, new peers and *belongings* – from the subjective experience to the collective identitary recognition that is part of the process of being *with*. Faced with the risk of 'being no one', youngsters can perform civic engagement at both the activist and subactivist levels. Ivo said:

> The first problem I faced was that, at the time, I didn't know anyone who was in the same situation as me, and so the internet worked as a means to meet more people who were in the same situation.

Debating how to deal with specific personal challenges, meeting possible love interests, joining an LGBT association and becoming acquainted with LGBT mass media are all valued resources, especially to those socially and *geographically* isolated.

> It was through a blog of a guy talking about [an LGBT] summer camp. Everything went well, it was fun, and I had never expected to see more than 30 LGBT people in a single room, because when you're going through this phase, you think it's only happening to you, but it never is! (Donald)

This meeting transformed his perception of himself, of the world around him and the limits of what is possible or expectable. Several respondents mentioned how they preferred engaging in face-to-face civic participation or subactivism. This highlights the importance of the bodily experience of being in a room surrounded by people who are seen as sharing an equivalent sexual truth and agency.

This also means that going from an experience of online contact to in-person meetings requires a certain degree of mobility and, thus, privilege:

> I wanted to join a friend of mine who was volunteering at ILGA, but at the time I didn't have the economic resources to do all that travelling... it's something I'd like to try one day. (Maria)

Maria is not the only one who said she would have liked to do something but ended up not being able to: Redgi also compliments *rede ex aequo*'s local youth LGBT groups, but was too far away from any group while growing up, and also claimed to have lacked the courage to go. Money, freedom and cognitive resources to cope with stress and the unknown are excluding factors for some youngsters, and although the internet can break down some isolation, it can also show them opportunities that are beyond their reach – *exclusion within inclusion*.

Beyond the affordances it brings, new media can also present youngsters with extra challenges and risks. Even though no respondent was older than twenty, several of them talked about feeling tired, burned out or drained by constant engagement around LGBT rights in social networks. 'We ended up having really heated discussions about this and that, and it got to a point where I simply disengaged, and left all the [Facebook] groups' (Subject A). The same technologies of the self which place these youngsters as empowered agentic citizens can also leave them open to a barrage of hate speech, draining social interactions and other onerous and toxic environments that mandate not only mastery over the discursive apparatus of human and LGBT rights, but also a physical and emotional labour associated with being online and doing civic engagement; this, in turn, can motivate a partial or total withdrawal from civic engagement and subactivism. Concerns about having to do a close monitoring of one's presence on social networks to avoid unwanted outings add yet another layer of complexity and risk.

Technology exists in a *floating* relationship between being a resource and a risk. Others, like Ivo, also see it as a resource which corresponds to a phase in an LGB person's life – important but 'not fundamental', as he puts it, in line with previous research (Szulc & Dhoest, 2013).

This experience is alien to straight-presenting respondents and they distance themselves from it. Joana: 'I have an interest [in LGBT rights], I support them, but maybe I just don't identify with it all that much'. The issue of *disidentification* is the basis for a double rhetorical move: firstly, the speaking subject can simultaneously disavow non-straightness *and* maintain straightness as the norm that need not be named; secondly, the speaking subject can use that othering as a way to rationalise their own disengagement with intimacy citizenship issues. Fighting for equal rights becomes the responsibility *only* of those affected by inequality, or must be done in terms that those who are privileged can recognise themselves in.

Sexting operates as an erotic and revealing mode of interpersonal engagement and content production. Both straight and non-straight respondents shared stories about private images being unduly shared, but all between former couples of people from different genders. Sexual alterity functions here as stigma and protection: LGB youngsters feel safer than straight ones. This can be related to how divulging a private image from a same-sexed person can lead to a homophobic backlash against the sharer, and also to how the power imbalance in sexting is often due to a gendered dynamics, where men draw surplus value from accumulating or having images of women. Still, navigating the dynamics of sexting requires not losing *self-control*, both over one's image and over one's displays of interest – another component of the moral fashioning that the subject has to govern.

Conclusion

That 'the personal is political' has a double meaning: on the one hand, formal politics needs to concern itself with issues which used to be relegated to the private sphere; on the other, political participation is never a wholly rational experience but rather exists in articulation with discursive systems of meaning making and identitary relationships of recognition and disidentification, and with non-discursive resources like emotions, money and freedom of locomotion.

New media create new venues for engagement but also operate as a technology of governing the self and others, producing both positive and negative results; the moral background against which a subject can claim success is also the background with which they can judge and exert power over other subjects. New media facilitate the epistemological and hermeneutic claims of the sexuality *dispositif* to essentialise sexual orientation by serving as sites where youngsters construct their sexualised identities when they are not straight and reinforcing the naturalness of straights' sexual orientation.

Taken together, these four usages of new media allow for the contestation of normative scientific epistemology as well as the power of schools and parents, and they fill the voids felt by LGB youngsters. Concurrently, they create their own expressions of pre-existing problems: homophobia, lack of awareness and information, as well as political disidentification from more privileged peers. Ultimately, the offline and the online are co-constitutive, and more research is needed to understand how they connect and what media affordances can be used to fight discrimination in both spaces. This fight against discrimination is fundamental for a full exercise of these youngsters' intimate citizenship.

Notes

1. All translations from non-English sources are by the author.
2. The respondents were: Subject A, 20, female, bisexual; Redgi, 20, female, gay; Ivo, 18, male, read as heterosexual; Tiago, 19, male, read as heterosexual; Miguel, 17, male, gay; Joana, 19, female, read as heterosexual; Miguel, 20, male, read as heterosexual; Beatriz, 20, female, read as heterosexual; Íris, 18, female, read as heterosexual; Donald, 20, male, gay; Maria, 20, female, read as non-monosexual.

References

Arnett, J. J. (2000). Emerging Adulthood: A Theory of Development from the Late Teens through the Twenties. *The American Psychologist*, 55(5), 469–480.

Attwood, F. (2002). Reading Porn: The Paradigm Shift in Pornography Research. *Sexualities*, 5(1), 91–105. http://doi.org/10.1177/1363460702005001005.

Bakardjieva, M. (2009). Subactivism: Lifeworld and Politics in the Age of the Internet. *The Information Society*, 25(2), 91–104. http://doi.org/10.1080/019722 40802701627.

Banaji, S. & Buckingham, D. (2013). *The Civic Web: Young People, the Internet and Civic Participation*. Cambridge, MA.: The MIT Press.

Blatterer, H. (2010). The Changing Semantics of Youth and Adulthood. *Cultural Sociology*, 4(1), 63–79. http://doi.org/10.1177/1749975509356755.

Buckingham, D. & Bragg, S. (Eds.) (2004). *Young People, Sex and the Media: The Facts of Life?* Basingstoke: Palgrave Macmillan.

Campbell, S. W. & Park, Y. J. (2014). Predictors of Mobile Sexting among Teens: Toward a New Explanatory Framework. *Mobile Media & Communication*, 2(1), 20–39. http://doi.org/10.1177/2050157913502645.

Cardoso, D. (2012). A Cultura do Quarto e o Uso Excessivo da Internet: Resultados Nacionais do Inquérito EU Kids Online. In C. Ponte, J. A. Simões, A. Jorge & D. Cardoso (Eds.), *Crianças e Internet em Portugal: Acessos, Usos, Riscos, Mediações: Resultados do Inquérito Europeu EU Kids Online* (pp. 57–73). Coimbra: Edições Minerva Coimbra.

Cardoso, G., Mendonça, S., Lima, T., Paisana, M. & Neves, M. (2014). *A Internet em Portugal - Sociedade em Rede 2014*. Lisboa: OberCom.

Castañeda, C. (2002). *Figurations: Child, Bodies, Worlds*. Durham: Duke University Press.

Chalfen, R. (2009). 'It's Only a Picture': Sexting, 'Smutty' Snapshots and Felony Charges. *Visual Studies*, 24(3), 258. http://doi.org/10.1080/14725860903309203.

Chalfen, R. (2010). Commentary: Sexting as Adolescent Social Communication. *Journal of Children and Media*, 4(3), 350–354. http://doi.org/10.1080/174827 98.2010.486144.

Cruikshank, B. (1993). Revolutions Within: Self-Government and Self-Esteem. *Economy and Society*, 22(3), 327–344. http://doi.org/10.1080/03085149300000022.

Döring, N. M. (2009). The Internet's Impact on Sexuality: A Critical Review of 15 Years of Research. *Computers in Human Behavior*, 25(5), 1089–1101. http://doi.org/10.1016/j.chb.2009.04.003.

Dumitrica, D. (2014). Imagining Engagement: Youth, Social Media, and Electoral Processes. *Convergence: The International Journal of Research into New Media Technologies*, 1–19. http://doi.org/10.1177/1354856514553899.

Eysenbach, G., Powell, J., Kuss, O. & Sa, E.-R. (2002). Empirical Studies Assessing the Quality of Health Information for Consumers on the World Wide Web: A Systematic Review. *JAMA*, *287*(20), 2691–2700. http://doi.org/10.1001/jama.287.20.2691.

Fae, J. (2015). *Taming the Beast*. Letchworth Garden City: Berforts Information Press.

Fahs, B. (2014). 'Freedom to' and 'Freedom from': A New Vision for Sex-Positive Politics. *Sexualities*, *17*(3), 267–290. http://doi.org/10.1177/1363460713516334.

Foucault, M. (1994a). *História da Sexualidade 1: A Vontade de Saber*. Lisboa: Relógio d'Água.

Foucault, M. (1994b). *História da Sexualidade 2: O Uso dos Prazeres*. Lisboa: Relógio d'Água.

Foucault, M. (2000). Technologies of the Self. In P. Rabinow (Ed.), *The Essential Works of Michel Foucault, 1954–1984: Ethics* (Vol. 1, pp. 223–251). London: Penguin.

Foucault, M. (2002). Governmentality. In J. Faubion (Ed.), *The Essential Works of Michel Foucault, 1954–1984: Power* (Vol. 3, pp. 201–222). London: Penguin.

Foucault, M. (2005). *The Hermeneutics of the Subject: Lectures at the Collège de France 1981–1982*. (F. Gros & F. Ewald, Eds.). New York: Picador.

Gomes, E. E. (2015). Práticas Socializadoras do Gosto Sexual e do Exercício do Sexo. *Etnográfica: Revista do Centro em Rede de Investigação em Antropologia*, *19*(1), 51–75.

Gray, N. J., Klein, J. D., Noyce, P. R., Sesselberg, T. S. & Cantrill, J. A. (2005). Health Information-Seeking Behaviour in Adolescence: The Place of the Internet. *Social Science & Medicine*, *60*(7), 1467–1478. http://doi.org/10.1016/j.socscimed.2004.08.010.

Hansen, D. L., Derry, H. A., Resnick, P. J. & Richardson, C. R. (2003). Adolescents Searching for Health Information on the Internet: An Observational Study. *Journal of Medical Internet Research*, *5*(4), 1–25. http://doi.org/10.2196/jmir.5.4.e25.

Hawkes, G. & Dune, T. (2013). Introduction: Narratives of the Sexual Child: Shared Themes and Shared Challenges. *Sexualities*, *16*(5–6), 622–634. http://doi.org/10.1177/1363460713497459.

Jäger, S. & Maier, F. (2010). Theoretical and Methodological Aspects of Foucauldian Critical Discourse Analysis and Dispositive Analysis. In R. Wodak & M. Meyer (Eds.), *Methods of Critical Discourse Analysis* (2nd ed., pp. 34–61). London; Thousand Oaks, CA.: SAGE Publications.

Jones, R. K., Biddlecom, A. E., Hebert, L. & Mellor, R. (2011). Teens Reflect on Their Sources of Contraceptive Information. *Journal of Adolescent Research*, *26*(4), 423–446. http://doi.org/10.1177/0743558411400908.

Keskenidou, M., Kyridis, A., Valsamidou, L. P. & Soulani, A.-H. (2014). The Internet as a Source of Information: The Social Role of Blogs and their Reliability. *OBS**, *8*(1), 203–228.

Kim, S. U. & Syn, S. Y. (2014). Research Trends in Teens' Health Information Behaviour: A Review of the Literature. *Health Information & Libraries Journal*, *31*(1), 4–19. http://doi.org/10.1111/hir.12057.

Klettke, B., Hallford, D. J. & Mellor, D. J. (2014). Sexting Prevalence and Correlates: A Systematic Literature Review. *Clinical Psychology Review*, *34*(1), 44–53. http://doi.org/10.1016/j.cpr.2013.10.007.

Kubicek, K., Beyer, W. J., Weiss, G., Iverson, E. & Kipke, M. D. (2010). In the Dark: Young Men's Stories of Sexual Initiation in the Absence of Relevant Sexual Health Information. *Health Education & Behavior*, 37(2), 243–263. http://doi.org/10.1177/1090198109339993.

Leong, W.-T. (1991). The Pornography 'Problem': Disciplining Women and Young Girls. *Media, Culture & Society*, 13(1), 91–117. http://doi.org/10.1177/016344391013001006.

Lesko, N. (1996). Denaturalizing Adolescence: The Politics of Contemporary Representations. *Youth & Society*, 28(2), 139–161. http://doi.org/10.1177/0044118X96028002001.

Lippman, J. R. & Campbell, S. W. (2014). Damned if You Do, Damned if You Don't… If You're a Girl: Relational and Normative Contexts of Adolescent Sexting in the United States. *Journal of Children and Media*, 1–16. http://doi.org/10.1080/17482798.2014.923009.

Livingstone, S. (2002). *Young People and New Media: Childhood and the Changing Media Environment* (1st ed.). London: SAGE Publications.

Livingstone, S., Mascheroni, G., Ólafsson, K. & Haddon, L. (2014). *Children's Online Risks and Opportunities: Comparative Findings from EU Kids Online and Net Children Go Mobile*. Retrieved from http://www.lse.ac.uk/media@lse/research/EUKidsOnline/Home.aspx.

Malamuth, N. M. & Donnerstein, E. I. (2000). Pornography and Sexual Aggression. *Annual Review of Sex Research*, 11, 26–91.

Marinho, S., Anastácio, Z. & Carvalho, G. S. de. (2011). Desenvolvimento e Implementação de Projectos de Educação Sexual: Análise das Dimensões Biológica, Psicológica e Social da Sexualidade. In *Atas do VI Congresso Internacional: Maia: AGIR – Associação para a Investigação e Desenvolvimento Socio-Cultural*. Chaves. Retrieved from http://repositorium.sdum.uminho.pt/handle/1822/12639.

Marques, A. M., Nogueira, C. & Oliveira, J. M. (2014). Lesbians on Medical Encounters: Tales of Heteronormativity, Deception, and Expectations. *Health Care for Women International*, 36(9), 988–1006. http://doi.org/10.1080/07399332.2014.888066.

Matos, M. G. de, Reis, M., Ramiro, L. & Equipa Aventura Social. (2011). *Saúde Sexual e Reprodutiva dos Estudantes do Ensino Superior: Relatório do Estudo - Dados Nacionais 2010*. Lisboa: FMH - UL.

Matos, M. G. de, Reis, M., Ramiro, L., Ribeiro, J. P. & Leal, I. (2014). Sexual Education in Schools in Portugal: Evaluation of a 3 Years Period. *Creative Education*, 5(15), 1353–1362. http://doi.org/10.4236/ce.2014.515154.

Matos, M. G. de, Simões, C., Tomé, G., Camacho, I., Ferreira, M., Ramiro, L., … Equipa Aventura Social. (2011). *A Saúde dos Adolescentes Portugueses: Relatório do Estudo HBSC 2010*. Lisboa: FMH - UL.

Mattoso, J. (Ed.) (2011). *História da Vida Privada em Portugal: Os Nossos Dias*. Maia: Temas e Debates.

McKee, A. (2005). The Need to Bring the Voices of Pornography Consumers into Public Debates about the Genre and Its Effects. *Australian Journal of Communication*, 32(2), 71–94.

McKee, A. (2007). The Relationship between Attitudes towards Women, Consumption of Pornography, and Other Demographic Variables in a Survey of 1023 Consumers of Pornography. *International Journal of Sexual Health*, 19(1), 31–45.

McKee, A. (2009). Social Scientists Don't Say 'Titwank'. *Sexualities*, 12(5), 629–646. http://doi.org/10.1177/1363460709340372.

McNair, B. (2002). *Striptease Culture: Sex, Media and the Democratisation of Desire*. New York: Routledge.

McNair, B. (2014). Rethinking the Effects Paradigm in Porn Studies. *Porn Studies*, 1(1–2), 161–171. http://doi.org/10.1080/23268743.2013.870306.

Neumayer, C. & Svensson, J. (2014). Activism and Radical Politics in the Digital Age: Towards a Typology. *Convergence: The International Journal of Research into New Media Technologies*, 1–16. http://doi.org/10.1177/1354856514553395.

Nogueira, C., Saavedra, L. & Costa, C. E. V. da. (2007). (In)Visibilidade do Género na Sexualidade Juvenil: Propostas para uma Nova Concepção sobre a Educação Sexual e a Prevenção de Comportamentos Sexuais de Risco. *Pro-Posições*, 2(19), 59–79.

OECD. (2015). *Adult Education Level (Indicator)*. OECD Publishing. Retrieved from http://www.oecd-ilibrary.org/education/adult-education-level/indicator/english_36bce3fe-en.

Ogas, O. & Gaddam, S. (2012). *A Billion Wicked Thoughts: What the Internet Tells Us about Sexual Relationships*. New York: Plume.

Owens, E. W., Behun, R. J., Manning, J. C. & Reid, R. C. (2012). The Impact of Internet Pornography on Adolescents: A Review of the Research. *Sexual Addiction & Compulsivity*, 19(1–2), 99–122. http://doi.org/10.1080/10720162.2012.660431.

Pais, J. M. (2012). *Sexualidade e Afectos Juvenis*. Lisboa: Imprensa de Ciências Sociais.

Pereira, M. do M. (2012). *Fazendo Género no Recreio: A Negociação do Género em Espaço Escolar*. Lisboa: Imprensa de Ciências Sociais.

Peter, J. & Valkenburg, P. M. (2006). Adolescents' Exposure to Sexually Explicit Material on the Internet. *Communication Research*, 33(2), 178–204. http://doi.org/10.1177/0093650205285369.

Peter, J. & Valkenburg, P. M. (2010). Processes Underlying the Effects of Adolescents' Use of Sexually Explicit Internet Material: The Role of Perceived Realism. *Communication Research*, 37(3), 375–399. http://doi.org/10.1177/0093650210362464.

Plummer, K. (1994). *Telling Sexual Stories: Power, Change and Social Worlds*. New York: Routledge.

Ponte, C. (2012). *Crianças & Media: Pesquisa Internacional e Contexto Português do Século XIX à Actualidade*. Lisboa: Imprensa de Ciências Sociais.

Ringrose, J., Gill, R., Livingstone, S. & Harvey, L. (2012). *A Qualitative Study of Children, Young People and 'Sexting': A Report Prepared for the NSPCC*. London: National Society for the Prevention of Cruelty to Children. Retrieved from http://www.nspcc.org.uk/.

Ringrose, J. & Harvey, L. (2015). 'BBM Is like Match.com': Social Networking and the Digital Mediation of Teen's Sexual Cultures. In J. Bailey & V. Steeves (Eds.), *eGirls, eCitizens: Putting Technology Theory, Policy & Education into Dialogue with Girls' and Young Women's Voices*. Ottawa: University of Ottawa Press.

Robinson, K. H. (2012). 'Difficult Citizenship': The Precarious Relationships between Childhood, Sexuality and Access to Knowledge. *Sexualities*, 15(3–4), 257–276. http://doi.org/10.1177/1363460712436469.

Rovolis, A. & Tsaliki, L. (2012). Pornography. In S. Livingstone, L. Haddon & A. Görzig (Eds.), *Children, Risk and Safety on the Internet: Research and Policy*

Challenges in Comparative Perspective (pp. 165–176). Retrieved from http://site. ebrary.com/id/10582900.

Scarcelli, C. M. (2014). 'One Way or Another I Need to Learn This Stuff!' Adolescents, Sexual Information, and the Internet's Role Between Family, School, and Peer Groups. *Interdisciplinary Journal of Family Studies*, 19(1), 40–59.

Scarcelli, C. M. (2015). 'It Is Disgusting, but … ': Adolescent Girls' Relationship to Internet Pornography as Gender Performance. *Porn Studies*, 2(2–3), 237–249. http://doi.org/10.1080/23268743.2015.1051914.

Selwyn, N. (2008). A Safe Haven for Misbehaving? *Social Science Computer Review*, 26(4), 446–465. http://doi.org/10.1177/0894439307313515.

Simões, J. A., Ponte, C., Ferreira, E., Doretto, J. & Azevedo, C. (2014). *Crianças e Meios Digitais Móveis em Portugal: Resultados Nacionais do Projeto Net Children Go Mobile*. Lisboa: Faculdade de Ciências Sociais e Humanas. Retrieved from https://netchildrengomobile.files.wordpress.com/2015/02/ncgm_pt_relatorio1.pdf.

Simon, L. & Daneback, K. (2013). Adolescents' Use of the Internet for Sex Education: A Thematic and Critical Review of the Literature. *International Journal of Sexual Health*, 25(4), 305–319. http://doi.org/10.1080/19317611.2013.823899.

Sloam, J. (2014). New Voice, Less Equal: The Civic and Political Engagement of Young People in the United States and Europe. *Comparative Political Studies*, 47(5), 663–688. http://doi.org/10.1177/0010414012453441.

Smith, C. (2010). Pornographication: A Discourse for All Seasons. *International Journal of Media and Cultural Politics*, 6(1), 103–108. http://doi.org/10.1386/ macp.6.1.103/3.

Smith, C. (2012). 'I Guess They Got Past Their Fear of Porn': Women Viewing Porn Films. In X. Mendik (Ed.), *Peep Shows: Cult Film and the Cine-Erotic* (pp. 155–167). London; New York: Wallflower Press.

Szulc, Ł. & Dhoest, A. (2013). The Internet and Sexual Identity Formation: Comparing Internet Use Before and After Coming Out. *Communications: The European Journal of Communication Research*, 4(38), 347–365. http://doi.org/10.1515/ commun-2013-0021.

Tanton, C., Jones, K. G., Macdowall, W., Clifton, S., Mitchell, K. R., Datta, J., … Mercer, C. H. (2015). Patterns and Trends in Sources of Information about Sex among Young People in Britain: Evidence from Three National Surveys of Sexual Attitudes and Lifestyles. *BMJ Open*, 5(3), 1–10. http://doi.org/10.1136/ bmjopen-2015-007834.

Temple, J. R. & Choi, H. (2014). Longitudinal Association Between Teen Sexting and Sexual Behavior. *Pediatrics*, 134(5), 1–6. http://doi.org/10.1542/peds.2014-1974.

Theocharis, Y. & Quintelier, E. (2014). Stimulating Citizenship or Expanding Entertainment? The Effect of Facebook on Adolescent Participation. *New Media & Society*, 1–20. http://doi.org/10.1177/1461444814549006.

Vieira, C. P. (2012). '*Eu Faço Sexo Amoroso*': *A Sexualidade dos Jovens pela Voz dos Próprios*. Lisboa: Editorial Bizâncio.

Vieira, P. C. M. (2010). *Silêncios Simultâneos: Currículo e Sexualidades* (Tese de Mestrado em Ciências da Educação). Universidade do Minho, Minho. Retrieved from http://repositorium.sdum.uminho.pt/handle/1822/14155.

Part V

Self-Presentation and Intimacy on Online Dating Sites

13 Exploring Networked Interactions through the Lens of Location-Based Dating Services

The Case of Italian Grindr Users

Lorenza Parisi and Francesca Comunello

LGBTQ people have made intensive use of digital media for their social interactions, having been among the first users to effectively explore the blurring boundaries between the online and the offline realms, with special regard to Location-Based Social Networks (LBSN) (de Souza e Silva & Frith, 2010). As Mowlabocus (2010a, p. 6) observes, 'the web has always been used by gay men as a means by which physical interaction could be sought, negotiated and organized. Gay men's digital spaces have historically provided an environment in which offline intimacies can be facilitated'. This chapter analyses the use of the gay male dating application Grindr to explore to what extent the use of a real-time location-based dating service affects the patterns and the flows of online/offline social interactions in urban spaces.

Our theoretical background relies on several contributions which explore the social use of mobile technologies within (urban) spaces and on the use of digital media to manage users' online visibility, self-presentation strategies and relational performances. We also introduce the context of empirical research that has been carried out in Rome and Milan (Italy) among Grindr users. Two main reasons led to this case study selection. Firstly, as Italian society is characterised by a strongly heteronormative culture, digital media seem to constitute effective environments where LGBTQ users can display and perform their sexual orientation and initiate interactions with other users, which could be continued both online and offline. In such a context, Grindr could be perceived as a tool to at least partially overcome hegemonic cultural and social constraints and to support visibility and sociability among gay users in Italy. Secondly, Grindr has been one of the first online platforms in Italy to support an actual and widespread interaction among users, linking online and offline realms. The literature on Social Networking Sites (SNS) has mainly described the social dynamics of moving from the offline to the online world, describing offline friends that interact also on digital platforms, basing their choices on pre-existing relations (boyd & Ellison, 2013); the online towards offline direction has been described as less widespread in the mainstream SNS. For this reason, location-based dating services such as Grindr represent an interesting case study for exploring practices which are oriented towards an online-to-offline shift.

Exploring Gay Male Dating Practices through LBSN

The conceptual framework adopted in this chapter relies on theories covering two main areas: the use of location-based mobile communication in (urban) spaces (Aurigi & De Cindio, 2008; Licoppe, 2015) and the use of digital media to manage users' online visibility, self-presentation strategies and relational performances (Baym, 2010). Within this framework we do not consider online and offline experiences as a dichotomy, as scholars used to do during the early years of internet studies (Wellman, 2004). On the contrary, we consider these two realms as a continuum (Comunello, 2011), understanding each (digital) platform as an 'environment' that offers specific affordances and constraints, where 'architecture shapes and is shaped by practices in mediated environments just as in physical spaces' (boyd, 2011, p. 55).

Each online environment is characterised by specific affordances and constraints negotiated by the users (boyd, 2011) and by specific 'media ideologies', a concept that refers to 'people's beliefs about how a medium communicates and structures communication' (Gershon, 2010, p. 21). Indeed, users rely on specific usage practices which can vary according to different social and cultural groups, as described by the concept of *communal common ground*, which refers to 'the facts, norms, procedures, and lexicons that can be assumed to be known to any member of a community' (Ellison, Hancock & Toma, 2012, p. 48).

Ever since digital technology became increasingly 'always on' and portable, users can shift rapidly between online and offline interactions. The use of mobile media has in fact transformed the perception of presence (Farman, 2012) as well as of proximity and distance (Urry, 2002). The user can experience different kinds of presence/absence, which have been described in terms of 'present absence' (Fortunati, 2002), 'absent presence' (Gergen, 2002) or 'connected presence' (Rainie & Wellman, 2012). 'Present absence' refers to the experience of people being present and absent at the same time: 'They are present in body, but their attention, mind and senses can at any moment, after a ring of the mobile phone, be drawn elsewhere by their communication network' (Fortunati, 2002, pp. 518–519). The 'absent presence' in turn refers to the virtual presence of members of one's personal network who are physically absent (Gergen, 2002).

Additionally, the intense use of digital media in everyday life has established the superimposition of physical and digital layers, a scenario that Manovich (2006, p. 233) defines as 'augmented (urban) space' – the 'overlaying of the physical space with dynamic data'. The emerging dialogue between location-based experiences and digital media produces interesting social consequences. To describe this scenario, de Souza e Silva (2006, p. 265) introduces the concept of 'hybrid space', a space 'built through the connection of mobility and communication and materialized by social networks developed simultaneously in physical and digital spaces'. This scenario has been extended by the rise of locative media (Tuters & Varnelis,

2006; Wilken, 2012) and by the diffusion of location-aware mobile media (Sutko & de Souza e Silva, 2011), all supported by the wide diffusion of GPS devices and smartphones. Indeed, through LBSN social interactions can be arranged according to users' location and users can meet people living nearby who share common interests (Sutko & de Souza e Silva, 2011). Following the networked individualism perspective (Rainie & Wellman, 2012), the emerging picture is that of a 'networked sociability' (Hampton, 2004); that is, a sociability 'breaking the organizational and spatial boundaries of relationships independent of spatial constraints' (Castells et al., 2007, p. 143). In this case, moving from communities to networks each user creates an 'individual-centered network based on choice and affinity' (Castells et al., 2007, pp. 143–144).

LGBTQ persons were among some of the first to embrace cyber resources (Wakeford, 2000) and to realise their potential (Gross, 2003, p. 260). In fact, 'the internet offers particular opportunities for marginalized and disenfranchised populations (Koch & Schockman 1998), such as among the lesbian, gay, bisexual, and transgender (LGBT) community, to meet and make connections' (Farr, 2010, p. 87). In particular, SNS for gay men facilitate both friendships and sexual activities among their users (Gudelunas, 2012). Digital platforms represent an evolution of Gay Public Space: 'The communication action context has moved, it now consists of online chatrooms, messageboards, dating sites [in a context in which] [...] online blogs and media outlets can help cement both local and global community relationships' (Usher & Morrison, 2010, p. 280).

Mowlabocus describes the strong interactions between gay male culture and digital technology:

> Gay male subculture (offline) and gay men's digital culture (online) are part and parcel of the same thing. While a bar or a club might be considered a physical gay space and a website a digital one, such boundaries are at best, difficult to maintain, and at worst, fabrications that conceal the truth of gay male subculture; that it is now both digitally and physically manifested, and that these multiple manifestations occur simultaneously and shape one another continuously.
>
> (Mowlabocus, 2010a, p. 15)

More specifically, online dating is popular among the LGBTQ community because it offers a useful tool for individuals 'who may have limited options for meeting people within their immediate geographic area or social circle' (Smith & Duggan, 2013). Gay men often use online means when they look for a partner (Hogan, Li & Dutton, 2011, p. 15) and in 2009 more than 60% of same-sex couples in the United States met online (Rosenfeld & Thomas, 2012). Moreover, thanks to the geolocalisation feature, real-time dating sites (Handel & Shklovski, 2012) play a relevant role in fostering offline intimacies. According to Licoppe (2015) mobile applications such as

Grindr enable encounters among 'pseudonymous strangers', namely 'people we have never seen but to the online persona of which we are connected through our mobile devices, and the proximity of whom mobile locative media make us aware of' (p. 26). As Batiste (2013) notices, Grindr 'allows gay men to interact with one another outside of specifically gay spaces' (p. 111), revealing the 'queer cartography' of any geographical location.

Literature on online dating has often focused on personal profiles and on the self-presentation and impression management strategies adopted by users (Ellison, Heino & Gibbs, 2006). Adopting the hyperpersonal theory framework, Ellison, Hancock and Toma (2012, p. 48) underline how the lack of physical cues in computer-mediated communication (CMC) 'gives the user more control over their self-presentational statements', but at the same time introduces pressures that are related to the need to explicitly document several identity characteristics which are implicitly expressed by physical cues in face-to-face encounters. The authors propose the *profile as promise* framework: 'the profile constitutes a promise made to an imagined audience that future face-to-face interaction will take place with someone who does not differ fundamentally from the person represented by the profile' (ibid., p. 56).

A relevant element for understanding user self-presentation strategies among online dating sites is the kind of information users are willing to share in their personal profiles. Research on gay men's personal profiles for instance has underlined that 'men seeking men are likely to emphasize physical characteristics and sexual relations' (Farr, 2010, p. 89); therefore the act of showing so-called 'face pics' (pictures showing a user's face) can affect the outcomes of an entire chat session (Jones, 2005) and can be considered as a 'signifier of authenticity' (Mowlabocus, 2010b, p. 206). Moreover, we should consider the role that algorithms play in supporting online dating practices, given that the software fixes in place several important social cues, such as the ranking order of the users according to the main user's localisation. Indeed the code is not neutral (Dodge, Kitchin & Zook, 2009). On the contrary, it opaquely determines the platform's sorting rules and filters, and therefore affects the social interactions.

Analysing dating practices supported by LBSN therefore offers the chance to explore several pertinent topics, including networked sociability processes, the blurring boundaries between the online/offline realms, user identity building and impression management strategies.

Homophobia in Italy

Many studies support the notion that Italian society is affected by homophobia (Trappolin, Gasparini & Wintemute, 2011). According to the LGBT Survey of the European Union Agency for Fundamental Rights (FRA, 2014) LGBTs experience a higher level of discrimination for their sexual orientation in Italy (54%) than in the EU on average (47%).

As Lingiardi et al. (2016) point out, in Italy there exists a common 'don't ask, don't tell' attitude towards homosexuality. Overall, Italian society is permeated by a heteronormative culture, suggesting conformist lifestyles where the traditional family, composed of a man and a woman, plays a central role. Recently this model has been questioned by an increasing representation in the media of different kinds of families (in terms of composition, family members and ethnicities). For example, after 2000 some LGBTQ characters appeared in prime-time Italian television series, even if in most cases they reproduced stereotypical roles (Malici, 2014). Very few Italian public figures publicly declare their homosexuality, so that the few examples that do come out are considered as atypical cases (Benozzo, 2013). As a result, even in the urban contexts which are more open to LGBTQ people (e.g. Rome and Milan; see Barbagli & Colombo, 2007) still many LGBTQs do not openly express their gender or sexual non-normativity to family members, friends and colleagues.

In the last ten years, the decision whether or not to extend civil union rights to LGBTQ people has been at the centre of the Italian public and political debate from time to time. In May 2016, the Italian parliament finally approved a same-sex civil union law, even if this does not allow for 'stepchild adoption' of the partner's biological child. Moreover, Italy is one of the very few countries among the current 28 European Union member states (still including the UK) which has not yet approved a hate crime law to protect LGBTQs. Some public figures (mainly right-wing politicians) and even brands, such as Barilla, explicitly express their views against same-sex civil unions through the mainstream media. In addition, members of civil society have organised public demonstrations to 'defend' the 'traditional family' composed of a man and a woman and founded on marriage (e.g. 'Family Day'). Numerous insults are addressed at LGBTQs in Italy (Vox, 2015), reaffirming the presence of stereotypes (Hall, 1997). As a result, a large majority of young people (83% in 2004) believe that Italian society stigmatises homosexual experiences (Zanutto, 2007). According to the European survey already mentioned (FRA, 2014), 92% of Italian LGBT respondents perceived the level of discrimination on the grounds of sexual orientation to be either 'very' or 'fairly widespread'. Currently, many Italian LGBTQs, especially under the age of 18, still hide their sexual and gender identifications in order not to upset their parents or to avoid social prejudices in their daily lives.

The Case Study: Grindr

Grindr is an application created in 2009 to support the dating practices of gay men (for early research, see Mowlabocus, 2010a). As claimed by its creators (Grindr, 2015), it recently reached seven million users worldwide (the top countries for users are the United States, the United Kingdom, France, Canada, Australia, Spain, Brazil, Italy, Germany and Mexico). Grindr shows a list of users who recently signed in, arranged in ascending order according to users' proximity. Through the platform, users can explore other men's profiles, chat with them and share their exact location. Thanks to Grindr's affordances they can decide to meet offline nearly in real time. The application is generally perceived as oriented toward short-term (generally sexual) encounters, even if some differences emerge in diverse social and cultural contexts. For example, in US culture Grindr was initially perceived as an app to procure sexual encounters (Blackwell, Birnholtz & Abbott, 2014) whereas nowadays it is oriented towards 'more social purposes' (Van de Wiele & Tong, 2014).

In Italy, Grindr started to gain popularity among the gay community in autumn 2010, a few years before the adoption of some of the currently most popular dating applications, such as Tinder, which are also used by heterosexual users. It was one of the first popular LBSNs which supported – although within a relatively small community – actual interaction among users, linking online and offline realms. Other LBSNs, such as Foursquare, were mainly used with a game-like attitude rather than as a tool for actual interactions with other users.

Research Questions and Method

This explorative research addresses the following research questions: 1) how do users manage self-presentation strategies, patterns of interaction and online visibility on Grindr?; and 2) how does the use of Grindr shape and become shaped by the perception of physical (urban) spaces?

In order to investigate self-presentation strategies and users' online visibility, we analysed two different corpora. In the winter and spring of 2012 we analysed 206 randomly selected user profiles, mainly observing the kind of information shared by users and their self-presentation strategies. More specifically we created a 'convenience sample', looking through the platform in different areas of Rome and Milan (Italy) and during different times of the day/week, both during working hours and in the evening, on weekdays and weekends. The cities of Rome and Milan were selected since they represent key cities for the Italian LGBTQ community. This non-probability sample aims to select a wide variety of urban Grindr profiles situated in Italy's biggest cities.

Although user data was recorded without explicit consent, we ensured that ethical guidelines were met by taking several measures. First of all, users' profiles were never 'collected' or archived. Secondly, we never recorded usernames nor any detail that could identify a user, even indirectly, limiting our analysis to the kind of information users shared online (but not tracking the specific information they shared). Thirdly, we never engaged in private conversations with users. Fourthly, the profile that was built for our research purposes was completely 'empty' (no profile picture, no personal information), thereby violating the shared 'idioms of practice' and overtly implying that we were not interested in engaging in some form of relation with other users. Finally, as interviewees confirmed, the platform – with the exception of private one-to-one conversations – is generally perceived as a 'public' space by their users, who calibrate their visibility according to such a consideration. In these ways we believe to have met the 'fundamental ethical principle of minimizing harm' (AoIR, 2012, p. 7).

From March 2012 until July 2013, we also administered twelve in-depth interviews with Italian Grindr users. In order to investigate users' perception of physical (urban) space, we decided to interview users living in the same city (Rome). Participants were recruited by using a snowball sampling method, and we stopped recruiting when we achieved saturation. The respondents' average age was 32. Although having contacted more than 50 users as well as some LGBTQ associations, we experienced several difficulties in finding respondents willing to engage in face-to-face interviews. This might have been related both to the social stigma within Italian society towards gay people and to Grindr's orientation towards 'fast-food sex' (a topic about which some people are not willing to share their experiences). Therefore we offered participants three interview options: face-to-face, Skype audio interviews and written interviews. As a result we administered four in-depth face-to-face interviews, four Skype audio interviews and four written (e-mail) interviews. We considered the methodological implications of virtual ethnography and internet inquiry (Hine, 2015; Markham & Baym, 2009) as applied to studying gay men's relationships (van Eeden-Moorefield, Proulx & Pasley, 2008), and the differences between face-to-face and computer-mediated interviews (in terms both of self-disclosure attitude and of communicative bandwidth), and accordingly adapted our administration strategy.

Two female researchers conducted the interviews. Whilst the participants were initially surprised, as they expected to be interviewed by a gay man, we believe that the study gained several benefits from the interviewers' outsider position, as participants provided us with background details when describing the application (Blackwell, Birnholtz & Abbott, 2014). Nevertheless, some of the respondents were hesitant to describe their sexual uses, being reluctant to admit that, as they later revealed, they like Grindr because it allows them to satisfy their sexual needs as quickly as possible. We transcribed and analysed the interviews using thematic analysis (Guest, MacQueen & Namey, 2011), identifying emerging patterns (themes) within the interviews.

Results and Discussion

The following section discusses the main results of our research. It addresses the first research question by focusing on users' self-presentation strategies and patterns of interaction as well as the role that Grindr plays as a place for the (public) display of sexual orientation and the implications of showing up in a location-based dating app. Subsequently the second research question is addressed, describing the interactions between the users' perception of physical (urban) space and their use of Grindr.

Users' Self-Presentation and Patterns of Interaction

In order to investigate self-presentation strategies and patterns of inter-action, we first analysed both the kind of information users included in their profiles and the responses to our interviews. As of spring 2012, Grindr offered a set of options for building user profiles, including profile pictures, age, relationship status, 'about' (self-description), looking for, height, weight and ethnicity. Such options, which are set in the platform's design, are not neutral; indeed they can steer the use of the application towards a 'preferred usage' (in analogy to the 'preferred reading' proposed by Hall, 1973), which might be shaped by a specific understanding of sexuality and sexual identity. Based on such a template, users can decide whether or not to give informa-tion on each of the topics and what kind of information to provide (e.g. true or false). Moreover some users rely on icons, or emoji (put in the 'about' section), in order to further personalise their profile, thus experiencing a form of 'negotiation' with the affordances and constraints provided by the platform.

As Cassidy (2015) notes in his analysis of Gaydar, another popular app for social networking among gay men, the presence of specific categorisa-tions and labels (and the absence of others) influences the users' perceived 'ideology' of the platform (Gershon, 2010). Each platform is characterised by intersubjective idioms of practice that describe the 'appropriate social uses of technology' (Gershon, 2010, p. 6). For example, Gaydar asks users to categorise themselves according to explicitly sex-oriented identity cues, e.g. 'indication of "cock" size and circumcision status, preferred sexual role and attitude towards practicing safe sex' (Cassidy, 2015, p. 6), thereby fos-tering specific patterns of user interaction. By contrast, the Grindr profile template lists more general traits (age, height, weight, ethnicity, etc.), as do most of the current dating sites. Most of the interviewees considered that these traits provide enough information. As a 25-year-old user explained: 'I found what I needed; it is not reductive [...] I mean, the application is very fast. You open it and you look for someone nearby that you can get to know better through face-to-face interaction'.

The prevalent information provided in the analysed profiles was age (81.1%), height (78.2%) and weight (74%) (see Figure 13.1). The youngest user stated he was 20 years old, the oldest user 53; the average declared age was 32.5 years old. Ethnicity (in Grindr defined as e.g. Asian, Black, Middle Eastern, White; for more information, see Shield in this volume) had been provided by nearly half of the users, maybe because this feature is perceived as redundant by many, as the great majority of Italian citizens are white. A minority of users made use of emoji (9.7%) to personalise their profile, which is not explicitly encouraged by the platform's design. The analysis of user profiles and the in-depth interviews confirmed that the majority of users fill in the requested information following Grindr's approach to sexual interactions. However, a 30-year-old user said he does not disclose his age in order to appear in the search results of younger users who may use age filters. Two interviewees moreover said they created an anonymous profile in order to maintain control over the interaction. A 39-year-old user explained: 'I don't publish information in my profile, I want to decide by myself whether or not to chat with someone'.

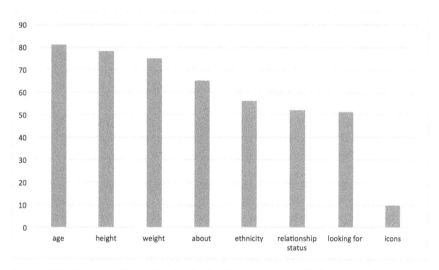

Figure 13.1 User profiles: What kind of information was filled in (out of 206 profiles).

All the twelve interviewees said they had come out of the closet at least to some family members, friends and colleagues. Half of them showed their facial picture on Grindr. During the interview they elaborated on the implications of appearing in a location-based dating application for gay men in terms of public presentation and visibility. For example, users' strategies concerning the choice of profile pictures clearly illustrate how carefully they manage their online visibility. At the same time, given the lack of several social cues that people usually get from face-to-face conversation (Ellison, Heino & Gibbs, 2006), the limited basic information that the user can add on their Grindr profile plays a crucial role in self-presentation strategies. In line with Brown, Maycock and Burns (2005, p. 67), interviewees said that pictures constitute important social cues among gay men's online interactions, given that they contribute to shaping expectations and assumptions. Unsurprisingly then, 93% of the 206 profiles we analysed included a profile picture. Only 53% of those however displayed the user's face. Our analysis disclosed that the decision to show a profile picture is influenced by several reasons, including the user's visibility as a gay person in everyday life, different cultural contexts and specific events (like the Gay Pride). This confirms that offline and online patterns mutually influence each other.

The decision to show a face picture plays an important role in negotiating online-offline interactions among users. Most of the interviewees who are not showing their face on the profile picture described the following conversation pattern. At the beginning of a chat session or whenever they perceive that the interaction could be engaging, they give up their anonymity and send some personal images (showing their face) to their interlocutor. This action is considered essential to continuing the interaction. Indeed the act of showing one's face to the partner is a relevant cue: it both expresses authenticity and the desire to continue the conversation, representing a necessary prelude to moving towards an offline meeting. Only if both participants are satisfied with the other user's picture are they going to arrange an offline meeting in the next few hours; otherwise in most cases the interaction rapidly fades way.

Consistent with Blackwell, Birnholtz and Abbott (2014), we found the presence of individuals with different goals on Grindr. The variety of goals is also reflected upon by some of our interviewees, as a 30-year-old interviewee explains:

> There are four different kinds of users: 'sex maniacs', who are already close to the door, already wearing their shoes; frustrated gay or bisexual users in a relationship just waiting for their partner to leave so they can quickly arrange a meeting (they generally do not publish a profile picture); people like me that just want to have fun with other guys only if the opportunity arises; and young people that use Grindr as the first place to disclose their sexual orientation.

Of course this quote does not provide an objective account of different Grindr users; rather it describes the perception that a variety of different uses and needs co-exists. In fact, all respondents said they perform a very individualised use of Grindr. Consistent with Cassidy's results (2015, p. 11), most of the interviewees do not perceive Grindr as supporting communal activities; as a 25-year-old user said, it is 'a very individualistic app'.

Grindr as a Place for the (Public) Display of Sexual Orientation

Several interviewees noted that Grindr is mostly used to arrange sexual encounters in almost real-time. Nevertheless, it also plays an important role as a place for (publicly) expressing users' sexual identity. Thus a 28-year-old interviewee stated that Grindr has helped him reveal his sexual orientation. Through the app he performed an online coming out within the 'community' of Grindr users belonging to the same city he used to live in; these users were perceived as his most appropriate audience, as they were not connected with his everyday life. Then, after he arranged his first date through Grindr, he decided to come out to his friends:

> I mean, Grindr has been the tool... has been a tool that I've used to meet another person and to have... let's say a date, outside of my friends' circles [...] And eventually, having a date with someone you've met on Grindr has been like an actual coming out in my life [...] these are my very first experiences.

According to this testimony, and other similar narratives, Grindr provides a protected environment where users who are still in the closet can express their sexual identity to their peers. Castañeda (2015) describes a similar use of Grindr by young Filipino gay men (in the age range of 17–25), who are using Grindr to articulate and perform their sexual identity and to share personal stories with people they perceive to be going through similar experiences. The gay men reported that they used Grindr to express concerns about family issues, school and faith, and to talk about sex and romance strategies and dilemmas.

Moreover, users are aware that Grindr supports the 'public' display of their sexual orientation, at least among the users who joined the app. At the same time, as Blackwell, Birnholtz and Abbott (2014) observe, they are aware that the app itself (the act of using it) indicates that the user is likely to be seeking sex. Therefore the users intensively consider the audience they can potentially chance upon while using Grindr. For instance, users evaluate the possibility that an outsider (especially someone living nearby, a colleague, etc.) would download the app and identify someone just by looking at the information published online. In this sense, the presence of several prejudices against LGBTQ people within Italian society and the general stigma towards one-time sexual encounters may influence users' decision to display personal information. Some interviewees for instance report that they share complete personal information (real name, profile image showing the face, etc.) only after they better realise whom they are talking to. As Woo (2006, p. 949) observes, 'affirmative acts of secrecy and deception regarding identity and identification might be the most effective way of ensuring privacy in the interactive environment'. At the same time, some interviewees showing their face pic said they did not want to chat with users who did not show their face, assuming they had not come out of the closet yet.

Most of the users have specifically considered the consequences of showing up in a location-based dating application for gay people. One 28-year-old user is not worried about the implications of being seen on Grindr:

> Visibility is what our society continuously demands from us; I've always thought that if someone sees me in such an application, it's because he or she is on that site him/herself, but I've never felt judged because of that.

On the other hand, another 28-year-old user is only partially concerned about the fact that Grindr publicly displays his sexual orientation:

> Actually my parents are my only problem because they don't know about me; in any case they wouldn't be on Grindr and, moreover, they live 80 km from here... honestly I don't care about the picture; otherwise, if I had these kind of problems, I wouldn't be here.

Grindr and the Perception of Physical (Urban) Space

The following section addresses the second research question, investigating to what extent the use of Grindr affects users' perception of physical (urban) space. Several respondents use Grindr as a sort of radar to get an idea of the extent to which specific areas of the city are populated by gay men. As Roth (2014) observes, location-based dating apps allow gay users to situate their interactions within the flow of their everyday life, even within heterosexual social spaces. Instead of users having to move to specific sexualised places to arrange social encounters (e.g. gay bars), Grindr transforms every corner of the city into a potential meeting opportunity with 'pseudonymous strangers' (Licoppe, 2015) who are available 24/7. Through Grindr gay men can overcome traditional community boundaries and remap heteronormative contexts.

As previously stated, each user gets a personalised composition of his Grindr network according to 1) geographical proximity, 2) density (in very dense areas the first 'page' displays only those users who are very close) and 3) other customised parameters (e.g. 'favourite' users are shown first, blocked users are removed). As a result most of the respondents use Grindr to explore the 'queer cartography' (Batiste, 2013) of different locations they are familiar or unfamiliar with; in fact they perceive Grindr as a tool, similar to magazines in waiting rooms, to pass the time when they are bored or want to relax for a few minutes. When they are moving into new urban areas for example they open Grindr just to look for new people hanging around. At the same time some users use Grindr to 'check' their home surroundings, whose cartography they are very familiar with (a 25-year-old user said: 'I always find the same people'). Using Grindr for the first time, some users said they were very surprised to realise their block was crowded with several 'gay people'. A 25-year-old user says: 'We are everywhere!' One user explains he uses the app to 'discover' if he has gay neighbours. He reports that he then checks out the offline realm to see if any of his neighbours match the characteristics (age, profile image, etc.) of his closest Grindr users. Two respondents are used to opening Grindr when visiting their hometowns, especially in rural areas, where gay social spaces do not exist and gay men are still in the closet: 'I open Grindr in my hometown out of curiosity, just to check how many people were there, and clearly they were all showing no picture given that they are all prudish' (a 28-year-old respondent).

Grindr makes gay men visible to each other even in very heteronormative places; the app itself redefines these places by making them more gay-friendly locations. Some users also said that the use of Grindr affected their perception of the surrounding areas and districts of their hometown: 'Well... I've realised that homosexuality in Rome is focused between Re di Roma and Colli Albani... Furio Camillo rocks, followed by Tiburtina [specific areas of Rome]' (a 28-year-old respondent). A 31-year-old user said: 'Definitely, it seems that gay people are everywhere, even when you are shopping, whereas you haven't noticed it before'.

On the whole, what emerges for the user is a very personal sense of place which is modified according to the social experiences carried out through location-based social media (Parisi, 2016). The use of Grindr establishes a strong connection with local urban spaces: even if the application is geolocalised (automatically showing the distance between users), 12.7% of users (out of the 206 analysed profiles) explicitly type the name of the district where they live (or work) in the 'about' section of their profile.

Finally, Grindr effectively connects online and offline contexts. Most of the respondents say they do not like to chat for a long time: the platform is used to find new people and when they encounter someone interesting they prefer to move quickly to the offline context. A 38-year-old interviewee describes Grindr as the fastest way to meet a guy in the surrounding area. A 28-year-old user explains: 'I don't chat for a long time... Never more than a couple of days... I prefer to meet quickly [...] Even the same night, if I'm not busy'. Given that sexual desire is generally one of the most important Grindr user motivations, many interviewees say that the geographical distance of users plays a key role in the decision to start an interaction. A 39-year-old user clearly explains: 'I don't want to chat with someone who is located 10 kilometres away. I'm not interested in chatting!'

Conclusion

The three main results of this research confirm that Grindr represents an interesting case study to illustrate how emerging digital media social practices (e.g. gay male online dating) support an intense online-offline shift. Firstly, in accordance with previous studies (Blackwell, Birnholtz & Abbott, 2014; Gudelunas, 2012; Mowlabocus, 2010a), Italian Grindr respondents use the application mainly to arrange offline local sexual encounters. Secondly, they perceive the app as a place for (public) displays of sexual orientation; some users say they have used the application to come out, perceiving Grindr as a 'protected' environment where they can easily manage their self-presentation. Thirdly, Grindr shapes the perception of physical (urban) space and its inhabitants, adding a new (gay) layer to the place which is superimposed on an otherwise heteronormative place. Whilst getting to know new people they might wish to meet offline, users also gather information about the offline context they are living in or going through in terms of the 'density' of gay people and other users' localisation, thus ceaselessly updating their 'queer cartography'.

This research confirms the importance of investigating the specific cultural context of each medium in order to better understand its actual role for users in terms of shared meanings and the range of experiences it supports. More specifically, some of the practices and motivations which were exposed during the interviews seem to be influenced by the heteronormativity of the Italian context. For instance, the practice of coming out on the platform or the way in which interviewees describe how they manage the (mediated) display of their sexual orientation seem to be connected to the tactics adopted by interviewees to deal with a context which is not perceived as 'gay friendly'. With regard to specific urban contexts, some interviewees use Grindr to assess the 'gayness' of different districts or to collect information about the presence of gay neighbours in their home surroundings. Some users moreover, when they visit their hometown (smaller towns or villages), use Grindr out of curiosity to reveal the gay cartography of a local area.

We are aware of the limitations of this research. As mentioned above, we experienced several difficulties to find respondents willing to engage in face-to-face interviews. This obstacle could be partially overcome in the future considering that Italian society is becoming more relaxed towards online dating and more accepting of LGBTQ people. As participation was accorded on a voluntary basis (and without any reward), people willing to take part in the research had a higher propensity for discussing topics related to their sexual orientation and online dating practices. As a result we interviewed only Italian users who openly declared their sexual orientation. Further research then could analyse identity-building and self-presentation strategies among Grindr users who are still in the closet. Finally, it would be interesting for future research to compare Grindr uses by men located in different cultural contexts.

References

AoIR – Association of Internet Researchers (2012). *Ethical Decision-Making and Internet Research*. Retrieved from http://www.aoir.org/reports/ethics2.pdf.

Aurigi, A. & De Cindio, F. (2008). *Augmented Urban Spaces: Articulating the Physical and Electronic City*. Aldershot: Ashgate.

Barbagli, M. & Colombo, A. (2007). *Omosessuali Moderni: Gay e Lesbiche in Italia*. Bologna: Il Mulino.

Batiste, D. P. (2013). '0 Feet Away': The Queer Cartography of French Gay Men's Geo-Social Media Use. *Anthropological Journal of European Cultures*, 22(2), 111–132.

Baym, N. (2010). *Personal Connections in the Digital Age*. Cambridge: Polity.

Benozzo, A. (2013). Coming Out of the Credenza: An Italian Celebrity Unveils His 'New' Gay Self. *Sexualities*, 16(3–4), 336–360.

Blackwell, C., Birnholtz, J. & Abbott, C. (2014). Seeing and Being Seen: Co-Situation and Impression Formation Using Grindr, a Location-Aware Gay Dating App. *New Media & Society*, 17(7), 1117–1136.

boyd, d. (2011). Social Network Sites as Networked Publics: Affordances, Dynamics and Implications. In Z. Papacharissi (Ed.), *A Networked Self: Identity, Community and Culture on Social Network Sites*. London: Routledge.

boyd, d. & Ellison, E. (2013), Sociality through Social Network Sites. In W. H. Dutton (Ed.), *The Oxford Handbook of Internet Studies* (pp. 151–172). Oxford: Oxford University Press.

Brown, G., Maycock, B. & Burns, S. (2005). Your Picture Is Your Bait: Use and Meaning of Cyberspace Among Gay Men. *Journal of Sex Research*, 42(1), 63–73.

Cassidy, E. (2015). Social Networking Sites and Participatory Reluctance: A Case Study of Gaydar, User Resistance and Interface Rejection. *New Media & Society*. Published online before print.

Castañeda, J. G. M. (2015). Grindring the Self: Young Filipino Gay Men's Exploration of Sexual Identity Through a Geo-Social Networking Application. *Philippine Journal of Psychology*, 48(1), 29–58.

Castells, M., Fernandez-Ardevol, M., Linchuan Qiu, J. & Sey, A. (2007). *Mobile Communication and Society: A Global Perspective*. Cambridge, MA: MIT Press.

Comunello, F. (2011). Preface. In F. Comunello (Ed.), *Networked Sociability and Individualism: Technology for Personal and Professional Relationships* (pp. xii–xxx). Hershey: IGI Global.

de Souza e Silva, A. (2006). From Cyber to Hybrid: Mobile Technologies as Interfaces of Hybrid Spaces. *Space and Culture*, 9(3), 261–278.

de Souza e Silva, A. & Frith, J. (2010). Locative Mobile Social Networks: Mapping Communication and Location in Urban Spaces. *Mobilities*, 5(4), 485–506.

Dodge, M., Kitchin, R. & Zook, M. (2009). Guest Editorial: How Does Software Make Space: Exploring Some Geographical Dimensions of Pervasive Computing and Software Studies. *Environment and Planning A*, 41, 1283–1293.

Ellison, N. B., Hancock, J. T. & Toma, C. L. (2012). Profile as Promise: A Framework for Conceptualizing Veracity in Online Dating Self-Presentations. *New Media & Society*, 14(1), 45–62.

Ellison, N., Heino, R. & Gibbs, J. (2006). Managing Impressions Online: Self-Presentation Processes in the Online Dating Environment. *Journal of Computer-Mediated Communication*, 11(2), 415–441.

Farman, J. (2012). *Mobile Interface Theory: Embodied Space and Locative Media*. London: Routledge.

Farr, D. (2010). A Very Personal World: Advertisement and Identity of Trans-Persons on Craigslist. In C. Pullen & M. Cooper (Eds.), *LGBT Identity and Online New Media* (pp. 87–99). London: Routledge.

Fortunati, L. (2002). The Mobile Phone: Towards New Categories and Social Relations. *Information, Communication & Society*, 5(4), 513–528.

FRA – European Union Agency for Fundamental Rights (2014). EU LGBT Survey. Retrieved from: http://fra.europa.eu/sites/default/files/fra-eu-lgbt-survey-main-results_tk3113640enc_1.pdf.

Gergen, K. J. (2002). The Challenge of Absent Presence. In J. E. Katz & M. Aakhus (Eds.), *Perpetual Contact: Mobile Communication, Private Talk, Public Performance* (pp. 227–241). Cambridge: Cambridge University Press.

Gershon, I. (2010). *The Breakup 2.0: Disconnecting over New Media*. Ithaca: Cornell University Press.

Grindr (2015). Grindr Press. Retrieved from: http://grindr.com.

Gross, L. (2003). The Gay Global Village in Cyberspace. In N. Couldry & J. Curran (Eds.), *Contesting Media Power: Alternative Media in a Networked World* (pp. 259–272). Lanham: Rowman & Littlefield.

Gudelunas, D. (2012). There's an App for That: The Uses and Gratifications of Online Social Networks for Gay Men. *Sexuality & Culture, 16*(4), 347–365.

Guest, G., MacQueen, K. M. & Namey, E. E. (2011). *Applied Thematic Analysis*. London: Sage.

Hall, S. (1973). *Encoding and Decoding in the Television Discourse*. Birmingham: Centre for Contemporary Cultural Studies.

Hall, S. (1997). The Spectacle of the Other. In S. Hall (Ed.), *Representation: Cultural Representations and Signifying Practices* (pp. 223–290). London: Sage.

Hampton, K. (2004). Networked Sociability Online, Off-line. In Castells, M. (Ed.), *The Network Society: A Cross-Cultural Perspective* (pp. 217–232). Northampton, MA: Edward Elgar.

Handel, M. J. & Shklovski, I. (2012). Disclosure, Ambiguity and Risk Reduction in Real-Time Dating Sites. In *Proceedings of the 17th ACM International Conference on Supporting Group Work* (GROUP '12) (pp. 175–178). New York: ACM.

Hine, C. (2015). *Ethnography for the Internet: Embedded, Embodied and Everyday*. London: Bloomsbury.

Hogan, B., Li, N. & Dutton, W. H. (2011). A Global Shift in the Social Relationships of Networked Individuals: Meeting and Dating Online Comes of Age. Retrieved from: http://www.oii.ox.ac.uk/publications/Me-MySpouse_GlobalReport.pdf.

Jones, R. (2005). 'You Show Me Yours, I'll Show You Mine': The Negotiation of Shifts from Textual to Visual Modes in Computer-Mediated Interaction among Gay Men. *Visual Communication, 4*(1), 69–92.

Licoppe, C. (2015). Seams and Folds, Detours, and Encounters with 'Pseudonymous Strangers: Mobilities and Urban Encounters in Public Places in the Age of Locative Media. *i3 Working Papers Series*, 15-SES-05.

Lingiardi, V., Nardelli, N., Ioverno, S., Falanga, S., Di Chiacchio, C., Tanzilli, A. & Baiocco, R. (2016). Homonegativity in Italy: Cultural Issues, Personality Characteristics, and Demographic Correlates with Negative Attitudes toward Lesbians and Gay Men. *Sexuality Research and Social Policy, 13*(2), 95–108.

Malici, L. (2014). Queer TV Moments and Family Viewing in Italy. *Journal of GLBT Family Studies, 10*(1–2), 188–210.

Manovich, L. (2006). The Poetics of Augmented Space. *Visual Communication, 5*(2), 219–240.

Markham, A. & Baym, N. (2009). *Internet Inquiry: Conversations About Method*. Thousand Oaks, CA: Sage.

Mowlabocus, S. (2010a). *Gaydar Culture: Gay Men, Technology and Embodiment in the Digital Age*. Farnham: Ashgate.

Mowlabocus, S. (2010b). Look at Me! Images, Validation, and Cultural Currency on Gaydar. In C. Pullen & M. Cooper (Eds.), *LGBT Identity and Online New Media* (pp. 201–214). London: Routledge.

Parisi, L. (2015). 'Where 2.0'. Exploring the Place Experience of 'Hyperconnected' Digital Media Users. *Sociologica, 3*, doi: 10.2383/82483.

Rainie, L. & Wellman, B. (2012). *Networked: The New Social Operating System.* Cambridge, MA: MIT Press.

Rosenfeld, M. J. & Thomas, R. J. (2012). Searching for a Mate: The Rise of the Internet as a Social Intermediary. *American Sociological Review,* 77(4), 523–547.

Roth, Y. (2014). Locating the 'Scruff Guy': Theorizing Body and Space in Gay Geosocial Media. *International Journal of Communication,* 8, 2113–2133.

Smith, A. & Duggan, M. (2013). Online Dating & Relationships. *Pew Internet & American Life Project.* Retrieved from: http://pewinternet.org/Reports/2013/Online-Dating.aspx.

Sutko, D. M. & de Souza e Silva, A. (2011). Location-Aware Mobile Media and Urban Sociability. *New Media & Society,* 13(5), 807–823.

Trappolin, L., Gasparini A. & Wintemute, R. (Eds.) (2011). *Confronting Homophobia in Europe: Social and Legal Perspectives.* Oxford: Hart.

Tuters, M. & Varnelis, K. (2006). Beyond Locative Media. *Leonardo,* 39(4), 357–363.

Urry, J. (2002). Mobility and Proximity. *Sociology,* 36(2), 255–274.

Usher, N. & Morrison, E. (2010). The Demise of the Gay Enclave, Communication Infrastructure Theory, and the Transformation of Gay Public Space. In C. Pullen & M. Cooper (Eds.), *LGBT Identity and Online New Media* (pp. 271–287). London: Routledge.

Van De Wiele, C. & Tong, S. T. (2014). Breaking Boundaries: The Uses & Gratifications of Grindr. In *Proceedings of the 2014 ACM International Joint Conference on Pervasive and Ubiquitous Computing,* 619–630.

van Eeden-Moorefield, B., Proulx, C. & Pasley, K. A. (2008). Comparison of Internet and Face-to-Face (FTF) Qualitative Methods in Studying the Relationships of Gay Men. *Journal of GLBT Family Studies,* 4(2), 181–204.

Vox (2015). La Mappa dell'Intolleranza. Retrieved from: http://www.voxdiritti.it/ecco-le-mappe-di-vox-contro-lintolleranza/.

Wakeford, N. (2000). Cyberqueer. In D. Bell & B. M. Kennedy (Eds.), *The Cybercultures Reader* (pp. 403–415). London: Routledge.

Wellman, B. (2004). The Three Ages of Internet Studies. *New Media & Society,* 6(1), 55–64.

Wilken, R. (2012). Locative Media: From Specialized Preoccupation to Mainstream Fascination. *Convergence,* 18, 243–247.

Woo, J. (2006). The Right Not to Be Identified: Privacy and Anonymity in the Interactive Media Environment. *New Media & Society,* 8(6), 949–967.

Zanutto, A (2007). Comportamenti Giovanili tra Rappresentazione degli Adulti e Gruppo dei Pari: La Moralità Situate. In C. Buzzi, A. Cavalli & A. De Lillo (Eds.), *Rapporto Giovani: Sesta Indagine dell'Istituto IARD sulla Condizione Giovanile in Italia* (pp. 209–224). Bologna: Il Mulino.

14 New in Town

Gay Immigrants and Geosocial Media

Andrew DJ Shield

'Most of my gay friends are from Grindr', reflected Ali from Iraq, who arrived in the greater Copenhagen area in 2015 as an asylum seeker. 'Actually a couple of them are really good friends. Either we dated and then became friends later or we were friends from the beginning'. Grindr – a geosocial smartphone app that lists men-seeking-men in one's exact location by order of proximity – was also the way Pejman from Iran met one of his earliest contacts in Denmark, a friend who eventually rented out his apartment to Pejman and found him a part-time job. Many users of gay dating sites blur the lines of friendship and romance when posting and responding to messages; some also discuss logistics like housing and employment or share information about local events or meeting-spaces. 'Looking for friends, dates, work', one user advertised, 'If u could help me find sth, I'd be thankful'.

For gay immigrants in particular, informal chats on gay dating platforms can be a useful way to engage initially with others in the host country and to build social and logistical networks. However there are some problems that immigrants and ethnic minorities face online, namely when encountering exclusionary or xenophobic messages. Caleb, originally from China, recurrently treads through profiles posted by men who announce that 'No Asians' need contact them. Şenol from Turkey was perplexed when an anonymous user called him a 'Turkish prostitute' before ignoring him entirely. In response to these negative experiences, both Caleb and Şenol have re-written their profile texts to address prejudicial comments on gay social media, thereby hoping to encourage users to problematise and be reflective about race-related communiqués.

As an exploratory study of recent immigrants' uses of and experiences on gay geosocial dating platforms in the greater Copenhagen area, this chapter analyses profile texts on Grindr and PlanetRomeo, and gives voice to ten recent immigrants who use these platforms. The first research question relates to the ways users form offline social networks through these media; in this regard, gay dating platforms can be viewed as 'social media' not unlike mainstream social networking sites. The second research question relates to discussions of race and exclusion online; with regard to the ways some users transform their public profiles into soapboxes to broadcast political messages, these gay dating platforms – not unlike YouTube and Facebook – can also be spaces for social media activism (Poell & van Dijck, 2015; Raun, 2016).

Migration, Sexuality and Online Media

In the early 2000s, scholarship on immigrants' use of online media in Europe often focused on internet news and emailing – which facilitate transnational communications with the country of origin – and whether these media hindered immigrants' interest in local politics in the host country and prevented the learning of the host country's language (e.g. Karanfil, 2007). But those who focused on immigrants' use of these media to connect both transnationally and to others within Europe noted that the relationship between online media, social networks and feelings of national belonging was more complex, particularly among young immigrants and the second generation (Madianou & Miller, 2012; Mainsah, 2010; Nikunen, 2010). Following these and recent studies of race in the Nordic context (e.g. Andreassen & Vitus, 2015), this chapter foregrounds affectivity, intimacy and emotion when exploring migrants' feelings of belonging, both online and offline (Ahmed, 2004).

When the seminal texts of 'queer migration' theory were published in 2005, scholars did not yet focus on actors' online social practices and identities (Epps, Valens & González, 2005; Luibhéid & Cantú, 2005). Subsequent studies of LGBTQ migrants in Europe have focused on migrants' processes of arrival and adaptation, with some attention to internet use in countries of origin (Peumans, 2012), on the unique challenges faced by LGBTQ people of colour in majority-white societies (El-Tayeb, 2012; Jivraj & de Jong, 2011) and most recently on Belgian gay men with a migration background who use social media to find positive information on and representations of homosexuality (Dhoest, 2016). Recent reports about LGBTQ immigrants and ethnic minorities in Denmark have touched on actors' uses of social media in Denmark, namely their strategies for remaining discreet or coming out on Facebook (Følner, Dehlholm & Christiansen, 2015; Østergård, 2015). But immigrants' social practices and experiences of building networks via dating platforms, where users interact mainly with strangers, remain areas for deeper investigation.

In *Gaydar Culture: Gay Men, Technology and Embodiment in the Digital Age* (2010), Sharif Mowlabocus argues that when gay men communicate online, 'physical interaction between users is the primary motivation' (p. 15). Studies of dating announcements often centre on users' self-identifications and their descriptions of ideal partners (e.g. with regard to race: Kaufman & Phua, 2003; or gay masculinity: Light, 2013). Drawing from Nicholas Boston's study of Polish immigrants in the UK who seek same-sex relationships with black locals on PlanetRomeo – a study that also connects sexuality studies, migration studies and online media – this chapter demonstrates how online communication between gay immigrants and locals can 'figure in processes of migrant adaptation and identity formation' (Boston, 2015, p. 293) in the greater Copenhagen area.

The empirical material in this chapter comes from my database of over 600 Grindr and PlanetRomeo profiles and semi-structured interviews with ten recent immigrants about their uses of gay social media, both collected in late 2015 and early 2016. The database includes both screen-grabs of profiles (tagged with time and location) and a spreadsheet with users' selections from various drop-down menus as well as references to migration status, race, jobs or housing. On weekday evenings, I recorded the data of all Grindr users within specific radii of Copenhagen centre (a high-traffic area with many hotels and gay establishments), Northwest Copenhagen (a neighbourhood characterised in part by decades of immigration) and Roskilde/Taastrup (suburbs with long immigrant histories). In each of these three locations, non-white users represented 12–14% of those on Grindr, though quantitative analysis is not central to this chapter. Extensive evaluation of profile texts allowed not only for discursive analysis but also for virtual ethnographic observations (Hine, 2000), as users updated their texts and interacted with me via private messages. Conscious of the ethics of internet research (Markham & Buchanan, 2015), I have removed all profile names.

By giving primacy to the voices of the users on the platforms, these profiles – as the primary sources for this chapter – show an appreciation for historical studies 'from below' that focus on the lives of common people (e.g. Thompson, 1966), as well as for feminist histories that explore gender, sexuality and race (e.g. Andreassen, 2015; Higginbotham, 1992; Stoler, 2010), which have encouraged me to foreground intersectionality in my research questions (Crenshaw, 1989). This research is also indebted to historical studies that use personal ads in order to understand dating and social networks (Cocks, 2009). Thus the conclusion utilises another source base: several hundred personal ads printed in Danish gay/lesbian journals in the 1970s, adapted from my dissertation research (Shield, 2015, pp. 279–311). In order to historicise my arguments about practices online, the conclusion compares and contrasts today's social trends with the practices of those who placed dating ads in the 1970s.

Interviewees mainly responded to announcements made on my researcher profiles on Grindr and PlanetRomeo, in which I identified myself as a scholar investigating the various uses of gay dating platforms, particularly newcomers' experiences. Additionally, I met three of the interviewees at public LGBTQ-themed events in Copenhagen. Drawing from anthropological imperatives of self-reflexivity in the field (Markham, 2013), I am aware that I often sympathised with the positions of my informants due in part to my own subject positions (Hesse-Biber, 2006; Sundén, 2012), but I aimed to remain critical in my analyses of the semi-structured interviews, which I recorded, transcribed and critiqued for discourses and narrative framings (Brinkmann & Kvale, 2015; Silverman, 2006).

The chapter refers to 'immigrants' who migrated and often received legal status through a variety of channels; the term 'newcomers' in this chapter refers also to internal (e.g. rural-to-urban) migrants and some tourists. My immigrant interviewees, who ranged in age from 23 to 40, arrived as students (two of them), by seeking asylum (two), through green card schemata (two), by getting a job (one) or through family reunification (one); the remaining two (both students) had European citizenship and could move freely within the EU. Non-European interviewees came from Egypt, Iran, Iraq, Turkey and China. All names, and some other identifying details, have been changed. All live in 'the greater Copenhagen area', which for the purposes of this chapter includes Malmö, Sweden (i.e. the Øresund region), where a few of the interviewees were based.

The chapter refers to 'gay' online platforms and users, although this term is imprecise as it oversimplifies the variety of ways users on these platforms identify (e.g. as bisexual, queer, straight or as one interviewee said, 'situationally' gay). While all of the interviewees identified as male, some users of these platforms are trans-women or non-binary. Unfortunately, the dating profiles and experiences of lesbian, bisexual, queer women and many gender-non-conforming people are not represented on these platforms or in this chapter.

Debuting in 2009 alongside the boom in smartphones, Grindr utilises a phone's global positioning system (GPS) to mark a user's location relative to other users. Since its first version, Grindr has permitted one profile photo, a short text (c. 50 words) and answers to a few drop-down menus such as age, height, weight, 'ethnicity' (a category problematised in this chapter) and 'looking for'. This simple format allowed Grindr to stand out from computer-centred dating profiles such as PlanetRomeo that did not limit users' photos or profile texts. Founded in 2002 in Germany, PlanetRomeo (originally called GayRomeo) took advantage of the web's affordances (i.e. unlimited space, advanced search abilities) and encouraged users to identify with dozens of drop-down menus, including gender/sexual orientation, safer sex strategies, fetishes, religion, 'ethnicity' (albeit with different options than on Grindr) and user-submitted location. Following the successes of Grindr and Scruff (a similar app), PlanetRomeo has since launched a GPS-based mobile version. According to their company websites, Grindr and PlanetRomeo each have 1–2 million active daily users worldwide, foremost in the United States and Germany/Austria, respectively; most features can be accessed for free on both platforms (Grindr, 2015; PlanetRomeo, 2015).

'Sometimes the Lines Are Not So Clear': Blurring the Sexual, Platonic and Logistical

Although platforms like Grindr and PlanetRomeo are often characterised as 'hook-up' applications that connect users primarily for sex (Race, 2015), there are a significant number of men who use these platforms for platonic connections (Katyal, 2011, p. 134; Race, 2014, p. 498–499), as shown in the following Danish ads:

> Looking for friends, fun and a gym partner. (Grindr)
> Coffee is a great start ☕. (Grindr)
> You will find a loyal, faithful friend in me. (PlanetRomeo)

A tally of profiles in central Copenhagen and Roskilde/Taastrup reveals some interesting trends: among Grindr users who selected what they were 'Looking for' from the all-that-apply checklist, the most commonly selected option was 'Friends' (over 'Dating', 'Relationship', 'Right now', etc.). Of 175 profiles which selected at least one desired interaction type, 126 (72%) included friendship among other possibilities and five users (3%) sought friendship solely.

Newcomers are no exception among those open to friendship. Perhaps as a strategy to stand out from the regular users in the area, tourists often change their display name to 'Visitor' or 'Hotel', or include explanations of their visit and how long they will stay. Similarly many recent immigrants introduce themselves as 'New in town'. In one tally of 140 Grindr profiles signed into central Copenhagen, ten of the users announced themselves as tourists and another ten as other newcomers. The latter did so in a variety of ways:

> New in town don't know anybody. Wanna meet up for a drink or something? (Grindr)
> Native English speaker. Just moved to Denmark. Show me a good time. (Grindr)
> I'm new to Copenhagen. Be nice. (Grindr)
> From Asia, relocated to Europe... (Grindr)

As the first two profiles show, newcomers are often explicit about their interest in making friends and can be eager for information about the city. These profiles demonstrate that many members of sexual minorities trust that a shared sexual identity, regardless of the promise of sex, might enable an intimate connection with a 'local'.

Yet not all immigrants, for example some LGBTQ asylum seekers, specify their immigration status in their profiles; they might instead introduce themselves as students and tourists so as to avoid confronting prejudicial notions about refugees. 'When someone asks, "Where are you from?", I reply, "Why does that matter?"', Ali from Iraq asserted. 'If you need to know what languages I speak, ask me that instead'.

Despite some anxieties, Ali had many positive experiences chatting and meeting with new people on Grindr, as the opening quotation in this chapter showed. In contrast, he has not made friends through more mainstream dating apps: 'I haven't met a lot of people through Tinder. But those I met were for dates and it didn't continue on to become friends'. Şenol from Turkey had similar experiences expanding his social network through Grindr: 'One of my best friends I met on Grindr. We started chatting and then we met up'. But Şenol did not think most people on Grindr favoured friendship over sex. '[It's] maybe both. Sometimes the lines are not so clear. Maybe the first thing that comes to mind is sex or dating. But in this case', where Şenol met one of his best friends, 'I thought: "He's interesting, he seems to do nice things in life, let's get a beer" and then it became a friendship'.

Although many users welcome friends via gay dating platforms, some expressed irritation that these friendships were the by-product of failed attempts at dating. Caleb, originally from China, was grateful for the many friendships he made through Grindr and PlanetRomeo but was sceptical that the platforms could actually match him with a boyfriend. Reflecting on his frustrations with these platforms, Caleb announced in our interview that he would delete his profiles in order to focus on other methods of finding a steady partner.

Especially in the later summer, before universities and other educational institutions begin a new semester, many ads can be found related to housing for newcomers. On PlanetRomeo, where profile text is not limited, users take the opportunity to introduce themselves and describe their housing needs; yet even on Grindr users still ask for help finding a place to live:

> Hey, I just moved to Copenhagen for my master studies. Looking forward to meeting new people and finding a place to stay... I try my luck here. Is there anyone with a room to rent?... I am the perfect roommate ☺. (PlanetRomeo)
> I am new in CPH so I am open to new adventures and also for some accommodations ☺ so if anyone has any offers I will be more than happy to hear... (PlanetRomeo)
> Currently looking for a room. Hit me up if you can offer anything ☺ Expat... (Grindr)

Those looking for a room on gay dating platforms trust they will find someone with whom they presumably share many interests, including a sexual identity. There are also some posts by those offering housing; one Dane wrote that he had a 'room to rent out... do you need a place to live?' But by writing only in Danish, he limited the pool of potential flat mates.

Asen, originally from Bulgaria, highlighted 'Looking for a room' on both Grindr and PlanetRomeo for over ten months, without success. Ideally he hoped someone would offer him an alternative to his student housing, but the few who messaged him about housing either offered to 'keep an eye out', provided a room which did not meet his criteria or wrote 'borderline sexual' messages, which turned him off from the housing offers. Although Asen was happy to post profiles that sought sex, friendship and a flat mate, he did not seek to blur the lines of sex/friendship with his flat mate. Despite many users' optimism about finding a flat mate via these dating platforms – something shared also by Caleb from China and Angelos from Greece – their success rate was lower than with other 'mainstream' housing platforms.

But Pejman from Iran found not only housing but also employment through a contact on Grindr. In 2013, shortly after arriving in Denmark, he wrote to someone on Grindr who was also Iranian: 'We met and made friendship, and after a few weeks I asked him if he knew someone that I can rent a flat or a room from'. Coincidentally the Iranian friend was looking to move out of his apartment and asked Pejman if he wanted to take it over. He did and he has lived there ever since. 'A few months later he introduced me to his boss', Pejman continued, 'and I got a part-time job', where he still works in 2016. Yet while Grindr was the technology that introduced the two contacts, it did not play a direct role in matching Pejman to a house or job; physical contact necessitated the building of a more 'traditional' social network that assisted with these practical logistics.

'I would rather look for jobs the right way', Angelos from Greece opined, naming a few mainstream job websites where he hoped to find an employer. To him, announcing that one sought work on Grindr or PlanetRomeo gave the impression that 'any job will do'. Like the men who offered Asen a room with sexual strings, some respondents might offer Angelos employment with sexual undertones. To the post-graduate the blurring of sex and employment represented the 'wrong' way to seek a job.

Immigrants from areas where sex work is more prominently found on these platforms would associate an announcement for 'a job' with sex work. Yet in the greater Copenhagen area only a handful of profiles offer or solicit sexual services for money, usually inconspicuously and alongside emojis with international monetary symbols (e.g.). Even though it is legal to offer sexual services in both Denmark and Sweden, these profiles risk being flagged by the online community and having the administrators delete them.

Despite or due to this ambiguity with job-seeking on gay social media, one finds users who seek job leads:

> Looking for a cleaning job, if u need it, i would do my best 🙏 🐝, also wanna make friends and have a date 👀 💑 💨 ... (Grindr)
> Brazilian looking for a friend, husband... A job would also be very helpful... I want a nice, sweet, generous caring older man... who would like to have a boyfriend live with him... (PlanetRomeo)

The first ad, which indicated that the user spoke a little Danish ('lidt '), from which one could infer that he was a recent immigrant learning the language, does not address transactional sex. The second ad was more ambiguous: elsewhere in his profile the user offered to 'show off' his body in exchange for housing and thus for financial support. Like the Grindr post cited at the end of this chapter's first paragraph, these ads blurred their announcements for 'friends, dates, work'.

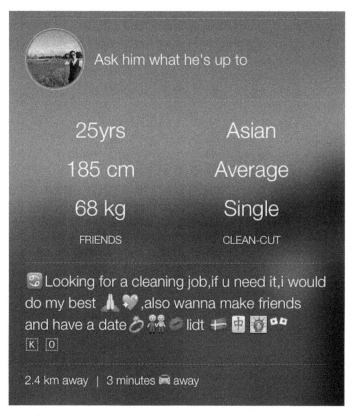

Figure 14.1 This recent immigrant squeezed an announcement seeking a job, friends and a date into one short Grindr profile. (Printed with permission from user.)

A final practical purpose of gay dating profiles is learning local information about a host country, including its subcultures, for people with minority expressions of sexual orientation or gender identity; in other words, users can gain 'cultural capital' on these platforms (Bourdieu, 2011 [1985]). Gay social media becomes a casual first step into conversations about LGBTQ identities and subcultures. Due to the informal nature of these chats, foreign users often feel comfortable practising their English, Danish or Swedish, while at the same time gaining insider knowledge about vocabularies, physical spaces and social practices of LGBTQ people in the greater Copenhagen area.

In the Country of Origin: Potential Immigrants and Online Speculation

Studies on gay social media in Tunis (Collins, 2012), Beirut (Gagné, 2012) and other cities with stricter laws and social regulations against public homosexuality have shown that digital technologies can be central to the formation of sexual and gender identities, and can connect users to a community of sexual minorities online and offline. In his dissertation about PlanetRomeo in India, Akhil Katyal (2011) also briefly explored the opportunities which gay dating platforms presented to same-sex-desiring men in rural areas who moved to cities like Delhi based on their positive experiences chatting online.

Interviewees from Egypt, Iran, Iraq and Turkey were all active with online communities for men-seeking-men in their countries of origin, via Grindr, PlanetRomeo and ManJam, a website popular among Arabic, Persian and Urdu speakers. Ali used Grindr in Iraq from 2010–2014 and described it as 'the main way to meet other people' and to get to 'know more about your sexuality'. However he acknowledged that many Iraqis feel insecure on gay dating platforms: a user never knows if he is chatting with someone who intends to threaten or blackmail him. For this reason Parvin never shared photos in Iran, even though he interacted with other Iranian men-seeking-men via Yahoo Messenger since 2005, some of whom used webcams. Parvin also chatted anonymously through a secondary profile on Facebook he made exclusively for cruising men. 'There are lots of them', he said about men with secondary Facebook profiles in Iran. 'I have about 600 friends' on that profile, none of whom he had met in real life.

Importantly, many gay dating platforms – PlanetRomeo, Scruff, ManJam, etc. – allow for international correspondence, which means that users can read the profiles and chat with men in Denmark, Sweden or another country to which they might relocate. In his study of Poles on PlanetRomeo in the UK, Nicholas Boston (2015) referred to the 'speculators' still living in Poland who cruised British profiles while considering a move or visit to the UK. While still living in Turkey, Şenol learned about Qruiser, a Swedish gay dating platform: 'I made a profile on Qruiser and made some friends, so when I came over we started hanging out actually, so it was great'. Other interviewees mentioned changing their PlanetRomeo profile locations to Denmark and Sweden to browse prior to moving there.

To sum up: in addition to the various sexual, platonic and logistical ways in which gay social media can assist immigrants in new countries – for example in finding friends, jobs, housing and information about LGBTQ subcultures – gay dating platforms can also help potential immigrants worldwide build social networks to assist with international migration and adaptation processes abroad.

'No Racist Guys Pls!': Encountering and Combating Prejudice

Although dating sites and apps can be a useful way to build social and logistical networks in the (future) country of settlement, immigrants (and ethnic minorities more generally) also face obstacles, more particularly when encountering exclusionary or xenophobic messages. On Grindr in Denmark the most commonly targeted group for ethnic/racial exclusion is Asians, with about one in every hundred profiles writing something along the lines of 'NOT into Asiens [sic]' or 'I apologise but Asians is a polite "no thank you"'. David Eng (2001) has described these speech patterns in psychoanalytic terms as the 'castration' of Asian men in white-majority societies, repetitions that negatively affect feelings of belonging to a gay or sexual community (see also Gosine, 2007; Peumans, 2014; as well as Douchebagsofgrindr.com in Woo, 2013). These exclusionary posts left a negative impression on many interviewees, especially Caleb from China: 'I don't want someone to have a fixed impression of me... You shouldn't need that to prove yourself to people'.

Yusuf from Egypt, who identifies as black, has also felt targeted on Grindr. 'You are close', a nearby user wrote to him one evening; Yusuf responded in the affirmative. The man continued: 'Are you a taxi driver?' The offhand comment about Yusuf's purported profession, with its implications about class and servitude, left Yusuf sickened. Yet he has also received half a dozen other offensive messages over the past two years, from slave jokes to being called an 'idiot'. These experiences show how immigrants and racial minorities can be targeted with public and private utterances – from racial-sexual preferences to hurtful jokes – which reinforce white associations between race and belonging in the gay community (see also Jivraj & de Jong, 2011; El-Tayeb, 2012).

When reading public statements about racial-sexual preferences, some feel indirectly targeted: 'I have not seen a profile that said "No Middle Eastern" or "No Muslims"', Ali remarked, but that did not make him feel better about the exclusionary posts he found against Asian, Indian and sometimes black men. Parvin from Iran felt that his ethnicity and status as a foreigner affected his popularity on Grindr: 'When I send more than 100 messages and no one responds, it must be some problem', he began. 'Am I so unfit in this society? Am I so ugly? What is the problem?' Feelings of rejection on gay dating platforms can exacerbate anxieties about belonging or exclusion more generally.

A study of dating ads in the United States in 2003 found that explicit references to racial-sexual preferences were quite common in men-for-men ads and were by no means limited to white men. Explicit references to race were indeed more common among black, Latino and Asian men-seeking-men, ranging from those who said they were only interested in their own race/ethnicity to those who were only interested in another specific race/ethnicity or those who stated they were open to all men in general. Kaufman and

Phua underscored that white men were not more likely to be 'colour-blind', even though they often ignored race in their ads; rather, many white users assumed 'a person of another race would not respond to them because of cultural differences and/or lack of encouragement' (2003, p. 984). In other words, white men who do not specify race in their ideal partner(s) assume that others will read the unmarked race as white (see also Blaagaard & Andreassen, 2012, p. 82).

Drop-down menus encourage users to identify by 'Ethnicity' (the preferred term on Grindr, PlanetRomeo, Scruff) by presenting the category alongside seemingly self-evident categories such as age, height and weight. Reflecting dominant US-American labels, Grindr and Scruff offer the racial identities 'White' and 'Black' as well as regional options like 'Middle Eastern' and one blanket category for 'Mixed' (Grindr) or 'Multi-Racial' (Scruff). Reflecting dominant German categorisations, PlanetRomeo offers the colour 'Black' but divides those of white European descent between 'Caucasian' and 'Mediterranean', the latter of which presumably excludes those who qualify under the ethno-linguistic category 'Arab'. On Qruiser (Swedish), whites are further subdivided into five regions – Northern, Southern, Eastern, Western or Central Europeans – under the category 'Looks and origin', while those with non-European backgrounds can choose from categories like 'African' and 'Middle East'. The Danish LGBTQ platforms Boyfriend and Girlfriend eschew ethnic/racial drop-down menus.

'What do I say? Asian? What's East? Who says that it's East?', laughed Parvin as he reviewed the Grindr labels. In Iran he was accustomed to identifying himself and his neighbours with labels like Iranian, Afghani or Azerbaijani. 'It's not like when you're in the Middle East it's one race. But now [here in Denmark] I'm "Middle Eastern"'. Boston also noted how immigrants in the UK incorporated PlanetRomeo's categories into their daily speech: 'Online, I'm usually looking for South Asian..., Arab, black and mixed-race', one Polish interviewee told Boston, who in turn noted that these terms corresponded to the 'preprogrammed options in the drop-down menu' (2015, pp. 304–305).

Choosing or eschewing the ethnicity drop-down was a matter of deep reflection for Ali: 'That's a very political power dynamic that I really don't want to support'. Şenol from Turkey, like Ali, refused to select an ethnicity on his online profiles: 'I don't believe in that. It doesn't make any sense to me'. Şenol linked these drop-down menus to the practice of announcing racial-sexual exclusions: 'Racism in the gay community is quite visible, and people get away with it because they say it's a preference... So I don't want to put that ["ethnicity" selection]'. The creators of these technologies, in tandem with the social practices of some users, reinforce hegemonic notions of racial difference online, which cannot be untied from their sociopolitical implications offline.

Having painted a picture of gay social media as a space overrun with problematic statements about race, this next section uncovers some of the techniques employed by users of these platforms to increase self-reflexivity or to shame those who post exclusionary messages.

'Dating based on racial preferences is racist', Caleb, originally from China, writes on his PlanetRomeo profile. 'Same goes for all races who prefer dating only one or a couple races, whether you like the argument or not. This is an uncomfortable topic for many, but it is a big challenge everywhere'. Caleb takes advantage of the extended space on PlanetRomeo to share his opinions on 'sexual racism' as well as links to blog posts on the topic (e.g. Allen, 2015). Reflecting on his decision to post these links, Caleb felt that Danes and Swedes were less accustomed to discussing race than for example US Americans: 'People are embarrassed to talk about their prejudice... They feel they can't be open about it, people will judge them. Not that they are more racist [than in the United States]', he asserted, but mainly 'I want people to think about it'.

Even within the limited space of Grindr profiles, users of various backgrounds will speak out against racial exclusions and other forms of prejudice, as the following Copenhagen-area profiles show:

> Foreigner... seeks chemistry. No racist guys pls! We are one big society. Everyone deserves to be happy :-) (Grindr)
> Ageism, fat shaming, racism and discrimination against feminine boys = go away! (Grindr)
> Please quit the nazi-aged rage!!! I don't fucking care!!!... where are all the Asians? (Grindr)
> I do not discriminate towards race or religion! All welcome and it does not matter if you are green, yellow, black... muslim, christian... (PlanetRomeo)

Şenol from Turkey recounted that a friend of his announced in his profile, 'Do not contact me unless you are an anti-racist feminist'. These statements counter hegemonic understandings of 'race' and 'sexual preference' circulated by other users on the shared interface, and demonstrate how gay profiles can be spaces for activism online.

'Those who write something inclusive, either they have experienced that [racism] first hand or they work with it', Ali asserted. He appreciated profiles that urged users, 'Don't say what you're *not* interested in, say what you *are* interested in', or else, 'I'm looking for someone I'm attracted to, not someone from a certain background'. Ali acknowledged that people might have their own specific preferences but felt these preferences often could be phrased in more positive ways. Altogether these users transform their dating profiles into soapboxes from which to broadcast messages of tolerance which could influence future users' communiqués on these platforms.

Historically Informed Conclusions

This chapter shows that immigrants utilise social media technologies – including dating profiles for gay/bisexual men and some gender-non-conforming people – as a means of developing social networks in, and

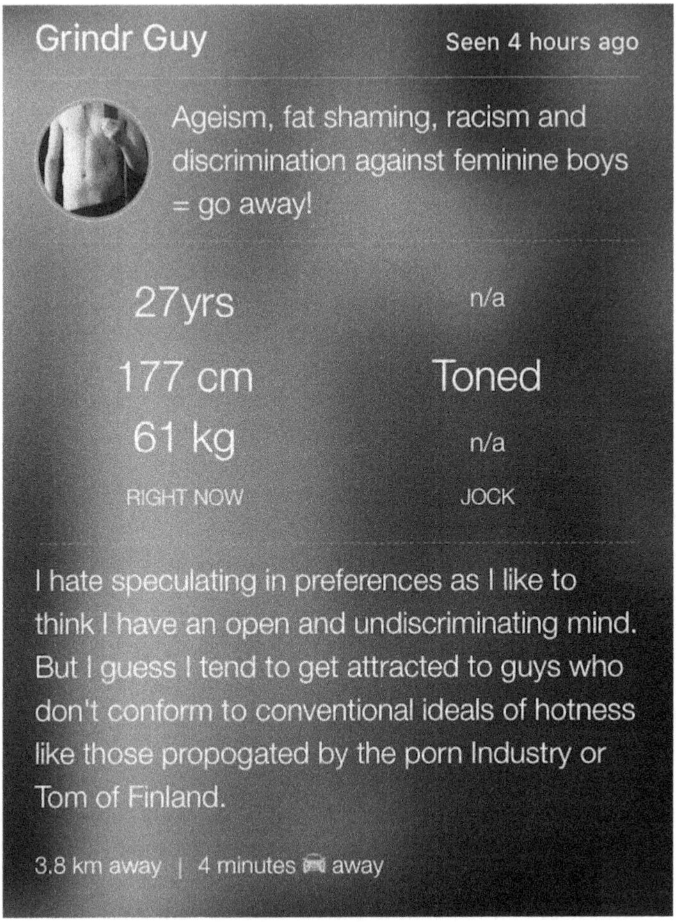

Figure 14.2 A Grindr user turns his profile into a soapbox to critique 'ageism, fat shaming, racism' and other problems he encounters on Grindr and offline. (Printed with permission from user.)

insider knowledge about, the greater Copenhagen area. Connecting to both locals and other immigrants in the host country, immigrants on Grindr or PlanetRomeo demonstrate that cultural immersion and adaptation involve not only government social services, community organisations and/or trade unions (e.g. Ager & Strang, 2008) but also individual and informal initiatives online.

These findings – foremost about the blurring of sexual, platonic and logistical announcements, but also about practices discussing race and belonging – must be qualified with two caveats. Firstly, one must not conclude that these findings are unique to Scandinavia, or even Europe. The ways immigrants use gay dating profiles in Denmark or Sweden do not differ greatly from the ways they used social media – even 'gay' social media – in their countries of origin. Thus, even if their abilities to use these technologies were limited by laws against homosexuality, it would be unwise to overemphasise a 'liberation narrative' (Lubhéid & Cantú, 2005) when describing immigrants' technological practices in Scandinavia. Secondly, one should not relegate these findings to the digital age. How locals and immigrants use gay online platforms does not differ significantly from many of the practices of people in the 1970s who printed dating ads in gay/lesbian magazines. Those working in communication history warn against overemphasising that new technologies necessarily bring about new social practices (Humphreys, forthcoming; Shield, 2015, pp. 263–264), so this final section provides food for thought from the archives of LGBT Denmark (originally called Foundation of 1948).

During the 1970s – the decade of radicalisation of gay, lesbian and feminist movements across much of Western Europe and North America – men and women submitted contact ads to gay/lesbian printed periodicals such as *Pan*, which was published by Europe's second postwar 'homophile' group, the (Danish) Foundation of 1948 (Edelberg, 2014a, 2014b; von Rosen, 1994). There were many obstacles in this communication: long time lags, limited privacy (when receiving letters at a shared address) and moderate costs (e.g. stamps, photo prints, private post office boxes). Nevertheless, *Pan* printed dozens of personal ads per issue from 1971–1977, and the following analysis looks at all 250 ads from selected spring/fall issues. 43 of these, or 17%, sought or offered housing and jobs.

As with dating profiles today, the lines between sexual, platonic and logistical ads sometimes blurred: one man posted (in Danish) 'for renting a house, and maybe erotic relationship' (*Pan* 4:1974), while another said he 'just bought a house in the country [with] tons of space', where he sought 'a young man to share the house with me' (*Pan* 6:1975). Whereas the first man sought a paying housemate who might occasionally or eventually desire sex together, the latter hoped his offer for free housing would entice a young man to move in with him and perhaps start a relationship. Though these housing offers might have been unstable, they could still be alluring for those with limited capital. Overall, the variety of ads printed in *Pan*, an archetypical 1970s gay/lesbian magazine, shows that the periodical was a 'social media', similar to Grindr or PlanetRomeo, which allowed readers occupying various social positions to interact with others who shared not only a sexual identity but also presumably other interests.

The majority of 'white' men in the 1970s did not identify with this label; one would instead assume that whoever posted a Scandinavian-language profile without racial markers had Nordic ethnicity. There were however a handful of people of colour who posted personal ads. (*Pan* was not the only magazine in Denmark with gay personal ads; there was also the pornographic *Eos*, which was one of the first legal explicit magazines for gay men and boasted the 'world's largest collection of personal ads', with around 350 per issue.) To provide just one example:

> [in English] COPENHAGEN, DK. Lonely young man from Asia, slim, discret [sic] and sincere, resident in Copenhagen, seeks good-looking friends in Europe. Correspondence also welcomed… Would also like weekend job for pasttime, perhaps as model. Have good face and profile.
>
> (*Eos* 1:1970)

Noteworthy here is not only that the gay 'scene' in Copenhagen already included some ethnic minorities in 1970, but also that newcomers had faith that the gay community would identify with and assist them. Not unlike the young Asian man on Grindr who posted for a cleaning job, friends and a wedding ring in Denmark, this newcomer hoped that a local social network could assist with both friendship and finances.

Finally, some users corresponded internationally in the 1970s through *Pan*, including some 'speculators' who hoped to move to Scandinavia. Approximately 16% of *Pan*'s advertisements in the 1970s came from outside of Scandinavia (as did half of the ads in *Eos*). Explicit about his desire to meet someone who could help him move, one man in Kenya posted three different times about his desire to migrate:

> [in English] KENYA: Afro-arab… wants to get in touch with friend of good will for assistance in travelling to Europe and getting settled there…
>
> (*Pan* 5:1972; see also *Pan* 5:1973, 9:1973)

Having somehow acquired a copy of a Danish-language magazine for gay/lesbian activists in Scandinavia, this Kenyan man sought to use the printed advertisements as a means for immigrating to Denmark permanently. Similarly, a teacher of Mexican descent in England hoped that a Danish reader could find him a job so he could move to Denmark (*Pan* 3:1975); and in Portugal the director of a local gay rights group posted an ad (in Danish, surprisingly) on behalf of a 21-year-old 'with bartender and pharmacy experience, who would like a job in Denmark' so that he could relocate during the early years of the Third Republic (*Pan* 4:1976). Writing in the context of economic recession across Europe, these readers hoped that the printed journals could connect them to a gay/lesbian social network which would support them with the logistics of international migration, not unlike the 'speculators' on PlanetRomeo.

In sum, gay dating platforms in Denmark and Sweden serve multiple purposes outside of sexual and platonic matchmaking. As in the 1970s, today's online dating platforms connect potential and recent immigrants to locals and enable cross-cultural social networks which can assist newcomers with friendship and logistical support. More recently in Denmark and Sweden, gay profiles have also doubled as public soapboxes from which users discuss political issues related to race and belonging, mostly in an attempt to subvert systems of power they encounter not only on these gay platforms but also in everyday life.

References

Ager, A. & Strang, A. (2008). Understanding Integration: A Conceptual Framework. *Journal of Refugee Studies*, 21(2), 166–191.

Ahmed, S. (2004). *The Cultural Politics of Emotion*. Edinburgh: Edinburgh University Press.

Allen, S. (2015, September 9). 'No Blacks' Is Not a Sexual Preference. It's Racism. *The Daily Beast*.

Andreassen, R. (2015). *Human Exhibitions: Race, Gender and Sexuality in Ethnic Displays*. Farnham: Ashgate.

Andreassen, R. & Vitus, K. (Eds.) (2015). *Affectivity and Race: Studies from Nordic Contexts*. Farnham: Ashgate.

Blaagaard, B. & Andreassen, R. (2012). Disappearing Act: The Forgotten History of Colonialism, Eugenics and Gendered Othering in Denmark. In B. Hipfl & K. Loftsdóttir (Eds.), *Teaching 'Race' with a Gendered Edge* (pp. 81–96). Utrecht: ATGENDER.

Boston, N. (2015). Libidinal Cosmopolitanism: The Case of Digital Sexual Encounters in Post-Enlargement Europe. In S. Ponzanesi & G. Colpani (Eds.), *Postcolonial Transitions in Europe: Contexts, Practices and Politics* (pp. 291–312). London: Rowman & Littlefield.

Bourdieu, P. (2011 [1985]). The Forms of Capital. In J. G. Richardson (Ed.), *Handbook of Theory and Research for the Sociology of Education* (pp. 241–258). New York: Greenwood.

Brinkmann, S. & Kvale, S. (2015). *InterViews: Learning the Craft of Qualitative Research Interviewing*. London: Sage.

Cocks, H. (2009). *Classified: The Secret History of the Personal Column*. London: Random House.

Collins, R. (2012). Efféminés, Gigolos, and MSMs in the Cyber-Networks, Coffeehouses, and 'Secret Gardens' of Contemporary Tunis. *Journal of Middle East Women's Studies*, 8(3), 89–112.

Crenshaw, K. (1989). Demarginalizing the Intersection of Race and Sex: A Black Feminist Critique of Antidiscrimination Doctrine, Feminist Theory and Antiracist Politics. *University of Chicago Legal Forum, 140*, 139–167.

Dhoest, A. (2016). Media, Visibility and Sexual Identity among Gay Men with a Migration Background. *Sexualities*. Published online before print.

Edelberg, P. (2014a). The Long Sexual Revolution: The Police and the New Gay Man. In G. Hekma & A. Giami (Eds.), *Sexual Revolutions*. New York: Palgrave Macmillan.

Edelberg, P. (2014b). The Queer Road to *Frisind*: Copenhagen 1945–2012. In J. Evans & M. Cook (Eds.), *Queer Cities, Queer Cultures: Europe since 1945*. London: Bloomsbury Academic.

El-Tayeb, F. (2012). 'Gays Who Cannot Properly Be Gay': Queer Muslims in the Neoliberal European City. *European Journal of Women's Studies, 19*, 79–95.

Eng, D. (2001). *Racial Castration: Managing Masculinity in Asian America*. Durham: Duke University Press.

Epps, B., Valens, K. & González, B. (2005). *Passing Lines: Sexuality and Immigrants*. Cambridge: Harvard University Press.

Følner, B., Dehlholm, M. & Christiansen, J. (2015). *Nydanske LGBT-Personers Levevilkår*. Copenhagen: Als Research.

Gagné, M. (2012). Queer Beirut Online: The Participation of Men in Gayromeo. com. *Journal of Middle East Women's Studies, 8*(3), 113–137.

Gosine, A. (2007). Brown to Blonde at Gay.com: Passing White in Queer Cyberspace. In K. O'Riordan & D. Phillips (Eds.), *Queer Online: Media Technology and Sexuality* (pp. 139–153). New York: Peter Lang.

Grindr (2015, March 25). Happy Birthday Grindr. Retrieved from grindr.com/blog.

Hesse-Biber, S. (2006). The Practice of Feminist In-Depth Interviewing. In S. Hesse-Biber & P. Leavy (Eds.), *The Practice of Qualitative Research* (pp. 111–148). London: Sage.

Higginbotham, E. (1992). African-American Women's History and the Metalanguage of Race. *Signs, 17*(2), 251–274.

Hine, C. (2000). *Virtual Ethnography*. London: Sage.

Humphreys, L. (forthcoming). *The Qualified Self: Social Media and the Cataloguing of Everyday Life*. Cambridge: MIT Press.

Jivraj, S. & de Jong, A. (2011). The Dutch Homo-Emancipation Policy and Its Silencing Effects on Queer Muslims. *Feminist Legal Studies, 19*(2), 143–158.

Karanfil, G. (2007). Satellite Television and Its Discontents: Reflections on the Experiences of Turkish-Australian Lives. *Continuum: Journal of Media & Cultural Studies, 21*(1), 59–69.

Katyal, A. (2011). *Playing a Double Game: Idioms of Same Sex Desire in India*. PhD Dissertation, University of London.

Kaufman, G. & Phua, V. (2003). The Crossroads of Race and Sexuality: Date Selection Among Men in Internet 'Personal' Ads. *Journal of Family Issues, 8*, 981–995.

Light, B. (2013). Networked Masculinities and Social Networking Sites: A Call for the Analysis of Men and Contemporary Digital Media. *Masculinities and Social Change, 2*(3), 245–265.

Luibhéid, E. & Cantú, L. (2005). *Queer Migrations: Sexuality, U.S. Citizenship, and Border Crossings*. Minneapolis: University of Minnesota Press.

Madianou, M. & Miller, D. (2012). *Migration and New Media: Transnational Families and Polymedia*. London: Routledge.

Mainsah, H. (2010). Transcending the National Imagery: Digital Online Media and the Transnational Networks of Ethnic Minority Youth in Norway. In E. Eide & K. Nikunen (Eds.), *Media in Motion: Cultural Complexity and Migration in the Nordic Region* (pp. 201–218). Farnham: Ashgate.

Markham, A. (2013). Fieldwork in Social Media: What Would Malinowski Do? *Qualitative Communication Research, 2*(4), 434–446.

Markham, A. & Buchanan, E. (2015). Ethical Concerns in Internet Research. In *The International Encyclopedia of Social and Behavioral Sciences, 2nd Edition*. Elsevier.

Mowlabocus, S. (2010). *Gaydar Culture: Gay Men, Technology and Embodiment in the Digital Age*. Farnham: Ashgate.

Nikunen, K. (2010). Satellite Living: Transnational Television and Migrant Youth in Finland. In E. Eide & K. Nikunen (Eds.), *Media in Motion: Cultural Complexity and Migration in the Nordic Region* (pp. 219–236). Farnham: Ashgate.

Østergård, E. (2015). *Livet i et Walk-in-Closet – Om Etniske Minoritetshomoseksuelles Håndtering af Deres Seksualitet*. Master thesis, Copenhagen University.

Peumans, W. (2012). To the Land of Milk and Honey: Migration to Belgium as a Stigma Management Strategy. *Studi Emigrazione, 187*, 541–559.

Peumans, W. (2014). 'No Asians, Please': Same-Sex Sexualities and Ethnic Minorities in Europe. In J. Boulton (Ed.), *Hand Picked: Stimulus Respond* (pp. 128–139). London: Pavement.

PlanetRomeo (2015, October 6). With More Than 1.8 Million Active Users.... Retrieved from twitter.com/planetromeo/.

Poell, T. & van Dijck, J. (2015). Social Media and Activist Communication. In C. Atton (Ed.), *The Routledge Companion to Alternative and Community Media* (pp. 527–537). London: Routledge.

Race, K. (2014). Speculative Pragmatism and Intimate Arrangements: Online Hook-Up Devices in Gay Life. *Culture, Health & Sexuality, 17*(4), 496–511.

Race, K. (2015). 'Party and Play': Online Hook-Up Devices and the Emergence of PNP Practices among Gay Men. *Sexualities, 18*(3), 253–275.

Raun, T. (2016). The 'Caspian Case' and Its Aftermath: Transgender People's Use of Facebook to Engage Discriminatory Mainstream News Coverage in Denmark. In J. Björklund & U. Lindqvist (Eds.), *New Dimensions of Diversity in Nordic Culture and Society* (pp. 79–99). Cambridge: Cambridge University Press.

Shield, A. D. J. (2015). *Immigrants in the Sexual Revolution: Perceptions, Participation, Belonging; The Netherlands and Denmark, 1960s–1980s*. PhD Dissertation, City University of New York Graduate Center.

Silverman, D. (2006). *Interpreting Qualitative Data*. London: Sage.

Stoler, A. (2010). *Carnal Knowledge and Imperial Power: Race and the Intimate in Colonial Rule*. Berkeley: University of California Press.

Sundén, J. (2012). Desires at Play: On Closeness and Epistemological Uncertainty. *Games and Culture, 7*(2), 164–184.

Thompson, E. P. (1966). *The Making of the English Working Class*. New York: Knopf Doubleday.

von Rosen, W. (1994). A Short History of Gay Denmark 1613–1989: The Rise and the Possibly Happy End of the Danish Homosexual. *Nordisk Sexologi, 12*, 125–136.

Woo, J. (2013). *Meet Grindr: How One App Changed the Way We Connect*. Self-published.

15 Strategic (In)visibilities and Bareback Subcultures

The Implications of Online Communication for HIV Transmission among Gay Men in Serbia

Zoran Milosavljevic

This chapter discusses the influence of online communication on HIV transmission among gay men in Serbia via unsafe sexual practices. It explores online communication practices, self-presentation strategies and identity constructions related to HIV status. Particular online self-presentations and unsafe sexual practices, together with specific understandings of intimacy, could have an effect on the possibility of HIV transmission among gay men. I will argue that the merging between technological/online/virtual and bio-medical advancements has implications for the transformation of sexual practices and representational modes among gay men in Serbia, in a way that potentially increases the risk of HIV transmission. My key research question is: what are the implications, if any, of the relative anonymity of the internet and of health disclosure strategies of gay men for HIV transmission? In particular I will look at the online practices of 'strategic (in)visibility' (Davis & Flowers, 2014), that is, at elusive disclosures of HIV status, as well as at the bareback (that is, condomless) sexual subcultures which are firmly anchored in the internet.

To contribute to a better understanding of those practices and cultures, I will draw on 25 interviews with gay men in Serbia on the use of communication technologies, online self-presentation strategies and unsafe sexual practices, as well as on virtual ethnography of gay dating sites and apps such as PlanetRomeo.com/Serbia (mostly known as 'GayRomeo' or simply 'Romeo' among gay men in Serbia), Gay-Serbia.com and Grindr. Giving voice to one of the most discriminated social groups in Serbian society is of the highest importance for understanding the dynamics of gay sexualities and sexual subcultures in virtual and 'real' (or unmediated) spaces. Serbian gay men use various strategies of self-presentation online, organised around the play with safe/unsafe sex and the disclosure of health status, in terms of their own translation of the dynamics of HIV status and specific 'strategies of protection' of potential sex partners. As I will show in this chapter, their self-presentation strategies online originate in technosexual and biomedical transformations of gay identities in which 'immunological equilibrium' (Preciado, 2013) – that is, the idea of a necessary balance of the immunological system for maintaining basic bodily functions – plays an important role.

Technosexuality, Identity and HIV/AIDS

The link between the online communication of gay men and HIV transmission is highly questionable. Is such a link even possible? How could it be that the internet becomes a transmitter, or at least an important facilitator of the transmission, of HIV? For many gay men in Serbia such a causal link would nevertheless seem to be a reality. Their (cyber)reality has created the possibility of HIV infection through unsafe sexual practices that follow what we could consider as the 'play' with health identity online, that is, with selective disclosure or non-disclosure of HIV status. Davis (2009) stresses the importance of 'technosexuality' – i.e. sexual uses of the internet and related technologies, especially creating online profiles for sexual purposes or having sex-related talks in chatrooms – for public health. The discourse of technosexuality has been explored in various forms (Davis, 2008; Preciado, 2013) and is well known since 1997, when Hamman coined the term 'cybersex' to examine sexual practices and behaviours among users of AOL chatrooms (as quoted in Davis et al., 2006). Since as Turkle points out, technology is 'the architect of our intimacies' (2011, p. 1), technosexuality strongly influences the shape of gay subjectivities today and is therefore a useful concept to explain the link between online communication and HIV transmission. This is particularly so in the context of the widespread and extensive use of online communication among gay men worldwide (Fox, 2012; Klein, 2014; McGlotten, 2013; Mowlabocus, 2010; Race, 2015). Attempts to find a sexual partner, but also to socialise in a broader community, are the predominant models of participation in online communication. The participation in online gay dating sites and apps allows for the establishment of identity positions which enable an individual to maintain such activities in different contexts.

People use virtual spaces for their identity constructions, with particular virtual 'hot spots' for sexual encounters that lead to various sexual practices in 'real' life. Rheingold argues that '[t]echnology doesn't have to dictate the way our social relations change, but we can only influence change if we understand how people use technologies' (2000, p. 346). Our own projections upon and desires for the other are incorporated into our virtual communication. As Fox (2012) discusses, the process of idealising the other is widely accepted as a measure against the incompleteness of the other person online. Our own perception of the other online in turn shapes the way we behave offline. Clearly there is no radical disjunction between online and offline realms. Sexual desires, as well as the desire for participation and sociability, have to be externally expressed both in 'real' and in virtual spaces. The two spaces are inseparable in the shaping of identities (Baym,

2010; Cerulo, 1997; Dodge & Kitchin, 2001; Gurak, 1997; McKenna & Bargh, 1998; Miller, 2012) and also of bodies. In researching the notion of technosexuality, Preciado (2013) envisions the bond between technologically produced bodies and representations, where biomedical and communicational technologies are incorporated into our bodies and become inseparable from everyday life practices. Those incorporated technologies help to define the processes of bodily transformation under the influence of desire (both sexual desire and the desire to be healthy).

Computer-Mediated Communication (CMC), with its core characteristic of relative anonymity, has introduced new modalities of intimacy and the formation of new online communities. Online identity is defined by the elusiveness of virtual space itself. Saraswati (2013) points out that the internet could be seen as a new epistemic point for research on sexuality and Turkle (1999, 2011) comments on the possibility of 'self-discovery' in virtual networking. In numerous internet studies the construction of the self and of identity has been seen as multiple and fragmented (Kolko & Reid, 1998; Miller, 2012; Turkle, 1999). The body politics behind such identity positions are also fragmented (Kolko & Reid, 1998, p. 226). Thus different profiles and different identity and body constructs may in fact originate in one 'real'-life subject under the influence of various discourses in different virtual spaces and networks. Such a play with the self-presentation of identities and bodies online may have serious consequences for HIV transmission offline, especially when it involves different degrees of disclosure or non-disclosure of HIV status and different degrees of safe-sex practice.

Gayness and HIV/AIDS in Serbia

In the Serbian context, gayness is mostly perceived as a deviation of sexuality that erodes heteronormative, patriarchal and re-traditionalised society. Even though an anti-discrimination law was introduced in 2009, its implementation is still a slow and painful process. Gay life is organised around big urban spaces, such as Belgrade, Novi Sad, Nis and Kragujevac, where greater anonymity (both online and offline) is easier to achieve. A politics of 'don't ask, don't tell' is the usual institutional and social response towards gay issues, but it is sometimes also accepted by gay individuals themselves as a politics of coping with social rejection. The silencing of gay sexuality results in insufficient social integration and impartial institutional and state strategies of supporting gay individuals, and the country's HIV/AIDS policy is a pertinent example of such social response (Milosavljevic, 2012).

As far as the HIV/AIDS epidemic is concerned, Serbia is a low-prevalence country with approximately 3,100 official cases of HIV/AIDS since 1984.[1] Unofficial estimates however put the actual figure at approximately five to ten times more than the official records. ARV (antiretroviral) therapy was introduced in 1997. Unfortunately, less than 4% of the population of 7.3 million Serbians have tested themselves for HIV and 25% of all registered people living with HIV (PLWH) in 2014 were in the last stages of AIDS when they decided to seek professional help. Those results were even worse in 2012 and 2013, when they reached 33% of newly registered cases. Gay men have consistently been the predominant social group in newly registered cases in the last five years (55–60%).[2] On 1 December 2015, the Public Health Institute of the Republic of Serbia reported an increase of newly registered HIV/AIDS cases in 2015 by 37%.[3] Such devastating results could not be worse news for gay men, as 80% of those cases were gay-sex-related transmissions.

The population group most affected by HIV/AIDS are younger gay men in their twenties and thirties.[4] The fear of discrimination and stigmatisation is driving these individuals to conceal their HIV status until the later stages of AIDS. Nevertheless, numerous NGOs are working with PLWH and the general population (mostly youths and students) to deal with issues of public health, discrimination, stigmatisation, ARV therapy and institutional support for PLWH. The biggest problems are continuity of ARV supplies and screening tests (the bio-technological impact on the evaluation of illness progression), access to health services (affected by welfare cuts and class) and sexual health education, thus placing those affected by HIV/AIDS in a situation of constant precariousness. PrEP and PEP (pre- and post-expositional profilaxis) are not available (occasionally gay men might get PEP in the Clinic for Infectious Diseases in Belgrade, but it is unavailable in general). For gay men moreover the issue of a forced coming out in social and medical institutions posits a problem for proper prevention practices against HIV/AIDS (Milosavljevic, 2012). All of these characteristics of the HIV/AIDS epidemic in Serbia, in particular discrimination and stigmatisation of gay individuals, tend to position the internet as a space of potential freedom for gay men (Milosavljevic, 2015). The number of users' profiles on gay dating sites in Serbia is constantly increasing.

Methodology

I chose a qualitative research methodology since the personal experiences of Serbian gay men are mostly absent from the public sphere and listening to their voices will contribute to a better understanding of the discursive field which shapes their subjectivities and unsafe sexual practices. I interviewed 25 gay men in Belgrade between September 2014 and November 2015. Participants were between 24 and 62 years old. I also conducted a virtual ethnography of the gay dating sites PlanetRomeo.com/Serbia, Gay-Serbia.com and Grindr as a contextual contribution to the narratives. Fourteen interviewees were recruited personally, online or in a gay club, while eleven were recruited by snowball sampling. All interviewees were introduced to the research and signed informed consent forms. They had the opportunity to choose pseudonyms or to be represented by their online user name, which 36% did. The majority of interviewees decided to keep their own names

(64%), mostly because they saw this 'representation policy' as their contribution to breaking the silencing of gay sexuality in Serbian society.

Semi-structured interviews furnished the basis of their narratives. Participants responded to ten open questions about their online habits (such as preferences for specific gay dating sites, frequency of online activity, specificity of online communication through them), their personal social context, attitudes towards intimacy, unsafe sexual practices and HIV/AIDS-related issues. The interviews lasted between 20 minutes and 1 hour 45 minutes. Interviewees were able to select a place where they preferred to talk: in my apartment, their place or any other place of preference. Most of them (21 out of 25) picked my apartment for the talk. Two interviewees decided to meet me in a third party's place (a friend's place). One interview was held in a public park and one in the interviewee's place. Four interviewees revealed they were HIV-positive; two of these have been on ARV therapy for several years.

The interviews were digitally recorded, transcribed and analysed using discourse analysis. The voices of participants offer a closer look at the everyday life of gay men, their problems and the politics of resistance towards dominant social (patriarchal) discourse in the Serbian context. Their answers contribute to a better understanding of different issues shaping gayness in the Serbian context, including the previously mentioned communicational habits, unsafe sexual practices, HIV/AIDS-related issues but also the abstract notion of intimacy.

Anonymity and Intimacy in Gay Online Communication

Extensive use of online communication among gay men in Serbia is not a novelty. Since 2000 the improvement of network coverage and computer availability has rapidly increased.[5] Easy access to networks, gadgets and apps has enabled gay men to enter virtual communities.

When we analyse the interviews, it becomes clear that the issue of multiple profiles and the dynamics of disguise/disclosure of personal information are extremely important in relation to health issues and HIV status, as part of the identity play which will be discussed later. The majority of participants recognise the anonymity of the other person online as a 'clear and present danger' and a matter of trust. The dynamics between anonymity and trust takes the form of a negotiation between two users, but also between each individual's beliefs, perceptions of the other person and responsibility. Some participants in this research are aware that HIV status plays an important role in negotiating safer-sex practices (or unsafe sex if bareback sexual practices are at stake). As a consequence, their level of anonymity online is closely connected to their health status, among other issues.

Sharing information with others online and possible unsafe sexual practices that follow online activities are also closely connected with the understanding of intimacy. Some internet researchers see intimacy as inherently virtual (McGlotten, 2013), but when asked to describe intimacy online only a minority of my interviewees saw online communication as intimate in nature (6 out of 25). For them the modalities of physical proximity, from sexual encounters to 'shared silence' between partners, are at the core of intimate relationships. Nevertheless, the predominant view of intimacy as the disclosure of thoughts and secrets considers this to be something extremely personal. The definition of intimate practices to which gay men in this research refer is what Orthon-Johnson and Prior call 'disclosing intimacy', conceived as a 'dialectic of mutual self-disclosure, a sharing of inner thoughts and feelings' (2013, p. 18). Embodiment in connection with intimacy and expression of this relation are seen as 'the intimacy of the self rather than the body, although it might be enhanced by bodily intimacy' which leads to 'the pleasure of co-presence' in a virtual space (ibid., p. 18).

How do internet users structure intimacy online? For Reid (1999) the context of the internet and the need for communication encourage users to be intimate or to simulate intimacy. The possibility of simulated intimacy, as well as the disclosure of identity online, enhances the possibility of online communication being based on wrong assumptions about the other. Thus one's HIV status and the interplay of intimacy and identity disclosure online could be a risk factor for HIV transmission. Indeed Davis suggests that internet-mediated sexual practices based on intimacy are structured around anonymity online, adding that 'anonymous intimacy' increases the possibility of transmission of HIV and other STDs in offline unsafe sexual behaviour (2008, pp. 53–54). These conclusions are clearly important for contemporary gay identities and body politics in the Serbian HIV/AIDS discourse, as well as for the use of online communication in this context.

For Ben-Ze'ev (2012) the offline/online difference of intimate relationships is structured around disembodiment online, which releases individuals from moral and mental constraints in relationships. It is important to underline that online communication allows people to disclose intimate information because 'anonymity and spatial distance reduce the risk of harmful consequences' (ibid., p. 37). Textual representations could be false or true, but the introduction of bodies as part of visual communication increases the level of information about the other. In that case, textual information is supported by the visual. The more information about the other we have, the less vulnerable we feel. Intimacy and vulnerability are in a constant dynamic, both online and offline. This is particularly evident on gay dating sites, where specific strategies of self-presentation emerge from different user profiles. In the remainder of this chapter, I will discuss examples of different strategies of self-presentation in connection with the risk of HIV transmission. I will start by discussing strategic (in)visibility of HIV-positive status and continue by investigating bareback sexual subcultures of generationing and stealthing that originate in online recruitment.

Strategic (In)visibilities

Gay online communication in search of potential sex partners frequently involves sexual health themes. A central issue in representing and negotiating online health status is HIV status. Whether positive or unknown, one's HIV status represents potential danger and may lead to an unwelcome outcome of online identity play and unprotected sexual practices. As HIV status is an important issue for many gay men in Serbia, its disguise on a user's profile brings in an element of untrustworthiness between potential sex partners. Users of gay dating sites whose profiles feature 'safer-sex needs discussion' statements demonstrate the risk of HIV transmission. As one of the interviewees reflected on this issue:

> 'Needs discussion' is 'absolutely without any discussion', as far as I'm concerned. I don't want to go into that at all. What does that mean if you have to discuss condom use today? That's crazy. (Vlada, 46 years old)

In this example, Vlada clarifies that he refuses to discuss the non-use of condoms with partners because he considers sex with condoms as the only possible option to protect himself against HIV and other STDs. However, the issues of unprotected sex and of representational modes of HIV/AIDS are not always clear on gay user profiles. In his discussion of the use of technological devices and the 'hook-up' online gay culture, Race (2015) explains how some gay men negotiate identities through 'veiled disclosure', where one user inquires into another's position regarding sexual practices, HIV status and other identity characteristics with a series of veiled signals and questions.

An interesting example of an online gay self-presentation strategy is that of strategic (in)visibility, which is closely connected with online disclosure of HIV status (Davis & Flowers, 2014). In using strategic (in)visibility online, individuals try to present one part of their identity by sending a message without saying or revealing too much. In the Serbian context, HIV status is frequently presented through strategic (in)visibility among gay men who are HIV-positive and want to meet or bond with other users online. Examples of such strategic self-presentations on PlanetRomeo in Serbia are 'Positive for Positive' and 'Stockrin-bg' – 'Stockrin' being the name of an ARV medicine for HIV and 'bg' a contraction of Belgrade, thus presenting a man from Belgrade who is on ARV therapy. One of the most original examples is the case of 'HIaVvatha'. HIaVvatha is a 37-year-old gay man from Belgrade who was HIV-positive for six years at the time of writing. He developed a specific strategy of self-presentation on gay dating sites which could be identified as strategic (in)visibility. By marking specific letters in his nickname with capitals (H, I and V) he sends a message about himself that he is somehow connected with HIV without explicitly saying he is HIV-positive.

This message shapes his connectivity with others but also arguably enables him to participate in online communication with fewer constraints. In our interview HIaVvatha explained:

> All of my gay connections are from online communication. You know... I don't know anyone whom I didn't meet online. Online communication is absolutely 'gay'. That's the place where I could hang around with other gay guys and talk about sex and other 'gay themes'. It's free communication. There is much more freedom in it.

Even if HIaVvatha's online self-presentation is a clear example of strategic (in)visibility, his online communication and offline sexual practices following online communication are not therefore as straightforward as we might conclude from his narrative. HIaVvatha continued:

> I've noticed that people who are aware of their HIV status, and who are also responsible, are clearly saying what their situation is. Even though there are many more guys... who have, as I would call it, 'civilian profiles'. Those are profiles, you know, where everything's right. You're healthy, all is well and you're ready to get married [*laughs*]. I mean... I have a 'civilian profile' too. I opened this one, HIaVvatha, in November 2009. I was confused, lost... you know? I wanted to know someone with a similar experience.

In terms of safer sex then HIaVvatha is a bit elusive. On the one hand, he is horrified by some users on gay dating sites and their practice of bareback sex, but on the other he has bareback sexual encounters with other gay men himself. First he made the following observation:

> Okay... you know... Some people are telling me – lucky you, you're positive now and you can have bareback sex. I don't comment on that. I'm not for bareback sex. I was horrified recently when one boy – he is 22 years old – stated on his headline that he wanted to have only bareback sex because he had it once and he liked it. It's shocking... I mean, I told him: 'Listen to me boy...' I was horrified.

Soon afterwards however, seemingly contradicting what he had already stated about barebacking and safer sex, HIaVvatha explained:

> I had sex with a couple of people this year and they didn't know about my HIV status. I had sex with one person... I mean bareback. He must be HIV-positive, otherwise he wouldn't do that. My viral load is low, almost like HIV-negative guys, and you know... If I have to save someone from infection... you know... the possibility is so small... I mean, let's live a normal life now. I know that I'm not quite sincere in that.

Volatile assumptions and personal translations of biomedical tests (specifically structured around the notion of viral load) and safer/unsafe-sex dynamics, as seen in HIaVvatha's case, are closely connected with disclosure online (Davis & Flowers, 2014). Although it is true that a low viral load reduces the possibility of HIV transmission, it is not true that it eradicates the possibility entirely. Thus the concept of 'immunological equilibrium' as a result of a controlled HIV infection, or simply having an unknown HIV status, are also used in self-presentation online, sometimes as part of a play with multiple (health) identities. 'Immunological equilibrium' could be defined as the necessary balance of the immunological system for maintaining basic bodily functions. Preciado posits 'immunological equilibrium' at the core of the 'battle for modern subjectivity' (2013, p. 360).

Victor, a 30-year-old HIV-positive man, elaborates on the specificity of health discussions among HIV-positive gay men online as follows:

> I mean, what they would like to know right now is whether your viral load is undetectable or not. HIV-positive guys discriminate between other HIV-positive people they would like to meet based on their level of CD4, PCR or whether they have some other disease that accompanies HIV. That's how they make a decision about who is going to be their sexual partner. I find that very funny in a way.

In this testimony Victor refers to biomedical tests such as the CD4 count (a specific group of lymphocytes whose low levels show viral progression in the body and high levels a good response to therapy) or PCR (the Polymerase Chain Reaction test, which provides evidence of viral presence in the body). Thus it would appear that 'undetectability' of the virus has brought a new era in the HIV/AIDS epidemic worldwide, in which biomedical screening markers of HIV are translated into a health paradigm closely connected with identity, which in turn remains very much rooted in beliefs, wishes and a re-enactment of one's previous (pre-infection) health status. 'Immunological equilibrium' is then seen by some gay men as a necessary balance of the body that could be used as a substitute for health. As a result, the qualification 'undetectable' sometimes equates with 'healthy' in self-presentations online, but also in negotiated safety, safer-sex decisions, chemsex (i.e. sex under the influence of recreational drugs) and gay men's identity and body politics in general. Victor reflected on attitudes towards viral loads as follows:

> There is lots of abuse of undetectability among HIV-positive gay men. What does that mean to be undetectable? It's so vague. The number of viral copies fluctuates. Possible HIV transmission also depends on a potential partner's own health… I think this is some kind of psychological defence mechanism to reassure themselves that they are healthy. They don't talk about it and they transmit the virus.

The translation of biomedical results into health status and identity constructions is influenced by numerous discourses – educational, media, sexual, technosexual, biomedical, institutional and so on – and seems to have become an inevitable part of online communication among gay men in Serbia.

Bareback Subcultures and Practices

A full exploration of bareback sexual subcultures exceeds the limits of this chapter, so I will only elaborate on the specificity of barebacking practices which originate from online communication. This does not make the task much easier, considering that the majority of bareback practices seem to have some kind of online connection, either in gay pornography's influence on gay sexual practices in general or in online communication as a known factor for organising bareback parties and orgies (Klein, 2014; Mowlabocus, Harbottle & Witzel, 2013; Race, 2015). The range in meaning of the term 'barebacking' posits a problem for the researcher as well. Numerous studies have explored not only the meaning of bareback sex but also the sexual subcultures of barebacking and their influence on gay subjectivity and gay communities in general (Adam, 2005; Bersani & Phillips, 2008; Carballo-Diegez et al., 2009; Davis et al., 2006; Dean, 2008, 2009, 2011; Dowsett et al., 2008; Klein, 2014; Mowlabocus, 2010; Mowlabocus et al., 2013; Race, 2010). Bersani and Phillips (2008) discuss barebacking as driven by internalised sexual shame among gay men and the reproducibility of cultural patterns and practices among gay men that lack any political meaning except individual beliefs structured around the virus and the death drive.

Discourses on the virus remain at the core of gay bareback practices. In their exploration of the meanings of HIV viral load across numerous disciplines and studies, Gagnon and Guta (2014) report that such viral load has specific meaning for PLWH and their presentation of the self in sexual decision-making. Regardless of the general meaning of the HIV viral load, for some sexual subcultures it is a specific 'ticket' for entering a community. The existence of bareback subcultures that revolve around the deliberate transmission of HIV among gay men, such as generationing and stealthing (Klein, 2014), is a clear example of the interconnectedness of online representations, health disclosure and HIV transmission. It is important to acknowledge that both these sexual practices originate from online recruitment. Generationing is a sexual practice whereby one HIV-positive gay man transmits the virus to an uninfected man and then the two collaborate in 'an effort to seroconvert another man and so forth', creating first, second and further generations of newly infected gay men ('sons' and 'grandsons', as participants in this practice call them) (ibid., p. 54). Stealthing is an unsafe sexual practice whereby an HIV-positive gay man who is in an active sexual role tries to infect an HIV-negative partner without the latter's consent. It is usually performed by taking off the condom deliberately during the sexual act without the knowledge of the sexual partner (ibid.).

Examples of generationing and stealthing in the Serbian context are discussed by one of the interviewees, Alexander, a 34-year-old HIV-positive gay man from the Central Serbia region:

> I've encountered a guy online who is HIV-positive… in this discussion of condomless sex and HIV-positive status disclosure… He said back then: 'I have already ten sons, or even more… all of them, they are all my children…' He is actually laughing about it, about having unprotected sex and infecting others deliberately.

The case of generationing that Alexander refers to is a typical bareback appropriation of the 'heterosexual breeding culture of impregnation or making babies', as Bersani and Phillips (2008) call it, whereby the virus is seen by gay bareback practitioners as a necessary link for kinship. Alexander himself was not eligible to be recruited for generationing since he was already HIV-positive. He is not on ARV and his viral load is low, but he denies his HIV positivity (even if several tests in the last five years have shown the presence of HIV in his blood, as he admits) on the ground of incorrect biomedical tests. Biomedical reasons (false initial or screening tests on HIV presence), religious reasons (having taken a pilgrimage to holy places, drinking holy water) or lifestyle (discipline in ARV-taking, healthy diet and exercise) are sometimes perceived as responsible for a 'better viral load' among HIV-positive gay men in Serbia. Nevertheless, to join the generationing practice initially one has to be negative in terms of HIV presence. Only then does the practice itself have a full 'ritualised' meaning for participants.

Continuing the narrative of his own HIV positivity and safer-sex practices, Alexander touches upon the issue of stealthing as well:

> A friend told me he met this guy online… a guy who is HIV-positive. They met in real life and started to have sex, but the guy took off the condom and my friend… at first, he didn't even notice it, but then he saw that this guy didn't have a condom on. He went crazy, you know? They had a fight… He yelled at the guy: 'Where did you get the idea to do that!!?' He simply took the condom off during sex, you know? People do that stuff. I simply don't get why.

Even though he is aware that the play with unsafe sex and HIV-positive status could potentially cause harm, Alexander follows his own logic of self-presentation online and implements his own 'politics of protection' towards the potential sex partners he meets online:

> I don't tell them I'm HIV-positive. Why should I? I always have safe sex, with condoms… I'm forced to think about it… you know… that I could potentially infect the other man, but also that I might get the other type of HIV, a superinfection.

In his narrative Alexander claims he protects younger gay men in their twenties, since according to him they do not have enough information about unsafe sex and HIV transmission. At the same time he did not say how he protects his older sex partners, even if he claims he always wears a condom when engaging in anal sex, though not if any other sexual practices are involved, such as oral sex.

This is another example that shows how volatile 'strategies of protection' of potential sex partners (online and offline) are, and how such volatility increases the risk of HIV transmission. Alexander does not have two user profiles, as HIaVvatha does, but we can recognise the same pattern of a 'dissociation of representation' online which affects the reality of their behaviour. While Alexander does not reveal to potential sex partners that he is HIV-positive and selectively protects younger men from getting HIV by using a condom (generational division of protection), HIaVvatha has two user profiles, one which displays strategic (in)visibility and the other – 'civilian', as he calls it – where he does not reveal his HIV status and sometimes performs bareback sex (division of protection based on 'multiple profiles'). Nevertheless the similarity between the two gay men is that both are HIV-positive and both use low viral load (HIaVvatha is on ARV, Alexander is not) to justify their multiple (health) identities online and different selective models of protection towards potential sex partners. These examples show that the spread of HIV among gay men may be influenced by the notion of 'immunological equilibrium' and its influence on online self-presentations. Selective strategies of self-presentation online and selective use of condoms and protection open a link between online communication and HIV transmission. The issue of shared responsibility between sex partners is at stake, but this will provide the focus of further research.

Conclusion

Gay men in Serbia use online communication extensively, mostly to find sex partners, but also to homosocialise and participate in the online gay community. Gay dating sites (PlanetRomeo.com/Serbia, Gay-Serbia.com, Grindr) provide the necessary infrastructure for such activities. Even if no precise data are available, the use of online communication among gay men in Serbia is clearly on the rise, as seen from the narratives of research participants and witnessed in everyday life. Online and offline communication are inseparably intertwined and are important parts of contemporary gay identities in Serbia. The participants in this research perceive intimacy among gay men as inherently physical proximity and closeness based on trust, but online communication plays an initial role in establishing intimate relationships.

Unsafe sex is widespread among gay men in Serbia and the strategies of protection of potential sex partners are unstable and elusive in nature. At the same time, the widespread use of online communication seems to provide new means for obscuring one's HIV status and thus has wider implications for HIV transmission. As the analysis demonstrated, anonymity and health disclosure are central elements of (health) identity play on the internet, which may result in HIV transmission through unsafe sexual practices following online communication. Self-presentations online depend on anonymous intimacy and health disclosure, with information about HIV status at its core. Strategic (in)visibility is one of the self-presentation techniques used by HIV-positive gay men in Serbia in online self-presentations, which adds ambiguity to disclosing health-related information online. What is more, the internet supports bareback subcultures which increase the risk of HIV transmission, such as generationing and stealthing. Finally, an important recent development in Serbia has been the rise of a discourse of viral load and 'undetectability' of the virus, which have become inseparable parts of HIV-positive gay men's self-presentations online. The personal 'translation' of biomedical tests and procedures organised around ARV use and viral load meaning, together with specific self-presentations online which include a health disclosure/disguise dynamic, introduce and promote the notion of 'immunological equilibrium' as a substitute for health among some gay men in Serbia. In the meantime, the number of registered HIV/AIDS cases among gay men in Serbia continues to increase and shows no sign of slowing down.

Notes

1. www.batut.org.rs: Official Serbian data on HIV/AIDS cases of the Public Health Institute of the Republic of Serbia, accessed on 03.12.2015.
2. www.aidsresurs.rs: Serbian HIV/AIDS info portal, accessed on 10.10.2015.
3. www.batut.org.rs.
4. aids-support.org/o-nama/: Serbian PLWH (people living with HIV/AIDS) NGO 'AS centar' info page, accessed on 10.10.2015.
5. www.pcpress.rs: Serbian internet coverage, accessed on 17.10.2015.

References

Adam, D. B. (2005). Constructing the Neoliberal Sexual Actor: Responsibility and Care of the Self in the Discourse of Barebackers. *Culture, Health & Sexuality*, 7(4), 333–346.

Baym, N. (2010). *Personal Connections in the Digital Age*. Cambridge: Polity.

Ben-Ze'ev, A. (2012). *Love Online: Emotions on the Internet*. Cambridge: Cambridge University Press.

Bersani, L. & Phillips, A. (2008). *Intimacies*. Chicago: University of Chicago Press.

Carballo-Diegez, A. et al. (2009). Is 'Bareback' a Useful Construct in Primary HIV Prevention? Definitions, Identity and Research. *Culture, Health & Sexuality*, 11(1), 51–65.

Cerulo, A. K. (1997). Identity Construction: New Issues, New Directions. *Annual Review of Sociology*, 23, 385–409.

Davis, M. (2008). The 'Loss of Community' and Other Problems for Sexual Citizenship in Recent HIV Prevention. *Sociology of Health & Illness*, 30(2), 182–196.

Davis, M. (2009). *Sex, Technology and Public Health*. Basingstoke: Palgrave Macmillan.

Davis, M. & Flowers, P. (2014). HIV/STI Prevention Technologies and Strategic (In)visibilities. In M. Davis & L. Manderson (Eds.), *Disclosure in Health and Illness* (pp. 72–88). London: Routledge.

Davis, M., Hart, G., Bolding, G., Sherr, L. & Elford, J. (2006). Sex and the Internet: Gay Men, Risk Reduction and Serostatus. *Culture, Health and Sexuality*, 8(2), 161–174.

Dean, T. (2008). Breeding Culture: Barebacking, Bugchasing, Giftgiving. *The Massachusetts Review*, 49(1/2), 80–94.

Dean, T. (2009). *Unlimited Intimacy: Reflections on the Subcultures of Barebacking*. Chicago: University of Chicago Press.

Dean, T. (2011). Bareback Time. In E. L. Callum & M. Tuhkanen (Eds.), *Queer Times, Queer Belongings* (pp. 75–99). New York: SUNY Press.

Dodge, M. & Kitchin, R. (2001). *Mapping Cyberspace*. London: Routledge.

Dowsett, G. W., Williams, H., Ventuneac, A. & Carballo-Diéguez, A. (2008). 'Taking It Like a Man': Masculinity and Barebacking Online. *Sexualities*, 11(1–2), 121–141.

Fox, R. (2012). *Gays in (Cyber-)Space: Online Performances of Gay Identity*. Saarbrücken: AV Akademikerverlag.

Gagnon, M. & Guta, A. (2014). HIV Viral Load: A Concept Analysis and Critique. *Research and Theory for Nursing Practice*, 28(3), 204–227.

Gurak, J. L. (1997). *Persuasion and Privacy in Cyberspace: The Online Protests over Lotus MarketPlace and the Clipper Chip*. New Haven: Yale University Press.

Kendall, L. (2002). *Hanging Out in the Virtual Pub: Masculinities and Relationships Online*. Berkeley: University of California Press.

Klein, H. (2014). Generationing, Stealthing, and Gift Giving: The Intentional Transmission of HIV by HIV-Positive Men to Their HIV-Negative Sex Partners. *Health Psychology Research*, 2(3), 54–59.

Kolko, B. & Reid, E. (1998). Dissolution and Fragmentation: Problems in On-Line Communities. In S. G. Jones (Eds.), *Cybersociety 2.0: Revisiting Computer-Mediated Communication and Community* (pp. 213–227). Thousand Oaks: SAGE.

McGlotten, S. (2013). *Virtual Intimacies: Media, Affect & Queer*. New York: SUNY Press.

McKenna, K. Y. A. & Bargh, J. A. (1998). Coming Out in the Age of the Internet: Identity 'Demarginalization' Through Virtual Group Participation. *Journal of Personality and Social Psychology*, 75(3), 681–694.

Miller, V. (2012). A Crisis of Presence: On-line Culture and Being in the World. *Space and Polity*, 16(3), 265–285.

Milosavljevic, Z. (2012). *AIDS and Its Discontents in Serbia: Silencing Gay Sexuality in the Age of Illness*. Unpublished Thesis, University of Hull, UK, and University of Lodz, Poland.

Milosavljevic, Z. (2015). Entropy of Desires: Gay Representations Online and HIV/AIDS Discourse in Serbia. In T. Rosic-Ilic, J. Koteska & J. Ljumovic (Eds.), *Representation of Gender Minority Groups in Media: Serbia, Montenegro and Macedonia* (pp. 283–298). Belgrade: Singidunum University.

Mowlabocus, S. (2010). *Gaydar Culture: Gay Men, Technology and Embodiment in the Digital Age*: Farnham: Ashgate.

Mowlabocus, S., Harbottle, J. & Witzel, C. (2013). Porn Laid Bare: Gay Men, Pornography and Bareback Sex. *Sexualities*, 16(5–6), 523–554.

Orton-Johnson, K. & Prior, N. (2013). *Digital Sociology*. Basingstoke: Palgrave Macmillan.

Preciado, B. (2013). *Testo Junkie: Sex, Drugs and Biopolitics in the Pharmacopornographic Era*. New York: The Feminist Press.

Race, K. (2010). Engaging in a Culture of Barebacking: Gay Men and the Risk of HIV Prevention. In M. Davis & C. Squire (Eds.), *HIV Treatment and Prevention Technologies in International Perspective*. Basingstoke: Palgrave Macmillan.

Race, K. (2015). 'Party and Play': Online Hook-Up Devices and the Emergence of PNP Practices Among Gay Men. *Sexualities*, 18(3), 253–275.

Reid, E. (1999). Hierarchy and Power: Social Control in Cyberspace. In M. A. Smith & P. Kollock (Eds.), *Communities in Cyberspace*. London: Routledge.

Rheingold, H. (2000). *The Virtual Community: Homesteading on the Electric Frontier*. Cambridge, MA: MIT Press.

Saraswati, A. L. (2013). Wikisexuality: Rethinking Sexuality in Cyberspace. *Sexualities*, 16(5/6), 587–603.

Turkle, S. (1999). Cyberspace and Identity. *Contemporary Sociology*, 28(6), 643–648.

Turkle, S. (2011). *Alone Together: Why We Expect More from Technology and Less from Each Other*. New York: Basic Books.

Afterword
Writing at the Precipice

Sharif Mowlabocus

As a scholar who is European by virtue of his British citizenship, writing an afterword for this book in February 2016 feels somewhat poignant. The mainstream media across Europe has been discussing the possibility of 'Brexit' (the British withdrawal from the European Union) ever since the Conservative Party won a second term in office in May 2015. Irrespective of whether the 'Vote Leave' campaign is successful in achieving this withdrawal, by the time this book is published, the UK's relationship with the EU will inevitably have changed. Even if the UK votes to stay in the Union, concessions will have been made, deals will have been struck and further animosity between Britain and the other EU member states will most certainly have been generated in the process. In writing this afterword to a collection of essays on LGBTQ European media, I sincerely hope I am not writing during the afterword of Britain's relationship with many of the countries featured in this book.

From beginning to end, this project has reflected the very best of what the European Union has to offer its citizens and demonstrated why the EU is important – for LGBTQ people and for scholars of all disciplines. Having been a reviewer of the original book proposal, I was invited by Lukasz, Bart and Alexander to speak at a workshop in Antwerp dedicated to the book in December 2015. Because those who have contributed to this book were based in Europe, travel to this workshop required no visas, no letters of invitation to be shown to border guards and (for many delegates) not even a change in the money they had in their wallets. Having previously experienced the collapse of conferences because half the delegates were denied entry to the host country, or because the keynote speaker was repatriated by immigration services, I never discount the freedom that the Schengen agreement provides academic researchers for face-to-face discussion and collaboration.

The workshop provided an opportunity for contributing authors to read the first drafts of each other's work, to present their own research and to discuss and critique methods, analyses and findings. I commend the editors of the collection for putting together such an event. Not only was it a dynamic and enjoyable couple of days, it also offered an opportunity for authors to identify similarities and differences between their work, to explore the broader themes that pervaded the different chapters and to learn more about the relationship between LGBTQ people, the media and the State across different national contexts. By the time we had finished our last bottles of Belgian beer, we had a much better understanding of each individual project and of the book as a whole.

I also left feeling that I had a much better understanding of *why* this collection was not just timely, but necessary. In their introduction the editors identify the dominance of the English-speaking world in LGBTQ media research and point towards the dangers of this predominantly Anglo-American hegemony. These dangers include what I term the proliferation of the 'Stonewall benchmark', whereby LGBTQ history (of whatever country) is measured (whether overtly or covertly) against the history of the North American LGBTQ civil rights movement. The fact that the UK's leading gay and lesbian rights organisation is named after an *American* historical event is just one example of this hegemony. Such dominance needs to be decentred if we are to fully understand the specific histories, identities and cultures of LGBTQ people outside of the USA – or indeed those who live in the USA but who are not included in the narrative of the post-Stonewall civil rights movement.

This is why the contributions of Herreman and Dhoest and of Brandão and colleagues, for instance, are so important here. Collectively these authors offer us an opportunity to step outside of the Anglo-American hegemony and explore hitherto hidden histories of LGBTQ lives in different parts of Europe. Such explorations also offer the researcher further evidence that the narrative of LGBTQ progress celebrated in, for example, the 'it gets better' campaign, requires further nuance and consideration. Brandão et al.'s chapter on the history of lesbian print media in Portugal is just one example that contradicts the rhetoric of Dan Savage's much-vaunted campaign.

Another reason why this collection warrants attention is because it helps us understand the specificity of media ecosystems at a time when digital communication platforms promote the belief that such specificity is being eroded. The global dominance of social networking sites such as Facebook, Twitter and Grindr cannot be ignored and these platforms are part of a long history of transnational media production and consumption. At the same time, and as demonstrated in the work of Milosavljevic, Shield, Parisi and Comunello and Cardoso (again, to name just a few examples), transnational media platforms do not prohibit or otherwise erode local identities, cultural practices, political discussions or sexual negotiations. Gay men may well be using Grindr to negotiate casual hook-ups in Serbia, but the details of these negotiations, including discussions (or silence) around sexual health issues is specific to Serbian men and men who live or work in Serbia. How a Serbian (or Danish or Italian) man negotiates a Californian dating application requires a recognition of the situated histories and politics that contribute to that man's understanding of self and of sexuality. The tension between local LGBTQ cultures and global (read USA) media platforms must be recognised if we are to move beyond linear, simplistic understandings of how such technologies impact the lives of their different users.

Singing for My Supper

I should at this point perhaps identify my role in the Antwerp workshop, considering I have not contributed a chapter to this collection. The evening before the workshop began, I was offered the opportunity to reflect upon the contributions to the book and to identify themes and commonalities between the chapters. Building on these themes, I also outlined directions for future research. What follows here is a summary of those directions. In no way can I map the horizons of new research – that would be impossible in an afterword of this length. Instead, I have collected together themes that I think point towards areas and fields where interesting and exciting new LGBTQ media research might lay.

Intergenerational Research

Much has been made of the purported death of the gay scene in scholarly writing, and the internet is often positioned as enemy number one when it comes to discussions of public gay culture (see e.g. Dean, 2009). Whether or not gay bars, clubs and social spaces are disappearing or in decline, it is the case that gay scenes are changing. In particular, the way in which we interact with them is shifting. Of course historically many people never had the opportunity to access (or the interest in accessing) commercial LGBTQ spaces. Either they did not have the resources (whether that be financial, human, cultural or social capital) to access those spaces, or those spaces did not exist. But where those spaces *did* exist, and when that 'smalltown boy' (or girl or trans person) was able to get themselves to that space, they often entered into a space that was populated by *generations* of queer people.

I remember the gay bars and pubs of my youth. I remember being terrified at first, but I also remember learning how to *be* gay. My education came from the older guys, the butch lesbians and the drag queens. I got a bit drunk and I made friends with some of them. I made out with some of them. I got to know what it was to be a young gay man in the early 1990s. LGBTQ fiction and oral history projects both evidence the way in which the gay scene offers an informal, subcultural education (Hall-Carpenter Archives, 1989). From Rechy's *Sexual Outlaw* (1977) to Maupin's *Tales of the City* (1978) to Bartlett's *Ready to Catch Him Should He Fall* (1990) and Feinberg's *Stone Butch Blues* (1993), the notion of younger people learning from their queer elders is a recognisable trope in queer literature.

It is easy to say that today it is easy for young people to come out, or by contrast, that it was better in the good old days. An acknowledgement of suicide rates among LGBTQ teens (Liu & Mustanski, 2012) quashes the first assumption while the briefest of glances back to the state-enforced homophobia of nations that now proudly claim to be LGBTQ-friendly dismisses the second (see Monro, 2015). At the same time, and while not positing a past that was never fully collective or shared, I do think we are at risk of losing an *intergenerational dialogue* between LGBTQ people.

We need to establish a dialogue between the past and the present in order to understand the 'longer history' of queer media use and queer media representation. One could say that this applies to broader society, but I can talk to my grandparents, my parents and my other relatives today about their media use. I think that families informally perform this kind of analysis and reflection on an almost daily basis. Every time my Dad and I watch a film together he ends up talking about a memory that the film has sparked. Often, given his racial position and his history, such a memory will be triggered by the representation of brown people in mainstream cinema. As uncomfortable as these recollections are, we both recognise that they are important. That this is a part of my inheritance and a part of his legacy. I can't easily perform this transaction with my queer forefathers. Queer people aren't able to 'recover' their media history in quite the same way. This then is my first 'headline'; we need more intergenerational work in queer media studies.

The work of Elizabeth Reed (forthcoming) which focuses on media use in 'queer families' and that of Dustin Goltz (2014), who uses writing workshops to engage gay men in intergenerational dialogue, are two examples of how this research might be carried out. I hope that, in the future, we see more of this intergenerational discussion.

Intersectional Research

A few years ago I was working on a project that was funded by a health charity and which explored the use of digital and social media by gay men. As part of the interview protocol, we recruited men who used bareback hook-up sites. Because the charity was interested in capturing the specificity of their experiences of sexual health services, we interviewed the bareback hook-up users separately from men who did not use such sites. While we used the same recruitment methods, demographic differences between the two groups quickly became obvious. While the age range was more varied among the mainstream cohort, the guys using bareback services were all over 45. Meanwhile nobody in the mainstream cohort identified themselves as having a disability, as having financial issues or as living on benefits or being socially excluded. All of these issues came to the fore in the focus groups dedicated to bareback service users.

The reasons for these demographic differences began to emerge when we discussed men's reasons for using the barebacking websites. Yes, sex was one factor, but for an overwhelming number of our interviewees, a sense of community was cited as a key reason for using these sites. In these spaces our participants felt accepted in ways that they weren't on apps such as

Grindr, Scruff and Growlr. Bareback websites have long been associated with the HIV-positive gay male community. It appears that the architecture of these sites (with chat rooms, group messaging and more space for user profiles), twinned with the more 'open' attitude of both the website and its users, is now offering something to gay men who face stigma not only because of their HIV status, but also because of their social class, financial status, geographical location and mental and physical health.

Intersectionality, a concept developed within the discipline of critical race studies, fell out of favour in the early 2000s as poststructuralist thinking favoured the altogether 'queerer' term 'assemblage' to discuss the multiple and fractured positions and politics that any one individual might occupy simultaneously (Puar, 2007). However, Crenshaw's (1991) earlier term has lately been reinvigorated as scholars begin to recognise that many people do in fact understand themselves in these ways – and that these intersections feel far more permanent and 'set' than perhaps 'queer assemblage' theory acknowledges.

LGBTQ media research needs to pay much more attention to the intersectional dimension of participant lives. Of course some scholars are in fact doing just that: Beetar (forthcoming) has recently explored how queer African migrants are using media technologies in South Africa to overcome rising levels of xeno- and homophobia. Dasgupta (2014) has examined the role that ethnicity, class and regionality play in the use of media by queer Indian folk. This work is emerging, but I think all LGBTQ work needs to pay further attention to the intersectional politics that frame the lives of our research subjects.

Spaces of/and Queer Media

The geographical dimension of this book cannot be overlooked. With chapters that focus on Germany, Sweden, Portugal, the Netherlands, the United Kingdom, Italy, Ireland, Denmark, Serbia, Russia, Latvia, Poland and of course Belgium, the spaces that come under the purview of this collection are diverse. Collectively they offer a rich analysis of how LGBTQ people use media. I think there is mileage in conceptualising the queer-space-and-media relationship in other ways, too.

The first is of course the use of media by queer people within physical spaces. Hook-up applications are perhaps the obvious example here (see Blackwell, Birnholtz & Abbot, 2015; Roth, 2014, 2016) but there are other ways in which media technologies are used by LGBTQ folk to locate safe spaces, to avoid sites of danger and to find comfort in strange and unknown spaces (see Mowlabocus, 2010). Having been denied (and in some cases continuing to be denied) legitimate space in society, LGBTQ people have long been sensitised to issues of space and have developed tools and strategies for cleaving spaces for themselves and others (Berlant & Warner, 1998; Browne, Lim & Brown, 2009; Knopp, 2004). How the media operates to enable such cleaving and space-making is, I think, something we need to continue to explore.

We must also consider how media technologies serve to expose and oppress LGBTQ people, rendering them vulnerable to judicial and extra-judicial violence. In spaces where sexually dissident people live precarious lives, the mobile phone has become a powerful tool for forming and maintaining loose ephemeral networks that connect queer people and allow them to operate under the radar. In the hands of their oppressors however, that same device can turn on its owner, placing an entire network of queer kinship in jeopardy. Such is the logic of the network (Castells, 2010) that one node can connect to all others – with horrific results. The internet is littered with videos showing neo-Nazi gangs and religious terrorists humiliating, torturing and murdering queer people. In almost all of these cases, the smartphone – and its associated apps – have provided easy access to their victims.

Beyond the fascist thugs, software itself can render queer people visible in ways that they never expected. In 2013, Grindr's 'backdoor' was found to be not just vulnerable to attack, but completely unbolted and left open (Cluley, 2012). Maps of Grindr usage began appearing on the internet. In an echo of the maps created during genocidal wars, these maps revealed the lack of control that queer people have over the technologies they use, and the lack of interest that some media producers have in protecting those who use their services. Future research into LGBTQ people's use of media technologies must include a critical investigation of the relationships of power that operate between user, interface, technology and developer. As digital media permeate ever deeper layers of our everyday lives, scholars must look beyond the reflection of the screen and unravel these complex (and often hidden) interactions.

Inter/Trans/National Queer Studies

Of course there is something powerful in not fully unravelling and extrapolating the meaning-making activities that queer people engage in on a daily basis. There is political mileage in not resolving the tensions, conflicts and negotiations of everyday life, but in letting them be as they are. The tensions that I am talking about here revolve around the local uses of transnational media by queer people that I mentioned in my introduction.

Many of us are familiar with Boellstorff's work on dubbing culture (2003) or Gray's work on queer rural youth (2009) or Kong's work on queer men in Hong Kong (2011) and Leap's work on queer South-African identities (2004). In all of these cases the role of transnational media flows has been highlighted in the identity work and meaning making of queer people. In each case the author offers the reader an informed and informative understanding of local queer cultures. These are texts to be celebrated. But they must not be seen as a conclusion. We need to continue such analyses and, at the same time, 'speak back' to the hegemony I alluded to earlier. Understandably, these scholars have spent time looking at processes of 'glocalisation' (Robertson, 2012), of how people from non-Western or non-urban contexts have assimilated, appropriated and apprehended texts, politics and identities that emanate from that hegemony. We now need to pay attention to how these appropriations and assimilations might rub up against that hegemony.

This is a challenging project, but there is a precedent for such work. The work of postcolonial scholars such as bell hooks (1992), Stuart Hall (1996) and Paul Gilroy (2000) comes to mind. In all three cases, these writers not only explored the ways in which whiteness came to shape racial 'otherness', but they also identified how the subaltern was, in turn, responsible for shaping the white centre.

It is vital that the voices at the margins (however we define that margin) are articulated by academics such as those who have contributed to this book. At the same time, such articulations often carry the risk of being considered *exceptional*. This is something I regularly witness at conferences, where there is a 'queer' panel and then a 'global queer' panel. While those from the latter panel cite the same work mentioned in the former, the reverse rarely happens. The traffic in ideas and critique often appears to flow only one way.

Responding to the 'tolerance' of black and lesbian women at a Humanities conference in 1979, Audre Lorde famously wrote that 'the master's tools will never dismantle the master's house' (1984, p. 110). In the essay of the same name, she demanded recognition that went beyond being given space on a conference panel, beyond being given a 'place at the table'. She wrote that 'difference must be not merely tolerated, but seen as a fund of necessary polarities between which our creativity can spark like a dialectic' (ibid., p. 112). What Lorde calls for here is not just recognition of the marginalised by the centre, but a critical self-reflection and re-organisation of that centre through the difference created by the margin. It is Lorde's critique that I echo when I refer to the risk of being exceptional. What is this risk? It is the risk that we all face when we explore cultures 'outside' of the Anglo-American hegemony; when we research sexualities 'outside' of the metropolitan concept of 'lesbian' and 'gay'; when we present on topics that are 'outside' of the spaces of traditional queer studies. It is the risk of being heard without actually being listened to. It is the risk of being tolerated, while not being allowed to influence. It is the risk of being 'local' colour that enlivens, but never encroaches upon, the centre of the (white, middle-class, male-dominated, ableist) queer academy.

I am not suggesting that we stop presenting on 'global queer' panels, but we owe it to our work, to our research participants and to 'the centre' to 'speak back' and influence thinking beyond the local. This is a grand ambition to finish on and no doubt there is much more to be said about such a project (not least that it has been tried before and may be almost impossible to achieve) but, returning to the book project that precedes these words, if there was one hope that I have for this collection, it is that it takes its place on the shelf of queer research not as a set of case studies about 'other places' but as a rallying cry to all interested scholars to consider how the findings from those 'other places' might cause us to reflect on our own research and consider how such ideas might have influence beyond the geographical borders mentioned in the titles and introductions.

References

Bartlett, N. (1990). *Ready to Catch Him Should He Fall*. London: EP Dutton.

Berlant, L. & Warner, M. (1998). Sex in Public. *Critical Inquiry*, 24(2), 547–566.

Blackwell, C., Birnholtz, J. & Abbot, C. (2015). Seeing and Being Seen: Co-Situation and Impression Formation Using Grindr, a Location-Aware Gay Dating App. *New Media & Society*, 17(7), 1117–1136.

Boellstorff, T. (2003). Dubbing Culture: Indonesian Gay and Lesbi Subjectivities and Ethnography in an Already Globalized World. *American Ethnologist*, 30(2), 225–242.

Browne, K., Lim, J. & Brown, G. (Eds.) (2009). *Geographies of Sexuality: Theory, Practices and Politics*. London: Routledge.

Castells, M. (2010). *The Rise of the Network Society* (second edition). Oxford: Wiley-Blackwell.

Cluley, G. (2012, January 20). Hacker Exposes Grindr User's Intimate Information and Explicit Photos. *Naked Security*. Retrieved from https://nakedsecurity. sophos.com/2012/01/20/grindr-hack/.

Crenshaw, K. W. (1991). Mapping the Margins: Intersectionality, Identity Politics, and Violence against Women of Color. *Stanford Law Review*, 43(6), 1241–1299.

Dasgupta, R. (2014). Parties, Advocacy and Activism: Interrogating Community and Class in Digital Queer India. In C. Pullen (Ed.), *Queer Youth and Media Cultures* (pp. 265–277). London: Palgrave Macmillan.

Dean, T. (2009). *Unlimited Intimacy: Reflections on the Subculture of Barebacking*. Chicago: University of Chicago Press.

Feinberg, L. (1993). *Stone Butch Blues*. New York: FireBrand Press.

Gilroy, P. (2000). *Against Race: Imagining Political Culture Beyond the Colour Line*. Cambridge, MA: Harvard University Press.

Goltz, D. B. (2014). 'We're Not in Oz Anymore': Shifting Generational Perspectives and Tensions of Gay Community, Identity, and Future. *Journal of Homosexuality*, 61(11), 1503–1528.

Gray, M. L. (2009). *Out in the Country: Youth, Media and Queer Visibility in Rural America*. London: New York University Press.

Hall Carpenter Archives (1989). *Walking After Midnight: Gay Men's Life Stories*. London: Taylor & Francis.

Hall, S. (1996). New Ethnicities. In D. Morley & K.-H. Chen (Eds.), *Stuart Hall: Critical Dialogues in Cultural Studies* (pp. 442–451). London: Routledge.

hooks, b. (1992). *Black Looks: Race and Representation*. London: Routledge.

Knopp, L. (2004). Ontologies of Place, Placeless and Movement: Queer Quests for Identity and Their Impacts on Contemporary Geographic Thought. *Gender, Place and Culture*, 11(1), 121–134.

Kong, T. (2011). *Chinese Male Homosexualities: Memba, Tongzhi and Golden Boy*. London: Routledge.

Leap, W. L. (2004). Language, Belonging and (Homo)sexual Citizenship in Cape Town, South Africa. In W. L. Leap & T. Boellstorff (Eds.), *Speaking in Queer Tongues: Globalization and Gay Language* (pp. 134–162). Chicago: University of Chicago Press.

Liu, R. T. & Mustanski, B. (2012). Suicidal Ideation and Self-Harm in Lesbian, Gay, Bisexual, and Transgender Youth. *American Journal of Preventative Medicine*, 42(3), 221–228.

Lorde, A. (1984). *Sister Outsider: Essays and Speeches*. New York: Crown Publishing.

Maupin, A. (1978 [1989]). *Tales of the City*. New York: Harper Collins.

Monro, S. (2015). History of LGBT/Queer Sexuality, Europe. *The International Encyclopaedia of Human Sexuality* (pp. 649–719). Wiley Online.

Mowlabocus, S. (2010). *Gaydar Culture: Gay Men, Technology and Embodiment in the Digital Age*. Farnham: Ashgate.

Puar, J. K. (2007). *Terrorist Assemblages: Homonationalism in Queer Times*. London: Duke University Press.

Rechy, J. (1977 [1989]). *The Sexual Outlaw: A Documentary*. New York: Grove Press.

Reed, E. (forthcoming). *Making Queer Families: Identity, LGBTQ Parents and Media Representation* (doctoral dissertation). Brighton: University of Sussex.

Robertson, R. (2012). Globalisation or Glocalisation? *Journal of International Communication*, 18(2), 191–208.

Roth, Y. (2014). Locating the 'Scruff Guy': Theorizing Body and Space in Gay Geosocial Media. *International Journal of Communication*, 8, 2113–2133.

Roth, Y. (2016). Zero Feet Away: The Digital Geography of Gay Social Media. *Journal of Homosexuality*, 63(3), 437–442.

List of Contributors

Joana Afonso has an MA in Sociology. She is a junior researcher of the Interdisciplinary Centre of Social Sciences – Pole of the University of Minho (CICS.NOVA.UMinho), Portugal. She is currently preparing her PhD thesis in Sociology at the University of Minho, which will focus on the career experiences of Portuguese LGB agents in the police and the military. Her research interests include gender, sexuality and identities.

Louis Bailey is a Research Fellow in the Medical Humanities, based at the University of Hull. His work explores the intersection of creativity and resilience in relation to marginalised and minority populations. He is the co-director of Artmob, a visual arts organisation committed to raising the profile of trans and gender-variant artists in the United Kingdom, and has worked with and for the trans community for a number of years. He was a strategic advisor to the NHS and the Department of Health on trans health equality issues and has published on a range of topics including ageing, embodiment, mental health, stigma, memorialisation and suicide prevention.

Evgeniya Boklage has recently completed her PhD at the Free University of Berlin, in which she studied the Russian LGBT community and their use of social media for the purposes of self-representation and mobilisation of social action. She is currently a researcher in the interdisciplinary project InfectContro2020 funded by the German Federal Ministry of Education and Research.

Ana Maria Brandão is a sociologist, an Adjunct Professor at the University of Minho and a Fellow Researcher of the Interdisciplinary Centre of Social Sciences – Pole of the University of Minho (CICS.NOVA.UMinho), Portugal. Her research interests include gender, sexuality and identities as well as social research methodologies. She is the author and co-author of diverse publications in national and international journals and books.

Daniel Cardoso is an Assistant Professor in the field of Communication Sciences and Journalism both at the Lusophone University of Humanities and Technologies and at the Faculty of Social and Human Sciences at the New University of Lisbon (UNL), Portugal. He has a PhD in Communication Sciences, with a thesis on how Portuguese youngsters use new media in relation to their sexual and intimate experiences. His master's thesis, also in Communication Sciences, deals with polyamory. He is part of the co-ordination team of ESA's Sexualities Research Network and an activist, both offline and online. His work can be accessed via www. danielscardoso.net.

Joanna Chojnicka is a Postdoctoral Researcher in the Postcolonial Language Studies team at the Faculty of Linguistics and Literary Studies, University of Bremen, Germany. She studied in Poland, Latvia, Lithuania and Germany. Having obtained her PhD in Latvian linguistics at the Adam Mickiewicz University in Poznan, Poland, in 2012, she has worked at the Herder Institute in Marburg, Germany (short-term postdoctoral scholarship, 2013) and at the Zukunftskolleg, University of Konstanz, Germany (Marie Curie ZIF fellowship, 2013–2015). In her research she currently focuses on gender and sexuality in postcolonial/postsocialist contexts from a critical-discursive perspective.

Francesca Comunello, PhD, works at the Sapienza University of Rome. Her research and publications focus on the intersections between digital technology and society. This includes research on network theories, digitally mediated social relations, mobile communication, social media, social network sites, digital media and disaster communication and digital inequalities.

Alexander Dhoest is Associate Professor in Communication Studies at the University of Antwerp, Belgium. He obtained an MA in Film and Television Studies from the University of Warwick (United Kingdom) and a PhD in Social Sciences from the Catholic University of Leuven, working on television drama and the construction of national identity. His research explores the significance of popular media culture in relation to social identities, focusing in particular on media and diversity. He has published widely on these issues in edited volumes and peer-reviewed journals such as *Media, Culture & Society, Television and New Media, European Journal of Communication* and *European Journal of Cultural Studies*.

Richard Dyer is Professor Emeritus of Film Studies at King's College London and Professorial Fellow in Film Studies at the University of St Andrews, UK. He has been honoured by the Society for Cinema and Media Studies, the British Association of Film, Television and Screen Studies, and Turku and Yale Universities, and is a Fellow of the British Academy. His many books include *Stars* (1979), *White* (1997), *The Culture of Queers* (2002) and *In the Space of a Song* (2012).

Bart Eeckhout is Professor of English and American Literature at the University of Antwerp, Belgium. He obtained an MA from Columbia University and a PhD from Ghent University and has been a visiting professor both at Fordham University and New York University. During the academic year 2016–2017 he is a Fellow-in-Residence at NIAS in Amsterdam. He teaches queer fiction as well as queer studies, and has been supervising

LGBT and queer research at the BA, MA and doctoral levels for years. His publications on LGBTQ issues, for which he draws frequently on his work as an activist, have appeared in a range of books (from *Queer in Europe* to *Approaches to American Cultural Studies*) and such journals as *CLCWeb*, *International Journal of Law, Policy and the Family* and *Journal of Homosexuality*.

Sonja J. Ellis is a Senior Lecturer in Psychology at the Australian Institute of Professional Counsellors, Brisbane, Australia. Graduating with her PhD from Loughborough University in 2001, she has an established career as an academic (social) psychologist with interests in gender, sexuality and mental health; and has published widely on lesbian, gay and trans issues. With Victoria Clarke, Elizabeth Peel and Damien Riggs she was co-author of the textbook *Lesbian, Gay, Bisexual, Trans and Queer Psychology* (Cambridge University Press, 2010), which won the 2013 British Psychological Society textbook award. She was also – with Jay McNeil, Louis Bailey and others – part of the research team for the *UK Trans Mental Health Study* (2012) on which her contribution to this volume is based.

Giulia Evolvi obtained her PhD in Media Studies in the College of Media, Communication and Information at the University of Colorado Boulder, where she was affiliated with the Centre for Media, Religion and Culture. She has a Bachelor in Asian Languages and Culture from the University of Venice and a Master in Religious Studies from the University of Padua, Italy. Giulia studied at the Denis Diderot University in Paris as an exchange student and was an intern at the press office of the Italian Embassy in Tokyo. She worked for two years as Project Officer for European NGOs in Brussels. Her current research interests are religious diversity in Italy, digital media and gender, and the role of media in the construction of national identity. Since June 2016 she has been a Postdoctoral Researcher at Ruhr University Bochum.

Robbe Herreman has a professional bachelor's degree in Music (2000, Hogeschool Gent) and a master's degree in Musicology (2004, Catholic University of Leuven). Currently he is finishing a PhD at the University of Antwerp on the functions and meanings of music in queer world-making processes in the city of Antwerp between 1960 and 2010. He is the co-editor and co-author of *Veel volk verwacht. Populaire muziek in Vlaams-Brabant sinds 1800*, a book on the history of popular music in the province of Flemish Brabant (Belgium), published by Uitgeverij Peeters (Leuven) in 2012.

Páraic Kerrigan is a doctoral student in the Department of Media Studies at Maynooth University, Republic of Ireland, where he is a John and Pat Hume and Irish Research Council Scholar. His research topic is *Gay (In) Visibility in Irish Media, 1974–2014*. He has presented at various international conferences and won a research impact award from Maynooth

University's Graduate Studies Office. He is the founder of the Project for Emerging Voices and Hidden Histories at Maynooth University, where he is currently working on a radio documentary about Ireland's first gay community hub, the Hirschfeld Centre, with Professor Maria Pramaggiore.

Tânia Cristina Machado is a sociologist and a junior researcher of the Interdisciplinary Centre of Social Sciences – Pole of the University of Minho (CICS.NOVA.UMinho), Portugal. She is currently conducting PhD research on lesbian motherhood in Portugal, funded by a fellowship from the Portuguese Foundation for Science and Technology (ref. SFRH/BD/89837/2012). Her research interests include gender, sexuality and identities. She is the author and co-author of diverse publications in national and international journals.

Jay McNeil is a clinical psychologist for the NHS and recently completed his PhD at Lancaster University. He is the co-founder of TransBareAll, an organisation working with the trans community to promote body positivity. In 2012 he led the Trans Mental Health study (recipient of the Gender Identity and Research Education Annual Award, 2013). He delivers training on the topic of trans empowerment, working with a range of NHS, government, public sector and independent organisations.

Zoran Milosavljevic is a medical doctor and researcher from Belgrade, Republic of Serbia. He holds a BA from the School of Medicine, University of Belgrade/Serbia, and an MA in Gender Studies (GEMMA) from the University of Hull (United Kingdom) and the University of Lodz (Poland). Currently he is a PhD candidate in the School of Social Sciences, University of Hull. His field of research is the interdisciplinary study of HIV/AIDS discourses in Serbia. He lives and works in Belgrade and Hull.

Sharif Mowlabocus is a Senior Lecturer based in the School of Media, Film and Music at the University of Sussex, United Kingdom. For the last fifteen years he has been engaged in research that explores the role which digital media plays in intimate daily life. His book *Gaydar Culture* (Ashgate, 2010) captured the experience of British gay men during the first ten years of the domestic internet. His more recent research has focused on the relationship between technology, pornography and sexual health. This work includes the Porn Laid Bare project and Reaching Out Online. He is a member of the Centre for the Study of Sexual Dissidence at the University of Sussex and is on the editorial board of *Porn Studies* and *Language and Sexuality*. Dr Mowlabocus collaborated on the 2009 Count Me In Too study and has also collaborated with Terrence Higgins Trust, the UK's longest-running HIV charity. His recent publications explore the role of app culture in the surveillance of sex offenders and the challenges of presenting health expertise online.

Lorenza Parisi is a Lecturer in Media Studies at John Cabot University in Rome, where she teaches 'Digital Media Culture'. She studies the interactions between digital technologies and society. In 2011 she received a PhD in Communication Studies from the University of Rome 'La Sapienza'. In her PhD thesis (*Where 2.0*) she explored the impact of digital media on place experience and urban space. Previously she was a visiting student at HIIT (Helsinki Institute for Information Technology) and at the MIT Media Lab (United States). Her research topics include mobile communication, social media, digitally mediated civic engagement and political activism, critical algorithm studies, social media and natural disaster and public communication.

Ulrike Roth is a Research Assistant and PhD candidate in the Department of Communication at the University of Münster, Germany. She holds an MA in Sociology, Science of Communications and Political Science. Her research interests include audience studies and digital media, queer, gender and cultural (media) studies and popular culture. In her PhD thesis she explores the gendering of online media technologies in everyday life.

Tim Savenije was trained as a sociologist and religious studies scholar at the University of Amsterdam, the Netherlands. Besides his studies about attitudes towards homosexuality at the University of Antwerp and the University of Amsterdam, he has done research on anti-gay violence, support needs of LGBTs, LGBT-employee networks, sexual health promotion and long-term care.

Andrew DJ Shield earned his PhD in History from the City University of New York (CUNY) Graduate Center and is currently turning his first dissertation into a book titled *Immigrants in the Sexual Revolution: Perceptions and Participation in Northwest Europe, 1960s–1980s* (Palgrave Macmillan, forthcoming), which is based on interviews and archival research in Arabic, Danish, Dutch and French. He is also completing a second PhD at Roskilde University (Denmark) in Communication as part of the 'New Media, New Intimacies' research group, which is funded through the Danish Council for Independent Research's prestigious Sapere Aude programme. He has published in the *History Workshop Journal* and taught courses in global history, sexuality studies and intercultural communication.

Jakob Svensson is Associate Professor, currently holding a position in Media and Communication Studies at Uppsala University, Sweden. He received his PhD in 2008 at Lund University with a dissertation on civic communication under the supervision of Prof. Peter Dahlgren. Today his research focuses on two areas: political participation on social media platforms and mobile communication in so-called developing regions.

Lukasz Szulc is a Postdoctoral Fellow of the Research Foundation Flanders at the University of Antwerp, Belgium, and a Marie Curie Fellow at the London School of Economics and Political Science, United Kingdom. Since June 2016, he has also been holding a two-year position of Student and Early-Career Representative at the International Communication Association's LGBTQ interest group. Lukasz was awarded a PhD in Communication Studies from the University of Antwerp in February 2015. His academic interests include the social and cultural role of new media, LGBTQ identities as well as nationalisms and transnationalisms. He has extensively published on these topics in international peer-reviewed journals such as *International Journal of Communication*, *New Media & Society* and *Sexualities*. His website is www.lukaszszulc.com and he tweets from @LukaszSzulc.

Marion Wasserbauer is a PhD student at the Faculty of Social Sciences of the University of Antwerp, Belgium. Her research project, 'Queer Voices', focuses on the role of music in the lives of LGBTQ individuals in Flanders, Belgium. Her research and activist interests include LGBTQs, music, identity, queer studies and oral history.

Index

For Product Safety Concerns and Information please contact our EU
representative GPSR@taylorandfrancis.com
Taylor & Francis Verlag GmbH, Kaufingerstraße 24, 80331 München, Germany

www.ingramcontent.com/pod-product-compliance
Ingram Content Group UK Ltd.
Pitfield, Milton Keynes, MK11 3LW, UK
UKHW020937180425
457613UK00019B/443